Party Politics in the Western Balkans

This book examines the development of party politics in the region of Western Balkans, describing party politics and analysing inter-ethnic or inter-party cooperation and competition.

Beginning with a thematic overview of the electoral systems and their link to the party systems, the authors consider the legacy of socialist/communist parties; compare the nationalist parties in the region; and explore opportunities for the national minorities. The book then provides detailed country case studies on Croatia, Bosnia and Herzegovina, Serbia, Montenegro, Kosovo, Macedonia and Albania that:

- provide an overview of the development of the respective political system since 1990, presenting key changes over time;
- depict important political issues in each of these countries and explain parties' particular policies in relation to these issues;
- discuss the level of democracy as well as ethnic minorities in the given states;
- explore the extent to which nationalism has dominated party organisation, the stability of the parties, important changes in the party policies, and their electoral performance and personalisation of the parties.

Bringing together a range of specialist experts on the Balkans, this book will be of interest to students and scholars of party politics, comparative European politics, post-communist politics, nationalism, Southern European and Western Balkan politics.

Věra Stojarová works as an Academic Researcher at the Institute for Comparative Political Research in Brno. The field of her professional interest is research on political and party systems in the Balkan countries. **Peter Emerson** works as the director of the de Borda Institute, an international NGO which specialises in promoting preference voting, especially in plebiscites on sovereignty. His work abroad has centred on conflict zones in the Balkans, the Caucasus, and East Africa.

Routledge research in comparative politics

Party Politics in the Western Balkans

Edited by Věra Stojarová and
Peter Emerson

Routledge
Taylor & Francis Group

LONDON AND NEW YORK

First published 2010
by Routledge
2 Park Square, Milton Park, Abingdon, Oxon OX14 4RN

Simultaneously published in the USA and Canada
by Routledge
270 Madison Ave, New York, NY 10016

Routledge is an imprint of the Taylor & Francis Group, an informa business

Typeset in Times by Wearset Ltd, Boldon, Tyne and Wear
Printed and bound in Great Britain by TJI Digital, Padstow, Cornwall

British Library Cataloguing in Publication Data
A catalogue record for this book is available from the British Library

Library of Congress Cataloging in Publication Data
A catalog record for this book has been requested

ISBN10: 0-415-55099-8 (hbk)
ISBN10: 0-203-86622-3 (ebk)

ISBN13: 978-0-415-55099-4 (hbk)
ISBN13: 978-0-203-86622-1 (ebk)

Contents

Illustrations

Figure

Tables

Contributors

Peter Emerson works as the Director of the de Borda Institute, an international NGO which specialises in promoting preference voting, especially in plebiscites on sovereignty. He speaks Russian, basic Serbo-Croat and some Kiswahili. His work abroad has centred on conflict zones in the Balkans, the Caucasus, and East Africa. His most recent work is *Defining Democracy*.

Florian Bieber is a Lecturer in East European Politics at the University of Kent, Canterbury. He received his MA in Political Science and History and his PhD in Political Science from the University of Vienna, as well as an MA in Southeast European Studies from Central European University (Budapest). Between 2001 and 2006 he worked in Belgrade (Serbia) and Sarajevo (Bosnia-Herzegovina) for the European Centre for Minority Issues. Florian Bieber is also a Visiting Professor at the Nationalism Studies Program at Central European University, at the Regional Masters Program for Democracy and Human Rights at the University of Sarajevo, and is Interdisciplinary Master in East European Studies, University of Bologna. He has been an International Policy Fellow of the Open Society Institute. His research interests include institutional design in multiethnic states, nationalism and ethnic conflict, as well as the political systems of South-eastern Europe.

Věra Stojarová works as an Academic Researcher at the Institute for Comparative Political Research in Brno. In addition she works as an Assistant Professor at the Department of Political Science of the Faculty of Social Studies, Masaryk University, Brno. She has been the executive editor of the Central European Political Studies Review since 2006. The field of her professional interest is research on political and party systems in the Balkan countries. For a semester in 1997, she completed a study stay in Haag. In 2004 she realised a granted stay at the J.F. Kennedy Institute in Berlin. She also realised a study stay in Heidelberg, supported by a grant from the Konrad Adenauer Foundation in 2005–2006. In 2009 she was a Visiting Fellow at the Institute for Human Sciences in Vienna.

Jakub Šedo is an Assistant Professor at the Department of Political Science FSS MU in Brno. At the same time he works as a post-doctoral researcher at the

Institute for Comparative Political Research at the FSS MU, where he leads a special section for electoral systems. His research is centred on the electoral systems in Central and Eastern Europe.

Daniel Bochsler is a post-doctoral researcher at the University of Zurich. He received his PhD (2008) from the University of Geneva, where his dissertation was on electoral systems and party systems in 20 Central and Eastern European democracies, with a special focus on party nationalisation. His research is centred on the effect of political institutions, namely electoral systems and referendums. He has stayed at universities in Tartu, Irvine (University of California), and Budapest (Central European University), and has conducted field research in Serbia.

Acknowledgements

This book has been undertaken as part of the Research Project 'Political Parties and Representation of Interests in Contemporary European Democracies' (code MSM0021622407).

The authors would like to thank the Institute for Comparative Political Research for provision of the workshop and the proofreading of the texts and Routledge for giving us the opportunity to publish the piece. Special thanks go to our parents, spouses, partners, friends and students. The authors' opinions do not necessarily reflect the opinion of the editors.

Abbreviations

AA/AS	Albanian Alternative (*Albanska Alternativa, Alternatives Shqiptare*)
AAK	Alliance for the Future of Kosovo (*Aleanca për ardhmërinë e Kosovës*)
AKR	New Kosovo Alliance (*Aleanca Kosova e Re*)
AMS	additional member system
AN	National Alliance (*Alleanza Nazionale*)
ANA/AKSh	Albanian National Army (*Armata Kombëtare Shqiptare*)
APV	Assembly of the Vojvodina region
AV	alternative vote
BC	Borda count
BDI	Democratic Union for Integration (*Bashkimi Demokratik për Integrim*)
BDL/DUD	Democratic Union of the Valley (*Demokratska unija Doline*)
BF	Union for Victory (*Bashkimi Për Fitore*)
BiH	Bosnia and Herzegovina (*Bosna i Hercegovina*)
BK	National Front (*Balli Kombëtar*)
BKK	Kosovo National Front (*Balli Kombëtar Kosovë*)
BLD	Liberal Democratic Union (*Bashkimi Liberal Demokrat*)
BNVS	Bosnian National Council of Sandžak (*Bošnjačko nacionalno vijeće Sandžaka*)
BS	Bosniak Party (*Bošnjačka stranka*)
CG	Montenegro (*Crna Gora*)
DC	Democratic Centre (*Demokratski centar*)
DNZ	Democratic People's Union (*Demokratska narodna zajednica*)
DOS	Democratic Opposition Serbia (*Demokratska opozicija Srbije*)
DPA	Dayton Peace Agreement
DPA/PDSh	The Democratic Party of the Albanians (*Partia Demokratike Shqiptarëve/Demokratska partija na Albacite*)
DPM	Democratic Party of Macedonia (*Demokratska partija na Makedonija*)
DPMNE	Democratic Party for Macedonian National Unity (*Demokratska partija za Makedonsko narodno edinstvo*)

DPS	Democratic Party of Socialists (*Demokratska partija socijalista*)
DS	Democratic Party (*Demokratska stranka*)
DSCG/LDMZ	Democratic Alliance of Montenegro (*Demokratski savez u Crnoj Gori, Lidhja Demokratike në Mal të Zi*)
DSHV	Democratic Union of the Croats in Vojvodina (*Demokratski savez Hrvata u Vojvodini*)
DSJ	Democratic Party of Unity (*Demokratska stranka jedinstva*)
DSP	Democratic Socialist Party Alliance (*Demokratska socijastička partija*)
DSS	Democratic Party of Serbia (*Demokratska stranka Srbije*)
DSS	Democratic Serb Party (*Demokratska Srpska stranka*)
DSVM	Democratic Party of the Vojvodina Hungarians (*Demokratska stranka Vojvođanskih Mađara*)
DUA/UDSH	Democratic Union of Albanians (*Demokratska unija Albanaca, Unioni Demokratik i Shqiptarëve*)
DUI/BDI	Democratic Union for Integration (*Bashkimi Demokratik për Integrim/Demokratska Unija za Integracija*)
DZVM	Democratic Union of the Vojvodina Hungarians (*Demokratska zajedinca Vojvođanskih Mađara*)
EC	European Community
EU	European Union
EULEX	EU Rule of Law Mission in Kosovo
FARK	Armed Forces of the Republic of Kosovo (*Forcat e Armatosura të Republikës së Kosovës*)
FBiH	Federation of Bosnia and Herzegovina
FBKSH	Albanian Front of National Unification (*Fronti Për Bashkim Kombëtar Shqiptar*)
FPP	first-past-the-post
FRY	Federal Republic of Yugoslavia
FYROM	Former Yugoslav Republic of Macedonia
GNU	Government of National Unity
GSS	Civic Alliance of Serbia (*Građanski savez Srbije*)
HB	Croatian Bloc (*Hrvatski blok*)
HČSP	Croatian Pure Party of Right (*Hrvatska čista stranka prava*)
HDB	Croatian Democratic Bloc (*Hrvatski demokratski blok*)
HDSSB	Croatian Democratic Assembly of Slavonia and Baranja (*Hrvatski demokratski sabor Slavonije i Baranje*)
HDZ	Croatian Democratic Union (*Hrvatska demokratska zajednica*)
HDZ-1990	Croatian Democratic Union 1990 (*Hrvatska demokratska zajednica 1990*)
HDZ BiH	The Croatian Democratic Movement BiH (*Hrvatska demokratska zajednica BiH*)
HGI	Croat Civic Initiative (*Hrvatska građanska inicijativa*)

HIP	Croatian True Revival (*Hrvatski istinski preporod*)
HKDU	Croatian Christian Democratic Union (*Hrvatska kršćanska demokratska unija*)
HND	Croatian Independent Democrats (*Hrvatski nezavisni demokrati*)
HNS	Croatian People's Party (*Hrvatska narodna stranka*)
HNZ	Croatian National Union (*Hrvatska narodna zajednica*)
HOS	Croatian Defence Forces (*Hrvatske obrambene snage*)
HPB	Croatian Rightist Brotherhood (*Hrvatsko pravaško bratstvo*)
HP-HPP	Croatian Rightists – Croatian Rightist Movement (*Hrvatski pravaši- Hrvatski pravaški pokret*)
HSLS	Croatian Social Liberal Party (*Hrvatska socijalno liberalna stranka*)
HSP	Croatian Party of Right (*Hrvatska stranka prava*)
HSP-1861	Croatian Party of Right 1861 (*Hrvatska stranka prava-1861*)
HSS	Croatian Peasant Party (*Hrvatska seljačka stranka*)
HSU	Croatian Party of Pensioners (*Hrvatska stranka umirovljenika*)
HZ	Croats Together (*Hrvatsko zajedništvo*)
IC	international community
ICG	International Crisis Group
ICTY	International Criminal Tribunal for the Former Yugoslavia
IDEA	Institute for Democracy and Electoral Assistance
IDS	Istrian Democratic Assembly (*Istarski demokratski sabor*)
IFES	International Foundation for Electoral Systems
JS	United Serbia (*Jedinstvena Srbija*)
KCD	Coalition for United and Democratic BiH (*Koalicija za cjelovitu i demokratsku Bosnu i Hercegovinu*)
KKCMTSH	National Liberation Front of Albanians (*Komitetit Kombëtar për Clirimin dhe Mbrojtjen e Tokave Shqiptare*)
KLA/UÇK	Kosovo Liberation Army
KNS	Coalition of People's Accord (*Koalicija narodnog sporazuma*)
KPC	Kosovo Protection Corps
KPH	Communist Party of Croatia (*Komunistička partija Hrvatske)*
KPJ	Communist Party of Yugoslavia (*Komunistička partija Jugoslavije*)
KPM	Communist Party of Macedonia (*Komunistička partija na Makedonija*)
LDD	Democratic League of Dardania (*Lidhja demokratike e Dardanisë*)
LDK	Democratic League of Kosovo (*Lidhja demokratike te Kosovës*)
LDP	Liberal Democratic Party (*Liberalno demokratska partija*)
LHL	Left of Croatia – Left (*Ljevica Hrvatske – Ljevica*)

LKÇK	National Movement for the Liberation of Kosovo (*Lëvizja Kombëtare për Çlirimin e Kosovës*)
LPM	Liberal Party of Macedonia (*Liberalna partija na Makedonija*)
LS	Liberal Party (*Liberalna stranka*)
LSCG	Liberal Alliance of Montenegro (*Liberalni savez Crne Gore*)
LSI	Socialist Movement for Integration (*Lëvizja Socialiste për Intigrim*)
LSV	League of Social Democrats of Vojvodina (*Liga socijaldemokrata Vojvodine*)
MBC	modified Borda count
MMP	multi-member proportional
MNVS	Muslim National Council of Sandžak (*Muslimansko nacionalno vijeće Sandžaka*)
MP	Member of Parliament
NATO	North Atlantic Treaty Organisation
NDH	Nezavisna država Hrvatska (Independent State of Croatia)
NHI	New Croatian Initiative (*Nova Hrvatska Inicijativa*)
NLA/UÇK	National Liberation Army
NS	New Serbia (*Nova Srbija*)
NS	People's Party (*Narodna stranka*)
NSDP	New Social Democratic Party (*Nova socijaldemokratska Partija*)
NSS	People's Socialist Party (*Narodna socijalistička stranka Crne Gore*)
NWG	national working group
ODIHR	Office for Democratic Institutions and Human Rights
OSCE	Organisation for Security and Cooperation in Europe
PAA	Agrarian Environmental Party (*Partia Agrare Ambjentaliste*)
PAD	Party of Democratic Alliance (*Partia Aleanca Demokratike*)
PBDNJ	Party for Unity and Human Rights (*Partia Bashkimi për të Drejtat e Njeriut, Κόμμα Ένωσης Ανθρωπίνων Δικαιωμάτων*)
PBKD	Democratic National Front Party (*Partia Balli Kombëtar Demokrat*)
PBKSh	Albanian National Unity Party (*Partia Bashkesia Kombetare Shqiptare*)
PDD	Party of Democratic Action (*Partija za demokratsko delovanje*)
PDI	Party for Democratic Integration (*Pokret za demokratsku integraciju*)
PDK	Christian Democratic Party of Albania (*Partia Demokristiane e Shqipërisë*)
PDK	Democratic Party of Kosovo (*Partia Demokratike e Kosovës*)
PDP	Party for Democratic Progress (*Pokret za demokratski progress*)
PDPA/PPDSh	Party of Democratic Prosperity of Albanians (*Partia per*

	prosperitet demokratik Shqiptarëve/Partija za demokratski prosperitet na Albancite)
PDR	New Democratic Party (*Partia Demokrate e Re*)
PDSh	Democratic Party of Albania (*Partia Demokratike e Shqipërisë*)
PDSH/DPA	Democratic Party of Albanians (*Demokratska partija Albanaca*)
PDSSh	Party of Social Democracy (*Partia Demokracia Sociale e Shqiperise*)
PES	Party of European Socialists
PGS	Alliance of Primorje – Gorski Kotar (*Primorsko–Goranski savez*)
PKSh	Communist Party of Albania (*Partia e Komunistëve e Shqipërisë*)
PKShR	Renewed Communist Party (*Partia Komuniste e Shqipërisë e Rindertuar*)
PLL	Legality Movement Party (*Partia Lëvizja e Legalitetit*)
PPS	Party of Danube Serbs (*Partija podunavskih Srba*)
PPSh	Albanian Party of Labour (*Partia e Punës e Shqipërisë*)
PR	proportional representation
PRPSh	New Albanian Party of Labour (*Partia e Re e Punës së Shqipërisë*)
PRSh	Republican Party of Albania (*Partia Republikane e Shqipërisë*)
PR-STV	PR single transferable vote
PSDSh	Social Democratic Party of Albania (*Partia Socialdemokrate e Shqipërisë*)
PSS	Movement of the Serbian Force (*Pokret snage Srbije*)
PSSh	Socialist Party of Albania (*Partia Socialiste e Shqipërisë*)
PUK	Party of National Unity (*Parti Unitet Kombëtar*)
PZ	Party of the Greens (*Partija na zelenite*)
PzP	Movement for Change (*Pokret za promjene*)
QBS	Quota Borda System
RKP-BiH	Workers' Communist Party of Bosnia and Herzegovina (*Radničko-komunistička partija Bosne i Hercegovine*)
RS	Republika Srpska
RSK	Republika Srpska Krajina
RS RS	Radical Party of RS (*Radikalna stranka Republike Srpske*)
RV	Vojvodina Reformists (*Reformisti Vojvodine*)
SAA	Stabilisation and Association Agreement
SBHS	Slavonia–Baranja Croatian Party (*Slavonsko–Baranjska Hrvatska stranka*)
SBiH	Party for BiH (*Stranka za Bosnu I Hercegovinu*)
SČP	Serbian Chetnik Movement (*Srpski četnički pokret*)

SD	Social Democrats of BiH (*Socijaldemokrati Bosne i Herce- govine*)
SDA	Party of Democratic Action (*Stranka demokratske akcije*)
SDH	Social Democrats of Croatia (*Socijaldemokrati Hrvatske*)
SDP-BiH	Social Democratic Party of BiH (*Socijaldemokratska partija BiH – socijaldemokrati*)
SDP	Sandžak Democratic Party (*Sandžacka demokratska partija*)
SDP	Social Democratic Party of Croatia (*Socijaldemokratska par- tija Hrvatske*)
SDS	Serbian Democratic Party (*Srpska demokratska stranka*)
SDS-BiH	Serbian Democratic Party BiH (*Srpska demokratska stranka BiH*)
SDSM	Social Democratic Union of Macedonia (*Socijaldemokratski sojuz na Makedonija*)
SDSS	Independent Democratic Serbian Party (*Samostalna demokratska Srpska stranka*)
SDU	Social Democratic Union (*Socijaldemokratska unija*)
SF	Sinn Féin
SFRY	Socialist Federal Republic of Yugoslavia
SI	Socialist International
SK CG	League of Communists of Montenegro (*Savez komunista Crne Gore*)
SKBiH	League of Communists of BiH (*Liga komunista BiH*)
SKH	League of Communists of Croatia (*Savez komunista Hrvatske*)
SKJ	League of Yugoslavian Communists (*Savez komunista Jugo- slavije*)
SKM-PDP	League of Communists of Macedonia (*Sojuz na komunistite na Makedonija*)
SKS	Union of Communists in Serbia (*Savez komunista Srbije*)
SL	Serb List (*Srpska lista*)
SLS	Independent Liberal Party (*Samostalna liberalna stranka*)
SMP	Union for Peace and Progress (*Savez za mir i progress*)
SNP	League of People's Rebirth (*Savez narodnog preporoda*)
SNP	Socialist People's Party of Montenegro (*Socijalistička nar- odna partija Crne Gore*)
SNS	Serbian National Party (*Srpska narodna stranka*)
SNS	Serbian National Union (*Srpski narodni savez*)
SNS	Serbian Progress Party (*Srpska napredna stranka*)
SNS RS	Serbian Progressive Party of RS (*Srpska napredna stranka Republike Srpske*)
SNSD	Alliance of Independent Social Democrats (*Savez nezavisnih socijaldemokrata*)
SPM	Socialist Party of Macedonia (*Socialistička partija na Make- donija*)
SPO	Serbian Renewal Movement (*Srpski pokret obnove*)

SPRS	Socialist Party of RS (*Socijalistička partija Republike Srpske*)
SPS	Serbian Socialist Party (*Socijalistička partija Srbije*)
SRJ	Federal Republic of Yugoslavia (*Savezna Republika Jugoslavija*)
SRP	Socialist Workers Party of Croatia (*Socijalistička radnička partija Hrvatske*)
SRPH	Croatian Socialist Labour Party (*Socijalistička radnička partija Hrvatske*)
SRS	Serbian Radical Party (*Srpska radikalna stranka*)
SRSG	Special Representative of the Secretary General
SRSJ BiH	Union of Reform Forces of Yugoslavia in BiH
SRSM	Union of Reform Forces of Macedonia (*Sojuz na reformski sili na Makedonija*)
SRS RS	Serbian Radical Party of RS (*Srpska radikalna stranka Republike Srpske*)
SSDS	Independent Democratic Serb Party (*Samostalna Srpska demokratska stranka*)
SSS	Independent Serb Party (*Samostalna Srpska stranka*)
STV	single transferable vote
SVM	Union of the Vojvodina Hungarians (*Savez Vojvođanskih Mađara*)
TRS	two-round system
UBHSD	Union of Social Democrats of BiH
UÇK	Kosovo Liberation Army (*Ushtria Çlirimtare e Kosovës*) or National Liberation Army *(Ushtria Çlirimtare Kombëtare)*
UK	United Kingdom
UN	United Nations
UNMIK	UN Mission in Kosovo
UNPREDEP	UN Preventive Deployment Force
UNPROFOR	UN Protection Force
USSR	Union of Soviet Socialist Republics
VMRO-DPMNE	Internal Macedonian Revolutionary Organisation – Democratic Party for Macedonian National Unity (*Vnatrešno – Makedonska revolucionerna organizacia – Demokratska partija za makedonsko narodno edinstvo*)
VMRO-NP	Internal Macedonian Revolutionary Organisation People's Party (*Vnatrešna Makedonska revolucionerna organizacija – narodna partija*)
VP	Vojvodina Party (*Vojvođanska stranka*)
WTO	World Trade Organisation
ZL	United List
ZPM	Green Party of Macedonia (*Zelena partija na Makedonija*)
ZZT	Together for Tolerance (*Zajedno za toleranciju*)

Introduction

Věra Stojarová

The first political parties in the Western Balkans in the post-bipolar era were founded back in the late 1980s. Nevertheless, the development of party politics was influenced by the turmoil of war, the subsequent installation of non-democratic regimes in several countries, and the delayed process of nation and state building in several of them. In Croatia, the winner of the transition happened to be the Croatian Democratic Union (HDZ) which ran the country in a not-fully-democratic manner throughout the 1990s. The HDZ at the time was aggregating the interests and preferences of the majority of the population, whose interest was the independence and sovereignty of Croatia. The opposition remained fragmented until the 2000 elections, when the position of the leading party was taken over by the Social Democrats (SDP) and the Croatian Social Liberal Party (HSLS). Nevertheless, the HDZ came back to power three years later, and in the 2007 elections was confirmed as the party of government. Croatia is now seeking EU accession very quickly, and hopes to integrate into the European structures by 2010 or at the latest 2011.

The war in 1992–1995 and the subsequent protectorate of the international community on Bosnia and Herzegovina (BiH) had a vast impact on its party landscape. The three ethnic groups have not changed their pre-war goals (the Serbs are still striving for an independent RS or annexation by Serbia; the Bosniaks want to have a unitary state, while the Croats are not really sure, some wishing to have their own entity within BiH). The political parties based on nationalism are therefore gaining popular support. The main party voted for by the Bosniaks remains the Party of Democratic Action (SDA); the Croats cast their preferences for the Croatian Democratic Union (HDZ) or HDZ-1990, while the party representing Serbian interests is the Union of Independent Social Democrats (SNSD) which replaced the previously prominent Serbian Democratic Party (SDS). The lack of a common goal in BiH is now being clearly reflected in the discussions over a new Constitution for Bosnia and Herzegovina. It seems for the moment that the European Union mission will stay in the country until a shared goal for all three ethnicities is found.

The adoption of nationalism helped the League of Communists of Serbia to re-orient itself in the post-bipolar world and remain in power as the Socialist Party of Serbia. Serbian engagement in four conflicts (the wars in Slovenia,

Croatia, Bosnia and Herzegovina, and Kosovo) brought economic embargos, political isolation and an enormous drop in the standard of living. Serbia lagged behind in terms of European integration, and furthermore the conflict with NATO in 1999 put Serbia out of favour with many European countries. National reconciliation has still not taken place in any country in the Western Balkans – nevertheless, in Serbia, it seems to be one of the preconditions for accession to the EU. At the very least, a public debate over national reconciliation is needed in Serbia in order to reach a consensus in the society about its future.

Montenegro decided at the beginning of the 1990s to stay with Serbia within the Federal Republic of Yugoslavia. Later, however, Montenegro began to split with Serbia, transforming the unit into a loose state of Serbia and Montenegro, and after a tight referendum, proclaiming independence in 2006. Montenegrin party politics has been dominated by the post-communist successor party, the Democratic Party of Socialists of Montenegro (DPS), led since 1998 by Milo Đukanović. Montenegro submitted its application for EU membership in December 2008. However, the EU demands that Montenegro engage in the fight against organised crime, nepotism, and the excessive intermingling of politicians with business affairs.

Macedonian party politics has been dominated by two parties – the Social Democratic Union of Macedonia (SDSM), and the Internal Macedonian Revolutionary Organisation – Democratic Party for Macedonian National Unity (VMRO-DPMNE). One of the main obstacles in its Euro-Atlantic integration is Greece's objection to the country's constitutional name, the Republic of Macedonia. According to the provisional interim agreement, the country name to be used in international organisations is the Former Yugoslav Republic of Macedonia (FYROM). Nevertheless, Greek officials have stated many times that Greece will object to Macedonian entry into EU and NATO until the name dispute is resolved.

Kosovo was under international auspices until it unilaterally declared independence on 17 February 2008. Subsequently it was recognised by more than 50 countries, while the process of governance is to be supervised by the newly-launched EU mission EULEX. Political parties were mostly formed as single issue parties with few programmatic policies. The ethnic Serbian party scene is divided – one part does not communicate with the newly proclaimed state, while some politicians consider that the only future for the ethnic Serbs in Kosovo lies in participation in local politics. Even though the international community has been operating in the region since 1999, Kosovo still has a long way to go towards being offered membership in the EU: the main EU objections are expected to be insufficient efforts in the fight against organised crime, clientelism, and nepotism.

In Albania a bipolar party system emerged, with the communist successor Socialist Party of Albania and the Democratic Party of Albania as the two main competitors. The lack of any democratic experience and a very low standard of political culture led to the establishment of not very democratic practices in the 1990s. Bearing in mind its starting point, Albania must be praised for its great progress. Nevertheless, when compared to other functioning democracies, there is still much work to be done in order to achieve the democratic standards of, and become fully integrated into, European structures.

Even though there has been an enormous output of books about the Balkans in recent years, the party systems of the Western Balkans as such have attracted little attention in the past. Probably the most comprehensive book dealing with party politics in the CEE is the IDEA publication *Political Parties in Central and Eastern Europe*, downloadable directly from the IDEA webpage. Another book covering selected Western and Eastern Balkan countries (minus Croatia and BiH) worth mentioning is the volume edited by Karasimeonov, *Political Parties and the Consolidation of Democracy in South Eastern Europe*, published in Sofia 2004. Among the books covering elections in the respective countries are *Izbori i konsolidacije u Hrvatskoj* edited by Goran Čular, *Izbori u SRJ od 1990 do 1998* by Vladimir Goati or *Izbori u BiH* by Herceg and Tomić, or most recently *Volební systémy postkomunistických zemí* written by Jakub Šedo. Besides these, mention must be made of case studies dealing either with the selected party systems or the state of transition – e.g. *Dileme demokratske nacije i autonomije* by Jovan Komšić, *Demokratija u političkim strankama Srbije* by Zoran Lutovac, *Kriza i transformacija političkih stranaka* by Anđelko Milardović *et al.*, *Partijski sistem Srbije* by Stojiljković, *Razvoj političkog pluralizma u Sloveniji i Bosni i Hercegovini* edited by Danica Fink Hafner and Mirko Pejanović or the latest *Politics of World Views* by Bojan Todosijević.

As we have seen, the only publications to date are case studies in local languages, and comparative studies in terms of the whole CEE (e.g. *Political Parties in Post-Communist Eastern Europe* by Lewis). *Party Politics in the Western Balkans* tries to fill the vacuum and satisfy the demand from both academic and more general circles. The authors not only describe party politics, but also try to analyse the different outcomes of similar situations on the level of inter-ethnic or inter-party cooperation or competition. The authors do not intend to offer a deep analysis or further conceptualisation of the phenomenon of party politics in the countries in transition; rather, the publication should serve as a starting point for further research or as essential literature for students of political science or Balkan studies.

The authors examine the development of party politics in the Western Balkans, an area defined in EU terminology as the ex-Yugoslavian states minus Slovenia, plus Albania.[1] The text encompasses the development of party systems in the given region, depicts important political issues in each of these countries, and explains the parties' particular policies in relation to these issues. The book also concentrates on the extent to which nationalism has dominated politics. It also considers party organisation, the stability of the parties, important changes in party policies, the parties' electoral performances and personalisation of the parties. In addition to the chapters on each of the countries, the book offers an overview of the electoral systems and their link to the party systems, the legacy of the socialist/communist parties, and a comparison of the nationalist parties in the region, as well as the opportunities for the national minorities in the given systems.

The book consists of an introduction, 12 chapters, and a conclusion. The first chapter focuses on the electoral systems and their possible impact on the party systems. The authors give an overview of the electoral structure in all the countries, and some concluding remarks about the link between the electoral systems and the shape of the party systems. The second chapter concentrates on the legacy of the communist/socialist parties, giving an overview of the transformation of the communist parties and their position in the current political system. The author explains why in some countries the transformed communist parties do not win elections while in other countries they do. Besides the successor parties, any new communist/socialist parties are spotlighted and presented in the overall context. The third chapter focuses on nationalist issues in the 1990s, and gives an overview of the nationalist parties in the assigned countries. It presents the highly fragmented Croatian nationalists, the tricky case of Bosnia and Herzegovina, and gives special attention to the nationalist approach of the Socialist Party of Serbia as well as the Serbian Radical Party. The author tries to assess the strengths and the potential of these parties along with their relevance in the system, and stresses the main differences between the ideologies of all the various parties. The fourth chapter focuses on the role and status of national minorities in the party systems. The text focuses on positive discrimination in favour of national minorities in terms of assigned seats in parliament, and the authors try to assess the ethnic and national minority parties in the region. The next nine chapters are intended as case studies of party politics in each country. Each chapter begins with an overview of the political system, and introduces the main points in the political development of each state (changes to the constitution, changes to the previous undemocratic system, involvement in wars, important political changes), and an overview of the national minorities and the latters' participation in the system. The authors focus on the countries' particular circumstances, and identify the main cleavages. The texts encompass electoral systems, personalisation of the parties, and other specific issues (coalition potential, party system fragmentation, centripetal/centrifugal tendencies, polarisation, party programmes etc.) As the authors regard Serbia as a unique case, an additional chapter about regional party systems looks at the political party landscape in Vojvodina, Sandžak and the Preševo Valley. The final chapter highlights the common themes which emerged from the complete text, and focuses on the issues presented in the introduction. The author draws some general conclusions, presents regional variations, and compares them with existing literature about party systems.

The book was written as a study of the area of the Western Balkans; a descriptive approach was used in the country study chapters, accompanied by an empirical–analytical approach regarded to be most appropriate. When trying to gain access to sources, the authors had to face poor accessibility of the primary sources, as well as their contradictory nature. Official materials very often offer subjective points of view, and the secondary sources tend to accept these. Access to the archives or current governmental documents is sometimes very problematic, and when interpreting *the facts* one has to keep in mind the origin of the author and the perception of his opponent as well. For the purpose of the third chapter on the nationalist parties, a questionnaire was used to obtain information about the parties and their processes, via high-level party officials. For the purposes of the other chapters, primary research was combined with the collection of a wide range of data. The sources used were printed, oral, and electronic. Most of the authors' sources are either directly from the political parties, or gained on research trips in the Balkans from the local institutions (e.g. Albanian Institute for International Studies in Tirana, the Euro-Balkan Institute in Ohrid, the Institute for Social Sciences in Belgrade, the Faculty of Social Sciences in Ljubljana, etc.).

Regarding the authors, Peter Emerson works as the director of the de Borda Institute, an international NGO which specialises in promoting preference voting, especially in plebiscites on sovereignty. Florian Bieber is a Lecturer in East European Politics at the University of Kent, Canterbury. Věra Stojarová and Jakub Šedo work as Assistant Professors at the Department of Political Science and as Academic Researchers at the Institute for Comparative Political Research at the Faculty of Social Studies, Masaryk University in Brno. Daniel Bochsler is a post-doctoral researcher at the University of Zurich.

As for terminology, the authors use the term Macedonia (when citing Greek sources then FYROM) and Bosniak (instead of Bošnjak or Muslim). Kosovo/ Kosova/Kosovo and Metohija (KiM) will hereafter be written as Kosovo, and it will be dealt with separately. Republika Srpska will be used (vs. the Republic of Srpska) in order to avoid confusion with the Republic of Serbia. Even though the term international community has been profaned (and not only in relation to the Balkans), and it does not actually reflect the IC, the authors opted to use this term in its prevalent meaning for the USA and the EU states. Terms appearing in the text have been adopted on the basis of party documents and do not represent any siding by the author with the rival parties.[2] The authors do not change the transcription of names; differences in transcription may occur in direct quotations (đ vs. dj; ç vs. č or q). If they do differ, all transcriptions of the toponyms were included in the text (e.g. Obiliq/Obilić). Albanian names are kept in the original Albanian transcription, while Serbian names are written according to the rules of transcription of Cyrillic into Latin alphabet.

The authors would like to thank the Institute for Comparative Political Research for institutional backing, proofreading of the texts, and the opportunity to arrange meetings among the authors. Further thanks go to all the scholars with whom the text was debated, our students who exposed our research to tricky questions, and last but not least to all of the beloved Balkan peoples.

Notes

1 The term does not correspond with the geographical interpretation, and is the product of social construction. Nevertheless, the term has become standardised and therefore will be used throughout the book.
2 NATO bombing vs. NATO air campaign or humanitarian intervention, Patriotic War vs. ethnic cleansing in Croatia, etc.

1 Electoral systems and the link to party systems

Peter Emerson and Jakub Šedo

There appears to be a general though unwritten rule which suggests that, if the people vote, *ergo* the process is democratic. The standard description of an election – 'free and fair' – applies not to the voting system itself but to all the other factors: the ability of parties to campaign on 'a level playing field'; the freedom with which the media give nationwide coverage to all contestants; the liberty of all voters to cast their votes unmolested; and the transparency of whatever counting system is being used. Be it an election, the voting system itself – whether the electoral system is to be FPP (first-past-the-post), AMS (additional member system), a list form of PR (proportional representation) or whatever, in constituencies large or small, with or without a top-up or set-asides, and with or without quotas based on gender and/or ethnicity – is seldom put under the international microscope.[1]

Electoral systems, then, do vary extensively, from FPP to the multi-preference systems like PR-STV (proportional representation – single transferable vote). Furthermore, some are single tier, like FPP and many PR-list systems; others are two tier, with either the one vote being counted twice (as in AMS) or with two votes (MMP – multi-member proportional). A further variation comes with gender quotas, which apply either in the nomination of candidates or in the conduct of the count. And the choice of electoral system often has a direct impact on the number of political parties which gain representation.

The legacy of an electoral system can be no less profound than the consequences of using the majority vote in decision-making. Indeed, the party system is directly related to the electoral system, and this is known as Duverger's Law.[2] If a country uses FPP or TRS (two-round system), it will probably have a two-party (or a 'two-large-and-some-small-parties') system; if it enjoys a form of PR, it will undoubtedly have a multi-party system, and the lower the threshold of that system, the greater the number of parties that will emerge.[3] Thus a country's choice of electoral system, and the adjustments it makes to that system, are a major factor in determining the number of parties which contest elections in that society.[4] This fact is generally accepted (whereas the consequences of majority voting in referendums and/or parliamentary votes are seldom recognised).

The degree of proportionality depends on the number of representatives elected per electoral district, and every system thus has its inherent threshold. In addition, governments sometimes impose a second, artificial threshold, usually to reduce the number of smaller parties gaining representation. As a general rule, the higher the threshold, the larger the coalitions, and the fewer the number of parties/coalitions which gain representation.

In many PR-list systems, some smaller parties tend to regard their list of candidates as campaign material: they submit lists which are as long as possible, with many names of political non-entities, so to compound what is already a fairly crowded market place. Preferential PR systems like PR-STV and QBS (Quota Borda System), in contrast, have the advantage that parties are not tempted to nominate more candidates than they can reasonably expect to get elected.[5]

Just as all the ex-communist countries decided to adopt the majority vote for decision-making, partly out of vested interest but also because this is the way Western democracies operate, so too they chose a party-based electoral system. Initially, most of the Yugoslavian republics opted for TRS, with many of the politicians concerned thinking it suited their vested interests. Later on, many jurisdictions moved to a form of PR-list which is fairly common in Western Europe.[6] One small exception that occurred is Slovenia, which in 1992 adopted a BC (Borda count) for the election of its Hungarian and Italian minorities.

Initially, too, there was a proliferation of parties, as those with principle or ambition manoeuvred for position: not so many parties with majoritarian systems like FPP and TRS; rather more with mixed systems – part FPP/TRS and part PR-list; and more again with fully proportional ones. Given the inherent and in some cases imposed thresholds associated with PR-list systems, many smaller parties manoeuvred themselves into blocs, alliances and coalitions. These often took place 'on negative grounds, where politicians agreed on what they opposed, but [not] on positive grounds' (Woodward 1995: 85). So relationships were often fickle, and coalitions sometimes varied quite considerably from one election to the next, as was the case in Macedonia. The usual trend for many emerging democracies, however, or at least the more stable ones, was for the number of parties to settle down to their respective electoral system's 'natural' level.

Croatia held its elections on 22–23 April, 1990 and 6–7 May; and many others came in the autumn, in the order shown in Table 1.1. In both Croatia and Serbia, the win-or-lose electoral system, TRS, helped the victory of Tuđman and Milošević. While using the same electoral system, Bosnia adopted a consociational form of decision-making, but not for the best of reasons: the Party of Democratic Action (*Stranka demokratske akcije*, SDA), the Serbian Democratic Party (*Srpska demokratska stranka*, SDS) and the Croatian Democratic Union (*Hrvatska demokratska zajednica*, HDZ) had 'secretly agreed before the elections to form a coalition government' (Silber and Little 1995: 232) and they then combined 'to defeat the reform communists and Marković's reformists on the second round' (Woodward 1995: 122).

As can be seen from Table 1.1, the electoral systems used in each country varied, with the trend as already noted moving from TRS, either directly or in stages, to full proportionality.

Table 1.1 Electoral systems in the Western Balkans

	TRS	Mixed FPP + PR	PR list (closed)	PR list (open)	Quota or divisor	Representatives per electoral district	Additional threshold %
Croatia	1990	1992–1995		2000	d'Hondt	14	5
Bosnia	1990		1996	1998	St. Laguë*	14 and 28[a]	3
Serbia	1990			2000	d'Hondt	250	5[b]
Macedonia	1990	1998	2002		d'Hondt	20	nil
Montenegro			1990/1998		d'Hondt	76 and 5[c]	3
Albania	1991	1992	2008*		Hare-Niemeyer[d]	40[e]	n[f]
Kosovo			2001	2008	St. Laguë*	100 and 10	5

Notes

The first four columns show the past electoral systems adopted in the respective countries for the lower chamber (if applicable). The last three columns present the most recently adopted electoral system.

a 14 in RS (Republika Srpska), 28 in the Federation.

b From 2007, this threshold no longer applies to national minorities.

c The five are reserved for a special electoral unit covering the region where mostly Albanians live, but they too are elected by PR.

d As in the 2005 elections.

e 100 single-member seats and 40 elected under PR.

f See http://www.electionguide.org/country. php?ID=3 as under the mixed electoral system used.

* The St. Laguë divisor tends to favour smaller parties.

Throughout Central and Eastern Europe, former Communists have tried to stay in power, adapting themselves as required in order to attract the voters' support. In the former SFRY, the League of Communists and the Reform League of Ante Marković competed with a proliferation of other parties and, generally speaking, the communists were stronger in rural areas. Sometimes, the former communists banged the nationalist drum, as in Serbia; in other republics, the nationalists were of the right, and the former communists and/or Reform League turned into a moderate, cross-community party, the Social Democratic Party (*Socijal demokratska partija*, SDP) of Bosnia being the obvious example.

The choice of electoral system has consequences, not only in the number of political parties which then emerge, but also in the form of government which follows. A two-party system such as FPP or TRS is likely to lead to single-party majority governments, as was initially the case in both Croatia and Serbia. Indeed, as often happens under such electoral systems, Tuđman came to power on the basis of a minority of the votes. Systems based on PR, in contrast, allow for the representation of many parties, often in a way that no one party has a majority of the seats. There may then follow a period of instability as the various parties wheel and deal in order to come to some sort of *modus operandi* based on a majority, but whether this stage of the proceedings is itself democratic is open to question. This is often seen as a disadvantage of PR.

We will now look at each jurisdiction in turn, and in the same chronological sequence, before then summarising with an overall assessment.

Croatia

Given the inter-ethnic tensions in Croatia/Yugoslavia in 1990, there were not as many parties as might otherwise have been expected to participate in a country's first post-communist election. Ivica Račan, the leader of Croatia's former communists, opted for TRS 'in the mistaken belief that his party would be its principal beneficiary' (Bennett 1995: 127). As it happened, Račan won just 28 per cent of the vote. The biggest winner was Tuđman who finished, with 'only 41.5 per cent ... [but] this winner-takes-all system translated 41.5 per cent into 58 per cent of the seats' (Woodward 1995: 119). He then formed a grand but not quite all-party coalition, i.e. every party except the SDS.

For the 1992 elections, the system was changed to a semi-proportional model: 60 seats were now to be elected by FPP, which suited the big parties; and 60 by PR-list, so any smaller parties still had a chance, for the additional threshold was only 2 per cent. Parties with levels of support less than this tended to form coalitions. The 60 PR seats, however, were awarded regardless of the results in the FPP election, so the system overall was only semi-proportional. In addition, 12 seats were reserved for ex-patriate Croats while a further 15 were set aside for minorities – 11 for Serbs, and four for the others.

In 1992, the dominant party was HDZ. And as can be seen from the table, it was the main beneficiary of this electoral system: with just 45 per cent of the vote, it gained 62 per cent of the seats. All the other parties and the one coalition suffered a disproportionate loss of representation and so, for the second time, the HDZ gained a majority of the seats on a minority of the votes.

Before the next election in 1995, the number of FPP seats was reduced to 28, and there were now to be 80 members of parliament elected under PR; the system was therefore a bit more proportional. But the threshold was raised from 2 to 5 per cent, and new thresholds for coalitions were introduced: a coalition of two parties now needed to jump an 8 per cent hurdle, while any grouping of three or more

Table 1.2 Election results in Croatia

Electoral system	TRS		Mixed				PR list					
Year[a]	1990		1992		1995		2000		2003		2007	
% of vote and seats	%	No.	%	No.	%	No.	%	No.	%	No.	%	No.
HDZ	42	55[b]	45	85	45	75		46	34	66	37	66
Democratic Centre	–	–	–	–	–	–	–	–			7	0
Christian Democratic, HKDU								1				
Party of the Right, HSP			7	5	5	4		4	6	8[c]	4	1
League of Communists, Party Democratic Change[d]	35	20	–	–	–	–	–	–	–	–	–	–
SDP	–	–	6	11	9	9		43	23	34	31	56
People's Party, HNS			7	6				2	8	11	7	7
Peasants' Party, HSS			4	3	18	20		17	7	10	7	8
Social Liberal Party, HSLS	15	3[e]	18	14	12	11		25		3		
Liberal Party, LS	–	–	–	–	–	–		2		2	–	–
Istrian Democratic Assembly	–	–	3	6[f]				4		4	2	3
Pensioners	–	–							4	3	4	1
Other	6	1		5				6[g]	5	7	2	3
Serbian Parties	2	1		3		3		1		3		3
Other minorities						4				3	2	5
TOTALS:		80		138		127		151		151		153

Notes

Tints in the left-hand column refer to parties which merged into, or emerged from, or were submerged by each other, and dashes in the body of the table indicate those elections when the parties did not function, either because they were not yet founded or were already defunct. Other shades of tint refer to coalitions which formed prior to the election, for the purpose of fighting that election, and not to any coalitions which might have occurred in government *after* the election.

a Social Political Council in 1990. The numbers for years 1992 and 1995 refer to the elections to the lower chamber.

b HDZ and HSS formed the Croatian Democratic Bloc.

c A coalition formed with two regional parties.

d The League of Communists became the Party of Democratic Change and then the SDP.

e In the Coalition of People's Accord

f A coalition with a regional party.

g Three of these belong to the SDP–SLP coalition.

parties had to clear 11 per cent. The slightly less popular HDZ still managed to gain a majority of the seats, but second place was now taken by a five-party coalition called *Novi Sabor* (New Parliament), the four shown plus one regional party.

In 2000, FPP was abandoned altogether. The system was now to be PR-list, with ten constituencies each electing 14 representatives with a 5 per cent threshold; in addition, there were a number of representatives for the ethnic minorities.

Like many other countries that use majority voting in decision-making, Croatia has witnessed the emergence of two dominant parties, but given the PR electoral system, there are also a few smaller parties. Croatia's more complex history has meant the process of coming to a 'two-plus-a-few' party system has taken rather longer than might otherwise have been the case. In the years to come, as has happened in other countries of the CEE where initially numerous parties competed for seats and then, in subsequent elections, rather fewer parties participated, the number of smaller parties will probably decrease further.

Bosnia and Herzegovina

As in every other post-communist country holding its first election, the field in 1990 was open. Anyone could set up a political party and contest elections. Radovan Karadžić, for example, started his political career by founding Bosnia's first Green Party, perhaps because the Greens elsewhere, most notably in Bulgaria, had been instrumental in their respective countries' campaigns for independence. It did not take long, however, before he gave up that idea and launched, instead, the SDS (Glenny 1999: 643). And in Bosnia as a whole, a number of parties emerged, some representing one or other of the three ethnic groups, while a few stood on other bases.

The electoral system, TRS, allows the voter to express only one preference. The measure of individual opinions was therefore inadequate, so the result, the expression of the collective opinion, was also inaccurate. It almost certainly did *not* represent the will of the people,[7] for while 'votes were cast most overwhelmingly for ethnonational parties, public opinion polls ... showed overwhelming majorities (in the range of 70 to 90 per cent) against separation from Yugoslavia and against an ethnically divided republic' (Woodward 1995: 228). The three nationalist parties gained votes and seats in ratios comparable 'to individuals' choices of national identity in the 1981 census' (Woodward 1995: 122). Of the 240 seats contested, they took over 200.

The post-Dayton 1996 election was also based on a single-preference system, closed-list PR. Bosnia was roughly 40:30:20 Bosniak:Serb:Croat if, that is, no account is taken of the thousands of mixed marriages and their offspring, let alone those of other ethnic groups, and any Yugoslavs. The resulting 1996 party structure in terms of percentage of seats in parliament was SDA:SDS:HDZ 45:21:19 (Tomić and Herceg 1998: 149).

In a word, the 1990 electoral system was one cause of the Bosnia war, just as the 1992 referendum was another. Similarly, the post-Dayton voting systems

Table 1.3 Election results in Bosnia

	TRS		PR – closed list				PR – open list + av (alternative vote)[b]					
Electoral system / Year	1990[a]		1996		1998		2000		2002		2006	
% of votes and seats	%	No.	%	No.	%	No.	%	No.	%	No.	%	No.
SKBiH		19	–	–	–	–	–	–	–	–	–	–
Reform League		12	–	–	–	–	–	–	–	–	–	–
SDP	–			3	9	4	18	9	12	5	15	5
SDA		87	38	19	34	17	19	8	24	10	20	9
Party for BiH, SBiH			4	2	9	4	11	5	12	6	18	8
SDS		72	24	9	12	4[c]	17	6	15	5	8	3
Serb People's Union, SNS					8	3						
Radicals SRS–RS and RS (RS)			3	0								
SNSD	–						1	1	10	3	16	7
PDP (RS) – Progress							6	2	5	2	2	1
HDZ		44	14	7	12	6	11	5	10	5	5	3
Christian Democrats	–	–									4	2
Croats together HDZ – 1990	–	–					2	1	1	1		
New Croat Initiative, NHI	–	–			2	1		1	1	1		
Pensioners' Parties									2	2		
People's Alliance/Community, DPA/DPC											2	3
Other		7		2		3		4		3	2	1
TOTALS:		240		42		42		42		42		42

Notes

Tints in the left-hand column refer to parties which merged into, or emerged from, or were submerged by each other, and dashes in the body of the table indicate those elections when the parties did not function, either because they were not yet founded or were already defunct. Other shades of tint refer to coalitions which formed prior to the election, for the purpose of fighting that election, and not to any coalitions which might have occurred in government *after* the election.

a Chamber of Citizens.

b AV is used in elections in RS only, for the presidency of RS.

c The SNS and SNSD, along with the smaller socialist party, SP RS, formed the coalition SLOGA.

were and still are a cause of instability. The electoral system has been subject to review by the NWG (National Working Group), and it has now been changed to a PR open-list format.

Many parties emerged in all of the three ethnic groups. Because nationalism was such a dominant factor, however, other more ideological parties tended to be squeezed out; and because majoritarianism was, and still is, so predominant in the internal workings of the parties, each of the three groups tended to split into two leading parties, just as they have in Macedonia.

Among the Bosniaks there were the SDA and the Party for Bosnia and Herzegovina (*Stranka za BiH*, SBiH); among the Bosnian Croats the supremacy of the HDZ was challenged by the New Croatian Initiative (*Nova Hrvatska inicijativa*, NHI) and later by HDZ-1990; while in *Republika Srpska*, a rather more complex situation saw the SDS competing first with the Serbian People's Union (*Srpski narodni savez*, SNS), then under Biljana Plavšić and later with the Union of Independent Social Democrats (*Savez Nezavisnih socijaldemokrata*, SNSD), under Milorad Dodik.

Bosnia, then, is far from being a settled country. There is still talk of secession in RS, and rumblings in Herzeg-Bosna for a third entity. Second, in both entities, the dominant players are the ethnic parties, with the important exception of the SDP. And third, there is still a large number of smaller parties, which only emphasises the overall instability of the political system.

Some observers had hoped the premiership of the SDP's Zlatko Lagumdžija in 2001 was to herald a new era of cross-community stability, but it was not to be. In the elections one year later, support for the SDP was down from nine to five seats. Maybe the nature of the Dayton Agreement was itself part of the problem. It does, after all, institutionalise sectarianism in so many different ways: in the ten cantons, the two entities, the three-person presidency, in the very formation of the institutions of government, and in the veto given to each of the three constituent nations. A further exacerbating component has been the single-preference electoral systems.

Serbia

In December 1990, Slobodan Milošević won 'a peculiar ballot. Less than half the electorate voted', not least because the Albanian-speaking population in Kosovo chose to boycott the poll, and 'the Serbian Socialist Party (*Socijalistička partija Srbije*, SPS) garnered 52 per cent of these votes, and 194 seats [78 per cent] in parliament' (Thompson 1992: 212). In retrospect, then, the Kosovar boycott was perhaps not the wisest ploy.[8] The 'ballot itself was not overtly rigged ... Milošević made sure of victory with a healthy electoral bribe, in the form of massive wage and pension increases, on the eve of the elections' (Bennett 1995: 121).[9]

Like many former Republics of the SFRY, Serbia started with TRS and then moved to a form of PR-list in 2000. The whole country was treated as one constituency, with a threshold of 5 per cent. This made it very difficult for any minority parties representing the Hungarians in Vojvodina, the Albanians in the Preševo Valley, and so on ... let alone the Kosovars, if and when they were to lift their boycott – unless, that is, these minority parties joined others in coalition. Which is often what happened. Indeed, in 2003, there was one coalition of two parties, two of four, three of five, and one of 15!

For a long time, the two dominant parties were Milošević's SPS and Šešelj's Serbian Radical Party, (*Srpska radikalna stranka*, SRS).[10] Slowly, a Western influence made its presence felt. In 2000, the Democratic Party, (*Demokratska stranka*, DS) and the Democratic Party of Serbia, (*Demokratska stranka Srbije*, DSS) came together, if but a little uneasily, so to spell the end of Milošević and, in turn, the decline if not the demise of the SPS. Koštunica was now President, although Đinđić had the more Western orientation.

In the latest contest, Serbia suffered yet another blow to what had been Milošević's dream: they lost Kosovo. But although Šešelj has followed Milošević to the Hague, the former's SRS party continues to play a major role, and the 2008 presidential race was a very divisive contest between the radical Tomislav Nikolić and the pro-European Boris Tadić; the latter won with just 50.5 per cent of the vote. And in the parliamentary elections, a DS-led coalition For a European Serbia gained power, although its overall majority in parliament was wafer-thin. Admittedly, the number of parties in parliament is relatively small, but Serbia is still far from being a stable country in which nationalism does not dominate the political debate.

Macedonia

Macedonia has been described as a lamb surrounded by four wolves. Not just for this reason, democracy has suffered some rather tumultuous birth pangs, and the weaknesses of its adopted party system are ably demonstrated in Table 11.1, where parties aligned themselves *against* those which are similar and *with* those which are not.

As in many other republics, Macedonia changed her TRS electoral system, first to a mixed system, and later to a fully proportional model. In 1998, then, 85 members of the 120-member parliament were elected in single-seat constituencies under the majoritarian principle, and 35 under PR with a 5 per cent threshold.

In the wake of the violence which spilled over into Macedonia, the Ohrid Framework Agreement was signed in 2001. Under its terms, the electoral system was changed to be fully proportional with six constituencies created. But one overall consequence was that 16 parties contested the 2002 contest, as opposed to eight in 1998.

Two years later, the situation settled down considerably, with just two major coalitions, and two unaligned parties. Not yet, however, can Macedonia be said to have a stable polity.

Table 1.4 Election results in Serbia

Electoral system	TRS								PR							
Year	1990		1992		1993		1997		2000		2003		2007		2008	
% of votes and seats	%	No.	%	No.	%	No.	%	No.	%	No.	%	No.	%	No.	%	No.
SPS	46	194	29	101	37	123	34a	110	14	37	8	22	6	16	8	20
SRS	28	22	23	73	14	39	28	82	9	23	28	82	29	81	29	78
DS	7	7	4	6	12	29	–	–	–	–	13	37	23	64	38	102
DSS	–	–		(19)	5	7	boycott		–	–	18	53	17	47b	12	30
G17+c	–	–	–	–	–	–	–	–	–	–	12	34	7	19	–	–
SPO	16	19	–	–	–	–	19	45	4	–	8	22d	3	–	–	–
LDP	–	–	–	–	–	–	–	–	–	–	–	–	5	15	5	13
SSJ	–	–	–	–	–	–	–	–	5	14	–	–	–	–	–	–
Democratic Movement of Serbia, DEPOS	–	–	17	50	16	45	–	–	–	–	–	–	–	–	–	–
Democratic Opposition of Serbia, DOSe	–	–	–	–	–	–	–	–	64	176	–	–	–	–	–	–
Hungarian	–	–	2	3	3	5	1	4	–	–	4	–	1	1	2	4
Bosniak Parties	–	–	–	–	–	–	–	–	–	–	–	–	1	2	1	2
Albanian Parties	–	–	–	–	–	–	–	–	–	–	–	–	1	1	–	1
Others	3	8	25	17	13	2	18	9	4	–	7	–	5	4	5	–
TOTALS:	100	250	100	250	100	250	100	250	100	250	100	250	98f	250	100	250

Notes

Tints in the left-hand column refer to parties which merged into, or emerged from, or were submerged by each other, and dashes in the body of the table indicate those elections when the parties did not function, either because they were not yet founded or were already defunct. Other shades of tint refer to coalitions which formed prior to the election, for the purpose of fighting that election, and not to any coalitions which might have occurred in government *after* the election.

a In 1997, SPS (85 seats) was in coalition with Jugoslav Left (20 seats) and New Democracy (five seats).

b A coalition with New Serbia, (*Nova Srbija*, NS).

c A coalition of 15 parties.

d In coalition with NS.

e DOS, a coalition of NS and 15 other parties, was led by Vojislav Koštunica who defeated Milošević in 2000.

f 2 per cent invalid.

NB The coalition Together, *Zajedno*, which included DS and SPO, fought the 1996 local elections only.

Table 1.5 Election results in Macedonia

Electoral system	TRS		Mixed		PR					
Year	1990	1994	1998		2002		2006		2008	
% of votes and seats	No.	No.	%	No.	%	No.	%	No.	%	No.
Social Democratic Union, SDSM[a]	31	58	25	27	–	60[b]	23	32[c]	24	27
New SDP, NSDP	–	–	–	–	–	–	6	7		(3)
Liberal Party	11	29	7	4	–	–	–	–	–	–
LDP – Liberal Democrats	–	–	–	–		(12)		(5)		(4)
Liberal Party of Macedonia, LPM[d]	–	–	–	–		(5)				
Democratic Party National Unity, VMRO-DPMNE	38	0 (31)[e]	28	49		33	33	43[f]	49	63
VMRO – People's Party, VMRO-NP	–						6	6		(3)
Socialist Party, SPM		8	5	1	2	1		3		
Democratic Alternative			10	13	1	0				
Party for Democratic Prosperity	17	10	19	14	–	2				
National Democratic Party, NDP	5	4								
Democratic Party of Albanians, DPA	–	–		10	–	7	8	11	8	11
Democratic Union for Integration	–	–	–	–		16	12	17	13	18
Parties of Turks, Romas, Serbs	1	2				1	1	1	1	1
Others	3	9					1	1	1	1
TOTALS:	<120	120	<120		120		120		120	

Notes

Tints in the left-hand column refer to parties which merged into, or emerged from, or were submerged by each other, and dashes in the body of the table indicate those elections when the parties did not function, either because they were not yet founded or were already defunct. Other shades of tint refer to coalitions which formed prior to the election, for the purpose of fighting that election, and not to any coalitions which might have occurred in government after the election. Election achievements of junior members of a coalition are shown in brackets.

a The SDSM emerged from the ranks of the former League of Communists.
b A coalition of ten parties.
c A coalition of nine parties.
d The Liberal Party came from the Reform League.
e Successful candidates from the first round withdrew prior to the second.
f A coalition of 14 parties.

Montenegro

Because Montenegro shares both a language and a religion with Serbia, the conflicts which have decimated other republics of the SFRY did not so trouble this mountain state, a land which has always enjoyed or endured a centralist system of governance. Since the Second World War, that rule has been wielded by the League of Communists or, since 1990, its successor, the Democratic Party of Socialists, (*Demokratska stranka socijalista*, DPS). The main political debates were, first, whether or not to support Milošević, and then whether or not to stay in union with Serbia. The first question came to an end in 2000; then, with the passing of the referendum in 2006, so did the second. Politics might now begin to focus on more ideological matters. Not yet, then, has Montenegro settled into a standard, Western style, party-based democracy. For the time being at least, while it had been a one-party state, it is now a bit of a contradiction in terms, a one-party democracy.

Albania

When visiting Albania in 1990, it was interesting to see how the powers that be had tried to cut their country off from the outside world, from *perestroika* and the wave of democratisation which was sweeping across Central and Eastern Europe. But, as the saying goes, nothing could stop the movement whose time had come. Democratisation was, as it were, inevitable. The process has, however, been a troubled one, at its worst at the time of the financial pyramid scandals.

The mixed system adopted for the 1997 elections consisted of 100 MPs elected in single-seat constituencies, while 40 seats were elected under PR, with a 2.5 per cent threshold for parties and a 4 per cent barrier for coalitions. In 2008, a further change was passed for a fully proportional system and a 3 per cent threshold for parties and 5 per cent for coalitions at constituency level.

Albania, then, has two major parties and, for the time being at least, several smaller ones. The two are the Socialist Party of Albania, (*Partia Socialiste e Shqipërisë*, PSSh); and the Democratic Party of Albania, (*Partia Demokratike e Shqipërisë*, PDSh).

Kosovo

> The [Kosovar] electoral system ... is quite straightforward. Seats will be allocated [by] PR (proportional representation) on the basis of closed lists. The Assembly will have 120 seats of which 20 have been set aside for minority communities: ten for the Serbian community, four for the Roma ... three for the Bošnjak, two for the Turkish community and one for the Gorani.[11]

The international community (IC) thus introduced the concept of 'set-aside' seats in order to ensure that at least some of the ethnic minority candidates would be successful, and governments throughout the world have adopted and adjusted voting procedures, for reasons not always benign.

But the party system which has evolved is very different from that which the proponents of the electoral system might have wished. Because the voter is

Table 1.6 Election results in Montenegro

Electoral system	PR – List													
Year	1990		1992		1996		1998		2001		2002		2006a	
% of votes and seats	%	No.	%	No.	%	No.	%	No.	%	No.	%	No.	%	No.
Reform League	14	17	–	–	–	–	–	–	–	–	–	–	–	–
Liberal Alliance or Party, LS, (LSCG)	–	–	12	13	6	–	6	5	8	6	6	4	4	3
SDP	–	–	4	4	–	–[b]	–	–	–	–	–	–	–	–
League of Communists, SKCG	56	83	–	–	–	–	–	–	–	–	–	–	–	–
DPS	–	–	43	46	50	45	49	42	42	36	47	39	49	41
Socialist People's Party, SNP	–	–	–	–	–	–	37	29	41	33	38	30	14	11[c]
Serbian List, SL	–	–	–	–	–	–	–	–	–	–	–	–	15	12
SRS	–	–	8	8	4	0	–	–	–	–	–	–	–	–
People's Party, NS	13	13	13	14	25	19	–	–	–	–	–	–	–	–
Movement for Change, PzP	–	–	–	–	–	–	–	–	–	–	–	–	13	11
SDA	10	12[d]	–	–	3	3	–	–	–	–	–	–	–	–
Democratic Alliance[e]					2	2	2	1	1	1	2	2	1	1
Various other Albanian Parties					1	2	1	1	1	1	2	2	2	2
TOTALS:		125		85		71		78		77		75		81

Notes

Tints in the left-hand column refer to parties which merged into, or emerged from, or were submerged by each other, and dashes in the body of the table indicate those elections when the parties did not function, either because they were not yet founded or were already defunct. Other shades of tint refer to coalitions which formed prior to the election, for the purpose of fighting that election, and not to any coalitions which might have occurred in government after the election.

a Of the 81 seats, five are for special polling unit inhabited mainly by the Albanian population. Two of the five were elected on the DPS list, one for the Democratic Alliance, and two others.

b Due to the electoral system, the SDP did not gain any seats, despite passing the threshold.

c A coalition of SNP, NS and DSS.

d A coalition of three parties.

e One of the larger Albanian parties.

Table 1.7 Election results in Albania

% of votes and seats	TRS						Mixed					
Year	1991		1992		1996		1997		2001		2005	
	%	No.	%	No.	%	No.	%	No.	%	No.	%	No.
Party of Labour	56	169	–		–		–		–		–	
PSSh	–		25	38	20	10	–	101	42	73	9	42
Socialist Movement Integration LSI	–		–		–		–		–		8	5
PDSh	39	75	62	92	56	122	–	25			8	56
Democratic Alliance PAD								2	3	3	5	3
New Democratic Party PDR									5	6		(4)
Albanian Republican Party PRSh			–	1	6	3						(11)
National Front BK					5	2		3			33	18[a]
SDP or PSDSh			4	7				10	4	4	13	7
Human Rights Party			–	2	4	3		4	3	3	4	2
Agrarian Party									3	3	7	4
Others	1	6						10	10	2	4	3
TOTALS:		250		140		140		155		140		140

Notes

Tints in the left-hand column refer to parties which merged into, or emerged from, or were submerged by each other, and dashes in the body of the table indicate those elections when the parties did not function, either because they were not yet founded or were already defunct. Other shades of tint refer to coalitions which formed prior to the election, for the purpose of fighting that election, and not to any coalitions which might have occurred in government *after* the election. Election achievements of junior members of a coalition are shown in brackets.

a An eight-party coalition; the BK itself won no seats.

allowed only one preference, the voting, as in BiH, is almost bound to be ethnically based. Second, within the Albanian electorate, many people vote from allegiances to families and clans, and here too, a majoritarian party system of politics is not necessarily the most appropriate.

In 2001, the first election after the war, the turnout of the Serb vote was 'patchy, with a higher turnout in the enclaves than in Mitrovica'.[12] By 2004, however, it was down to 0.25 per cent. Of the other ethnic minorities, in contrast, the Turks and the Bosniaks sometimes gained a seat in the main (100 seat) contest as well as in the set-asides – see Table 1.8.

Meanwhile, among the Albanian parties, changes are underway. The fortunes of the more pacifist party Democratic League of Kosovo (*Lidhja Demokratike te Kosovës* LDK), are beginning to wane, not least in the wake of the death of its charismatic leader, Ibrahim Rugova, in 2006. In its place, the more militant Democratic Party of Kosovo (*Partia Demokratike e Kosovës* PDK), under Hashim Thaçi, the former leader of the KLA has come to dominate parliament. With the 17 February 2008 declaration of independence, some degree of internal stability has been achieved, except in Mitrovica.

Kosovo is now, both *de jure* and de facto, almost an independent nation. It is not yet, however, at peace with itself. Meanwhile, of course, the implications of its nationhood stretch well beyond its borders: not only to Preševo and RS, but also to the Caucasus and the conflict in South Ossetia.

Conclusion

In the immediate wake of the Dayton Agreement, many commentators held the almost naïve assumption that, once the elections were held in September 1996, Bosnia would then be democratic and everything would be all right. It was not.[13] When it came to Kosovo, the IC was a little more reticent, so elections were held but not with quite the same haste.

As in Bosnia so too in Kosovo, the choice of electoral system was entirely in the hands of the IC and, in both jurisdictions, the prevailing concept was of a simple, single-preference form of list-PR, albeit, as was noted earlier, with a number of set-aside adjustments for Kosovo's national minorities.

For the moment at least, then, most ex-Yugoslav countries have adopted a single-preference PR-list system, albeit with adjustments to cover ethnic minorities, and/or thresholds to influence the number of parties or coalitions gaining representation in parliament. In so doing, they have predicated a multi-party system. In normal circumstances, TRS would cater for two larger parties; a mixed electoral system would allow for two larger parties, and a few smaller ones; while a fully proportional single-preference system, which tends to entrench the existing parties, may lead to a multi-party system, depending on the size of electoral districts and the existence of any threshold: the smaller the electoral district, and the higher the threshold, the fewer the number of parties and/or coalitions which gain representation.

If and when stability is achieved, the outcome of a PR-list system is usually a two-big-plus-a-few-small-party system, with the main differences between the

Table 1.8 Election results in Kosovo

Electoral system	100 PR + 20 set-aside					
Year	2001		2004		2007	
% of votes and seats	%	No.	%	No.	%	No.
LDK	46	47	45	47	23	25
New Kosovo Alliance, AKR	–	–	–	–	12	13
PDK	26	26	29	30	34	37
Alliance for the Future, AAK	8	8	8	9	10	10
Reformist Party, ORA	–	–	6	7	4	0
Christian Democrats			2	2	10	11
Democratic League of Dardania, LDD	–	–	–	–		
Others	9	7 + 10	7	5 + 10	5	4 + 10
Coalition Return	11	12 + 10				
Other Serb Parties*			2	10		10
TOTALS:	91	100 + 20	99	100 + 20	98	100 + 20

Note
*The Serb vote was split in 2004 between two different groups, while in 2007, there were five.

parties/coalitions being, at least in theory, ideological. Slovenia has achieved such a situation but, as we have seen, many of the countries under current discussion have not (yet). A comparison of the number of political parties/ coalitions gaining representation in parliament, for all the former republics, is as shown in Figure 1.1.

The electoral systems of the Western Balkans have often undergone complicated development. None of the countries maintained the rules which were used during the first elections. Generally, we can observe the continuation of a trend which was identified in the mid 1990s by Dieter Nohlen and Mirjana Kasapović (1996: 213–59) – a gradual reform as follows: two-round majoritarian system → mixed system → list proportional system.

Albania stands out as the only country which has adopted different variants of a mixed system,[14] though the next elections in 2009 will take place according to a list proportional system.

When judging the changes adopted in the usage of a list proportional system, we do not come to any general conclusion. When countries decided to reform their systems in the beginning of 1990s, we could identify the trends depicted by Nohlen and Kasapović (1996: 242) – the adoption of rules which limited the chances of small political parties in the electoral competition. Nevertheless, in subsequent years many countries adopted changes which are hard to assess objectively. Montenegro and Serbia have often changed the legal threshold and the size of their electoral districts, and these rules were more favourable for some small parties and less favourable for others. Croatia and Macedonia revoked the legal threshold at the national level when changing from mixed to proportional system. Another example in favour of small parties is the change in

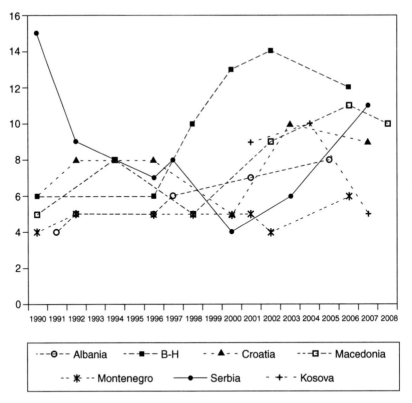

Figure 1.1 The number of political parties in parliament.

Note
The figures for Kosovo refer to the Albanian parties only. Initial information taken from Fink-Hafner and Pejanović 2006: 164.

the modus of recount of votes into mandates in Bosnia and Herzegovina before 1998 elections – see Šedo 2007: 58–67, 72–4, 88–9).

Overall, among the electoral systems in the region, we find various levels of inclusiveness, from the very inclusive one (Kosovo, Montenegro, Macedonia, Bosnia and Herzegovina) to quite disproportional ones (Albania, Serbia), due to the high legal threshold on the national level. A specific feature of the electoral systems in the Western Balkans relates to regulations which are designed to ensure the representation of ethnic minorities. Some countries reserve mandates for certain ethnic minorities (Croatia, Kosovo); minimal representation of all constituent nations is guaranteed on the level of entities in Bosnia and Herzegovina; Montenegro ensures representation of Albanians through the special electoral district inhabited mainly by Albanians in which the 3 per cent national legal threshold is not applied; while ethnic minorities in Serbia do not have to comply with the 5 per cent national legal threshold (Šedo 2007: 58–79).

The evaluation of the impact of the electoral systems on the party systems is rather complicated. The first reason is the particularity of the development of political systems in many Western Balkan countries. In some countries and at certain times, presidential elections (or rather the position of the political parties vis-à-vis the president or the regime which he symbolised) played rather an important role. So, for example, when Croatia introduced a more inclusive system for the 2000 elections, the party system changed in a completely different direction than expected. The number of parties which entered parliament decreased while the will of the parties to cooperate in the framework of electoral coalitions increased (Šedo 2007: 212–19). The reason was that the elections were perceived as a certain kind of plebiscite about the regime of recently deceased Franjo Tuđman and the HDZ, and so the parties in opposition united in broad coalitions. An analogical situation was observed in Serbia in the 2000 elections, which were supposed to confirm the end of the Milošević regime, even on the parliamentary level. In effect, the opposition united under the electoral coalition DOS, which led to a substantial concentration of the party system and the number of coalitions. Subsequent elections no longer had the character of a referendum (Šedo 2007: 240–5).

A second complication in some countries is the frequency of electoral reforms which limited the impact of the electoral system on the party system. Before the voters and the parties could 'adapt' to certain rules and 'learn' to assess the changes, another reform came with the need to adapt to yet more new rules.

A third factor in some countries concerns electoral fraud which often deformed the results of the elections. The chances of objectively evaluating the impact of an electoral system are thus diminished as the results could have been affected by factors not related to the actual electoral system.

There have also been frequent boycotts of elections by some parties in certain countries, which again hamper our assessment. This was probably most visible during the Macedonian elections in 1994 when after the first round of the elections, two of the opposition right-wing parties agreed to a boycott even though one of those parties had long been one of the two strongest parties representing ethnic Macedonians. Therefore, during one electoral term, the party spectrum was reduced and the elections resulted in an overrepresentation of the winning party (cf. Šedo 2007: 257).

Finally, the splitting of society and political culture have had a key impact on the formation and further development of party systems (Chytilek 2005: 611–12). For example, the division of ethnic Macedonian parties into two blocs, or the predominance of the DSP in Montenegro despite all the electoral reforms which, according to the theory (Duverger 1954: 205), should have supported tendencies to multi-partyism.

Developments of the electoral systems in the Western Balkans and their impact on the party systems present an interesting study, and due to fluctuations of both are still taking place, even 20 years after the fall of the communist regimes.

Notes

1 The main power brokers in the world – most notably the USA with their majority-vote decision-making and FPP elections – would hardly agree to an international agreement which criticised their own systems of governance. Thus international

charters on human rights are invariably rather glib when it comes to the question of democratic rights. Furthermore, the OSCE and other organisations responsible for laying down standards and observing elections operated initially only in the emerging democracies. In the wake of Florida in 2000, however, the OSCE now sends missions to the USA. In like manner, it first came to the UK in 2003.

2 '...a plurality [vote] election tends to produce two-party systems, whereas PR systems tend to produce multiparty systems' (Duverger 1972: 23). His law considers electoral systems only; he did not consider the influence of decision-making, and whether or not decision-making could be taken in other than binary voting procedures.

3 In an FPP election with only two candidates, (i.e. a straight majority vote), a candidate needs at least 50 per cent + 1 of the valid vote. In such a two-party democracy, other minor parties can and do compete, but given the dominance of the two major players, the threshold for success is normally taken as 35 per cent (Lijphart, 1994: 17). Under single-preference PR-list systems, in a two-seater constituency with three candidates, the theoretical threshold is 33 per cent + 1; in a three-seater with four candidates, it is 25 per cent + 1 support. And so on. Thus, in the Netherlands, where the entire country is just the one constituency electing 150 representatives, a party can get its first MP with only 0.7 per cent of the vote. Little wonder, then, that the Dutch have a multi-party system. The precise threshold of any PR-list system depends upon the formula which is used for determining how many votes cast equate to how many seats: the two most common quota formulas are Droop and Hare, while d'Hondt and St. Laguë are the most frequently used divisors.

4 For example, in the German two-vote system, MMP, some members of the Bundestag are elected under FPP while in the second vote other members are chosen under a form of regional PR-list. As a result, Germany tends to have two large parties, and two to three smaller ones.

5 If a party has two quotas of votes in a constituency and yet nominates three candidates, it might find that each candidate gets only two-thirds of a quota of first preference votes.

6 PR-list systems are used in Austria, Belgium, the Netherlands, Spain and throughout Scandinavia. Today they are also the chosen system in Estonia, Latvia, Poland, the Czech Republic, Slovakia, Romania and Bulgaria. Most of these open-list systems allow the voter a single preference, but systems used in Luxembourg and Switzerland are multi-preference, so enabling the voter who so wishes to vote for more than one candidate, and also for more than one party.

7 In a similar way, FPP is sometimes hopelessly inaccurate. In February 1974, in the UK parliamentary elections in Northern Ireland, the Unionists with but 53 per cent of the vote got 92 per cent of the seats. FPP, therefore, was one of the forms of discrimination which caused and/or exacerbated the Troubles.

8 The boycott was perhaps even more ill-advised at the time of the 1992 presidential elections, after Milan Panić had attacked Milošević and when opinion polls 'found that only one third of the electorate supported Milošević' (Woodward 1995: 361).

9 An interesting comparison of how roughly the same percentages of votes can produce quite different percentages of parliamentary seats under a different electoral system is shown on: http://parties-and-elections.de/serbia2.html.

10 The author witnessed an SRS pre-election rally, albeit in RS, in 1996. Šešelj was of course the star attraction, but the build-up included a Serbian Orthodox priest.

11 *Kosovo Assembly Election 2001, Administrative Procedures*, OSCE (Organisation for Security and Cooperation in Europe) and UNMIK (UN Mission in Kosovo), p. 16. All the parties competed on an equal basis for the 100 seats, but the ethnic minority parties also competed, amongst themselves, for the set-asides. A full report, *2001 Electoral Administration and Performance*, is available from IFES (International Foundation for Electoral Systems): www.ifes.org/publication/712b791bb0a27120cec 1d7777d727e3b/04_09_2002_kosovo_survey_english.pdf. According to Article 64 of

the new 2008 constitution, the electoral system is now open list, and while all candid-
ates/parties compete on an equal basis, the Serb parties 'shall have the total number of
seats won through the open election, with a minimum ten seats guaranteed if the
number of seats won is less than ten', and a similar provision is made for the Roma/
Bosnian/Turkish/Gorani minorities, in the same ratio of 4:3:2:1.
12 www.un.org/peace/kosovo/news/kosovo2.htm.
13 In the 1996 election in Bosnia, the count took place in regional counting centers.
'Serious violations were reported in a number of cases … [including] deliberate spoil-
ing of valid ballots' (*The Elections in Bosnia and Herzegovina, 14.9.1996*, Second
Statement of the Co-ordinator for International Monitoring. www.osce.org/docu-
ments/odihr/1996/09/1194_en.pdf).

Accordingly, the procedures were changed to allow the count to take place, not in
some centralised centre but inside the polling station. This is possible with the simpler
electoral systems but not with the more complex PR-STV or QBS. The fact that PR-
list is now common to many OSCE-observed elections may well have a direct impact
on any future choice of electoral system, and thus an indirect one on the resulting
party system.
14 The electoral system used in the elections in 1992, 2001 and 2005, mixed-member
proportional system, is not considered by some authors (Sartori 2001: 31–2; Lebeda
2004: 41) as mixed but rather as personalised proportional system.

2 Legacy of communist and socialist parties in the Western Balkans

Věra Stojarová

As Ishiyama and Bozóki note, the development of communist successor parties[1] in post-communist politics has had an important effect upon the development of democracy (Bozóki and Ishiyama 2002: 393). In some countries the communist party was outlawed; in many cases it was transformed into a party of a socialist or social democratic character; elsewhere, the communist party began to take part in the democratic process, which led to varying results; in some cases, the party transformed itself into a classic socialist or social democratic party; while in other cases it retained a communist ideology. As the literature reveals, the type of the regime, the modus of transition, the manner of financing political parties, the organisation of the parties, as well as the whole political context, all matter. Ishiyama suggests that the patrimonial communist regime (as in Serbia) produced communist successor parties which had to distinguish themselves from the previous communist system and hence turned towards nationalism, while in a national-consensus regime (Slovenia, Croatia), the successor parties developed policies that divorced the party from the past, and led to the emergence of a social democratic identity (Ishiyama 1998: 81–2). Nevertheless, the application of the above-mentioned theory reveals the exceptionality of the Western Balkan countries. In Bosnia and Herzegovina, the ethnic structure and the different goals of the three ethnicities had a great impact on the formation of political parties, which were mainly based on ethnic grounds, and left little space to the parties with a social democratic orientation. A special case is Macedonia – when the issue of independence was resolved, the Social Democratic Union of Macedonia left the nationalist discourse to the re-established VMRO-DPMNE; the transformed party moved significantly to the centre of the political spectrum, and regained its position in the party system. The case of Montenegro is specific as well – the main question was *to be or not to be with Serbia* and the successor Democratic Party of the Socialists of Montenegro (after an internal split) has managed to stay in power up to the present day (2008). Albania is an outstanding example of a country where nationalism was left out, and the socio-democratic orientation was a case of later transformation.

With the exception of Albania, the countries of the Western Balkans adopted a uniform approach towards their communist parties. Albania followed the pattern of Latvia, Lithuania, Romania, Bulgaria and Moldova[2] and outlawed the communist party as early as 1992. Nevertheless, a couple of parties claiming a communist legacy remain active underground, though they have no political impact. The other countries of the region opted for toleration of the extreme left political parties, and occasionally the latter take part in local politics.

New parties which identify with communism emerged on all the party scenes. In Croatia it was the Communist Party of Croatia (*Komunistička partija Hrvatske*, KPH), which was set up at the end of 2005. Nevertheless, the state authorities prevented the party from becoming registered and so the party is functioning underground.[3] Another Croatian party which could be classified as extreme left is the Croatian Socialist Labour Party (*Socijalistička radnička partija Hrvatske*, SRPH) which was founded in 1997.[4] In BiH there is the Workers' Communist Party of Bosnia and Herzegovina (*Radničko-komunistička partija Bosne i Hercegovine*, RKP BiH) formed in June 2000.[5] In Serbia, the most 'successful' revival party happened to be the League of Communists – Movement for Yugoslavia (*Savez komunista- Pokret za Jugoslaviju*) which was founded in 1990s out of the Yugoslav National Army (*Jugoslovenska narodna armija*, JNA) part of the Yugoslav League of Communists. It later became the core of Yugoslav Left Party (*Jugoslovenska levica*, JUL), which governed together with SPS after 1993 (and formally after 1996). A New Serbian communist party was founded in March 1992 – the Party of Labour (*Partija rada*, PR), which since then has striven 'to overthrow the capitalist social system and replace it with the socialist social system'.[6] The party that claims to be the only ideological and legal successor of the Communist Party of Yugoslavia is the Union of Yugoslavian Communists in Serbia – Communists of Subotica (*Savez komunista Jugoslavije u Srbiji – Komunisti Subotice*).[7] Another party which relates its legacy to the previous communist league fighting for Marxism–Leninism is the New Communist Party of Yugoslavia. In Montenegro, the New League of Communists of Montenegro was founded in 1993 and renamed itself the League of Communists of Yugoslavia – Communists of Montenegro.[8] In the case of Kosovo, a radical Marxist group, the National Movement for the Liberation of Kosovo (*Lëvizja Kombëtare për Çlirimin e Kosovës*, LKÇK) was among the first in the 1990s which advocated either independence for Kosovo or the creation of a Greater Albania.[9] In Macedonia, the League of Communists of Macedonia (*Sojuz na komunistite na Makedonija*), founded in 1992, represented the extreme left. In Albania, a group of firm Stalinists announced the foundation of the new party, the Communist Party of Albania (*Partia Kommuniste ë Shqipërisë*, PKSh), whose official date of founding was put at 8 November 1991 – the fiftieth anniversary of the Albanian Party of Labour.[10]

The communist parties in the Western Balkans have retained their internationalism or in many cases Yugoslavism, and so actively cooperate on the regional as well as international levels. One example is the Balkan Conference of Communist and Workers' Parties of the Balkans,[11] with the anti-imperialist struggle being one of its main goals. The less radical parties joined the Socialist International.

This text will look only at the successor parties as conceptualised by Ishiyama, and not the newly born communist parties. Some parties claim to be the only legal successor parties (due to personnel or adherence to ideology), but as they are only partially related to the former ruling parties' resources and personnel, they will only be mentioned in passing. Many scholars claim that the historical legacies and points of departure are important factors explaining transition, while others prefer the type of transition or other criteria (cf. Merkel 1999; Dawisha and Parrot 1997; Linz and Stepan 1996; Beyme 1996; Ishiyama 2002, etc.). This text deals with the factors mentioned by most scholars as influencing the transformation path of the regimes as well as that of the communist parties: the legacy of the previous regime, the type of transition, the electoral performance of the parties, the financing of political parties, their internal organisation and programmatic orientation, external relations abroad, lustration laws, relations to ethnicity and the church, and electoral laws. The chapter concentrates on the legacy of the communist/socialist parties; it gives an overview of the transformation of the communist parties and their position in the current political system.

Successor parties: new European left or communists?[12]

The transition from the communist regimes, as well as the transformation of the communist parties in the Balkans, followed different patterns. Kitschelt has classified the Croatian regime as a national consensus communism, where national competition and interest articulation were permitted and accompanied by a certain degree of bureaucratic professionalisation (Kitschelt 1995). Nevertheless, this categorisation can be questioned, as the League of Communists of Croatia (*Savez komunista Hrvatske*, SKH) was one of the conservative parties where no changes in the terms of democracy were expected due to the fact that most liberals were purged out of the party after the Croatian spring in the beginning of 1970s, when the leadership of the party was dominated by Serbs (disproportionately to the Serbian population in Croatia), who were not willing to take a pro-reform approach. As Pickering and Baskin note '...the waxing and waning of the liberal tradition in Croatian socialism turned more on questions of nationality, autonomy and federalism than on questions of genuine political pluralism and the autonomy of the individual in social life' (Pickering and Baskin 2008: 524). Nevertheless, when the transition eventually happened it came from above, when the reformed communists started to oppose the central Yugoslavian regime and introduced the necessary measures to implement political pluralism.

Even though the party eventually regained the liberal and reformist spirit (with Ivica Račan's victory as President at the 11th Congress of the League of Communists of Croatia in 1989, and in the context of the implosion of other East European regimes and following the example of Slovenia), the party failed to attract voters in the 1990 elections. In 1990 the party added to its name the Party of Democratic Change, and four years later it merged with the Social Democrats of Croatia to create the Social Democratic Party of Croatia (*Socijaldemokratska partija Hrvatske*, SDP).[13] The party remained in opposition till the end of the Franjo Tuđman regime, after which it somehow transformed and recovered, and then came to power in 2000–2003. The 2003 as well as 2007 elections were again victorious for the Croatian Democratic Union (*Hrvatska demokratska zajednica*, HDZ).[14]

When assessing the performance of the SDP, one has to bear in mind that the Tuđman regime monopolised all national policy, and led Croatia in a not fully democratic manner. Politics was nationalised – the HDZ was presented as the winner of the *Homeland war* and the party which helped Croatia to become an independent, sovereign state. Parties which stood against the HDZ were presented not as the political opposition but rather as national traitors who failed to acknowledge the merits of HDZ in the struggle for national self-determination. The elections were by no means considered free and fair – only in 2000 was the OSCE able to declare that the elections to the parliament had made progress towards meeting the country's commitments to democratic governance, while three years later it stated that the elections were conducted generally in line with OSCE commitments and international standards for democratic elections (OSCE 2000: 2 and OSCE 2004a: 1). The same non-democratic pressures were applied to the checks and balances in the Croatian political system, judicial system, and media. Another characteristic of the non-democratic regime was the non-transparent manner of financing political parties. The main problems seem to have been the non-existence of any kind of disclosure obligation for regular campaign funds of the political parties, and non-transparent and limitless donations from the business sector (Petak 2003). The new law on the financing of political parties intended to improve the corrupted environment was only passed in 2006, with the whole process being supervised by the Venice Commission (European Commission for Democracy through Law).

Since the beginning of the transition, the SDP was led by Ivica Račan (1990–2007), a reformed communist who managed to transform the party into a social democratic one. The structural conditions, the great outflow of members of the League of Communists of Croatia,[15] and the position of the SDP in the opposition helped the party to transform itself from the clientelistic type to a programmatic party.[16] The programme of the SDP is that of a modern social democratic party, where no legacies of the communist past are visible. The party distinguishes itself from the HDZ, stressing its civic orientation (e.g. it claims to be willing to revoke the right of the Croatian diaspora to vote in Croatian elections).

The party is now not only part of the Socialist International, but (together with the Macedonian SDSM as the only Western Balkan representatives) an associate member of the Party of European Socialists (PES) as well. As all proposals for a lustration law were removed from the agenda of the parliament, there is no lustration law in Croatia in force which could have an impact on the performance of the SDP. At the very beginning of the transition, the Croatian League of Communists realised that its stance towards the church was harming its popular support, which was reflected in the founding statute of the SDP (1990) which states that religious belief is a private affair and therefore has no impact on party membership. The SDP then extended this provision in its programme: the SDP recognises the freedom and equality of all religions and all religious communities and free expression of religious belief (cited from Markešić 2007: 50 in Milardović *et al.* 2007). The party switched from a completely atheist stance to neither atheist nor theist, and is now capable of welcoming all citizens of a pluralist society.

The winner-take-all electoral law of 1990 helped the HDZ to achieve absolute victory in the initial phase of Croatian transition. Even though the mixed electoral system was used for elections to the lower chamber of the Croatian parliament in 1992, the atmosphere of war and the fact that the HDZ was presented as a movement embodying the whole nation again aided the HDZ victory. The elections of 1995, which confirmed the trend of transforming the electoral system towards a more proportional one (nevertheless disadvantaging the smaller parties), were held in a post-war atmosphere in which the HDZ presented itself as the winner of the war, helping it to a repeat victory. The next elections (2000 and 2003) were held under a fully proportional system with a 5 per cent threshold on the level of the electoral districts. The prevalence of the majoritarian system up to 2000, the non-democratic practices during elections and the extraordinary post-war atmosphere favouring populism, all helped the ruling HDZ hold on to power, while hindering access of the other parties to the political contest.

The death of Franjo Tuđman opened the way for transforming the regime and for the victory of the SDP. The SDP government introduced many changes which moved Croatia more towards the ideals of democracy. Nevertheless, the government comprised of six parties broke down into factions, and was not able to reach important decisions. The indecisiveness of the government, along with other issues (such as turning war indictees over to the ICTY) discredited the party in the eyes of the public, and led to a comeback by the HDZ.

Bosnia and Herzegovina could probably be classified under Kitschelt terminology as patrimonial communism, as one could observe very little inter-elite competition. The transition was the result of events in Slovenia and Croatia. Nevertheless, instead of political pluralism, an ethnic pluralism emerged in BiH (Pejanović in Hafner and Pejanović 2006: 50), and the transition was hindered by the war. The political outcomes after 1995 have been highly influenced by the post-war environment and the fact that BiH is in effect a protectorate under UN, OSCE, NATO and EU auspices. The post-communist parties in BiH did not get much attention, and were in the shadow of ethnic parties in existence at the outbreak of the war (SDA, SDS, HDZ), or which were later founded again with a nationalist appeal (SNSD). The Law of Financing Political Parties was passed in 2000, but the controlling mechanisms incorporated are still followed in practice only with difficulty.

The successor parties in Bosnia Herzegovina have not been as triumphant as elsewhere. The Social Democratic Party of Bosnia and Herzegovina – Social-Democrats (*Socijaldemokratska partija BiH – Socijaldemokrati*) gains more votes only at the Federation of BiH level, while on the level of the parliament of BiH and the parliament of RS it has been represented by only four or fewer members of parliament.[17] The party has failed to win strong support among Croats and Serbs, and is mostly voted for by Bosniaks. Nevertheless, the party has never achieved more seats in the parliament of FBiH than the Bosniak SDA, unlike the Serbian Independent Social Democrats (SNSD)[18] which overwhelmingly won in the 2006 elections over the Serbian Democratic Party,[19] To conclude the overall picture of BiH, it should be added that there is neither a Croatian nor a Serbian political party that could be linked somehow to the former Communist League of BiH; the former communists are dispersed among all the parties. In terms of personnel and party infrastructure, the only relevant post-communist party in BiH to be identified is SDP BiH.

The SDP BiH is a member party of Socialist International and an observer party in PES; it tries to present itself as a multi-ethnic, supranational, and modern social democratic party, recalling the SDP BiH which was founded back in 1909. It promotes social security, social justice, equality (regardless of sex, religion, national or social status), solidarity and accountability, freedom, and equal opportunity for all (SDP BIH 2002). Nevertheless, intra-party democracy is quite weak, as it is with other parties in the region.

No proposal for a lustration law has ever been adopted in BiH. Since 1990 the electoral law has stipulated (on the state as well as entity level) the list proportional system[20] so that pluralism would be ensured. Nevertheless, the systems used resulted in a fragmented political spectrum where the parliaments are composed of more than seven political parties.

Kitschelt categorised the regime in Serbia in the pre-transformation period as patrimonial communism, relying heavily on hierarchical chains of personal dependence between leaders and followers, and with low levels of inter-elite competition, popular interest articulation, and rational bureaucratic professionalisation. The transition, imposed from above, was a transmutation (communism changing to nationalism) rather than what we understand as a transition (transformation to a democratic regime).

In 1990, the League of Communists of Serbia (LCS) was reborn as the Socialist Party of Serbia; technically the party represented a merger of LCS and the Socialist Alliance of the Working People of Serbia. Between 1989 and 1991, membership in LCS/SPS declined by half, but one-third of the 430,000 members in 1990 were new, indicating a real transition, and probably picking up portions of the nationalist electorate. (Goati not dated, cited in Miller 1997: 155). As the party presented itself as the only legitimate representative of the national interest, it succeeded in remaining in power, leading the country until the October revolution in 2000. It must be pointed out, however, that the party dominated politics due to the facts that the regime was not fully democratic, and that elections were not reasonably free and fair. It is highly disputable whether this party could be categorised as socialist, as its policies in the 1990s were mainly based on nationalism, so one might classify the party as extreme-right as well.[21] Furthermore, the party is not really keen on nationalisation of property, or the instalment of socialism in Serbia, and instead supports private property, keeping state control over strategic branches of industry.

The financing of political parties in Serbia did not meet even minimum democratic standards. The legislation was underdeveloped and not enforced. As experts from the Centre for Free Elections and Democracy (CeSID) mention, the parties conformed to the situation, and wealthy people got involved in politics, so determining the very nature of multi-partism and particularly the opposition parties (CeSID not dated). A new Law on Financing Political Parties was passed in 2003; it increased the funds allocated to the parties, and intended to comprehensively regulate the financing of the parties, which was seen as vital for the further development of democracy. Until 2003 the parties were receiving only small amounts of money, and were forced to rely on other sources. Experts from Transparency International state that before the collapse of the Milošević regime there was a wide system of arbitrary utilisation of state resources as the SPS spent state budget funds as if they were their own, which was the reason why Serbia at that time could be called 'a party state' (Goati *et al.* 2004: 13).

The SPS does not give much power to its leader; his main task was to coordinate the work of the party organs and develop set programme goals. Nevertheless, the 1992 statutes enlarged his authority so that the party president also coordinated the relationship between the party organs and the President of Serbia and other state functionaries, provided they were SPS members. The 2000 statutes again enlarged his authority by making the president head of the main committee, and entitled to propose party functionaries; the 2003 status cut back the power of the president for the first time: the right to propose party functionaries returned to the main committee, and the president was no longer ex officio head of the main office (Ristić 2008: 347). Radojević emphasises that the extended leadership character of SPS during the 1990s was not based on SPS statutes but on the authority of the chairman of the party (Radojević 2006: 91 in Lutovac 2006). The personalisation of the party is quite visible considering that from 2001 until his death in 2006, the former leader Slobodan Milošević led the party remotely from the Hague. As Orlović mentions, party leaders in Serbia can lose elections but not their party positions (Orlović 2006: 103 in Lutovac 2006). The party is neither a member of Socialist International nor has any affiliation to the PES. As regards the SI, the party stressed it would like to join, nevertheless the conditions were set as follows – to support the integration of Serbia into the EU, and the renouncement of ultra-nationalist policies. The entry of SPS into SI is hindered not only by internal factions within the party, but by protests from SDP BiH as well.

Along with Albania, Serbia is the only country in the Western Balkans where lustration laws have been passed. However, the law was passed only in 2003, with the main criterion concerning human rights violations; the departure point for the lustration laws was set for the day the International Covenant on Civil and Political Rights in Yugoslavia came into effect (23 March 1976), unlike in other CEE countries where the starting point was usually the time of the communist takeover, explicitly stipulating the prior holding of state or party position (Hatschikjan *et al.* 2005: 24).

The Serbian Orthodox Church played an important role during the 1990s, providing support for Serbian involvement in the wars, although it was not an unconditional supporter of Milošević and his regime (Bardos 1992, cited in Miller 1997: 173). In 1999 the leaders of the Serbian Orthodox Church condemned Yugoslav President Slobodan Milošević as 'the root of all evil'.[22] Nevertheless, ever since the Hague Tribunal was founded, the Synod and the Assembly of the Serbian Orthodox Church have categorically insisted that the tribunal was illegitimate and unfair, and that it places on trial the entire Serbian people and subjects them to a sort of collective guilt (RFE/RL South Slavic, How strong are the Catholic Church in Croatia and the Orthodox Church in Serbia? 31 January 2002, Volume 4, Number 4).

Serbia has carried out four reforms of the electoral system since 1990: the first two corresponded with trends in other post-communist countries in moving from the majority system to a proportional one. In the last reform, however, relatively small electoral units were replaced with a single electoral unit encompassing the whole state, which worsened the position of the small parties (Šedo 2007: 69). In regard to fairness, Goati often cites the violation of the principle of equality of parties in official media, the review of voting material, the rearranging of data by municipal electoral commissions, omissions in the electoral register, substantial electoral manipulation, and great numbers of cases of names of deceased persons in some electoral registers etc (Goati 2001: 108–11, 122–3, 138–9).

In neighbouring Montenegro, the communist regime strongly resembled its Serbian counterpart, with a low level of inter-elite competition, and personal dependence between leaders and followers; it was classified as patrimonial communism under the Kitschelt terminology. The Communist League of Montenegro was renamed in 1991 as the Democratic Party of Socialists of Montenegro (*Demokratska partija socijalista Crne Gore*, DPS) and has been leading the country continually since then. In 1998, the present leader Milo Đukanović took over the party, while former chairman Momir Bulatović formed a new Socialist People's Party of Montenegro (*Socijalistička narodna partija Crne Gore*, SNP)[23] advocating closer ties with Serbia and against the secession supported by Đukanović; this was the major opposition party in Montenegro until the first parliamentary elections in the independent state in 2006. As in the case of Serbia, the successor DPS remained in power and only slowly adapted to the new situation by opening political competition to the other parties. The party retains a chameleonic nature, and is very flexible in adapting to new settings. Until 1997 it was very much under the Serbian yoke, while since then the policy has been to distinguish Montenegrin politics from Serbian ones, and slowly endorsing political and economic reforms. Unlike the SPS, the goal of the DPS is not only integration into the European Union but into NATO as well (DPS 2007).

The Election Monitoring Centre (CEMI) points out that control of financing political parties in Montenegro did not begin until 2006.[24] Even though the 1997 law already saw some provisions about public access to information on the political parties, the law did not specify a mechanism and procedures for the fulfilment of these provisions. A new law introduced in 2004 implies that financial reports will be public, and therefore available to all who show interest, to check the accuracy of these statements. This significantly improved the level of availability of information on the gathering and expenditure of party political funding, not only for election campaigns but regular financing as well (CEMI 2005). The lack of controlling mechanisms allowed too much space for linking up between the political parties and the business sector. New rich elites emerged, closely tied to the ruling party and organised crime (Vreme 14.12.1994 in Bieber 2003a: 25).

The party has been led since 1998 by Milo Đukanović, who served four terms as Prime Minister from 1991–1998, and then again from 2003–2006, in the meantime serving as president of the republic (1998–2002). No other leader in post-communist Europe has dominated the political life of his country for such a long time. He has been dogged by charges of nepotism and shady links to tycoons. Critics point out that Đukanović has never had a consistent ideology beyond merely staying in power. But he has weathered some tumultuous times, and brought his country through two perilous decades without violence (RFE/RL, Pejic: *The Smartest Man in the Balkans*, 17 October 2008). The party is a full member of the Socialist International, and has no affiliation with the PES. Taking the transition into account, it is quite natural that no lustration law has been passed in Montenegro, and no draft lustration bill has been proposed in the Montenegrin parliament.

The party's relationship to the church is quite peculiar, bearing in mind that the Montenegrin Orthodox Church has yet to be recognised as an official church by the communion of Orthodox churches; it is blocked by Serbia, which claims the church's property in Montenegro. Milo Djukanović, pursuing the Montenegrin national identity, was quite careful in supporting the existence of the Montenegrin Orthodox Church, and it was only in 2000 that the state authorities allowed for the recognition of the Montenegrin Orthodox Church. Regarding the stance of the party towards the church, communist atheism was abandoned, and the current DPS party programme calls for ethnic and religious equality (DPS 2007).

The PR party-list system has been in force with minor changes in Montenegro since 1990. In 1992 the 20 very small electoral units were replaced with one large one, which even with a 4 per cent threshold has opened more space for the minor parties. Further changes in the electoral system were rather questionable, and it cannot be said with certainty which parties they favoured (Šedo 2007: 72). Regarding fairness, there were no serious allegations of manipulation of the vote; nevertheless the elections in 1992 cannot be deemed free and fair since the DPS had supremacy over the opposition in the economic and media spheres. The subsequent parliamentary elections in 1998 saw a systematic effort by the state administration to provide all the conditions for fair elections, and they were pronounced 'fair and honest' (Goati 2001: 151; 169–70).

The Macedonian communist political elites were the ones which promoted the preservation of the status quo in Yugoslavia, i.e. a decentralised and communist Yugoslavia. From the mid-1980s on, however, the pro-reform communist elites began to prevail, thus changing the course of Macedonian politics and setting it on the path to political and economic liberalism (Daskalovski 1999: 26). In the Kitschelt terminology the regime until 1985 would probably fall under patrimonial communism, then slowly evolving into one of national consensus. The transformation was started by the communist elite themselves, and seemed inevitable in the course of development in other CEE countries. The League of Communists of Macedonia (LCM) transformed itself into the Social Democratic Union of Macedonia (*Socijaldemokratski sojuz na Makedonija*, SDSM), which then became the main party of government from 1992–1998 and 2002–2006; it currently (2008) holds the position of the second largest party on the political party scene in Macedonia.[25]

The current president of Macedonia, Branko Crvenkovski (2004–present), was the leader of the SDSM in the period 1992–2004. Since then three chairmen have served, with Zoran Zaev leading the party since 2008.[26] As the party was in power during the decisive years of the transformation, it had a decisive role in the economic transformation, and has turned from a socio-democratic orientation towards neo-liberalism. Nevertheless, the party scene in Macedonia is closely tied with ethnicity, and disputed steps taken during the process of implementing the Ohrid Framework Agreement (together with corruption scandals and dissatisfaction of the people with the economic situation) led to the defeat of the party in the 2006 elections. The financing of political parties in Macedonia is regulated by a law passed in 2004 by the Macedonian parliament; this introduced more regulatory measures and opened the way for more transparency in the financing of political parties in the country. As lustration laws were not introduced in Macedonia, the reform leaders from the 1980s managed to stay in power throughout the transition. The relaxed stance of the social democrats towards the Macedonian Orthodox Church played a certain role as well. The electoral system followed a similar pattern as in other countries in the region, moving from the prevalence of majoritarian components to a more proportional one. SDSM is a full member of the Socialist International and an associate member of the PES.

The League of Communists of Kosovo ceased to exist in 1990 and there has been no relevant successor party in Kosovo; the only parties which received attention from the ethnic Albanians in the aftermath of 1999 were those striving for the independence of Kosovo. Many of the parties in Kosovo were formed mainly by communists purged from the LCK during the 1980s, and its former prominent politicians are dispersed among all parties; nevertheless, these latter can not be classified as classical successor parties because they did not inherit the preponderance of the former ruling parties' resources and personnel as conceptualised by Ishiyama.[27]

Along with the Romanian regime, the Albanian communist regime was one of the toughest in Europe, and would be classified under the Kitschelt terminology as a patrimonial system. Even though some *liberalisation* policies were launched after the death of Enver Hoxha in 1985,[28] the transition started somewhat later, and mainly because of the domino effect. It came from below with student protests. The communists, however, pursuing only cosmetic changes, did not want to give up absolute power, arguing that Albania was not ready for democracy. The first elections in 1991 favoured the APL (in terms of party internal structure, nationwide network, resources, and the electoral system); the next elections in 1992 were more democratic, though by no means completely *free and fair*.

The turning point for the Albanian Party of Labour was its tenth congress, which took place on 10 June 1991.[29] The party rejected Marxism–Leninism and its former goal of forming a communist society, and changed its name to the Socialist Party of Albania. The party distanced itself from the APL and tried to present itself as a different party. Some parts of the programme remained in the socialist format (e.g. preservation of farm cooperatives), while some propagated capitalist mechanisms (e.g. privatisation). Neither radical nationalism nor strong ties with any church are advocated for Albania by the Socialist Party.[30]

This party was the leading party of government from 1997–2005, but it lost the most recent elections in 2005 due to internal splits and disagreements. From 1991 the Socialist Party was led by Fatos Nano, a charismatic leader who kept most power in his own hands, allowing no intra-party democracy.[31] Although from time to time some internal opposition against him emerged, he succeeded in suppressing it.[32] Thus Nano was able to hold power until a new person emerged on the party scene – a young, controversial, modern artist and former mayor of Tirana, Edi Rama, who was elected party chairman in 2005, whereupon Nano left to set up a new party. The Socialist Party is a full member of the Socialist International and has no affiliation with the PES.

Albania has no contribution limits from the business sector to the political parties, but a partial ban on foreign donations. Even though public disclosure was introduced, the parties are reluctant to reveal their financing sources and keep the identities of their donors secret. The Socialist Party had great advantage in comparison with other newly established parties in inheriting great resources as well as a well-established network. Although the Democratic Party tried to get rid of its rival by every means, the Socialist Party remained a relevant actor of Albanian politics.

As the leader of the Albanian transition until 1997, Sali Berisha was a fierce opponent of the Socialist Party, and a comprehensive lustration law was passed. In 1993, a law was passed affecting the licensing of private lawyers, and in 1995 further legislation was enacted on state officials. The lustration law was supposed to terminate at the end of the transition, and the law expired on its own terms in 2001 except for one article (Hatschikjan *et al.* 2005: 23).

Albania is one of those countries which has a most unstable electoral system, as each and every election was held according to new rules. The first modifications moved Albania towards a more proportional system. As some majoritarian components of the electoral system were strengthened in the last electoral reform, the Socialist Party will remain along with the Democratic Party as one of the two strongest, forming a bipolar structure and it might even become a two-party system in the next elections.[33]

Communist parties: from pariah to legitimate forces?

All of the communist political parties in the Western Balkans successfully transformed and metamorphosed into socialist or socio-democratic groupings, except the Communist League of Kosovo which ceased to exist in 1990.

The successor parties in the Western Balkans could be grouped according to their development into three categories:

- Parties which lost the initial elections, restructured, and after one or two electoral terms returned to (coalition) governments (Croatia, Albania, BiH);
- Parties which reformed, accepted a socio-democratic orientation, and retained power (Macedonia[34]);
- Parties which adopted nationalist policies and so remained in power (Serbia, Montenegro).

In the Croatian case, the Social Democratic Party came to power after the death of Franjo Tuđman in 2000 and stayed in power until the 2003 elections, while the Albanian Socialist Party won the elections in 1997 after the collapse of the pyramid schemes, and retained power till 2005. The Macedonian Social Democratic Union of Macedonia remained in government until 1998, and returned to government in 2002. The Socialist Party of Serbia kept its position till the October revolution in 2000, while the Montenegrin Democratic Party of Socialists has been in government without pause up to the present (2008). The Social Democratic Party of Bosnia and Herzegovina–Social Democrats is being represented on all levels of the BiH administration, but lacking a nationalist approach it does not appeal much to the voters.

All of the analysed parties except SPS are members of the Socialist International, while only the Croatian SDP and the Macedonian SDSM are associate PES members, and the SDP BiH is an observer party of the PES. One could try to classify the parties according to ideology; in that case we would come to this categorisation.

- Parties with a socialist ideology (Albania approximately until the mid 1990s);
- Socio-democratic parties (Macedonia, Albania, Croatia, BiH);
- Nationalist socio-democratic parties (Serbia, Montenegro).

Most of the parties retained their charismatic or clientelist character, and only in the Croatian case and possibly to some extent in the Macedonian case could one observe a move towards a more programmatic spirit. Nevertheless, all categorisation has to be taken with caution, as the categories remain fluid, and all of the party systems are still developing.

In most cases the communist parties transformed successfully into parties of a (national) social democratic nature. But what about the communist ideas – were they completely abandoned? New communist parties re-emerged in all of the

Table 2.1 Communist successor parties in the Western Balkans

	Previous regime	Transition	Retained power during transition/ got back to power later	Charismatic/clientelist/ programmatic	Socialist/Social Democratic/Nationalist Socio-Democratic	SI/PES	Lustration
SDP	National consensus	Above	No/back later	Charismatic/programmatic	SD	SI/PES associate	–
SDP BiH	Patrimonial	Above	No/partially	Clientelist	SD	SI/PES observer	–
SPS	Patrimonial	Above	Yes/–	Charismatic	NSD	–/–	L
DPS	Patrimonial	Above	Yes/–	Charismatic/clientelist	NSD	SI/–	–
SDSM	Patrimonial/National Consensus	Above	Yes/–	Clientelist/programmatic	SD	SI/PES associate	–
PSSh	Patrimonial	Pressure from below, collapse	Yes/back later	Charismatic/clientelist	SD	SI/–	L

tracked countries. But whether operating legally or from underground, it seems that communist ideology does not appeal any more to the voters and communist parties everywhere remain on the margin of the political spectrum.

Notes

1 Ishiyama defined the successor parties as 'those parties which were the primary successors to the former governing party in the communist regime and inherited the preponderance of the former ruling parties' resources and personnel'(Ishiyama 1998: 62).

2 The Communist Party of Moldova was legalised again in 1993.

3 Quite interestingly the party does not reject democracy, and states that democracy is the basis for original Marxism. Even though the party has anti-capitalist and anti-liberal stances, it advocates Croatian integration into the EU, with a referendum as a precondition (KPH 2005).

4 The party uses the classical communist newspeak (imperialism, exploitation of masses etc.). Regarding the EU, the party would like to see Croatia within the EU, but as an equal member not only *as the ground for cheap labour and a place for investments with non-competitive slaves* (SRPH 2002: 51).The party remains on the margin of the political spectrum (www.srp.hr/).

5 In its programme the party rejects Stalinism, and praises to a certain extent the Yugoslavian model of socialism. One of the main aims of the party is the re-establishment of socialist federal Yugoslavia as a decentralised state. The party does not accept parliamentary democracy as 'it is based on partiocracy – the rule of power parties and their leaders' (www.rkp-bih.org/).

6 Interestingly, the party has stood against Serbian nationalism, and has been striving for peaceful relations among the Yugoslavian nations. For this reason it denounced Serbian policy in Kosovo, and supported the ethnic Albanians during the 1990s (www.partijarada.org/).

7 The party achieves minor successes on the local level, participating in municipal governments.

8 The party takes part in elections but has no representation at the higher level of Montenegrin administration.

9 The party has been taking part in elections since 1999, trying to gain support but with no significant results. The party opposed the presence of the international community in Kosovo and is one of the most radical left political organisations (www.lkck.net). The US Department of Treasury has issued an Executive Order blocking property of persons 'who threaten international stabilization efforts in the Western Balkans' in which LKÇK is listed (United States Department of Treasury. www.treas.gov/offices/enforcement/ofac/actions/20010627a.shtml).

10 The leader of the party Hysni Mylloshi strove to establish a party of the Stalinist type. After the ban on all parties based on Enverism and Stalinism, the PKSH started to operate underground, and split into factions under the leadership of Hysni Mylloshi, Razi Brahimi and Krastaq Mosk. The last-named established the independent Renewed Party of Labour in 1996 under the leadership of Sami Meta. The victory of the Socialists in 1997 meant the legalisation of the communist parties, and so from the PKSH factions there emerged three parties which became legal in August 1998: the Communist Party of Albania (PKSH), the Renewed Communist Party of Albania (PKSHR), and the New Albanian Party of Labour (PRPSH). The programme of these three parties does not differ much – they all admire the era of Enver Hoxha and the role of the Albanian party of Labour in the previous regime. The PKSH was the only communist party to gain one seat in the parliament. In 1998, the United Communist Party of Albania emerged criticising Hysni Mylloshi, the party leader with the highest support of the communist movement abroad.

11 It unites among others the Labour Party of Albania, the Reformed Communist Party of Macedonia, the Labour Party and the League of Communists of Yugoslavia in Serbia. (www.balkanconference.net/english/index.html).

12 For conceptualisation of the term 'left' see March and Mudde 2005; Fiala *et al.* 2007; Schirdewan 2004.

13 For the political party quotas in SDP see Leaković 2004.

14 Pickering and Baskin suggest that the HDZ might be included in the group of successor parties, as it was composed of communists purged from the party in the early 1970s despite the fact that the HDZ's message was ardently anti-communist. The same would go for the Independent Democratic Serbian Party (*Samostalna demokratska Srpska stranka*, SDSS) which was founded only in 1997, again by the ex-communists (Pickering and Baskin 2008: 528).

15 Between the end of 1989 to June 1990, membership in SKH-SDP fell from 298,000 to 46,000 and during 1990 roughly 70,000 members of SKH-SDP joined the HDZ (Goati 1991 cited in Cohen 1997: 115).

16 *Charismatic* parties revolve neither around collective action nor collective choice problems. Only the party leader's charisma holds the party together. *Clientelistic* parties revolve only around the collective action problem. They organise and exchange electoral support (votes and money) for policy favours, but do not present ideological platforms. *Programmatic* parties address both problems. They both organise electorally and present an ideological platform (Kitschelt 2000).

17 For exact numbers see www.republikasrpska.net/skupstina.

18 The SNSD is not a classical successor party, and was created only in 1996. It has transformed since then, and now could also be classified as an extreme right-wing nationalist and secessionist party.

19 The SDS was very popular within the Serbian community in the 1990s.

20 For complex indexing and results of electoral laws used in BiH on all levels, see Šedo 2007.

21 For the position of the SPS on the 'left–right' scale see Branković in Bozóki and Ishiyama 2002: 214–15.

22 'If the only way to create a greater Serbia is by crime, then I do not accept that, and let Serbia disappear. Milošević has done a lot of evil to everyone, but he has done the most evil to the Serbian people', said Artemiye, the Bishop of Kosovo. (RFE/RL *Watch List*: 1 July 1999, Volume 1, Number 24).

23 Momir Bulatović was ousted from the party and formed a new People's Socialist Party of Montenegro (*Narodna socijalistička stranka Crne Gore*, NSS CG) in 2001.

24 The Law on financing political parties was adopted in 1993, followed by the anti-corruption law. A new law was approved in 1997. The last two changes occurred in 2004 with the approval of a new law, and a year later with its revision.

25 To some extent the League of Communists of Macedonia – Freedom Movement could be classified as one of the successor parties, as it was founded by a minor group from the former LCM. The same applies to the Socialist Party of Macedonia, which claims to be the successor of the Socialist Alliance of Working People of Macedonia, a minor party which used to ally with SDSM, but which is now in coalition with VMRO-DPMNE. From the ethnic Albanian parties the Party of Democratic Prosperity (*Partija demokratskog prosperitet* – PDP, *Partia e Prosperiteti Demokratik* – PPD*)* might be included as a successor party in Macedonia, as its founding fathers were former members of the League of Communists of Macedonia, with a different view on the treatment of the ethnic Albanian minority in Macedonia.

26 Interestingly in Balkan terms, the party was led by a woman (Radmila Šekerinska) in 2006–2008.

27 Among others we could cite prominent members of the League of Communists of Kosovo: Azem Vllasi and Kaqusha Jashari (both members of the central committee of LCK in the 1980s) joined the Social Democratic Party of Kosovo (PSDK) and the

Democratic Party of Kosovo (PDK) respectively; Mahmut Bakalli (leader of the League of Communists of Kosovo till 1981) was one of the founding fathers of the Alliance for the Future of Kosovo (AAK); while a founding father of the League for Democratic Kosovo (LDK), Ibrahim Rugova, was a member of the League of Communists of Kosovo. It should also be noted that the origins of the PDK and the UÇK (Kosovo Liberation Army, KLA) were with Marxist groups which were in opposition to Titoist Yugoslavia and which had closer ties to Hoxha's Albania.

28 Liberalisation should understood in the terms and conditions of Albania in the late 1980s, and not compared to the liberalism in other CEE countries.

29 From 1986 till the tenth congress of the APL the membership fell from 147,000 (1986) to 100,000 (1990) (Hoppe 1993: 12, in Zëri I popullit, 19.12.1991, p. 1).

30 Albanians claim that the only religion of the Albanians is the Albanian nation. Despite this, Albanian leaders from Albania have never expressed their desire for the creation of a Greater Albania.

31 Nano was imprisoned in mid-1993 on charges of misappropriation of foreign assistance; his father served as a close Hoxha adviser and director of state television. Nano used to work at the Institute of Marxism–Leninism alongside Nexmejije Hoxha. He rejected political pluralism and the free-market economy, emphasising that Albania had to develop its own political and economic model, within the existing social system (Biberaj 1999: 281 in Drita 1990).

32 See e.g. Schmidt 2000b: 32–50.

33 Another party which is not a classical successor party but stems from the original APL, or rather its reformist wing, is the Social Democratic Party of Albania (*Partia Socialdemokrate e Shqipërisë*, PSDSh), whose chairman Skendër Gjinushi, became the minister of education (1987–1991), famous for negotiations with the opposition. In the economy the party pursues a social market format (PSDSh undated). Since 2005 the party holds seven seats in the parliament.

34 Macedonia is a tricky case, as in the initial phase of the transition the party gained due to the drive towards independence.

3 Nationalist parties and the party systems of the Western Balkans

Věra Stojarová

The aim of this chapter is to depict the chief issues and problems surrounding research of nationalism in the Western Balkans. The analysis of each country includes more than one party whenever applicable. The author has decided to look at the party documents (party programmes, manifestoes and other texts), and to assess actual party policy. In addition, the author circulated a questionnaire adapted from a book by Cas Mudde (Mudde 2007). The outcome, however, was less than satisfactory: 26 party questionnaires were sent out but only five were filled in and returned.[1] The parties will be treated as one unit and only when relevant will significant factions be mentioned. The text will focus only on the political parties; political movements, paramilitary formations and other groupings will only receive passing comment.

The author had to face a couple of questions with regard to the unfinished state-building process in the region. How should nationalism be defined, and how too nation and state building? Is nationalism the promotion of an independent Bosnia and Herzegovina (BiH), or that of an independent Republika Srpska? Does it consist in a state of its own for the Croatian entity? Is the Croatian entity a first step towards the creation of a Greater Croatia? Does nationalism mean striving to create a Greater Serbia? The last question should certainly be answered in the affirmative. But what about the others? The key to these questions is the delineation of the border between nationalism and ethno-regionalism, keeping in mind that the classification will only have validity temporarily, since the political backdrop will change over time. Cas Mudde claims that 'regionalism is best limited to groups that call for more autonomy of a region within a larger state structure' while interpreting 'nationalism in a holistic way including both civic and ethnic elements' (Mudde 2007: 29, 17). For the purposes of this study, we understand nationalism in terms of internal homogenisation (by assimilation, genocide, expulsion, separatism) as well as external exclusivity (bringing all members of the nation into the territory of the state by means of territorial expansion or, e.g. population transfer). In other words, those parties will be considered nationalist that strive for their own state. The text will also deal with those parties that strive for their own entity within already defined borders (e.g. the Croatian entity in BiH or Albanians in Macedonia). In the case of Montenegro, the analysis will concentrate on the period after independence was achieved (2006).

Nationalism in Croatia

Croatian nationalism

The post-war setting and inter-ethnic relations within society are far from being *normalised* even though 13 long years have passed since the end of the war in Croatia. The political and party landscape seems to be stable for the moment; the party system is bipolar with two main actors – Croatian Democratic Union (*Hrvatska demokratska zajednica*, HDZ) and the Social Democratic Party (*Socijaldemokratska partija Hrvatske*, SDP), in addition to some other minor parties. There seems to be a consensus about the future orientation of Croatia throughout the entire political spectrum and relevant parties support rapid integration into the EU. The leading post-war party, HDZ,[2] has transformed itself and moved towards the centre on the right–left axis, and seems to be becoming a standard conservative party. Even though the HDZ strives to take on the appearance of a pro-European, pro-democratic party, it retains some relics of its nationalist past.[3] Looking at other nationalist subjects of the political spectrum in Croatia, the fragmentation becomes clear at first glance. The most visible nationalist actors on the party scene are the Croatian Party of the Right (*Hrvatska stranka prava*, HSP)[4] and the Croatian Bloc (*Hrvatski blok*, HB)[5]; other nationalist parties remain without political representation in parliament: the Croatian Pure Party of the Right (*Hrvatska čista stranka prava*, HČSP),[6] Croatian Right-wing Movement (*Hrvatski pravaši- Hrvatski pravaški pokret*, HP-HPP),[7] Croatian Party of the Right 1861 (*Hrvatska stranka prava-1861*, HSP-1861),[8] Croatian True Revival (*Hrvatski istinski preporod*, HIP),[9] Croatian Right-wing Brotherhood (*Hrvatsko pravaško bratstvo*, HPB).[10] We might possibly include some factions of the Croatian Peasant Party (*Hrvatska seljačka stranka*, HSS).[11] Regionalist features are apparent with the Istrian Democratic Assembly (*Istarski demokratski sabor*), which focuses on the acquisition of a cultural and economic identity for Istria, as well as for equal status for Italians and Croatians living on the Peninsula (IDS 2007).

In looking at the Croatian electorate, we must also keep in mind the unfinished transition, as well as a couple of other specific features. When the Croatian political scientist, Ivan Šiber, analysed electoral behaviour since 1989, he concluded that it is not yet possible to bind the social structure with a political orientation, due to the process of transition, the institutionalisation of a new sovereign and independent state, and the war.[12] Family roots played a role in the elections – families with partisan ancestors gave their votes mostly to parties of the left, while families with *Ustasha* and *Domobrana* ancestors voted for parties of the right. As Šiber concludes, voters for parties of the right (HDZ, HSP and HKDU) are religious and conservative, with authoritarian tendencies, and voters of the Croatian Party of the Right are mainly young, between the ages of 18 and 28. The older a voter is, the less he or she tends to vote for the HSP (Šiber 2007: 152–84). The Croatian right-wing electorate with its strong state-conservativism is more active in the elections than those of the left and other voters. This state-conservativism, which is typical for the most active voters, encompasses support for the Croats in BiH, protection of the dignity of the Patriotic War, a strengthening of military power and state security, spiritual renewal and support for demographic growth (Čular 2005: 31). Dissatisfaction with democracy is constantly growing among HSP voters, while HDZ voters began to be dissatisfied with the state of democracy after the 2003 elections (Čular 2005: 151–3).

The Croatian extreme right political scene demonstrates specific features such as a Greater Croatia, Tuđmanism, the dignity of the patriotic war, a negative stance towards the ICTY, Serbianism, and the EU and NATO, and a positive stance towards the Croatian Independent State from the Second World War, (*Nezavisna Država Hrvatska*, NDH). Issues specific to the Croatian political scene which continue to be repeated in party documents are Croatian ethnic space and the protection of Croats abroad. The most radical parties such as the Croatian Party of the Right, Croatian Pure Party of the Right, Croatian Bloc and the Croatian Right-wing Movement would like to see the unification of Croatian ethnic space and the creation of a so-called Greater Croatia, while other parties promote equal rights for Croats in BiH with Serbs and Bosniaks, and therefore their right to their own entity – a Croatian republic in BiH. Another controversial issue on the Croatian political scene is relations towards Franjo Tuđman. The parties of the right admire him since he succeeded in gaining independence for Croatia and won the Patriotic War; other parties denounce him for his authoritarian tendencies and lack of respect towards the Serbian minority. The only party on the right which stands in opposition to Tuđmanism is the HSP-1861. Whereas the so-called Patriotic War has become another controversial issue for society, for the nationalist parties their stance is clear: one must protect the dignity of the war and stand against the ICTY. Most of them demonstrate strong anti-Serbian feelings. The stance of the parties towards the EU is becoming less negative, and such parties tend to promote the EU, subject to a referendum and with the right to withdraw, and a guarantee that Croatian national values will be protected. The position of the parties towards NATO is more negative; parties either promote a referendum on NATO or demand military neutrality for the country. The only parties demonstrating positive feelings towards NDH and the *Ustashas* used to be the HSP and HČSP. The HSP has been abandoning its revisionism recently and it is not an issue for the party any more.

It is evident that the former repository of nationalism and xenophobia in Croatia, HDZ, has moved to the centre, while the other nationalist parties remain fragmented. The only party which has successfully kept its representation in parliament is the Croatian Party of the Right. Even this party, however, is abandoning its *Ustasha* rhetoric, nationalism and xenophobia, and is now trying to find issues more attractive to the Croatian voters, such as ecology. The party in parliament which was furthest to the right was the Croatian Bloc. Nevertheless, this party has not gained a single seat in later elections and has thus joined the fragmented spectrum of far-right parties which are not represented in the Croatian assembly.

As can be seen, with the consolidation of the party system, Croatian parties tend to abandon strong nationalism and xenophobia and move closer to the centre. The parties which stick to these old stances remain irrelevant and neither succeed in gaining seats in parliament nor in achieving stronger membership. Currently, we may conclude that Croatian nationalism is fading away from the party system. This could nevertheless change with accession into the EU, with the opening of borders, and with having new issues arise which the political centre does not wish to deal with.

Serbian nationalism in Croatia – Republika Srpska Krajina 1991–1995

The most important party in RSK was the Serbian Democratic Party (*Srpska demokratska stranka*, SDS). The SDS was set up in Knin as a party uniting ethnic Serbs in Croatia under the leadership of Jovan Rašković[13] and later on under the president of the Knin municipality Milan Babić. With its propaganda, it was inciting the Serbs living in Croatia with populist rhetoric about 'the restoration of Ustasha, genocide over the Serbs, Croatia-Albanian agreement about the breaking of SFRY', so to remind them of the German bombardment of Belgrade in 1941, the 'Ustasha concentration camps' and the 'hundreds of holes filled with the killed Serbs' (Barić 2005: 113, 125). Even though the SDS tried to present itself as the main united force against Croatia, the party was in factions. Already in 1991, one of the regional party leaders Milan Djukić left and organised the Serbian National Party (*Srpska nacionalna stranka*, SNS).[14] After Rašković left, the main rivalry took place between Milan Babić and Milan Martić. Babić was against Slobodan Milošević and his interfering into Krajina matters, while Martić sided with Belgrade and was obedient to Milošević's decisions. The personal enmity between these two was transposed even onto the RSK governmental level and Babić was replaced as president of RSK with the more loyal Goran Hadžić. The main aim of SDS was

> the creation of RSK as modern state, internationally recognized and equal with all other states which emerged after the dissolution of SFRY. At the end, RSK should be part of united Serbian state, which should be constituted on the ethnic and historical Serbian lands.
>
> (Programme SDS cited from Barić 2005: 229)

After the end of the war in Croatia, the SDS ceased to exist. Some of its supporters, together with the Independent Serb Party (*Samostalna Srpska stranka*, SSS) set up a new party in 1997 – Independent Democratic Serb Party (*Samostalna Srpska demokratska stranka*, SSDS).[15]

Besides the SDS, which occupied the main place in the RSK party system, other parties have to be mentioned as well. Based upon the Serbian Radical Party (*Srpska radikalna stranka*, SRS) pattern of Vojislav Šešelj, the SRS RSK was founded in Vukovar in 1992 under the leadership of Rade Leskovac. However, the SRS RSK did not evade internal rivalry either. Leskovac tried to get rid of the link to the mother party in Belgrade and make the party independent, but he was soon replaced by the more loyal Branko Vojnica. The party was in tow to Vojislav Šešelj and the SRS for its whole existence (Barić 2005: 230–3). After the signing of the Erdut agreement and the re-incorporation of Eastern Slavonia into Croatian territory, the party was in 1998 re-constituted as the Party of Danube Serbs (*Partija podunavskih Srba*, PPS) while the leadership remained the same.[16]

Nationalism in Bosnia and Herzegovina

It is fairly difficult to assess the situation in Bosnia and Herzegovina since the main parties present at the outbreak of war are still in power; they are all based on ethnic identity and nationalism. The Party of Democratic Action (*Stranka demokratske akcije*, SDA) is a Bosniak party which has been striving for a single, united Bosnia and Herzegovina. Even though the party claims to be open to other nationalities as well (e.g. the electoral slogan 'we are the party even for beer drinkers'), its electorate is chiefly composed of Bosniaks. The party defines itself as a party of the political centre, and of the creation of a Bosnian identity which would be at a higher level than, but complementary to, the Serbian, Croatian and Bosniak identities (SDA 2005). The Croatian Democratic Union BiH (*Hrvatska demokratska zajednica BiH*, HDZ BiH) strives to change the Dayton Peace Agreement and to adopt a new constitution for BiH, since it does not agree with a country based on two entities when it is in reality composed of three ethnicities. The party advocates BiH integration into the EU and NATO; it further wishes to have special relations with Croatia and would like to see dual citizenship for inhabitants of these two countries. The party declares that it is open for anyone regardless of ethnicity (HDZ BiH 2007). Last but not least, the Serbian Democratic Party (*Srpska demokratska stranka BiH*, SDS BiH) defines itself as a Serbian national party and belongs with the most nationalist parties. The party has been obstructing the peace process in Bosnia and Herzegovina and has continually dreamt about linking Republika Srpska (RS) with Serbia; the recent programme talks about special relations and about the right of RS to self-determination, as soon as the Dayton Peace Agreement passes out of effect. (*Politička platforma Srpske demokratske stranke. Prijedlog*. SDS 2007). In addition to these three parties, there are other parties based on strong nationalism. These are mainly factions of the endemic or paternal parties from Croatia or Serbia. As the state-building process in Bosnia and Herzegovina is not yet finished, most of the political parties include nationalistic features – mainly on the part of the Serbians and Croatians as the Bosniak political scene[17] strives (due to the current conditions and state) rather for regionalisation and multi-ethnic Bosnia and promotes neither internal homogenisation nor external exclusivity.

As for the Croatian political scene[18] in BiH, besides the above mentioned Croatian Democratic Union, there are several minor political parties which fulfil our criteria of nationalistic.[19] Almost all of them seek a different configuration of Bosnia and Herzegovina and have different proposals for redrawing the constitution.[20]

Almost all ethnic Serbian political parties in BiH[21] display nationalist features. The main role has been played by the above-mentioned Serbian Democratic Party, together with what is currently the largest player on the Serbian political scene in BiH – the Party of Independent Social Democrats (*Stranka nezavisnih socijaldemokrata*, SNSD), led by the former Prime Minister of Republika Srpska, Milorad Dodik. The party programme touts BiH 'as one state built on international agreements' and essentially speaks of BiH as a federation with RS as one entity. However, the current leader has many times mentioned the possibility of a referendum on independence for Republika Srpska (SNSD undated). The ethnic Serbian political space remains fragmented[22] and only the strongest players are able to compete on the federal level or in the Federation of BiH, while the smaller parties continue to acquire only one or two seats in the Assembly of RS. Most of the ethnic Serbian parties in BiH seek the constitution to be redrawn to form a confederation of sovereign states with RS having special ties with Serbia.

As the state-building process is not yet complete in Bosnia and Herzegovina, the situation is quite difficult to assess. The political scene continues to be divided along ethnic lines, with most parties lobbying for their own ethnicity, while the chief subject of controversy is the Dayton Peace Agreement and the continued involvement of the international community in Bosnian state affairs. Most of the parties wish to rewrite the agreement which ended the Bosnian war. But each ethnicity has a different vision. The Bosniak parties wish to abolish the entities and create a centralised BiH. The Croats wish to create a third entity within BiH and thereby have one federal state composed of three entities. The Serbs wish to have stronger centralisation on the entity level and the right to leave the federation. Some of the Serbian political parties talk openly about an independent Republika Srpska tied to Serbia, while Croatian political parties seek the creation of their own entity within BiH. But would that be just the first step towards the creation of an independent Croatian Republic (Herzeg-Bosna) tied to Croatia?

Nationalism in Serbia

Serbian nationalism

The rough division of the Serbian party system could be nationalist vs. modernist. The first radical and populist group[23] would encompass SRS,[24] SPS,[25] SPO,[26] NS[27] and DSS[28] while the second, pro-Western group would comprise DS,[29] G17+,[30] LDP,[31] LSV[32] and SDU.[33] For simplification we will call the first group radical and the second one modest. If we wanted to be more precise we would have to go more deeply into this issue. The most nationalistic and populist party, the SRS, is propagating the creation of a Greater Serbia, that is, the annexation of Republika Srpska and Republika Srpska Krajina into a new national state. The SPS uses populist means as well, however it does not want to revise the Dayton Peace Agreement or existing borders. All parties in Serbia see the future of Kosovo within Serbian borders. Radical groups demand the return of Serbian nationals and the Serbian army into Kosovo while the modest groups demand dialogue leading to consensus which could mean the autonomy of the Serbs in an autonomous province in Kosovo and special protection of the property of the Serbian Orthodox Church.

The SRS is usually lumped in together with the Socialist Party of Serbia to create the third pole of the Serbian party system, sharing such themes as 'criminal usurpation of the country', 'anarchy', the return of 'national-patriotic politics' and a 'system of law, work and responsibility' (Komšić 2006: 175). The voters of this red–black pole, in contrast with DS voters, identify themselves much more with the nation, do not like Americans, tend towards authority, are traditional, patriarchal, passive, and anti-Western; in addition, they are against privatisation, giving rights to minorities and membership of Serbia in the EU (Mihailović in Lutovac 2006: 158). The SRS and SPS are most radical when talking about cooperation with the ICTY. Neither of these two parties talks about national reconciliation but rather about genocide committed on the Serbian nation. The SPO and NS do not want to deal with the past in order not to repeat the mistakes of the previous regime. The DSS has a kind of middle position while the modest group talks about the need to cooperate with the ICTY and to acknowledge the crimes committed by the Serbs.

In foreign policy, all parties except the SRS talk about integration into EU while DS, G17+, LDP, LDV and SDU support NATO accession as well. Most of the parties talk about supporting the Serbian diaspora in the neighbouring countries, while DSS refers to special relations with Republika Srpska. Most modern parties support regional cooperation.

Besides the party scene, there are other nationalist groups – e.g. the Guard of Tzar Lazar (*Garda Cara Lazara*) or the National Machine (*Nacionalni stroj*). These ideological platforms serve as a meeting point for those nationalist groups (presumably having ties with skinheads from Blood and Honour Serbia) recruiting volunteers for the defence of Kosovo.

Regional nationalism – Vojvodina, Sandžak and Preševo valley – nationalism of Hungarians, Bošnjaks and Albanians

Hungarian parties in Vojvodina focus on political and cultural autonomy for the ethnic Hungarians living there, while regional parties focus on decentralisation issues. So far, there are a couple of ethnic Hungarian political parties though none of them demand separatism. The Sandžak presents the same picture – the Bosniak parties focus on decentralisation but do not present a security threat in a form of separatism. This can not be said about the Preševo valley region – sometimes described by the ethnic Albanians as Eastern Kosovo (*Kosova Lindorë*). There is a strong tendency in the three municipalities of Preševo, Medvedja and Bujanovac for either gaining more attention from the central government of Belgrade or for accession to Kosovo. Hungarian, Bosniak and Albanian political parties are exclusively elected by their own ethnic community, although the Vojvodina political parties are more multicultural focusing on Vojvodina issues rather than ethnic Hungarian issues, which is in sharp contrast with the situation in Preševo Valley where the Serbian and Albanian communities vote for their respective ethnic parties.[34]

Nationalism in Kosovo

Each and every ethnic Albanian political party in Kosovo promotes independence, and therefore the whole spectrum could be labelled as nationalist. In the same sense, part of the ethnic Serbian political spectrum promotes the creation of a Greater Serbia or at least the idea that Kosovo is part of Serbia.[35] Parties promoting a Greater Albania are marginalised. The Kosovo National Front (*Balli Kombëtar Kosovë*, BKK) has succeeded the original Kosovo Front, which was set up in 1939 by the patriotic writer Mid'hat Abdyl Frashëri. The BKK is 'a continuation of all movements which are fighting for unification of Albanian nation'. In the section entitled The National Question, the BKK states that it 'has a deeply national character and proposes to unite all Albanian ethnic places under one state'. The party declares that it protects the rights and liberties of all Albanians in the world, wherever they live or work. The BKK emphasises that the priority is the national question, and that it will cooperate with those states and political forces which respect the sovereignty and independence of Kosovo as a first step in solving the Albanian national question. It also seeks full integration into Europe. The programme states that the BKK respects the rights of national minorities as enshrined in international agreements; however it would not fulfil requests by national minorities if those requests went against the Albanian national interest. The programme ends with the motto *Albania for the Albanians* (BKK 2001).

In addition to the party scene, there are paramilitary formations striving for the creation of a Greater Albania or independent Kosovo.[36]

Nationalism in Montenegro

Since Montenegro ceded from the Federation of Serbia and Montenegro only in 2006, it is once again quite difficult to determine which parties are nationalist. There is not only state building, but also nation building going on – the Montenegrin nation was recognised only after the Second World War, while the Montenegrin language seems to have existed only since 2007, when the new Constitution of the Republic of Montenegro was passed. In 2003, 43 per cent of people claimed to have Montenegrin identity, while 32 per cent of inhabitants claimed to feel Serbian (*Popis stanovništva, domaćinstava i stanova u 2003*, 2004). These figures remain fluid as the processes of nation and state building have not yet consolidated. Therefore, if we look at the political scene in Montenegro before 2006, we must take into account that half of the political scene had irredentist tendencies, demonstrating nationalism accompanied with xenophobia and that we would therefore have to analyse most of the entities on the political scene. However, as independence was declared, the only nationalist entities depicted are those of a sub-regional character (Albanian formations claiming a Greater Albania) or the sister parties of Serbian radical entities, seeking the creation of a Greater Serbia (SRS or SNS[37]). At one stage, the nationalist right-wing parties met in Montenegro with nationalist left parties, as the Serbian Radical Party formed a coalition before the elections of 2002 with the People's Socialist Party of Montenegro and YUL (the Yugoslavian Left, led by Mirjana Marković – the wife of Slobodan Milošević). The same happened four years later, when the People's Socialist Party of Montenegro[38] allied with the Serbian Radical Party, the Party of Democratic Unity, the Socialist Party of Yugoslavia, the Serbian National Council and Academic Alternative, in order to create the platform Serbian List, which subsequently received 12 seats in the 81-seat parliament.

To conclude, state building and nation building in Montenegro looks as if it is reaching its end; however, identification with either Montenegrin or Serbian identity remains fluid. Nationalism is still present and corresponds to the regional Albanian problem, as well as the identity problem in Montenegro. There is nothing like a relevant ethnic Montenegrin nationalist party in the country. The only parties which could be depicted as nationalist are the ethnic Serb parties, since their aim is a Greater Serbia. The Serbian People's Party as well as the SRS are typical examples of nationalist parties; they remain relevant actors in parliament while having almost no significant coalition potential but with the perspective of significant blackmail potential in the future.

Nationalism in Macedonia

If we look at Macedonia's political scene, most nationalist formations are on the ethnic Albanian side. There is one ethnic Macedonian political party which used to be depicted as nationalist in the beginning of the 1990s – the VMRO-DPMNE.[39] However, with the finalisation of independence and the setting up of an independent Macedonian state, the party moved more to the centre of the political spectrum and gave birth to the marginal faction VMRO-NP.[40] If we look at the party system of the last decade, we most likely conclude that all ethnic Albanian formations could be classified as nationalist.[41] However, because the relevant political parties have been part of the political process since the Ohrid Peace Agreement and therefore do not wish to redraw the borders, and their chief aim is full implementation of that Agreement, we will not here focus on the entire ethnic Albanian political scene. As already stated above, the formations which strive for the creation of either a Greater Albania or a Greater Kosovo operate sub-regionally. In addition to the political scene, one could focus on paramilitary formations which operate across the entire ethnic Albanian territory or only in Western Macedonia, e.g. the Army of the Republic of Ilirida or the Macedonian National Liberation Army (*Ushtria Çlirimtare e Kombatarë*, UÇK).[42]

To sum up, most ethnic Albanian political parties seek full implementation of the Ohrid Framework Peace Agreement and do not wish to redraw the borders. However, it is quite unpredictable what kind of reaction the proclamation of

Kosovo independence (and the reactions in south-eastern Serbia and in Republika Srpska) will have on the ethnic Albanian political scene. Demands for federalisation of the country or for the creation of a greater Kosovo have already appeared and cannot be ruled out, which could mean a strengthening of nationalism in both ethnicities. The current situation could be the calm before the storm; as the Albanian question remains unresolved and ethnic Albanians make up almost 25 per cent of the population, there is still space for the nationalist subjects.

Nationalism in Albania

The bipolar Albanian political scene is dominated by the Democratic Party (PDSh) and Socialist Party (PSSh) with some other minor parties on the right as well as on the left of the political scene. Political parties which would fight for unification of ethnic Albanian lands are marginalised. Ethnic Albanian formations operate in Kosovo, south-eastern Serbia, Albania and western Macedonia; they communicate together and presumably with the political wing of AKSh – the National Liberation Front of Albanians (*Komitetit Kombëtar për Clirimin dhe Mbrojtjen e Tokave Shqiptare*, KKCMTSH), which is based in Tirana. It merged with the Party of National Unity (*Parti Unitet Kombëtar*, PUK[43]) in 2002, in order to create the Albanian Front of National Unification (*Fronti Për Bashkim Kombëtar Shqiptar*, FBKSH).[44] There are a couple of political parties in the political spectrum which in some respects demonstrate nationalist features – the National Front (*Balli Kombëtar*, BK), Legality Movement Party (*Partia Lëvizja e Legalitetit*, PLL) or Albanian National Unity Party (*Partia Bashkesia Kombetare Shqiptare*, PBKSh). The only one which has ever surpassed the threshold to enter the Albanian Assembly is BK.[45]

To conclude, the Kosovo question is not very appealing to voters in Albania and they are not interested in electing a party which would like to redraw the borders and, in so doing, create a Greater Albania. Even though the political system is far from being consolidated, the party system, with its bipolar configuration, seems to be quite well established. At the moment, the nationalist parties do not attract enough voters to be elected to parliament and they remain negligible. The only threat comes from the fact that Albania, together with Kosovo, is the centre of pan-Albanian political and military formations, and some Albanians who are being sought in Kosovo or Macedonia are enjoying asylum in Albania.

Conclusion

The Croatian nationalist scene is highly fragmented and there are more than ten parties located on the far right of the political spectrum. From among those which have ever gained representation in the Croatian Assembly, the most radical seems to be the Croatian Bloc. The Croatian Democratic Union has transformed itself into a classical conservative party, while the Croatian Party of the Right is also staking out issues other than nationalist hatred. Other parties in the political spectrum seem to have abandoned nationalist issues.

The Bosnian political scene is tricky – the Bosniaks achieved their aim (an independent Bosnia and Herzegovina within the former borders), so we would hardly expect to find any ethnic Bosniak striving for redrawing the borders, for example. The same cannot be said about the Croatian and Serbian political scene. Croats would like to see a different configuration of BiH and strive for their own entity within the state, which would have the right to be more closely attached to Croatia. Serbs seek more powers on the entity level and the right to be closely attached to Serbia; some parties champion referenda concerning the incorporation of RS into Serbia. To sum it up, the main focus of the parties is to achieve their national goals. Most of the ethnic Serb and Croat parties could, then, be labelled as strongly nationalist. Nevertheless, neither the political nor the party system is consolidated yet; what we say today does not necessarily have to be applicable and valid tomorrow.

In Serbia, the Serbian Radical Party together with the Socialist Party of Serbia, New Serbia, and the Democratic Party of Serbia, all demonstrate nationalist features. The strong position of nationalist SRS is caused by a frustration of the voters from the dreary economic situation as a result of wars and economic blockades. Serbian citizens have the feeling that Serbia is in disgrace in the West, which is always siding with Serbia's enemies. The strength of the SRS is demonstrated when the SRS stands for elections even in Croatia, BiH and Montenegro.

Nationalist parties in Montenegro are logically represented by ethnic Serb parties. If we had analysed the party system a decade ago, it would have been the opposite – Montenegrin parties striving for independence. Kosovo is a very similar case – one will have to wait until consolidation in order to assess the overall party system. Up until now, most political parties have promoted Kosovo independence and one cannot clearly distinguish the political right, left or any party family. In Macedonia, probably the most nationalist parties are VMRO-NP and PDSh. Nevertheless, most of the parties demonstrate some level of nationalism. The only party in the region which promotes the creation of a Greater Albania and has surpassed the parliamentary threshold is the National Front in Albania. However, the idea of all Albanians within one state is not very attractive for Albanian voters and the party remains on the margins of the political spectrum.

As we have seen, research in the Western Balkans is complicated due to the incomplete process of state and nation building, and it is very difficult to apply any theory to an unconsolidated political (party) system. Most of the parties we have analysed have an ideological core made up of nationalism as it still prevails due to the late process of state building.

Linz and Stepan concluded as far back as 1996, that 'one of the most dangerous ideas for democracy can be summed up in the maxim that every state should strive to become a nation-state and every nation should become a state' (Linz & Stepan 1996: 29–30). This paradigm is very visible in the Balkans, where the nation and state-building process was slowed down and it only comes to an end in the beginning of the twenty-first century, whereas other European nations had succeeded in forming their own states more than 100 years earlier. Nationalism in the Western Balkans demonstrates the same features: a striving for mono-ethnic countries in expanded borders, accompanied with xenophobia towards other local ethnic groups.

Notes

1 This chapter draws from Stojarová (forthcoming). The author would like to give special thanks to Cas Mudde for his consent to use the questionnaire translated into local languages from his latest book, *Populist Radical Right Parties in Europe.*
2 The Croatian Democratic Union was set up in 1989 and became the major party in Croatia during the 1990s – it ruled from 1990 till 2000 and has been in power again since 2003. In the 1990s, the party or rather government policies were heavily influenced by the wars in Croatia and in BiH, and therefore heightened nationalism was the dominant philosophy. For the HDZ policies during the 1990s see e.g. Irvine 1996.
3

> HDZ was an endeavour of the Croatian national and democratic movement in the last decade of the last century, led by the salvation idea of reconciliation of the Croatian national being, introduced and divided during the political and military storms of the 20th Century, the idea of the unity of inland and extraterrestrial Croats, that Croatians in Bosnia and Herzegovina are an indivisible part of the united Croatian national being.

The current standpoint of the party is protection of the Croatian minority in BiH and promotion of their rights to become a third entity; the party promotes the right to vote and to stand for office for Croats living abroad (HDZ 2002).
4 The Croatian Party of the Right (founded in 1990) belonged originally to the extreme far right. Its former vice-chairman and current leader, Anto Đapić, was one of those who organised the Croatian Defence Forces (*Hrvatske obrambene snage*, HOS), one of the first defence forces organised by Croats at the onset of the Croatian war. Party members used to present themselves in black shirts, openly wearing *Ustasha* symbols and recalling the leader of the Independent Croatian State, Ante Pavelić. Recently, however, the party has started a process of reform and now presents itself as a modern (sometimes even pro-European) conservative right-wing party, similar to the CSU in Germany. Instead of controversial issues such as the ICTY and the Patriotic War, the party has started to deal with legal state issues, protection of the environment, pollution of the Adriatic and the use of genetically modified food (Pleše 2003). As regards the party programme, the HSP presents itself as a party promoting ethnic nationalism (early party policies could be labelled external exclusive – seeking the inclusion of all members of the Croatian ethnic community within a single Croatian State). Even though some party representatives presented themselves as pro-European, the party programme contained anti-European components, advocating referenda as a precondition for joining any other (supra-) state structure, and paraphrasing the *Father of the Homeland*, Ante Starčević: *Not Hague, not Bruxelles, not Dayton, but free independent Croatia!* (www.hsp.hr/content/view/6/6/lang,hr/).
5 The Croatian Bloc was founded in 2002 and was thought to be more a movement than a party. Since the party evolved as an HDZ faction, it was present in parliament from 2002 until the elections of 2003, even though it had never gained a single seat in an election. In two subsequent elections the party failed to enter parliament. The party defines itself as a patriotic, national, state-building, conservative party based on the ideological roots of the former Croatian president, Franjo Tuđman – *Tuđmanism.* Party ideology is based on the free development of individuals in society, protection of the Central European–Mediterranean identity of Croatia and protection of the Croatian language. The party supports the equal membership of Croatia in the EU (but not at all costs), and wants to keep an eye on, and hinder the sale of natural

resources to foreign firms. It wants to promote the strengthening of relations with Croats living abroad and one of the key components of the programme is the protection of the dignity of Patriotic War and the fight against *detuđmanisation* (*100 Pitanja i odgovora. HB-pokret za modernu Hrvatsku* 2003). The party promotes active participation by Croatia in the Partnership for Peace (PfP), but it is against integrating the country into NATO, and states that if NATO integration should come, it should only be on the basis of a broad national consensus. The party is against global solutions which would threaten the Croatian national interest, sovereignty, or integrity and is against any regional Western Balkan association. It wishes to have strong relations with the USA and is open to cooperation with the ICTY and other UN agencies, on condition of depoliticiation. The party sees the main security problems in pressure to create a Western Balkan union, politiciation of ICTY cases, the economic situation, organised crime, the state of the judiciary, Croatian monetary policy, the state of the Croatian nation in BiH, unsolved border disputes, global terrorism, migration, refugee crises, ecological incidents of a transnational character, and an unstable and violent world (HB 2006).

6 The party was re-established in 1992 due to the personal rivalry in the original Croatian Party of the Right. It campaigns for 'the liberation of the entire Croatian ethnic space, for a completely independent and free Croatia in the entire territory' (*Temeljna načela* HČSP 2007, par. 8).

7 HP-HPP was founded in 2003 and 'the party does not renounce the Croatian historical lands where the genocide over Croatian citizens took place: BiH, Gulf of Croatian Saints (Zaljev Hrvatskih Svetaca), Srijem and Bačka' (*Temeljna načela* HP-HPP). The party uses clear signs of nationalism and xenophobia directed mainly against the Serbs in its documents.

8 The party was founded in 1995; it presupposes the creation of a (con)federation with BiH in order to tighten relations with the Croatian minority there (*Temeljna načela Hrvatske stranke prava-1861*, par. 6).

9 HIP was founded in 2001, and the son of the former president, Miroslav Tuđman, became its first leader. The party is against any de-tuđmanisation and the Hague prosecutions; and is for preserving the dignity of the Patriotic War, protecting Croatian generals, promoting special relations with BiH and protecting the Croatian nation there (HIP 2001).

10 The party was set up in 2004, and promotes the dignity and values of the Patriotic War, the merits of the first modern president Franjo Tuđman, the heroism of Croatian soldiers and HOS volunteers in the war (HPB 2004).

11 HSS is a traditional conservative party, recalling the pre-Second World War party leader, Stjepan Radić. The party is for integration into the EU, a referendum on NATO integration, protection of the national identity, a 12-year moratorium on the sale of land to foreigners after the EU accession, and protection of the Patriotic War and Croatian heroes (HSS 2007).

12 Therefore the workers and craftsmen supported the right in the first elections in 1990 (HDZ, HSP, HKDU), but changed their support in the elections in 2000. Young voters gave their support to the right-wing parties in 1992 and 1995, then switched to the left in 2000 and then again in 2003 voted for the right. The same goes for unemployed people. The police and army gave their votes in the first elections in 1990 to parties of the left and then, with the HDZ in power, they completely turned and since 1992 have supported right-wing parties (Šiber 2007: 152–76).

13 Rašković became discredited within Serbian society after some of his secret statements about Serbs ('Serbs are mad nation') and Milošević ('great Bolshevik, communist and despot') were made public (Barić 2005: 212). Some of his pronouncements were clearly pacific ('I do not want to lead you into war, I can lead you into peace and if you want war you shall be led by someone else'). However, e.g. a Serbian intellectual S. Livada stated that Rašković's declarations were a 'product of myth mania and

even necrophilia', that Rašković is a 'bloodthirsty necrophyl' who 'wants to spill Croatian blood' (Livada cited in Barić 2005: 219).

14 The nickname of the party was 'Party of Tudjman's Serbs', because it was loyal to Croatia and did not really stand in opposition to the regime.

15 For the current programme of SDSS see www.sdss.hr/dokumenti/PROGRAM%20 SDSS-a.doc. The current critique of RSK government in exile Milorad Pupovac belongs to the SDSS leadership.

16 For a summary of its programme see www.hidra.hr/STRANKE/programi/028426. htm.

17 SDA (nine mandates out of 42 in the House of Representatives on the federal level and 28 out of 98 on the FBiH level in 2006), SBiH (eight mandates out of 42 in the House of Representatives on the federal level and 24 out of 98 on the FBiH level in 2006) and BPS (one mandate out of 42 in the House of Representatives on the federal level and four out of 98 on the FBiH level in the 2006 elections).

18 The electoral coalition HDZ-HNZ (three mandates out of 42 in the House of Representatives on the federal level and eight out of 98 on the FBiH level in 2006); HDZ-1990 and its allies (two mandates out of 42 in the House of Representatives on the federal level and seven out of 98 on the FBiH level in 2006).

19 This would relate to the Croatian Party of the Right in Bosnia and Herzegovina (*Hrvatska stranka prava BiH Đapić-dr.Jurišić*, HSP) which strives for the regionalisation of BiH and 'protection of the vital interests of all nations, above all the Croatian nation, which is most endangered' though supporting integration into the EU and NATO. The New Croatian Initiative (*Nova Hrvatska inicijativa*, NHI) clearly displays nationalism as well: 'BiH and Croatia make one geopolitical unity so they are necessarily tied to each other' (Bilic 1998). The same would go for the Croatian Bloc in Bosnia and Herzegovina (*Hrvatski blok Bosne i Hercegovine*, HB BiH). As do other Croatian parties, HB BiH seeks nullification of the Dayton Peace Agreement and sees the Croats having a third entity within BiH with its own legal, executive and judicial powers.

20 Probably the only party which does not demonstrate strong nationalist features is the Croatian National Community (*Hrvatska narodna zajednica*, HNZ) which wants to stop marginalisation of the Croatian nation and strives instead for a sovereign, independent, united and decentralised country with power on regional and local levels (HNZ HNŽ: BiH treba biti … 2005).

21 The SDS HDZ-HNZ (three mandates out of 42 in the House of Representatives on the federal level and eight out of 83 on the RS level in 2006); the SSND (seven mandates out of 42 in the House of Representatives on the federal level and 41 out of 83 on the RS level in 2006). The RS (two mandates out of 83 on RS level in 2006).

22 The Serbian Radical Party of RS (*Srpska radikalna stranka Republike Srpske*, SRS RS), the Radical Party of RS (*Radikalna stranka republike Srpske*, RS RS), the Serbian National Union (*Srpski narodni savez*, SNS), the League of People's Rebirth (*Savez narodnog preporoda*, SNP), the Serbian Progressive Party of RS (*Srpska napredna stranka Republike Srpske*, SNS RS) fight for an independent, free and democratic Serbian state and the unity of the Serbian nation (SNS RS 1997).

23 In the past, another party which presented strong nationalism was the Party of Serbian Unity (*Stranka Srpskog jedinstva*, SSJ). The SSJ was led (until his assassination) by Željko Ražnatović Arkan and later on by Borislav Pelević; its aim was the unity of the Serbian nation (Komšić 2006: 172–4). The SSJ merged late in 2007 into the Serbian Radical Party (for further information see e.g. Komšić 2006: 171–5).

24 During the regime of Milošević, the Serbian Radical Party (*Srpska radikalna stranka*) was sometimes in opposition, sometimes in coalition with the SPS. Since 2000, the party has been very successful at attracting voters and in both the 2003 and 2007 elections, it gained more than 27 per cent of the votes. Vojislav Šešelj has been leading his party from its foundation to the present. Since Šešejl left for the Hague, the party

has elected a second leader to substitute for him – Tomislav Nikolić. The Serbian Radical Party seeks the unification of all Serbian territories and protection of all Serbs; this entails the unification of Serbia, Republika Srpska, Republika Srpska Krajina, Montenegro (SRS does not talk about the Montenegrin nation), Kosovo of course and, if it wished, Macedonia as well. The main idea of the SRS's ongoing campaign is that 'those who are not with us are against us' or, better put, those who are not Serb are against us.

25   The Socialist Party of Serbia (*Socijalistička partija Srbije*) was the party in power till 2000. The party was led by Slobodan Milošević (1990–1997), Milan Milutinović (1997–2002) and, since 2002, Ivica Dačić. The nationalist course combined with socialism makes up the main part of the party programme.

26   In the beginning of the 1990s the Serbian Renewal Movement (*Srpski pokret obnove*) strove for a Greater Serbia; since the fall of the Milošević regime and with the participation of the party in government, its nationalist and xenophobic features have disappeared.

27   New Serbia (*Nova Srbija*) was formed in 1998 by a group splitting from the SPO. The party programme contains monarchist and nationalist features. It is expected that the party could form a coalition with SRS and DSS if they win in the May 2008 elections. The party is led by Velimir Ilić.

28   Democratic Party of Serbia (*Demokratska stranka Srbije*, DSS) was founded in 1992, and the current leader is the charismatic Vojislav Koštunica. The DSS openly claimed the unification of Serbian territories in the beginning of the 1990s, thus demonstrating strong nationalistic features. At present, the party is against any cooperation with the EU or trading Kosovo for EU membership, and in certain circumstances could ally with the radical SRS.

29   Democratic Party (*Demokratska stranka*, DS) is a successor to the Democratic Party which was founded in 1919 and re-launched in 1990. The party is led by the current president of Serbia, Boris Tadić, who shows more pro-European stances than his counterpart in the DSS, Vojislav Koštunica. The DSS sees a chance for Serbia in EU membership and supported the signing of the SAA agreements with the EU.

30   Originally an NGO, the G17+ was set up as a party in 2002. It is led by Mladan Đinkić and the core of its programme is economic liberalism and fast accession of Serbia to the EU.

31   The Liberal Democratic Party (*Liberalno-demokratska partija*) was founded in 2005 by Čedomir Jovanović and presents a classic example of a neo-liberal party supporting EU membership. In April 2007, the party merged with the Civil Union of Serbia (GSS, led by Vesna Pešić).

32   The League of Social Democrats of Vojvodina (*Liga socijaldemokrata Vojvodine*) is a minor party on the right of the political spectrum; it is led by Nenad Čanak.

33   Social Democratic Union (*Socijal-demokratska unija*).

34   See chapter on political parties in Serbia's regions.

35   See Chapter 10, The party system of Kosovo.

36   The most famous is the Albanian National Army (*Armata Kombëtare Shqiptare*, AKSh or ANA), striving for the creation of a Greater Albania. It encompasses around 200 members and it does not really have support among the Kosovars. The Army for the independence of Kosovo (*Ushtria për Pavarësinë ë Kosovës*, UPK) was classified as a criminal gang rather than paramilitary formation. (http://sweb.cz/messin/upk.htm; www.serbianna.com/). Even though the UÇK has been dissolved, the last incident it claimed responsibility for was a bomb attack on a government building in Prishtina on 19 February 2007 as revenge for the death of two Albanians who were killed during the previous demonstrations in the Kosovo capital (www.tkb.org/Incident. jsp?incID=35446).

37   The Serbian People's Party (*Srpska narodna stranka*, SNS), founded in 1997, promotes the rights of Serbs in Montenegro with the motto 'Montenegro – land of Serbs'.

The party advocates the 'realization of our national goal of a unified state from Subotica to Bar'. The programme goes on to say that it wishes dual citizenship (with the right to vote) for the inhabitants of Montenegro and Serbia, a system of special relations with Serbia (economic and military union) and Republika Srpska, a constitutional definition of the Serbian language with the Cyrillic alphabet deemed to be official, along with the right to use the national symbols of Serbia. As for foreign relations, the party promotes EU membership unconditionally, and NATO membership subject to a referendum, with special relations with Serbia, Republika Srpska and the Russian Federation. The party promotes the preservation of ethnic values and national traditions. The party succeeded in securing nine seats (out of 81 MPs) in the 2006 parliamentary elections and represents one of the main opposition parties. The party was blocking the approval of the new Constitution and has certain blackmail potential.

38 The party strived for preservation of the union with Serbia. The current leadership as well as their programme is oriented on pro-European voters breaking with the past.

39 VMRO-DPMNE recalled the nationalist revolutionary organisation of the beginning of the twentieth century, which transformed itself into a terrorist organisation with elements of fascist ideology (Stojar 2006: 225).

40 The VMRO-People's Party (*Vnatrešna Makedonska revolucionerna organizacija – Narodna partija*, VMRO-NP) was formed by a faction of VMRO-DPMNE in 2002, and in subsequent elections gained six per cent of the votes (six mandates). Vesna Janevska was elected its first president. The party defines itself as a right-wing conservative, patriotic party and seeks, among other issues, celebration of the Day of Patriotism in Macedonia. The programme is populist-oriented against the main parties in Macedonia; the party fights for a strong state. We can identify some kind of nationalism; however the party does not strive for an ethnically clean Macedonia or even a Greater Macedonia (VMRO-NP 2006). Many of the party's interviews and texts include xenophobic statements against the Albanian minority.

41 One of the most radical relevant actors used to be labelled the Democratic Albanian Party (*Partija Demokratik Shqiptare*, PDSh) which was created in 1997 under the leadership of the influential Arben Xhaferri; the current chairman is Menduh Thaçi. The party stands strongly against its main rival, the Democratic Union for Integration (*Bashkimi Demokratik për Integrim*, BDI), which has continually boycotted parliament since the last elections because PDSh was chosen as coalition partner, even though it received fewer seats in parliament. Ironically, the party allies with the VMRO-DPMNE which is far more nationalist than the Social Democratic Union of Macedonia. The party wants to improve the rights of ethnic Albanians in the country and supports the proclamation on the independence of Kosovo. The party wants the Ohrid Peace Framework Agreement to be implemented and sees the future of Macedonia in stronger relations with the USA, EU and NATO (*Perspektiva e Maqedonisë varet nga të drejtat e Shqiptarëve* 2007).

42 The Army of the Republic of Ilirida was set up in 2002 in Macedonia. It fights for the incorporation of western Macedonia into a Greater Albania or Greater Kosovo. Over-rated sources indicate there are around 200 members. Some of these stated that the combatants took an oath to Albanian King Leka Zogu. However, Leka Zogu denies that. UÇK is led by Avdil Jakupi and he claims to control a paramilitary formation encompassing around 3,000 men.

43 Idajet Beqiri, the founder of the political party, writes in his article 'Albanian nationalism is the national reunion' that the party does not wish to change the borders aggressively, that its politics calls for peaceful solutions, and it opposes changing the borders with the law of the jungle. The main argument from the article is that if the Helsinki Declaration had already existed in 1912, Albania would have been complete and united (Beqiri 2002).

44 The pseudonyms of the leaders are Valdet Vardari, Alban Vjosa, Vigan Gradica, and Ramadan Verikolli. While Valdet Vardari is presumably a former collaborator of Ali

Ahmeti (real name Gafurr Adili) from Macedonia, who was arrested by the Albanian police while illegally passing through the borders from Macedonia and accused of creating terrorist organisations, Vigan Gradica is a former general of the Albanian army (www.fbksh-aksh.org/; http://akshalb.ifrance.com/statuti.htm; Spiro 2004).

45 The National Front follows on its historical predecessor from the Second World War; the president of the party is Abas Ermenji. The current programme calls for the creation of an ethnic Albania, with the motto Albania for the Albanians (BK undated). The party states that Albanians are not chauvinist nationalists and the mentality of BK is oriented toward a Western political vision supporting American politics in the Balkans. The BK does not wish to fight for the creation of a Greater Albania, but asks for compliance with international charters and respect for the right of the Albanian nation to place its frontiers where its natural borders lie. The party seeks integration into Europe. The BK gained two seats in 1996, three seats in 1997, and in subsequent elections in 2001 it was part of the greater coalition of Union for Victory (PDSh, PRSh and others), which gained 46 mandates, though the mandates for BK remained on very much the same level as after previous elections. In 2005, the party did not succeed in gaining a single seat.

4   National minorities in the party systems[1]

Florian Bieber

National minorities form a significant aspect of the social reality and political systems of the Western Balkans. During the transition from communism to multi-party rule, minorities have formed their own political parties across the region. In addition, some mainstream parties have managed to incorporate members from minority communities. The emergence of national minorities as a key political actor in the region has been a challenge for the countries under consideration. In particular in Yugoslavia, members of some national minorities violently opposed the emergence of new countries and their very status as minority. Other minorities for the first time acquired the possibility to autonomously formulate their political projects. Altogether, the period since the introduction of multi-party systems in 1990 in Yugoslavia and a few years later in Albania is characterised by strong 'nationalising nation-states', which showed in law and/ or in practice little respect towards national minorities. Since the late 1990s with the consolidation of statehood in many parts of the region and the end of (semi) authoritarian regimes in Croatia and Serbia, there has been a general normalisation where minority parties have increasingly participated in governments in the region and state borders have been less contested. Nevertheless, the degree of inter-ethnic accommodation varies greatly across the region and in some parts, such as in Kosovo, communities live mostly segregated.

During the communist rule in both Yugoslavia and Albania, many minorities were not particularly excluded from the system. In Albania, the Greek community, by far the largest minority, was well represented in the Party of Labour. This was not the result of particular minority rights provisions, but rather the consequence of the Southern origins of the Communist party, coinciding with the area of settlement of the Greek minority. The Albanian communist experience was, however, not only characterised by Stalinist repression until the late 1980s, but also by a strong ethnonationalist slant of the regime (i.e. cult of Skenderbeg or the Illyrians). In Yugoslavia, the League of Communists more explicitly sought to cater for the different communities. With the hierarchy of nations (*narodi*), nationalities (*narodnosti*) and ethnic groups (*etničke grupe*), Yugoslavia did not recognise minorities as such. Thus Serbs in Croatia, for example, were a nation equal to Croats in Croatia and Yugoslavia. As such, they were often well represented in the League of Communists, although this applied less to intra-Yugoslav migrants, such as Bosnians or Macedonians in Croatia or Slovenia. The larger nationalities, such as Hungarians and Albanians in Vojvodina and Kosovo respectively enjoyed a substantial degree of representation in the party, borne out of their substantial numbers and the institutional autonomy of the two provinces. However, their inclusion in the structures of power, institutions and the party came later than for others, as especially the Albanians were not given full rights until the late 1960s. The controversies over the future of Yugoslavia and its republics tore not only the Federal League of Communists apart, but also alienated members of different ethnic groups within the republican and provincial party organisations from each other. While a majority of Serbs in 1990 voted for the Social Democratic Party rather than the nationalist Serb Democratic Party, the ruling Croatian Democratic Union (HDZ) accepted the claim of the SDS to represent Serb interests, while the SDP undertook new efforts to represent the urban Serbs who did not support the policies of Slobodan Milošević (Caspersen 2006: 51–69). The emergence of a multi-party system across Yugoslavia in 1990 saw the creation of minority parties which sought to represent the interests of one particular group. While the claim to represent one particular group was at times not confirmed by electoral choice, parties representing Serbs entered the first Croatian *sabor*, while Albanian minority parties took seats in the Macedonian *sobranie* and the Serbian *skupština*. Similarly in Albania, a Greek minority party entered the first multi-party parliament in 1991. Minority parties thus emerged before countries instituted any type of reserved seats or other positive measures to promote the representation of minorities. And in fact, parties seeking to represent minorities were the consequence of the nationalist climate which emphasised ethnic differences over other political cleavages. The emergence of ethnically defined parties also harks back to the inter-war period, when most political parties appealed to one particular nation or ethnic group (Banac 1984).

Political parties and alternate forms of minority representation

National minority political parties have become the primary pillars for minority representation in the region. They are, however, not the only institutional mechanisms through which minorities have been able to articulate their interests. This has been especially true since the late 1990s, when new forms of political representation emerged, and these often formed a part of comprehensive minority laws. Minorities have achieved representation in three different forms in addition to minority parties. First, minority associations can have a formal role in representing minority interests; they have the advantage of depoliticising certain minority-relevant decisions. At the same time, minority associations are not necessarily representative and might exclude parts of the community. Second, minorities can be represented through specific institutions which are established to represent minority interests. A problem these institutions often encounter is the form through which they are elected. Direct elections by minorities raises a plethora of problems, from questions on who can vote (and who can determine who can vote) to potential discrimination, whereas indirect elections can be used by one particular party to exclude others. Third, minority interests can be articulated by parties or bodies which do not represent minorities per se, but rather a broader constituency which also includes a particular minority. In theory, such an inclusive form of representation can avoid overemphasising difference and ethnicity. In reality, the record suggests that minority interests are easily ignored in this format and thus do not address the challenge of minority representation. Despite these alternative forms of minority inclusion, minority parties have been the dominant feature of minority politics in the Balkans, especially in the case of larger and geographically concentrated minorities, whereas others have withdrawn from the political system altogether. Withdrawals have occurred when a significant portion of the minority does not agree with the larger political system or the state, as was the case for Kosovo Albanian parties in Serbia during the 1990s; when the minority is very small and/or it has insufficient political mobilisation and organisation, as is the case with Roma parties. With the partial exception of Montenegro, the majority of mainstream parties have been unable to attract the votes of minorities. The configuration of the party system along ethnic lines is largely a consequence of the unwillingness of majority parties to seriously incorporate minority community concerns, often due to fears of alienating the majority.

While the larger minorities are generally represented in the parliaments of the countries of south-eastern Europe, smaller minorities are often excluded due to the electoral threshold or the absence of a political organisation. Of the larger minorities, the Roma generally suffer from a lack of political representation and, with rare exceptions as in Macedonia, are not represented in parliament or, if so, only occasionally. While Bulgaria and Macedonia do not have specific electoral laws to ensure minority representation, other countries have adopted some degree of positive discrimination in the electoral system. Romania has set aside one seat for every minority which does not manage to cross the threshold. As a result some 20 MPs hail from minorities other than the larger Hungarian minority. Similarly in Kosovo, 20 seats in the 120-member parliament have been set aside for minorities:[2] irrespective of any seats the minorities might gain in the main PR election, ten seats are reserved for Serbs and ten for all the other minorities. Croatia has established a special countrywide electoral district for minorities, allowing minorities to choose whether to vote for their minority MPs or for representation in the electoral district of their residence. Curiously, of the seats reserved for minorities some are 'shared' between several minorities, i.e. between Albanians, Bosniaks, Slovenes and Montenegrins. Montenegro has also established a special polling unit, covering a geographical area where most Albanians live and thus ensuring that this community can elect its own representatives.[3] In Serbia, the 5 per cent threshold was abolished in 2004 for minority parties, meaning that only the 'natural' threshold for each parliamentary seat applies.[4] The systems of choice have thus largely ensured minority participation. At the same time, they have a number of flaws, either in terms of abuse by politicians arguably not belonging to the minority in question (Alionescu 2004: 64), or because of the systems which favour some minorities over others (Montenegro). An additional problem associated with the parliamentary representation of smaller minorities is the lack of influence these MPs have. Generally, they cannot impact parliamentary procedure and at times have been described as mere 'window-dressing'. In some cases, the minority MPs, relying on the parliamentary majority to preserve their seats, might be little more than bolstering the government coalition without being of any benefit for their respective minority.

In the first half of the 1990s, the only country to include minorities in its government was Macedonia. In the rest of the region, such a form of recognition of minorities seemed unlikely and often unimaginable. More than a decade later, all countries in the region have included minorities in government, ranging from the Serb minority party joining the HDZ government in Croatia in 2007, the Hungarian minority party's participation in the DOS government in Serbia (2000–2003), the various Albanian parties participating in Macedonia since 1991, and the predominantly Greek Union for Human Rights Party in Albania has also been included in government since 2001.

In addition to the minority-specific bodies such as minority councils, parties have been at the forefront of representing minority interests. Through these political parties, minorities have achieved representation in parliaments and government. The power of these parties is consolidated by electoral systems based on proportional representation and closed electoral lists.

Minorities and the party system of the Western Balkans

In terms of the interrelationship between parties and minorities, one can identify four different types of parties:

1   Mono-ethnic parties
2   Ethnic parties with minority candidates
3   Diversity-sensitive civic parties
4   Multi-ethnic parties.

In order to classify parties effectively, one needs to consider the programmatic orientation, the leadership and candidates of the parties, as well as the members and voters of the party.

Mono-ethnic parties generally appeal to only one community. Their programme, membership and voters thus largely hail from only one group, be it the majority or minority. Often with conservative or nationalist parties, any inclusion of other groups is purely tokenistic and minimal. Thus, the Serb Radical Party (*Srpska radikalna stranka*, SRS) has had MPs of a non-Serbian background. Such minority candidates, however, if nominated at all, are not chosen to represent minority interests but to prove the supposed inclusiveness of the party.

In order to obscure the promotion of the interests of only one community, *Ethnic parties with minority candidates* often do not include the protection of minorities in their programme or have candidates from other communities. Such a step might be a policy to overturn a ban in countries where ethnically based parties are prohibited or an effort to gain votes from other communities. In Bosnia and Herzegovina, for example, the different nationalist parties have run candidates from other groups to control certain reserved seats. Such policies do not prevent parties from being classified as mono-ethnic. One thus needs to examine the effective inclusion of other groups rather than focusing only on formal elements.

Diversity-sensitive civic parties are not explicitly dominated by one group and seek to down-play the role of ethnicity in their programmes and member-ships. In most countries, these parties might still be dominated by a large group, but they are able to effectively recruit candidates from, and offer programmatic incentives to, their minorities. Such parties often include left-wing or liberal parties such as the Social Democratic Party (*Socijal demokratska partija*, SDP) in Montenegro or the Liberal Democratic Party (*Liberal demokratska partija*, LDP) in Serbia.

The final category comprises *multi-ethnic parties*; this is largely an aspira-tional category. A number of parties, such as the Social Democratic Party (*Socijal demokratska partija*, SDP) in Bosnia and Herzegovina, aspire to be inclusive and represent their different communities. Considering the dynamics of party formation, however, few parties have been able to consistently represent different ethnic groups. Instead, coalitions between minority and civic parties have been more likely.

The success of minority parties has been considerable. With few exceptions, a significant proportion of minorities vote for parties which appeal explicitly to minority communities. Of course, minority parties vary widely, but most of them fall into the first two categories described above. As the table below indicates, the largest minorities in most countries are represented by one or two significant political parties. In some countries, the party might exceed the percentage of the minority, indicating either a high degree of mobilisation for elections among the minority (or at least higher than among the majority) or the ability to gain votes from other minorities or the majority.

Minority parties across the Western Balkans and in the broader region are not cast out of a single block. Their agendas have changed over more than 15 years of democratic transition, and most parties now encompass divergent political views. Having their origins in broad anti-communist coalitions or representing different political platforms, most minority parties are brought together not only by the common interest of representing a minority group, but also by the need for cohesion to secure parliamentary representation. Many strong and competing minority parties, as in Macedonia, are exceptional and only possible among a numerically strong minority.

The internal differences between minority parties in the region are apparent in their divergent views on how to secure minority interests and different positions along larger political cleavages. The first issue often juxtaposes views that seek greater inclusion in state institutions and minority rights, with demands for political and territorial autonomy.[5] The second expresses itself in terms of support for larger ideological concepts, such as conservatism or liberalism. Thus some minority parties, such as the larger Hungarian minority parties, tend to represent more conservative options, whereas others, like the Movement for Rights and Freedoms in Bulgaria, cast themselves as liberal. These ideological variations, however, are often not strongly developed, as the overall political systems in most post-communist countries lack clear ideological differentiation.

Minority parties and electoral systems

In designing their electoral systems, all the countries opted for PR, either with their first multi-party elections or by later shifting from majoritarian or mixed systems to PR. Albania was the last to do so, changing from a mixed to a PR system only in 2008. The prevalence of PR has had a significant impact on minority representation. Conventional wisdom on minority representation suggests that proportional systems tend to be superior to majoritarian ones. In fact, a great variety of electoral systems can ensure minority representation (Venice Commission 2000). The experience in south-eastern Europe suggests that, in combination with relatively high thresholds, PR rather than majoritarian systems might actually be a greater disadvantage to minorities when the latter are geographically concentrated. In Albania for example, the Greek minority party has been able to enter parliament only due to the mixed electoral system; similarly Albanian and Roma minority parties entered the Macedonian *sobranie* through the single-member constituencies used until 1998 (Friedman: 2005: 381–96). It appears that the majoritarian electoral system in use from 1990 to 1998 in particular helped Roma representation due to a high geographic concentration of Roma in the Skopje neighbourhood Šuto Orizari (60.6 per cent in 2002). Nevertheless, Roma continue to be underrepresented at local and national level.[6] This effect is difficult to replicate elsewhere, however, as Roma mostly lack such geographic concentration and electoral units to match it.

By contrast, most of the largest minorities in the region are geographically concentrated and have performed relatively well, irrespective of the electoral system. In Serbia, for example, Hungarian, Albanian and Bosniak/Muslim parties regularly succeeded in entering parliament while gaining less than 2 per cent of the vote during the 1990s. After the change to PR from a majoritarian system in 2000 in Serbia, minority parties failed to enter parliament in 2003 and only returned in 2007 once the threshold for minorities was lifted. With thresholds of 3 to 5 per cent in most countries, minorities with a smaller share of eligible voters have no chance of entering parliament independently. Thresholds, however, were not established to prevent minority participation, but rather to avoid excessive fragmentation of parliament.

Table 4.1 The most significant minorities and minority political parties in the Western Balkans

	Census in %	Parties in %	Seats in parliament %
Albania (census 1989, elections 2005)	1.8 Greeks	Union of Human Rights Party, 4.13	1.43 (2 of 140)
Macedonia (census 2002, elections 2006)	25.2 Albanians	Democratic Union for Integration, 12.12	14.16 (17 of 120)
		Democratic Party of Albanians, 7.50	9.17 (11 of 120)
Montenegro (census 2003, elections 2006)	32.0 Serbs	Serb List, 14.7	13.58 (11 of 81)
	11.7 Bosniaks/Muslims	Liberal Party/Bosniak Party, 3.8	3.70 (3 of 81)
	5.0 Albanians	Democratic Alliance, 1.3	1.23 (1 of 81)
		Democratic Union of Albanians, 1.1	1.23 (1 of 81)
		Albanian Alternative, 0.8	1.23 (1 of 81)
Serbia (census 2002, elections 2007)	3.9 Hungarians	Alliance of Vojvodina Hungarians, 1.3	1.2 (3 of 250)
	1.8 Bosniaks	List for Sandžak, 0.84	0.8 (2 of 250)
	1.4 Roma	Roma Union of Serbia, 0.42	0.4 (1 of 250)
		Roma Party, 0.36	0.4 (1 of 250)
	0.8 Albanians	Albanian Coalition of Preševo Valley, 0.42	0.4 (1 of 250)

Notes
The election data is taken from official election offices and the ODHIR reports. The census data is taken from the statistical offices of the countries. Note that only countries and minorities are included where minority parties secured parliamentary representation by other means than reserved seats (i.e. Serbs and other minorities in Croatia, and smaller minorities in Kosovo). Bosnia and Herzegovina is also excluded as the ethnification of the political system renders such a categorisation problematic.

Table 4.2 Minority provisions in the electoral systems in the Western Balkans (2008)

	Electoral system	Special minority representation	Threshold %
Albania	Mixed Proportional	n/a	2.5
Bosnia and Herzegovina	List PR	House of Representatives (42); House of People (15): reserved seats (5 Bosniaks, Croats, Serbs)	3
• Federation	List PR	House of Representatives (98): reserved seats (min. 4 Bosniaks, Croats, Serbs); House of Peoples (58): 17 Croats, Bosniaks, Serbs, 7 Others	3
• Republika Srpska	List PR	National Assembly (83): reserved seats (min. 4 Croats, Bosniaks, Serbs); Council of Peoples (28): reserved seats (8 Croats, Bosniaks, Serbs, 4 Others)	3
Croatia	List PR	8 reserved seats (of 151), 1 Czech & Slovak, 1 Hungarian, 3 Serbian, 1 Italian, 1 Bosniak, Albanian, Montenegrin, Macedonian and Slovene, 1 Austrian, Bulgarian, German, Polish, Roma, Romanian, Ruthenian, Russian, Turkish, Ukrainian, Vlah and Jew minority	5
Kosovo	List PR	20 reserved seats (of 120), 10 Serbs, 4 Roma/Ashkali/Egyptians, 3 Bosniaks, 2 Turks and 1 Gorani	–
Macedonia	List PR	n/a	–
Montenegro	List PR	4 reserved seats from Albanian electoral unit (of 81)	3
Serbia	List PR	No threshold (of 250)	5

Preventing and promoting minority parties: the politics of institutional engineering

The failure of blocking minority parties

Since the introduction of multi-party systems, no single country has completely prevented the representation of minorities in parliament. Nevertheless, reducing the representation of minorities in the political system has been an implicit and at times explicit policy of numerous governments. Here, we shall examine restrictions to minority parties in the form of first, bans and other restrictive measures directed against minority parties; second, gerrymandering; and third, electoral thresholds.

Outright bans have been the exception, enacted only in Albania and Bosnia and Herzegovina. The briefest experiment was in Bosnia, where mono-ethnic parties were briefly prohibited during the pre-election period in 1990. The Constitutional Court lifted the ban before the elections, thus having no impact on the outcome, which resulted in an overwhelming victory for the three nationalist parties (Arnautović 1996). In Albania, experience with such bans has been longer but not much more effective, as the main party of Greeks in Albania, the key minority, has not been prohibited.

As the Venice Commission notes, bans are ineffective, unusual and incompatible with human rights standards (2000). Bans on ethnic parties have been clearly instituted to prevent what the state and the ethnic majority considers threatening, rather than as a tool for moderating or de-ethnicising the political system, and the one short-lived ban on ethnic parties in Bosnia failed to prevent the emergence of ethnically based parties.

Most measures to hinder minority representation do not take the form of explicit bans, but rather express themselves through a number of obstacles, which inadvertently and/or intentionally seek to preclude or reduce minority representation. As the Venice Commission notes in its study of electoral systems and their impact on minorities, '[i]t is not always easy to identify which of these general rules promote and which hinder representation of minorities' (2000).

A common tool has been ethnic gerrymandering, i.e. creating electoral units which reduce the representation of minorities in parliament. As electoral commissions or other institutions charged with the establishment of electoral units have been dominated by majorities, electoral districts have often been drawn to reduce minority representation (Venice Commission 2000). One poignant example is electoral district 61 in Macedonia's 1998 elections. In the ODIHR monitoring report, the observers note that this snake-shaped district 'curls around the mountains in the north west of the country, joining ethnic Macedonian villages together in a mainly ethnic Albanian area'. As a consequence, electoral engineering secured additional seats for the majority and prevented the creation of a minority voting block (ODIHR 1998). In fact, gerrymandering was so widely recognised as disadvantaging Albanians that it was explicitly addressed in the demands of the Albanian National Liberation Army during the 2001 conflict (Rusi 2004: 4).[7]

Similarly, the size of constituencies has been a tool to disadvantage minorities. A number of countries, such as Serbia, have held elections in one country-wide constituency.[8] Registration requirements also constitute a potential obstacle for minority parties. A high number of signatures for either registering a party or running in parliamentary elections can also be an obstacle. In Serbia again, the electoral commission dropped the requirement to submit 10,000 signatures for national minority parties in order to participate in national elections to 3,000.[9] Only then could the abolition of the electoral threshold of 5 per cent for national minority parties effectively advance their representation. This rule, which had presented a considerable obstacle for parties representing smaller minorities, was abolished in a controversial decision by the Constitutional Court in April 2008 (B92 Vesti 2008).

The most frequent obstacle for minority parties in the Western Balkans is the electoral threshold. All countries have an effective threshold, which generally varies between 3 and 5 per cent. As there has been a general trend towards PR since the 1990s, the importance of thresholds has increased. In most countries, only the parties of the largest minority could secure parliamentary representation, and only then if they were to run on a single ticket. Thresholds have thus stifled party formation among smaller minorities and at times resulted in the consolidation of a single minority party. Coalitions among several smaller minority groups to overcome the threshold have been rare. The most significant attempt failed in 2003 in Serbia, when the 'Coalition for Tolerance', composed of parties from the Hungarian and Bosniak minority and regional parties, failed to cross the 5 per cent threshold by only winning 4.2 per cent of the vote (B92 2003).

Instead, thresholds prompted minority parties or associations either to form pre-election coalitions or to secure seats on lists of majority and mainstream parties. In particular, parties of Roma and other small minorities have only been able to secure representation through such means, if no specific mechanisms favouring minority parties are in place. The regional experience with such representation through mainstream parties has been modest. If majority parties were willing to include minority candidates on electoral lists, such candidates were often placed at low positions on the ballot, resulting in only a few seats being gained by minorities.

The difficult promotion of minority parties

The most common mechanism for promoting minority inclusion is reserved minority seats in parliament: Croatia, Bosnia and Herzegovina, Montenegro, and Kosovo have set-aside seats on the basis of ethnic affiliation. The mechanisms for distributing such seats, however, vary greatly. Reserved seats seek to secure representation of smaller minorities which would not be able to achieve representation without such special measures. As the number of reserved seats is generally small, they have not been a major distortion of proportionality and equal representation.

Montenegro has been setting seats aside for the Albanian minority since 1998.

While the whole country was treated as one electoral district in parliamentary elections, one special district was established with first five and since 2002 four reserved seats. The fact that neither the voters in the affected polling stations are exclusively Albanian, nor are all Albanians included in these special polling stations, is rather unusual. Furthermore, other minorities such as the much larger Muslim/Bosniak minority have not benefited from a similar treatment. ODIHR has thus criticised this electoral mechanism for its legal uncertainties and for singling one minority out (ODIHR 2006b: 15–16). As the system does not prescribe *who* gets elected, but only *how*, not all of the reserved seats have been held by Albanian minority parties. Half of the seats have generally been won by the governing parties, which usually do not have Albanian minority candidates (Pavićević 2002: 35–6).

In Croatia the key challenge since independence has been the representation of Serbs, and the 1990s saw numerous changes to the election law. Since 2000, minorities have the choice between voting for a general candidate list or for the specific minority list, amounting to a current total of eight reserved seats. Confronted with this choice, a majority among all larger minorities opts for the general list; in the case of the Serb minority, less than a quarter voted for the minority list in 2003. Curiously, a number of minority MPs represent not only their own ethnic group, but also other communities. The Croatian Constitutional Law on Minorities and the Election Law reserves one to three seats for minorities larger than 1.5 per cent; de facto only Serbs qualify. Among the five seats reserved for smaller minorities, only the Hungarians and Italians hold a seat in parliament; the other minorities 'share' the remaining three reserved seats. Candidates of the minorities assigned to the same seat thus compete with each other, with the candidate receiving the most votes winning the seat. Nikola Mak, for example, elected to the Croatian *Sabor* in 2003, not only represented his own German community, but also the country's Austrians, Bulgarians, Poles, Roma, Romanians, Ruthenians, Russians, Turks, Ukrainians, Vlahs and Jews (Petričušić 2002/2003: 618–19).

In Kosovo minorities have been able to receive representation through reserved seats, in addition to a share in the overall proportional voting for the assembly: ten seats are reserved for the Serb community and an additional ten seats represent other communities. As a result, in the 2001 elections, minority parties gained an additional 15 seats in the parliament, increasing their share from 16.7 per cent (20 of 120 seats) to 29 per cent (35 seats). In practice, this has only benefited the larger Serb minority. However, as Serbian parties have mostly boycotted subsequent elections in 2004 and 2007, the number of seats taken by Serb MPs has been limited to the ten reserved seats. The case of Kosovo also highlights the legitimacy of reserved seats when a community boycotts the elections. Thus the ten deputies elected to the seats reserved for the Serb community in 2007 gained only between 31 and 281 votes, a total of 1,700 votes for ten seats (CEC 2007a).

Similar mechanisms are in use in the entities and at the municipal level in Bosnia and Herzegovina where a minimum number of seats are set aside for all communities whose candidates do not reach the threshold through the regular electoral procedure (see Bieber 2006: 128–31).[10]

With the exception of Macedonia, all countries have some means of promoting the parliamentary representation of minorities. This trend is not only a reflection of the conflicts in the 1990s, but more a continuation of the elaborate institutionalisation of ethnic representation which took place under communism. As affirmative policies by definition favour minority parties which would be at risk of not being represented through the regular electoral system, the main beneficiaries tend to be the smaller minorities which generally do not have great weight in parliament. The impact on policymaking of minority MPs has thus been generally weak. Only when minority parties have been able to participate in government has the importance of the minority parties increased. This, however, has been largely reserved to the largest minorities. While smaller minorities have been included in government, governments commonly do not rely on their support, thus reducing their weight. Minority parties have been part of governing coalitions from Croatia (since 2007) to Albania. In Macedonia, the inclusion of an Albanian party has become part of the unwritten rules of inter-ethnic accommodation, and any government without an Albanian party would result in serious instability. In Kosovo, the inclusion of Serb and other minorities in government is a constitutional requirement, which was first established in 2001 and re-affirmed in the 2008 constitution. The Serbian and other minority members of government have not been able to transform the constitutional requirement into significant weight within the Kosovo government. In Bosnia and Herzegovina, the constitution dictates the inclusion of all three 'constituent' peoples, but other minorities have no guaranteed space in government, even if some ministers have hailed from one of these smaller minorities. Elsewhere, the inclusion of minority parties has been less a part of any power-sharing arrangement, but the consequence of the formation of a parliamentary majority. In a polarised environment among majority parties, as in Albania or Croatia, minority parties can become king makers and punch well above their weight.

Conclusions

Political participation of minorities in the Western Balkans has been largely channelled through minority parties. As the regional experience suggests, the largest minorities have been represented by relatively strong parties, which have participated in government in all countries. Neither the electoral system nor the promotion of minority rights, nor bans of ethnic parties have significantly altered the importance of these parties. Smaller minorities have been largely unable to secure representation in parliament, except where special affirmative measures are in place. The larger minorities have generally not been able to benefit from positive measures promoting minority representation, which mostly favoured smaller minorities. In fact, at times, minority representation through reserved seats has been established to promote smaller minorities over larger minorities.[11]

Parliamentary representation is often just one aspect of a broader parcel of minority rights; it entails representation at municipal and regional levels and in some cases also some degree of cultural autonomy (e.g. Slovenia, Croatia). Parliamentary representation, though symbolically important, has often not been the most significant form of minority inclusion, as the impact of minority members in parliament has been marginal. The most marginalised minority in the region, the Roma, has been the least able to benefit from efforts to promote minority parties. Struggling with a fragmented Roma party landscape in most countries, suspicion towards mainstream politics and distrust in their own political elites, the Roma have been consistently underrepresented. In some cases, reserved seats or reduced thresholds have assured the Roma's inclusion in parliament, whereas elsewhere, the Roma have either failed to be represented at all, or had to rely on majority party support. The number of Roma parties and members of parliament still lags behind the share of Roma in the population. While many Roma vote for majority parties, this voting pattern is hardly a reflection of the integration of Roma into mainstream politics, but rather of the political and social marginalisation of the community. The cause and remedies for the political underrepresentation of Roma thus lie beyond the field of electoral systems.

The widespread existence of minority parties has meant that minority concerns are commonly aggregated through political parties rather than through other institutions such as extra-institutional movements or NGOs. However, here one can observe considerable variation among minorities. While larger minorities find their primary voice through minority parties, smaller minorities more frequently articulate their concerns on minority-specific interests through institutions for cultural autonomy, minority associations, or local-level political activism. As with smaller minorities, the Roma have often found their interests aggregated by NGOs, both from within the community itself and via larger national and international organisations. Only in exceptional circumstances have mainstream parties, often small liberal or regional groups, effectively represented minority-specific concerns.

Political parties of larger minorities have been a relatively stable fixture in highly volatile political party systems. Whereas there has been an overall degree of moderation in the demands of minority parties, linked to their inclusion in the mainstream political system through coalitions, such parties have not disappeared, even in countries which do not promote or actually discourage ethnically based parties. This consistency has been a reflection first of the cleavages between majorities and minorities, especially in the early phases of transition; and second of the positive view taken by international organisations, in particular the EU, of minority interest articulation through minority parties. While minority parties have not always been successful, the larger minorities have achieved a firm place in the political system, including in the executive, and this has arguably improved the legitimacy of both the state and the political system for minorities, and contributed to the institutionalisation of minority grievances. This process has generally moderated majority–minority relations, as well as minority demands themselves, bringing about greater institutional stability. At the same time, however, minority parties have not generally been able to meet the needs of smaller communities and of the Roma, which find their needs inadequately addressed through state institutions, be they parliament or the executive.

Notes

1 This chapter draws on Bieber 2008a and Bieber 2008b. I would like to thank Věra Stojarová and Daniel Bochsler for their helpful comments.
2 The June 2008 constitution abolishes this system of double representation, but still sets aside 20 seats for minorities, but these are not assigned in addition to seats gained through regular voting. The old system remains in place for two elections following the enactment of the constitution (Art. 64, 148, Constitution of Kosovo 2008).
3 The 2006 minority law also establishes reserved seats for other minorities, but these provisions of the law have been suspended after the Constitutional Court found them to be in breach of the constitution.
4 However, minority parties still require the same number of signatures in elections as mainstream parties, creating a significant obstacle for some minorities. In 2008 a coalition of Albanian parties could only register with the support of some Serbian NGOs gathering signatures in their support in Belgrade.
5 Bugajski distinguishes between minority parties on the basis of their primary political platform: 1. Cultural revival; 2. Political autonomy; 3. Territorial autonomy; 4. Separatism; and 5. Irredentism. Generally speaking most large minority parties would fall in categories 2 and 3, whereas smaller minority groups often opt for category 1. Secessionist and irredentist minority parties are few, especially since the mid-late 1990s (Bugajski 2002: li–lii).
6 While the Roma continued to be represented in parliament after the introduction of PR, Roma candidates only entered parliament through pre-election coalitions with majority parties (Friedman 2005: 392).
7 Iso Rusi, 'From Army to Party – the Politics of the NLA', p. 3.
8 ODIHR, 'The Slovak Republic Parliamentary Elections, 25 and 26 September 1998', 26.10.1998.
9 Republička izborna komisija, Uputstvo za sprovođenje Zakona o izboru narodnih poslanika, 15.11.2006, Available at: www.rik.parlament.sr.gov.yu/latinica/propisi/ Uputstvo210107Lat.doc.
10 At the state-level reserved seats benefit the three dominant groups, Serbs, Bosniaks and Croats to the disadvantage of other minorities. Thus, in the second chamber of parliament, the House of Peoples, five seats each (of 15) are reserved for the three dominant nations.
11 For example in Macedonia in 2007, the VMRO-DPMNE-led government launched an initiative to reserve seats for minorities in a clear bid to undermine the dominance of Albanian parties among non-majority MPs.

5 The party system of Croatia

Jakub Šedo

Political system of Croatia

In the nineteenth century, contemporary Croatia belonged to the Austrian–
Hungarian monarchy: the coastal regions of Dalmatia and Istria were part of the
Austrian Empire, and the central part of present Croatia as well as Slavonia (the
eastern part of Croatia) belonged to the Hungarian Kingdom. Today's borders
were established after the Second World War, when Istria and that part of Dalmatia which had been a part of Italy between the two wars, were joined to the
Federative People's Republic of Yugoslavia.

The beginning of democratisation meant the 'awakening' of Croatian nationalism. The Serbian minority (approximately 12 per cent of the population living
in the Eastern Slavonia and next to the borders of north-western Bosnia and
Herzegovina) began to mobilise themselves against it (Hloušek 2003: 85).

Reminders of the late Nazi puppet Independent State of Croatia (*Nezavisna
Država Hrvatska*, 1941–1945) headed by Ante Pavelić, a leader of the fascist Ustaša
Movement, were an important symbol for both sides. During the domination of the
Ustaša regime in Croatia and Bosnia and Herzegovina, hundreds of thousands of
Serbs were massacred. Croatian campaigns for independence were answered by the
Serbs setting up paramilitary troops supported by the Federal Yugoslav People's
Army. After the landslide of a coalition led by the nationalist Croatian Democratic
Union (HDZ) in 1990, Croatia declared independence in the summer of 1991, and
almost immediately afterwards, a civil war broke out. Serbians declared the Repub-
lika Srpska Krajina. The war was terminated by a Croatian offensive (Operation
Storm – *Oluja*) in the summer of 1995 which led to the annexation of the Serbian
Krajina. The majority of the Serbs escaped from Croatia, and their share of the
population fell to less than 5 per cent (Søberg 2006: 61; Hloušek 2002: 172).[1]

During the civil war a semi-presidential political system was established,
closely connected with the former dissident and later the founder and leader of
the HDZ, Franjo Tuđman, who became the first president of the independent
Croatia. The regime during the period of his government may be classified as a
hybrid democracy or an authoritarian system. At that time, the HDZ controlled
both the state institutions and the media; they interfered with the activities of
political parties and non-profit groups, committed electoral manipulations, and

managed a course of privatisation which did not take place in a desirably transparent way and brought undeserved privileges to selected groups of people (Hloušek 2003: 115–16; Helmerich 2008: 176; Haughton and Fisher 2008: 443–4; Søberg 2006: 54–6).

The Tuđman regime collapsed right at the end of the 1990s. Franjo Tuđman died in 1999, and the HDZ lost the following parliamentary as well as presidential elections in January 2000 – first to the coalition of the Social Democratic Party of Croatia (SDP) and the Croatian Social Liberal Party (HSLS)[2] led by Ivica Račan (Račan, a former leader of the League of Communists of Croatia, was elected in 1989 and he led the party during its transformation into the SDP). The HDZ lost again in the presidential elections to Stjepan Mesić (from the Croatian People's Party – HNS). Moreover the HDZ nominee, Mate Granić, was placed third and thus failed to enter the second round. The HDZ's defeat was due to numerous circumstances; apart from Tuđman's death, there was increasing dissatisfaction among the population (a bad economic situation, corruption scandals) and also changes in the strategy of the opposition parties: they suddenly succeeded in putting together two great cooperating alliances which offered a real alternative to the HDZ government (Haughton and Fisher 2008: 445; Hloušek 2003: 146–7). The subsequent process is called the second Croatian transition. Its ingredients were constitutional changes leading from a semi-presidential system to a parliamentary one. The return of the HDZ to power in 2003 (now led by Ivo Sanader, former Deputy Minister of Foreign Affairs) did not mean the return of authoritarian practices; the 'second' democratisation in Croatia was successful, and the country was offered membership in NATO in 2008 and became an EU candidate country. The effort to achieve integration with western European structures represented an important influence on the consolidation of democracy in Croatia. According to the present constitution (the Croatian Constitution was adopted in 1990; crucial amendments were put through in 2000 and 2001), the political system in Croatia is a parliamentary republic with a directly elected president. The key role in the administration, however, is played by the government, which is accountable to a one-chamber parliament (until 2001 Croatia had a bicameral administration). The parliamentary electoral system experienced frequent changes during the 1990s. These were carried out by the HDZ and they were targeted – for example the change in 1992 of the two round majority–plurality system to a mixed-member majoritarian system with FPP in the nominal tier, prevented cooperation among the opposition in the second round of the elections (see Kasapović 2000; Helmerich 2008: 169). Since 2000 a List PR system has been in use, with minimum changes. The number of members of parliament is not fixed; the decisive share of 140 is elected in ten constituencies of equal magnitude; a 5 per cent legal threshold has been introduced only at constituency level, and seats are distributed using the d'Hondt method. Apart from these 140 seats, a share (five at the moment) is given to the Croatian diaspora in a special constituency. The number of MPs in this group is based on the turnout of the diaspora voters in comparison with the intra-Croatian constituencies. The establishment of the diaspora constituency in

1995 was another of the targeted changes introduced by the HDZ, which has won all the seats of this constituency in every election (the majority of the diaspora voters live in Bosnia and Herzegovina). Eight seats are reserved for constitutionally recognised minorities: three seats for the Serbs, one for the Italian, one for the Hungarian minorities, and the remaining seats for three groups of minorities (Šedo 2007: 58–61; Antić and Gruičić 2008: 752).

Development of party system in Croatia

Most of the currently relevant parties in Croatia have either been represented in parliament continuously since at least 1992, or they originated by secession from these parties. Development of the party system can be divided into three phases. From 1990 up to the end of the 1990s the HDZ was predominant. The opposition was dispersed in a number of smaller parties (Haughton and Fisher 2008: 442–3; Hloušek 2003: 85–8, 112–16; Hloušek 2002: 173–4; Helmerich 2008: 171–5). The second phase began at the end of the 1990s. Previously separated opposition parties came together in two coalitions, and after the 2000 elections they came to power (Hloušek 2003: 146–8; Hloušek 2002: 174–5; Helmerich 2008: 176–7). The third phase started with the 2003 elections. The significance of electoral coalitions decreased, and the relevant political parties ran in elections in minor coalitions or independently. The HDZ retained its position as a big party, and among the parties in opposition to the regime of Tuđman the SDP became the strongest (Helmerich 2008: 167; Šedo 2007: 219–20). The 2007 elections were almost exclusively a duel between the HDZ and the SDP; the rest of the parliamentary parties were seen merely as potential coalition partners for one of the main parties (see Antić and Gruičić 2008).

In the 2007 elections 54 parties took part, either as coalition members or independently. According to the electoral law, it is not obligatory for coalitions to consist of the same members in all electoral districts; therefore individual parties run in coalitions in some constituencies and separately in others. Neither the HDZ nor the SDP were in coalitions in all the electoral districts. After the 2003 and 2007 elections, greater attention was paid to parties which seated at least two members of parliament because of the large number of parties.[3]

Party families

Communist and radical left parties

Since the transformation of the League of Communists of Croatia at the beginning of the 1990s, this party family has had no representation in parliament. In the 2007 elections, the coalitions containing communist and radical left parties, the Left of Croatia – Left (*Ljevica Hrvatske – Ljevica*, LHL) and the Socialist Workers Party of Croatia (*Socijalistička radnička partija Hrvatske*, SRP) achieved less than 1 per cent of the votes; the SRP received a similar share in both the 2000 and 2003 elections.[4]

Socialist and social democratic parties

Social Democratic Party of Croatia (Socijaldemokratska partija Hrvatske, SDP)

The governing communist party took part in the 1990 elections as the League of Communists of Croatia – Party for Democratic Changes (*Savez komunista Hrvat-ske – Stranka demokratskih promjena*, SKH-SDP), and only later did it adopt the party's current name (Hloušek 2003: 85; Hloušek 2002: 177). In 1994 it joined with the marginal Social Democrats of Croatia (*Socijaldemokrati Hrvatske – SDH*). After the initial relative success (second place in the 1990 elections), the party experienced a deep crisis during which they had only minimum parliament-ary representation. At the end of the 1990s, its popularity began to grow again, and in the 2000 elections the party won in coalition with the Croatian Social Liberal Party (HSLS); in selected electoral districts there were two more regional parties added to the coalition. After those elections the party chairman Ivica Račan became the Prime Minister (Hloušek 2003: 147–8; Hloušek 2002: 177).

Račan's government introduced a series of reform measures that led to the democratisation of the country after the Tuđman regime. However, it did not succeed in finding solutions for the difficult economic situation, which contrib-uted to the government parties' defeat in 2003 (Helmerich 2008: 177–8). The SPD took part in those elections as a member of a coalition with the Istrian Democratic Assembly (IDS) and the Liberal Party (LP), and thus it managed to retain its position as one of the two strongest parties in the country (Šedo 2007: 216–17). Before the 2007 elections, Zoran Milanović became the new party chairman after Račan's resignation (I. Račan died soon afterwards). Elections for party chairman showed the party's internal coherence, as Milanović's rivals did not leave the party and remained members of the party presidium. In the 2007 elections, the SPD had no coalition partner, and won second place with 56 seats (Helmerich 2008: 178). Considering that the minor parties are far behind, the SPD can be seen as one of the two large Croatian parties which are either in gov-ernment or leaders of the opposition (cf. Antić and Gruičić 2008: 752–4).

The SDP declares support for the traditional themes of social democracy (solidarity, social justice); it is clearly pro-European, and it is an associate member of the Party of European Socialists.[5] During the electoral campaign in 2007 the SDP had two major themes: the introduction of a capital income tax, and the legitimacy of participation by the traditionally pro-HDZ diaspora in elec-tions (Antić and Gruičić 2008: 753).

Liberal parties

Croatian People's Party – Liberal Democrats (Hrvatska narodna stranka – Liberalni demokrati, HNS)

The HNS was founded in 1990 by the leaders of the Coalition of People's Accord (*Koalicija narodnog sporazuma*, KNS), an alliance of several minor parties which in the 1990 elections achieved only very small representation (Hloušek 2003: 87–8). Those leaders were Savka Dabčević-Kučar (who became the first party chairman) and Miko Tripalo. From the very beginning the HNS was in opposition to the HDZ government. It took part in the 1992 elections independently; in 1995 it joined the electoral coalition New Parliament (*Novi Sabor*) which was formed by five centrist opposition parties. Before the 2000 elections it took part in the electoral alliance Opposition Four with the Croatian Peasants' Party (HSS), the Istrian Democratic Assembly (IDS) and the Liberal Party (LS). The Opposition Four came third, and their members joined the SPD-led government of Ivica Račan. A member of the HNS, Stjepan Mesić, was elected president of Croatia in 2000. The HNS remained in Račan's government for the entire electoral term (Kasapović 2005: 196; Hloušek 2003: 147–8; Hloušek 2002: 179; Helmerich 2008: 179; Buljan and Duka 2003: 30, 44). In the 2003 elections the party ran in elections in a majority of districts independently; only in selected regions did it form coalitions. From 2003 on the HNS was in opposition, while before the 2007 elections it declared its intent to form a coalition with the SDP. In 2006 the party merged with a minor party called the Party of Liberal Democrats (Libra). In the 2007 elections, they remained in opposition, ran in elections independently, and came in third in number of votes, and fourth in terms of parliamentary seats (seven) (Antić and Gruičić 2008: 753). The chairman of the party is Radimir Čačić who also held the post from 1994–2000 and who replaced Vesna Pusić. This replacement did not lead to a party split; instead V. Pusić remained in the presidium of the party, and is a chairperson of the parliamentary party of the HNS.[6]

The HNS defines itself as a liberal and centrist party; its main themes are a legally consistent state, integration into NATO and the EU, decentralisation and economic growth. It is a member of the European Liberal Democrat and Reform Party.[7]

*Croatian Social Liberal Party (*Hrvatska socijalno liberalna stranka, HSLS*)*

The HSLS was founded in May 1989 as the Croatian Social Liberal Union (*Hrvatski socijal liberalni savez*) and took part in the 1990 election under the present name as a member of the Coalition of People's Accord (KNS). During the first half of the 1990s it was the strongest opposition party (it was second in the 1992 elections and third in 1995, in both elections running independently). In 1997 the party experienced a split – the wing headed by the former chairman from 1996–1997, Vlado Gotovac, left the party and founded the new Liberal Party (*Liberalna stranka*, LS). The latter took part in the 2000 and 2003 elections in various coalitions; it won seats in parliament but its achievements were not of major significance, and in 2006 the party merged back with the HSLS. Meanwhile, the HSLS took part in the 2000 elections in coalition with the SDP and won (Hloušek 2003: 14; Hloušek 2002: 179–80). The HSLS then joined Račan's government but in 2002 they left because of conflicts concerning levels of cooperation with the international court in The Hague (the HSLS criticised the extraditions of Croatian generals), and also the unfulfilled ambitions of the HSLS chairman Dražen Budiša, who failed to win the post of president in 2000 and was not even given a post in government. One of the consequences of the HSLS's abandonment of government was another party split – a wing headed by the Minister of Defence Jozo Radoš founded a new party, the Party of Liberal Democrats (*Libra – Stranka liberalnih demokrata*) (Kasapović 2005: 196, 201–2; Helmerich 2008: 177–8; Buljan and Duka 2003: 38–9, 48–51). The HSLS then made a shift towards the right (Buljan and Duka 2003: 17); it took part in the 2003 elections in coalition with the Democratic Centre and regional parties, but the coalition won just three seats. In the 2007 elections the HSLS joined the Croatian Peasants' Party (HSS) and the regional parties. This coalition became the fourth strongest subject in terms of the number of votes and third in seats won. The HSLS, however, got just two of the total of eight seats won by the coalition. Already before the election the members of this coalition preferred to cooperate with the HDZ rather than the SDP, and after the election they joined the HDZ-led Sanader government (Antić and Gruičić 2008: 754–5).

The HSLS combines social and liberal themes (transparent privatisation, civic and social rights) and defines its position at the centre of the party system.[8] The HSLS is a member of the European Liberal Democrat and Reform Party.

Christian democratic parties

*Croatian Democratic Union (*Hrvatska demokratska zajednica, HDZ*)*

The inclusion of the HDZ in this party family is somewhat questionable. During the 1990s it was possible to define it as a nationalist or populist right-wing party, but after the death of Franjo Tuđman its orientation began to change. The HDZ now declares itself to be a modern Christian Democratic and Conservative Party (Haughton and Fisher 2008: 448; Hloušek 2002: 181–2). The change in its pro-gramme, rhetoric and policies is obvious, and the HDZ has begun to be accepted by the western European Christian Democrats as a partner (Haughton and Fisher 2008: 449).

The HDZ was founded in June 1989, and in 1990 its branch in Bosnia and Herzegovina came into existence too. Before the first free elections, the HDZ put together the Croatian Democratic Bloc (*Hrvatski demokratski blok*, HDB), which became the unambiguous winner of the election (Hloušek 2003: 86–7).

In 1992 and 1995, the party ran independently, and in both cases it achieved decisive victories resulting in large majority representations in the parliament. The reason was the popularity of the HDZ, which presented itself as a key force in the fight for gaining and sustaining the independence of Croatia (the civil war ended in 1995). In addition, the HDZ misused its dominant position in parlia-ment and the state administration, and the elections were thus manipulated in favour of the HDZ; tactics included targeted changes in the electoral law and the timing of elections (those of 1995 were in fact premature, the HDZ wanted to exploit its popularity after Croatia's victory in the war). In 1994 a moderate wing headed by Josip Manolić and Stjepan Mesić left the HDZ and founded the Croatian Independent Democrats (*Hrvatski nezavisni demokrati*, HND) (Hloušek 2003: 114). After the 1995 elections failure of the HND, Mesić joined the HNS and in 2000 was elected president.

The popularity of the HDZ decreased during the second half of the 1990s; moreover, in 1999, its founder and long-term chair, Franjo Tuđman, died. After a transitory period in 2000, Ivo Sanader was elected his successor, and he has been the chairman of the party ever since. In the same year of 2000, the HDZ suffered two heavy electoral defeats: they achieved less than one-third of the seats in the parliamentary elections, and in the presidential elections their candidate Mate Granić failed even to advance to the second round (Hloušek 2003: 146–9). Afterwards Granić together with some other HDZ representatives founded the Democratic Centre (*Demokratski centar*, DC), a party of more centrist and moderate politics than that of the HDZ (Hloušek 2002: 178, 182; Buljan and Duka 2003: 40–1). The DC has had only minimum parliamentary representation; after 2003 they participated in the Sanader HDZ-led government (Helmerich 2008: 181; Šedo 2007: 216–22), and after the 2007 elections they held no parliamentary seats at all.

The HDZ managed to succeed in its internal consolidation and modernisation during the period 2000–2003. In the 2003 elections it won again, and party chairman Ivo Sanader became the Prime Minister (Haughton and Fisher 2008: 447; Helmerich 2008: 180). Another victory for the HDZ came in the 2007 elections in which it got 61 out of 140 seats in Croatia, and all five diaspora seats (Antić and Gruičić 2008: 753–5).

The HDZ is a member of the European People's Party as a Christian Democratic party. It is still a nationalist party, but moderate and pro-European, making it possible for the HDZ-led government to cooperate not only with the EU but also with the ICTY. The HDZ defends the unity of the Croats and supports the participation of the Croatian diaspora in the election. The other main themes for the HDZ are the social–market economy and integration into the EU and NATO.[9]

Radical right-wing parties

Croatian Party of the Right (Hrvatska stranka prava, HSP)

The HSP continues the heritage of the radical nationalist party of the same name that existed in the nineteenth and the first half of the twentieth centuries, not only in name but also in its rhetoric and programme. The party was founded (renewed) in 1990. In the first elections it participated in the HDZ-led Croatian Democratic Bloc (HDB) (Hloušek 2003: 87). At the beginning of the civil war the HSP managed its own paramilitary troops called the Croatian Defence Forces (*Hrvatske obrambene snage*, HOS) which was involved in ethnic cleansing. On the political scene, the HSP did not have much success (Hloušek 2002: 184; Helmerich 2008:

181). Although it had permanent parliamentary representation, the other parties did not accept it as a partner due to its radicalism. In the elections it ran mostly by itself; only in 2000 and 2003 did it enter into coalition with minor parties, in 2000 with the Croatian Christian Democratic Union (*Hrvatska kršćanska demokratska unija*, HKDU), and in 2003 with two minor regional parties (Šedo 2007: 216–17). The 2007 elections brought its worst electoral result; it gained only one seat, and it lost many voters to the HDZ, which 'mobilised' right-wing voters against a potential SDP victory (Antić and Gruičić 2008: 753).

The party is described as an extreme right-wing nationalist party; it declares strong support for the independence of Croatia without any limits, opposes the pro-integration policy of the government, and is against cooperation with the international court in The Hague.[10] It is not acceptable as a member of the government for either the left or the moderate right, although the HSP indirectly supported the HDZ-led government in 2003–2007 (Antić and Gruičić 2008: 754–5).

Agrarian parties

Croatian Peasants' Party (Hrvatska seljačka stranka, HSS)

The original HSS, founded in 1904, was a dominant Croatian party in the past. In post-war Yugoslavia, it was active in exile, and at the end of 1989 it was re-established in Zagreb, as exile management handed power to the domestic party. In the 1990 elections the HSS cooperated with the HDZ in the Croatian Democratic Bloc (HDB) (Hloušek 2003: 87). In the 1992 elections it ran independently, and from 1995 it participated in coalitions aimed at uniting the opposition against the Tuđman regime. Thus in 1995 the party ran in the electoral coalition New Parliament (*Novi Sabor*). Before the 2000 elections the HSS joined the electoral alliance Opposition Four with the Croatian People's Party (HNS), Istrian Democratic Assembly (IDS), and Liberal Party (LS) (Hloušek 2003: 147–8; Hloušek 2002: 185). After the elections that brought the end of the HDZ government, the HSS became a member of the government coalition headed by Ivica Račan (SDP) and remained in coalition for the entire electoral period. In the 2003 elections HSS ran independently, but in 2007 it entered into coalition with the HSLS and two minor regional parties. After the elections the party joined the Sanader government (Antić and Gruičić 2008: 753–5).

The HSS is a member of the European People's Party. Its programme combines the agrarian (the importance and support of the rural sector are the first and foremost themes in the party programme), conservative, and social themes.[11]

Single issue parties

Croatian Party of Pensioners (Hrvatska stranka umirovljenika, HSU)

The HSU was founded in 1991, but until the 2003 elections it had no parliamentary representation. In that year, however, the party succeeded in obtaining three seats, and although it did not become a direct participant in government, it supported the Sanader government in several key situations. In 2007 the HSU was unable to repeat its previous achievements, and took only one seat (Antić and Gruičić 2008: 753–5). The HSU is a single issue party; it focuses on all topics related to the interests and living standards of pensioners (according to its manifesto, not only of already retired persons, but also of the people who will retire in the future).[12]

Regional parties

Istrian Democratic Assembly (Istarski demokratski sabor/Dieta democratice Istriana, IDS)

The IDS was founded in February 1990 and initially, it acted only at the local level. It took part in national elections for the first time in 1992 when it established an electoral alliance with the Slavonia–Baranja Croatian Party (SBHS). In the following years, the IDS has participated in coalitions opposing the Tuđman regime, and with its strong regional position, it was also able to win in the nominal tier. During the entire period, it retained three to four seats. In 1995 it participated in the New Parliament (*Novi Sabor*) electoral coalition, and in the 2000 elections it was a member of Opposition Four, with the Croatian People's Party (HNS), the Croatian Peasants' Party (HSS) and the Liberal Party (LS). The IDS joined the Račan government after the elections, but left the government one year later (Hloušek 2003: 146–7; Hloušek 2002: 186–7; Helmerich 2008: 179–80; Buljan and Duka 2003: 56–7). In 2003 it was in coalition with the SDP and two minor parties (Šedo 2007: 216–17; Buljan and Duka 2003: 57–8), in 2007 it ran independently and took three seats (Antić and Gruičić 2008: 753).

The IDS declares itself to be a liberal and regionalist party; it is a member of the European Liberal, Democrat and Reform Party. Its oft-repeated topics are civil rights and freedoms, decentralisation, and defence of the specific identity and interests of Istria.[13]

Croatian Democratic Assembly of Slavonia and Baranja (Hrvatski demokratski sabor Slavonije i Baranje, HDSSB)

The HDSSB was founded in 2006, and its activities are limited to Slavonia, i.e. the inland part of Croatia. Before that – since 1992 – the Slavonia–Baranja Croatian Party (*Slavonsko–Baranjska Hrvatska stranka*, SBHS) was successful on the national level, joining electoral alliances against the HDZ government (Hloušek 2002: 187). In the 2003 elections, the SBHS in coalition with the Croatian People's Party (HNS) did not achieve any significant success, and in the 2007 elections it was a total failure.[14]

The founding of the HDSSB was preceded by Branimir Glavaš's leaving the parliamentary party of the HDZ. Glavaš was among the prominent organisers of the defence of the town of Osijek during the civil war and, accompanied by many other members of the HDZ, he later became a direct commander of the defenders. One of the reasons why he left the HDZ was because of a disagreement with the HDZ policy in relation to the ICTY, as he was also threatened with being charged for war crimes.[15] In the 2007 elections the HDSSB got three seats. The HDSSB is a regional populist party, which demands decentralisation and support for the Slavonia and Baranja region (the eastern part of Croatia which was war-torn during the war).[16]

Other regional parties

Apart from the IDS and the HDSSB which have maintained a long-term parliamentary representation, a number of other regional parties also take part in elections. In some cases they have managed to achieve minor parliamentary representation (one or two seats), always in coalitions. Since the 2007 elections, however, none of them has been represented except for the IDS and the HDSSB. The only exceptions are the ethnic minority parties which obtain seats within special contests reserved for the ethnic minorities. In 2000–2007 parliamentary seats were held by the Alliance of Primorje – Gorski Kotar (*Primorsko – Goranski savez*, PGS), which in 2007 cooperated unsuccessfully with the electoral alliance of the HSS and the HSLS. The region Primorje – Gorski Kotar is situated in the north-west of the country (east of Istria) and is a part of the two electoral districts (No VII and VIII) in which the PGS runs candidates.[17]

Ethnic minority parties

*Independent Democratic Serbian Party (*Samostalna demokratska Srpska stranka, *SDSS)*

The SDSS was founded in 1997 as a party focusing on the Serbian minority, and it competes for the votes of those Croatian Serbs who returned home after the war. Its main political target and topic is therefore support for the Serbians' return. Its political approach to the Croatian majority has always been cooperative, and at present the SDSS participates in the HDZ-led coalition government (Antić and Gruičić 2008: 755). It competes only for the seats reserved for the Serbian minority. Both in 2003 and 2007 it won all three seats, and thus it replaced the Serbian People's Party (*Srpska narodna stranka*, SNS) which had represented moderate Serbs on the political scene in the 1990s (Hloušek 2002: 187).[18]

The SDSS describes itself as a liberal and social democratic party. Its main topics are support for the return of Serbian refugees, defence of the Serbian minority, its language and culture; but it does not oppose Croatian independence. Its programme and politics are cooperative.[19]

Interim conclusions

Croatia experienced different phases of development in both its political and its party systems after the fall of the communist establishment. The initial democratisation at the beginning of the 1990s was not successful. The regime of President Tuđman in the 1990s only faked a democratic environment, but in fact it violated many democratic standards. At the turn of the millennium Croatia experienced its so-called second democratisation, which was relatively success-ful compared to what was happening in other Western Balkan countries, and one of its consequences was the gradual integration of Croatia into western European structures. Croatia is now a member of NATO; accession to the European Union is not yet finished. Croatia had been aiming to join along with Bulgaria and Romania in 2007. A fixed date for accession has still not been determined; in November 2008 the end of the year 2011 was being mentioned as the latest date for its membership in the EU. The most complicated disputes concerned Croatia's cooperation with the ICTY, because Croatia was to extradite its citizens indicted of war crimes to the ICTY (for many Croats they are not crimi-nals but heroes of the War of Independence). Also, there is a dispute between Slovenia (an EU Member state) and Croatia over the maritime borders in the Piran Bay and Slovenia's access to international waters.

The most important change in the demographic nature of post-communist Croatia was the decrease in the numbers of the Serb minority. According to the last pre-war census in 1991 there were more than 518,000 Serbs (over 12 per cent of the population) living in Croatia; in the 2001 census only about 201,000 citizens declared themselves as Serbs (4.54 per cent). According to data of the OSCE Mission in Croatia, at least 300,000 Serbs left Croatia during the war. About 120,000 of them have returned to Croatia, leaving more than 180,000 still living in Serbia, Montenegro, and Bosnia and Herzegovina. About 120,000 have retained refugee status, others have changed their status through the acquisition of citizenship in other Western Balkan countries. The return of refugees to Croatia is a complicated process not only in terms of potential conflict between Croats living in the territories of the former Republic of Serbian Krajina, but also as a result of the activities of the Croatian army during and after the decisive victory, which forced the Serbian population to leave their homes and which sys-tematically destroyed these houses. The infrastructure of the former Serbian Krajina was also seriously damaged. Returning refugees therefore have many social problems (housing, employment etc.).[20]

Just as the political system experienced various stages in its development, so too did the party system. The present can be seen as a duel between two large and internally quite consolidated parties – the HDZ and the SDP. Apart from these there are numerous minor parties which, except for the HSP, act as pro-system parties. Among these minor parties we find both national actors and purely regional alliances. The position of the minor national parties, however, may be threatened in the future if the proportion of voters for the large party increases. In spite of the fact that the political and party system of Croatia can be assessed more or less positively, it would be wrong to neglect the set of difficulties which exist in Croatia and which are typical of all post-communist countries, such as frequent suspicion of corruption and clientelism among prominent politicians (many times well-founded).

Notes

1 Leaders of the Republika Srpska Krajina, including the President of the Republic, Milan Babić, were indicted for war crimes by the ICTY. Babić was sentenced to 13 years and in 2006 committed suicide in prison. His successor in the office of President, Milan Martić, was sentenced to 35 years. After the war, the Government of Republika Srpska Krajina in exile was established in Serbia, and in 2005 re-established; it was led by Milorad Buha, former Member of Parliament of Republika Srpska Krajina.

2 In addition two regional parties participated on the SDP-HSLS coalition – Alliance of Primorje – Gorski Kotar (*Primorsko–Goranski savez*, PGS) and Slavonia–Baranja Croatian Party (*Slavonsko–Baranjska Hrvatska stranka*, SBHS).

3 www.osce.org/documents/odihr/2008/04/30928_hr.pdf.

4 www.izbori.hr.

5 www.sdp.hr. See for example Buljan and Duka 2003: 7–14.

6 www.hns.hr/modules/news.

7 www.hns.hr/modules/news, for 2003 elections see Buljan and Duka 2003: 30–5.

8 www.hsls.hr, for 2003 elections Buljan and Duka 2003: 36–9.

9 www.hdz.hr, Buljan and Duka 2003: 15–22.

10 For the party position in the 2003 elections see Buljan and Duka 2003: 52–5.

11 www.hss.hr, for previous elections see Buljan and Duka 2003: 23–9.

12 www.hsu.hr.

13 www.ids-ddi.com.

14 www.izbori.hr.

15 www.branimirglavas.com/index.php?option=com_content&task=view&id=22&Itemid=2.

16 www.hdssb.hr.

17 www.izbori.hr.

18 www.izbori.hr.

19 www.sdss.hr.

20 www.osce.org/documents/mc/2005/07/15886_en.pdf.

6 The party system of Bosnia and Herzegovina

Jakub Šedo

Overview of the political system

Bosnia and Herzegovina (BiH) was established after the Second World War as a republic within the Federative People's Republic of Yugoslavia. The borders of BiH approximately follow the model of former borders that were designed at the Berlin Congress in 1878 and were valid until 1929 (Hladký 2005: 181, 207).

The process of democratisation of the Socialist Federative Republic of Yugoslavia in the beginning of 1990s rapidly descended into the disintegration of the state. BiH became an independent state after the 1992 referendum; independence was supported by 63.4 per cent of all voters (98 per cent of those who actually participated). The referendum was boycotted by the Serbs (approximately 32 per cent of the population). The Serbs voted earlier in their own referendum for maintaining BiH within Yugoslavia. The stability of the newly established state was further undermined by the efforts of the Croats, who wanted the western part of BiH to join Croatia (Kasum 2007: 89–93). War soon broke out, lasting until 1995. More than 100,000 people were killed, and almost half the inhabitants left their homes to escape the fighting, ethnic cleansing and economic collapse. BiH was actually divided into two de facto independent entities – Republika Srpska (RS), and the Federation of Bosnia and Herzegovina (FBiH) consisting of the self-declared Croatian Republic of Herzeg-Bosnia and that part of the country which was controlled by the Bosniaks. The merger took place in 1994 (Herceg and Tomić 1999: 97–102; Kasum 2007: 93–105; Hladký 2006: 283–4; Robinson and Pobrić 2006: 238). The war ended after negotiations in Dayton in 1995, where the Dayton Peace Agreement (DPA) was concluded.[1]

The DPA confirmed the autonomy of both FBiH and RS, and national institutions were re-established. Since 1999 the Brčko District (in the north-eastern part of Bosnia) has enjoyed special status – it is a self-governed district existing outside the entities but within BiH (Hladký 2005: 302–3). The situation in the whole of the territory is still marked with tension. None of the ethnic groups has actually reached all of the goals for which they struggled during the war. Demands for independence (the Serbs), an effort to establish a third entity (the Croats) or the desire to abolish the entities and strengthen the national institutions (the Bosniaks) are often used to mobilise voters.

The political system in the post-Dayton period is based on a complicated institutional structure which combines both parity and proportional representation for all the three main ethnic groups (constituent nations). Two-chamber parliaments have been established on the national level and in both entities. The lower chambers are elected directly by PR, the upper chambers indirectly with parity representation of the constituent nations. There is a directly elected presidency with three members on the national level; the members of the presidency rotate in the post of president. On the level of the entities, each constituent nation is represented by the president or one of two vice-presidents. In addition, FBiH is divided into ten cantons with their own governments and one-chamber parliaments (Herceg and Tomić 1999: 102–7; Hladký 2005: 299–301; Kasum 2006: 329–36).

An important role in the post-war period has been played by the international community. Apart from the deployment of international military forces in BiH, an institution of the High Representative for BiH was also established. This institution is charged with overseeing the implementation of the DPA, and is authorised to directly influence political events, even to the point of removing local representatives. For example, in 1999 the president of RS Nikola Poplašen (from the ultra-nationalist Serb Radical Party) was removed from office; in 2001 the same action was taken against a Croat member of the presidency Ante Jelavić from the Croatian Democratic Union, HDZ, (Kasum 2006: 336–7; Hladký 2005: 314–15).

The term of the House of Representatives of BiH, the House of Representatives of FBiH, and the National Assembly of RS was two years in the period of 1996–2002; afterwards it was extended to four years. The House of Representatives of BiH consists of 42 members: two-thirds of them (28) are elected in FBiH, and one-third (14) in RS, regardless of electoral turnouts. The House of Representatives of FBiH consists of 98 members (until 2000, 140 members), and the National Assembly of RS has 83 members. Since 2000, both entities have been divided into constituencies (before that, each formed a single constituency). Approximately one-quarter of the seats are reserved as compensatory; consequently representation is clearly proportional. The high inclusiveness of the electoral system is strengthened by the Sainte-Laguë method, which has been in use since 1998 (both on the national level and in the entities). Especially after the 2000 and 2002 elections, numerous parties in the parliaments were represented by one member only. Thereupon the participation in the distribution of the compensatory seats has been conditioned upon a 3 per cent legal threshold at the entity level since 2006. This measure led to the elimination of some marginal parties in the last elections on the entity level; the impact on the national level is limited to only a small number of parties from FBiH (Šedo 2007: 62–7, 222–37).

The governments of BiH are broad coalitions representing all the constituent nations and usually at least two of the three nationalist parties which won in the 1990 elections. The only exception was the government which was established in 2001 after the 2000 elections. This government, called the Alliance for

Change, was led by Zlatko Lagumdžija (Social Democratic Party of BiH) and did not include the trio of nationalist parties (Burwitz 2004: 332).[2]

All of these governments have had to face unfavourable economic and social conditions in the country. A big problem has been clientelism and bribery; bribery scandals are frequently connected with prominent politicians (Hladký 2005: 307–8).

Development of the party system

Research on the contemporary party system of BiH is complicated by the fact that there are actually two different party systems in the country, which meet on the national level. This is easy to see when counting the effective number of the parliamentary parties. There are more parties represented in the parliaments of the entities than on the national level, but the effective number of parties is relatively low. On the entity level, only a limited number of large parties are represented, and the others have a minimum of seats. The situation on the national level is just the opposite, because this is where the large parties meet (see Table 6.1).

The results deduced just from the tendencies on the national level may be distorted mainly in the case of the Serb political parties. RS has only 14 seats in the House of Representatives of BiH, some of which (one to three) are held by non-Serb parties (this is partly because voters have the right to vote in the place where they lived before the civil war, which ensures that the SDA gets at least one seat in Eastern Bosnia). It is therefore more sensible to follow the development of the party system simultaneously on both the national and the entity level. Elections have been held on all levels simultaneously, except for one early election in the RS in 1997 (Šedo 2007: 222–37).

For the party system of BiH, there is visible continuity from 1990 when the first free elections were held. Before the 1990 elections, three political parties representing the main ethnic groups in the country were formed. The Bosniaks were represented by the Party of Democratic Action (SDA), founded by Alija Izetbegović, the former dissident who became the first leader and most important and influential person in the SDA in the 1990s. The Serbs had the Serb Democratic Party (SDS), whose first leader was Radovan Karadžić, and the Croats the Croatian Democratic Union of BiH (HDZ), a branch of the strongest party in Croatia at that time. Their main rivals in the first elections were two parties

Table 6.1 Effective and absolute number of parliamentary parties on national and subnational level

Year	1996	1997	1998	2000	2002	2006
National level	3.40 (6)		4.59 (10)	7.30 (13)	7.96 (14)	7.17 (12)
FBiH	2.57 (6)		3.35 (14)	5.00 (17)	5.44 (18)	5.33 (11)
RS	2.90 (9)	5.02 (7)	6.82 (12)	5.22 (13)	5.64 (15)	3.30 (9)

Source: Šedo 2006: 352.

which emerged out of the former communist establishment. The communists entered the elections as the League of Communists of BiH – Social Democratic Party (SKBiH-SDP), and the other competitor was the Union of Reform Forces of Yugoslavia in BiH (SRSJ BiH), which supported Yugoslavian Prime Minister Ante Marković. The nationalist parties won 98 of 130 seats, and the two post-communist parties 27 seats (Herceg and Tomić 1999: 76–8).

The parties which were formed before the war prevailed even in the post-Dayton era. New parties have been successful mostly in cases where they have separated themselves from the large parties. Personal rivalry is a more frequent reason for party splits than programme conflicts. Parties in BiH are very person-alised, with the party leader playing a crucial role (especially in Serb parties, which present the name of the leader as part of the party name). Intra-party democracy is very limited. There are large numbers of political parties partici-pating in the political process – 36 parties and eight coalitions took part in the 2006 elections; most of them remain marginal.

During the war a confrontation broke out between the BiH government (with Alija Izebegović) and Fikret Abdić (one of the seven members of the presidency elected in 1990). In 1993 Abdić founded the Autonomous Province of Western Bosnia in the town of Velika Kladuša (North-West BiH). The province built up its own army and joined the RS forces to fight against those Bosniaks who were loyal to the BiH government. Abdić also founded the Democratic People's Union (DNZ), which is represented as a regional party on the canton, entity, and national levels (Herceg and Tomić 1999: 251–2; Kasum 2007: 97). In 1996 Haris Silajdžić, a former SDA vice-chairman and the Prime Minister of BiH in 1993–1996, founded the Party for BiH (SBiH). His reasons for leaving SDA were mainly personal. Silajdžić is a very ambitious person whose expectations were not fulfilled in SDA. SBiH entered the national parliament in the 1996 elec-tions, strengthened its position during the following years, and later became one of the largest parties.

The SDS was unambiguously the strongest and the most important Serb party in the 1996 elections. Its predominance was so clear that the Bosniak SDA was the second strongest party of RS in these elections. In the course of the follow-ing months, however, clashes occurred between the RS president Biljana Plavšić and the leaders of the SDS among whom the influence of former RS president and the party leader Radovan Karadžić was still strong. Karadžić was charged with war crimes; therefore he could not participate in political life. Until July 2008 he successfully hid himself, but was then arrested and extradited to The Hague.[3] Plavšić founded the Serbian Popular Alliance (SNS). Early elections in RS were held in 1997, after which Plavšić and her SNS closely cooperated with the smaller Serbian socialist parties (Socialist Party of RS, SP RS and the Party of Independent Social Democrats, SNSD). The chairman of the SNSD, Milorad Dodik, was nominated for RS Prime Minister even though his party had only two seats in the RS National Assembly. Later on the SNSD became stronger than its partners. In the 2006 elections, the SNS and SPRS became only marginal parties, and the SNSD is now the dominant Serb party (Šedo 2007: 223–35). In

2001, after a merger with the small Democratic Socialist Party (DSP), the SNSD changed its name to the Alliance of Independent Social Democrats, keeping the same abbreviation as before.[4]

Out of the three 'traditional' nationalist parties in their ethnic group, the HDZ was able to hold its dominance for the longest time. Its position remained unshaken even when Krešimir Zubak left the HDZ and founded the New Croatian Initiative (NHI). The latter has had only limited representation, and after failing in the 2006 elections (only one seat in the coalition on the entity level) it merged with the Croatian Peasant Party (HSS) (Šedo 2007: 223–35).

The unsuccessful candidacy of Božo Ljubić for the party chairman against Dragan Čović in 2005 was more crucial for the position of the HDZ in the party system. In 2006 Ljubić founded the Croatian Democratic Union 1990 (HDZ-1990). Even though HDZ-1990 won fewer votes than the HDZ-led coalition in 2006 elections,[5] it ended the HDZ predominancy among Croatian voters.

After the 1990 elections the SKBiH-SDP shortened its name to SDP. It began to cooperate with the SRSJ BiH, which changed its name to the Union of Social Democrats of BiH (UBHSD), and later to the Social Democrats of BiH (SD). The SDP and the SD entered the 1996 elections together with smaller partners as the coalition United List (ZL). In the 1998 elections they acted independently, and after the election both parties (SD and SDP) merged as the Social Democratic Party of BiH (SDP) (Šedo 2002a: 69).

An exception to the scheme where parties are either the successor parties of 1990, or splinter groups from those parties, is represented by the Party of Democratic Progress of the RS (PDP). It was founded in 1999 by Mladen Ivanić. An important role was also played by the Serb Radical Party for a certain time; in 1998 it even won the position of RS president (Šedo 2002a: 73, 76).

Before and for a short time after the war, the ethnic parties SDA, SDS and HDZ dominated the ethnic groups. The only alternatives were the left-wing post-communists and, in the case of the Serbs after 1996, their own left-wing parties (cf. Kasapović 1997: 119–21). The loss of dominance of the three ethnic parties was preceded or accompanied by their splitting apart, which became the basis for the Bosniak SBiH, the Serbian SNS and the Croatian HDZ-1990 (Šedo 2007: 238). In spite of the relative inclusiveness of the electoral system, a narrow group of large parties remained clearly out in front, followed by a huge number of minor parties that could still achieve representation in the entity parliaments or even in the national parliament. The big parties maintained their connection to the individual constituent nations, although some of them made an effort to obtain a non-ethnic character (the SDP has perhaps got closer to it than others). With a certain degree of simplification it is possible to say that the votes of the Bosniak voters are won mainly by the SDA, SBiH and SDP. For a long time Croatian voters clearly preferred the HDZ, which had no real competitor within this segment of the party system. Although some of its voters left for the small parties, the HDZ remained the dominant Croatian party until the foundation of the HDZ-1990.

The SNSD, originally a minor coalition partner with other moderate Serbian parties that tried to compete with the SDS, holds the strongest position, but the

SDS still remains a relevant player. Since 2000 the third strongest party has been the PDP (moderate), which is clearly stronger than the other remaining parties, although it experienced significant losses in the last elections. Apart from the above mentioned parties, only the radical nationalist SRS party managed to obtain two seats on the national level in 1998. Dozens of minor parties were represented on the entity level in 1996–2006, but none of them ever got more than five per cent of the seats (Šedo 2007: 223–35).

Party families

Any research on political parties in BiH should consider several basic limitations that make any analysis fairly complicated. First, political parties are connected with ethnicities whether or not they try to appear non-ethnic, and whether or not their candidate lists are representative of other ethnicities. Their electorates clearly reflect the links of these parties to ethnic groups (Stojarová *et al.* 2007: 73). The Bosniak parties are especially problematic, as they declare only their ideological standpoints and thus may seem to be non-ethnic. On the other extreme, the Serbian and Croatian parties show their ethnic background directly in their names, while the Serbians usually end their party names with the addition of 'RS'. Second, political parties often adapt their orientations, strategies, and positions significantly between elections. Instead of building up a firm programme and ideological orientation, parties have changed their approaches so that their leaders could fulfil their ambitions. Third, the programmes of the parties or orientation declared by them may be different from their actions in reality. Moreover, some topics and policies are suppressed due to the High Representative's actions against individual parties or politicians. It is therefore desirable when analysing the party families to define the connection of the party with an appropriate ethnicity first, and to consider their programme orientation as secondary. Except for the SDP, which is the closest of all the relevant parties to having a non-ethnic character, the primary classification of the parties follows the criterion of the constitutive nations each party belongs to. Based on the results of the last elections, the list of relevant parties consists of the SDA, SBiH, SNSD, SDP, HDZ and HDZ-1990, which managed to obtain at least two seats (4.8 per cent) in the House of Representatives, either as independent subjects or within coalitions, which is mainly the case with the Croatian parties.

Socialist and social-democratic parties

*Social Democratic Party of BiH (*Socijaldemokratska partija Bosne i Hercegovine*, SDP)*

The SDP is a party whose orientation is the closest to being non-ethnic or supra-ethnic, and is currently being described as such. Although it is connected first of all with Bosniak voters, in 2006 their party vice-president Željko Komšić was elected as a Croat member of the BiH presidency. To a certain extent, his success was due to two favourable circumstances, one of which was competition between HDZ and HDZ-1990 candidates who together obtained more aggregate votes; the other was the electoral system which allows an FBiH voter to choose the Croatian or the Bosniak member of the presidency. It can be assumed that some Bosniak SDP voters preferred the Croatian candidate for the presidency member, especially since the SDP did not nominate any Bosniak candidate for the presidency at all.[6]

The party arose out of the transformation of the Communist Party, and it has taken part in all the elections since 1990, each time succeeding in winning at least minimum representation both on the national level and in the two entities. The most significant organisational change in the course of the party history was the merger with the Social Democrats of BiH (*Socijaldemokrati Bosne i Hercegovine,* SD) after the 1998 elections. After the Dayton Peace Treaty the SDP was in opposition to governments consisting of nationalist parties. Its support gradually grew, and in 2000 it won the national elections plus a narrow second place in FBiH. Its chairman Zlatko Lagumdžija (1997–present) became Prime Minister in 2001 (Šedo 2002a: 69–70). In the 2002 elections it lost again and returned to the opposition. In 2006 it succeeded in winning five seats on the national level, its second best result since 1996. In the House of Representatives of FBiH the SDP is the third strongest party, with 17 seats (Šedo 2007: 223–35). Its representation in the National Assembly of RS has always been minimal, and after the last elections it holds just one seat there. In the territory of FBiH, the party has the biggest support in the Tuzla canton (north-east of Bosnia), while in the cantons with a Croatian majority its support distinctly decreases, and its worst results are in the canton of West Herzegovina where, in 2006 in the entity parliamentary elections, it had even less support than in the majority of RS electoral districts.[7] The SDP makes an effort to appear as a modern left-wing social-democratic party with a multi-ethnic character. It cooperates with the Party of European Socialists, but the main features of the other BiH parties are relevant for them as well (strong position of the chairman, clientelism and weak intra-party democracy) (Hladký 2005: 321–2). In their documents they emphasise the classic social democratic topics (social justice, human rights), and also a need to support the multi-ethnic character of the country. In common with other Bosniak parties, it supports the unitary character of the state (with decentralised self-government on the regional and local levels – the regions, as it suggests for the new republic constitution, do not comply as they should with the borders of the entities).[8] The other constituent nations and their parties reject such proposals (Kasum 2006: 340).

Bosniak parties

*Party of Democratic Action (*Stranka demokratske akcije, *SDA)*

Since its foundation, the party has been perceived as a nationalist party for Bosniaks/Muslims. The word Bosniak came into use only during the war; before that they were referred to as Muslims in the ethnic sense. This party seeks the role of main spokesman for this constituent nation (Herceg and Tomić 1999: 257–8).

The SDA declares itself to be a conservative party being an observer member of the European People's Party. The party was founded in 1990 and local branches have also been active in other republics of the former SFRY. The SDA was the strongest party in all elections on the national level except for the year 2000, and they always won the elections to the House of Representatives of FBiH. The party has always run independently except for 1998 when it headed the Coalition for a United and Democratic BiH (*Koalicija za cjelovitu i demokratsku Bosnu i Herce-govinu*, KCD). The KCD also took part in early elections to the National Assembly of RS in 1997, when they cooperated with SBiH and two minor parties. With the exception of the government of the Alliance for Changes in 2001–2002, the SDA has always been one of the key parties in the coalition governments (Šedo 2002a: 75).[9] Both chairman Alija Izetbegović and his successor Sulejman Tihić held the post of the Bosniak member of the presidency. Tihić, however, suffered a fatal defeat by Haris Silajdžić (SBiH) in 2006.[10] In the parliamentary elections held at the same time, the SDA won nine seats which meant a loss of one seat from the 2002 elections. In the House of Representatives of the FBiH, the SDA won 28 seats, historically its second worst result. In the National Assembly of RS, the SDA has only three seats, just half of what it had after the previous elections (Šedo 2007: 223–35). Support for the SDA is concentrated in the Bosniak cantons of the FBiH, and it gets its best support in the Una-Sana canton, Zenica-Doboj canton and Tuzla canton (except for the town of Tuzla and its surroundings where the SDP dominates). Within the RS its support is clearly bigger in the north and east, in districts that include the town of Srebrenica.[11]

The party has tried to preserve a politically and economically unified BiH and to build a BiH civic identity. According to their programme, BiH should be transformed into a unitary decentralised state. The rights of individual ethnic groups are subordinate to more general individual human rights, and also the interests of the country (such an attitude is quite logical for a party which represents the majority ethnic group in an ethnically divided country). Emphasising a unitary and multi-ethnic BiH does not by any means suggest a weakening of the party connection with the Bosniak ethnicity, which is also a target for the SDA. The party also advocates bringing BiH closer to Western democracies and implementing their standards (human rights and freedoms, religious freedom, market economy and social rights). Its image is meant to be that of a Bosniak catch-all party.[12]

*Party for Bosnia and Herzegovina (*Stranka za Bosnu i Hercegovinu, *SBiH)*

The classification of the SBiH enables us to demonstrate the problems of exact definition of party identity in BiH. Considering the fact that it took part in the Alliance for Change and declared its support for democratic values (liberty, equity, respect for human rights of all citizens regardless of ethnicity and religion), it is sometimes classified as a non-ethnic liberal party. At the same time such a classification is open to doubt because the party is dependent on

Bosniak voters; its effort to abolish the entities (accompanied by a critical assessment of attitudes of politicians in RS) can be explained as support for Bosniak nationalism. If we consider the opportunistic behaviour of its founder and chairman Haris Silajdžić, it always depends on which elements of its programme or campaign momentarily prevails, whether liberal and non-ethnic, or Bosniak nationalist (Šedo 2002a: 77–8; Burwitz 2004: 332–5). The party was founded in 1996 and was initially considered a small moderate Bosniak party. It gradually succeeded in improving its position, and since 2000 it can be undoubtedly seen as one of the major actors on the political scene. It runs mostly independently, with the exception of 1997 and 1998 when it cooperated with the SDA in the KCD (Šedo 2002a: 77–8). The 2006 elections brought the greatest success for the party so far. Silajdžić was elected the Bosniak member of presidency by a clear margin, and the SBiH achieved its best result on the national level (eight seats) and in FBiH (24 seats), and they managed to keep four seats in the RS (Šedo 2007: 223–35). The SBiH has participated in all national governments since the beginning of 1997 (the first post-war government), but it has not held the post of Prime Minister since 2000.[13]

The voters of the SBiH are concentrated first of all in the central parts of Bosnia (Sarajevo canton, Bosnian Podrinje, around the town of Goražde, and in the Zenica-Doboj canton). As with the SDA and SDP, support for the SBiH in the cantons with a bigger share of Croatian population is very limited.[14]

The main topic of the SBiH in recent years has become the future arrangement of the country. Its target is the formation of a unitary, decentralised state. It should be noted that in its preliminary proposal of the constitution, the constituent nations are not mentioned, and the text does not deal with them at all. The SBiH also sharply criticises the division of BiH into entities. It is possible to follow a decline of the SBiH away from 'neutral' liberal topics, and the party now presents itself as the defender of the interests of the Bosniak ethnicity.[15] In some cases it is questionable whether it is not more nationalist than the SDA, which is undoubtedly classified as a Bosniak nationalist party.

Serbian parties

Alliance of Independent Social Democrats (Savez nezavisnih socijaldemokrata, SNSD)

Classification of the SNSD represents another problem which can help to demonstrate the development of perceptions of a party's politics and policy. In the 1990s, when the SNSD was among those in RS who accepted the DPA and cooperation with the international community, it was seen positively (Šedo 2002a: 76). Considering the name of the party, its orientation towards the Socialist International (it obtained full membership in 2008), and its programme focused on support for a market economy as well as an active social policy, the party was classified as a moderate party, both in the family of ethnic and regional parties, and in that of social-democratic and socialist ones. However, the SNSD has not given up consistently referring to the DPA, and their defence of the federal structure with wide autonomy for the RS became a key element of the party's external presentation. This is now criticised because the SNSD with its sharp attacks do not contribute to the diminishing of tension. When strengthening and making national institutions more efficient is being debated, the SNSD rejects anything that would weaken the position of the entities. The SNSD repeatedly emphasises the threat of the Bosniaks institutionalising their majority, and it exploits this threat in its programmes and campaigns to mobilise the voters. The party chairman Milorad Dodik even threatened to hold a referendum on independence for the RS (Kasum 2006: 339). In autumn 2007 the Prime Minister of the national government Nikola Špirić of the SNSD submitted his resignation to protest a measure by the High Representative to reform government voting rules; the move was intended to prevent blockage of negotiations and thus was a de facto weakening of the position of representatives of the individual constituent nations (Špirić was restored to his post later on, and still holds the office of Prime Minister).[16] Therefore it is possible to classify the SNSD also as an extreme right-wing nationalist and secessionist party. The contemporary SNSD thus integrates the elements of a social democratic party with populism and nationalism.[17]

The SNSD was founded in 1996 following cooperation in the Independent Members of Parliament Caucus in the National Assembly of RS (*Klub nezavisnih poslanika u narodnoj skupštini Republike Srpske*), which was in opposition to the SDS during the war (Herceg and Tomić 1999: 268). The club and later on the party was chaired by Milorad Dodik, the Prime Minister of RS in 1998–2001 and again since 2005. The party participated in the 1996 elections in the coalition Union for Peace and Progress (*Savez za mir i progress*, SMP) along with the Socialist Party of RS (*Socijalistička partija Republike Srpske*, SPRS) and one minor party; in the early elections in 1997 it cooperated with the SPRS and the Serbian People's Union (*Srpski narodni savez*, SNS) of the president of RS Biljana Plavšić as part of the Sloga (Concord) Coalition. Sloga compiled a common candidate list for the national elections while in the elections to the National Assembly of RS its members ran separately. In the 2000 elections the SNSD ran on the national level in coalition with the small Democratic Socialist Party (*Demokratska socijastička partija*, DSP), with which it merged in 2001, changing one word in the name: 'Party' to 'Alliance'. In the 2002 and 2006 elections, the SNSD ran independently. The latter contest brought a decisive victory in the RS, where they hold 41 out of 83 seats. In the House of Representatives of BiH they have seven seats (however, it won the largest number of votes in the elections). In the House of Representatives of FBiH they have consistently held one seat since 2000 (Šedo 2007: 223–35). The SNSD also succeeded in obtaining the Serbian seat of the presidency of BiH (Nebojsa Radmanović), and it kept the post of RS president. As of 2007, the SNSD has not participated in the national government, but since 2007 it has held the post of Prime Minister.[18]

In the past, the SNSD's main support was found in Northern Bosnia around the town of Banja Luka. In 2006 it succeeded in all the electoral districts of RS, thus disrupting the previous hegemony of the SDS in the north-east and next to the Serbian border. It is also active in the FBiH elections, where it has held one seat in the House of Representatives of FBiH since 2000. It is supported in Canton 10 in the West, from which the majority of the Serbs fled during the Croatian attack in 1995.[19]

*Serbian Democratic Party (*Srpska demokratska stranka*, SDS)*

The SDS has been classified since its foundation as an extreme right-wing nationalist party which seeks support exclusively from Serbian voters. Its officials headed the RS during the war, and those people are now charged with war crimes; they include former party chairman Radovan Karadžić. Even after the war, the party presented itself as a right-wing traditionalist and patriotic party, both in its programme and in its officials' presentations (Herceg and Tomić 1999: 266). Therefore its classification is not difficult.

The SDS has been the strongest party representing the Serbian ethnicity since 1990. Only in the 1998 elections did the Sloga coalition prevail in terms of numbers of votes, but the number of seats was the same for the SDS and Sloga in the House of Representatives (Šedo 2002a: 72–3). After the 2002 elections, the SDS began to lose support. First of all, as a key party in the government, it was seen as responsible for the unsatisfactory economic and social situation in the country. Second, because the SNSD ran a very strong campaign, the SDS lost supporters quickly, and the 2006 elections saw it heavily defeated. Both on the national level and in the RS, it achieved its historically worst result when it obtained three and 17 seats respectively (the SDS has never been represented in FBiH) (Šedo 2007: 223–35). The party also lost its executive offices in the RS and in the BiH presidency, and is now in opposition. It participated in national governments in 1996–1999 and 2002–2007, as the smallest of the three 'traditional' ethnic parties.

The SDS is supported traditionally in north-eastern Bosnia and in the east of the country next to the Serbian border, where there are few large urban centres. The SDS took part in the electoral campaign of 2006 in FBiH, but only in selected cantons.[20] In these last elections the SDS presented itself primarily as a nationalist party consistently rejecting any tendency towards centralisation in BiH; on the contrary it would welcome further strengthening of the entities and a co-federative arrangement for the country.[21]

Croat parties

*Croatian Democratic Union of BiH (*Hrvatska demokratska zajednica Bosne i Hercegovine*, HDZ)*

The HDZ has declared itself a nationalist party since its foundation. It has some elements of Christian Democracy in its programme, and also refers to social topics (the HDZ is an observer member of the European People's Party). In the early 1990s its target was for the western part of BiH to join Croatia; later on it limited its ambitions to the establishment of a third, Croatian, entity in BiH (Herceg and Tomić 1999: 252–3; Šedo 2002a: 71–2). At the beginning of 2001, the HDZ attempted to bring about the establishment of the third entity through an appeal by Ante Jelavić, the chairman of the party and the Croatian member of BiH presidency, to disobey the national authorities and institutions of FBiH. The High Representative, Wolfgang Petritsch, then forced Jelavić's removal from his post. When the HDZ continued in its efforts, he (Petritsch) ordered the occupation of the Herzegovina Bank in Mostar by soldiers of the international mission SFOR, and he froze the financial resources of the HDZ (Hladký 2005: 314–15). Despite this failure in spring 2001, the HDZ still did not abandon the idea of strengthening Croatian autonomy in BiH, including the possibility of establishing a third entity, but they ceased any practical steps that could lead to this goal. In every election the HDZ has been the strongest Croatian party, clearly ahead of all the others, although its support has moderately decreased. It ran independently until the 2002 elections, when it took part in a coalition with two minor Croatian parties. Likewise in 2006 the HDZ headed a three-member coalition of Croatian parties. The last elections brought the worst results for the HDZ, when it obtained just three seats in the House of Representatives of BiH and eight seats in the House of Representatives of FBiH (Šedo 2007: 223–5). This was obviously a consequence of HDZ-1990 splitting off from the party, and also the bad reputation of party chairman Dragan Čović, who is said to be one of the most corrupt politicians in the country (Kasum 2006: 338).[22] The conflict between him and Ljubić, who tried to win the chairman's post in the party and pointed out the suspicions of bribery connected with Čović, triggered the party split of the HDZ. Until 2006, candidates of the HDZ had always won in the elections for the Croatian member of the presidency. During the post-Dayton period, the HDZ participated in all national governments with the exception of 2001–2002.[23]

Support for the HDZ is concentrated in the cantons with a Croatian majority, i.e. in Herzegovina and western parts of Bosnia; this corresponds to the ethnic character of the party. The party achieved its best election results in 2006 in the West Herzegovina canton, than in the Neretva canton and in Canton 10. The HDZ usually does not run in the RS, neither in the elections to the House of Representatives nor in the National Assembly of RS.[24]

Even in the latest version of its programme in 2007, the HDZ criticises the model of three constitutive nations and only two entities, and it would like to introduce symmetry in this respect. Apart from that, the programme reflects the party's efforts to be the only really catch-all party of the Croats in BiH: it proclaims a pro-Western orientation, Christianity, individual freedom, and freedom for the nation as well as social justice.[25]

*Croatian Democratic Union 1990 (*Hrvatska demokratska zajednica *1990, HDZ-1990)*

HDZ-1990 tries to present itself as the genuine successor to the original HDZ, and a more authentic defender of Croatian interests than the HDZ. Support has also been declared by the Croatian HDZ and the Catholic Church. It presents itself as a national, social and Christian democratic party.[26] HDZ-1990 can be seen as a Croatian nationalist catch-all party, the programme and topics of which are very similar to those of the HDZ.

HDZ-1990 took part in the 2006 elections as the leading member of the coalition Croats Together (*Hrvatska zajedništvo*, HZ). There were four other minor Croatian parties in the coalition. The HDZ-1990 failed to replace the HDZ, as it won only two seats in the House of Representatives of BiH and seven seats in the House of Representatives of FBiH, and its chairman Božo Ljubić took only third place in the elections for the Croatian member of the BiH presidency.[27] Since 2007 the party has been part of the national government.[28]

Support for the HDZ-1990 and the HZ is distributed in a similar way as the support for the HDZ; they achieved their best results in the same three cantons. HDZ-1990 usually won fewer votes than the HDZ, but in two cantons with a Croatian majority (Herzegovina-Neretva and Canton 10), its achievements were better. Unlike the HDZ, HDZ-1990 also ran candidate lists in some districts of the RS, but it totally failed in those elections.[29]

Interim conclusion

The political system of BiH faces a series of problems. A complicated structure and decision-making process prevents effective administration. A potential solution can be seen in reforms which would strengthen the positions of the national institutions at the expense of the entities, but such a reform is rejected both by the Serbs, who insist on preserving or even strengthening the autonomy of the RS, and the Croats whose target is to strengthen their influence in the FBiH institutions or even to establish a third entity. In spite of the fact that the war ended more than ten years ago, and ordinary citizens must face everyday problems caused by the adverse economic situation, nationalist topics are still dangerous potential triggers for disturbance.

Within the political party system, during the second half of the 1990s there developed a rather copious spectrum of parties, and thanks to the high inclusiveness of the electoral system, numerous minor political parties are represented. The successful parties appeared mostly at the beginning of the 1990s, or came into existence by splitting away from the original ones. All the big parties are connected with particular ethnic groups, and can be mostly classified as nationalist in light of their programmes and presentations. More difficult is their assignment to party families, as their proclaimed orientations and general targets (usually economic development, social justice, the fight against the crime, or integration into Western structures) are in fact just cover-ups for their actual attitudes and actions. In reality all the parties are controlled by narrow groups of individuals strongly fixated on the person of the party leader, and the prominent politicians are frequently accused, correctly, of clientelism and bribery.

Notes

1 For the full version of the Dayton Peace Agreement see www.ohr.int/dpa/default.
  asp?content_id=380.
2 www.terra.es/personal2/monolith/bosnia.htm.
3 http://news.bbc.co.uk/2/hi/europe/7518543.stm.
4 www.snsd.org/dnn/Default.aspx?tabid=54&language=en-US.
5 www.izbori.ba.
6 www.izbori.ba.
7 See results of 2006 elections on www.izbori.ba, especially on the level of the constituencies or cantons.
8 www.sdp.ba.
9 www.terra.es/personal2/monolith/bosnia.htm.
10 www.izbori.ba.
11 www.izbori.ba.
12 www.sda.ba.
13 www.terra.es/personal2/monolith/bosnia.htm.
14 www.izbori.ba.
15 www.zabih.ba.
16 http://news.bbc.co.uk/2/hi/europe/7072908.stm.
17 For the programme and other details see www.snsd.org.
18 www.terra.es/personal2/monolith/bosnia.htm.
19 www.izbori.ba.
20 www.izbori.ba.
21 www.sdsrs.com.
22 See also www.sudbih.gov.ba/?id=896&jezik=h.
23 www.terra.es/personal2/monolith/bosnia.htm.
24 www.izbori.ba.
25 www.hdzbih.org.
26 www.hdz1990.org.
27 www.izbori.ba.
28 www.terra.es/personal2/monolith/bosnia.htm.
29 www.izbori.ba.

7 The party system of Serbia

Daniel Bochsler

Some aspects of Serbia's history and its political system[1]

Contemporary political discussion in Serbia sometimes reads like a history book of Serbia in the twentieth century. Figures such as Dragoljub 'Draža' Mihailović (Chetnik[2] leader in the Second World War), Josip Broz 'Tito' (Partisan leader and then president of the Socialist Federal Republic of Yugoslavia, SFRJ), Slobodan Milošević (Serbian and Yugoslav president in the 1990s), or Vojislav Šešelj (paramilitary leader in the 1990s) would fit in very well among the members of today's parliament. Indeed, the most recent bloody episodes of Serbia's history are so little distant that the two latter persons on this list were still both influential players in Serbian party politics in the early twenty-first century, which is the subject of this chapter. Šešelj is still running in parliamentary elections, and would be an MP if he were not facing trial for war crimes at the International Criminal Tribunal for the former Yugoslavia (ICTY).

Serbian independence and democratisation

Compared to most of the other post-communist countries in Europe as well as to most of its neighbours, Serbian democracy is much younger. Full democratisation in Serbia dates to 2000, ten years later than the peak of post-communist democratisation in 1990. When the Socialist Federal Republic of Yugoslavia broke apart in 1990 and 1991, Serbia under the rule of Milošević steered towards a decade of nationalist ideology, aggression against its neighbours and internal minorities, and an authoritarian system with elections that fell short of democratic standards. After four former Yugoslav Republics (Slovenia, Croatia, Macedonia, and Bosnia and Herzegovina) had declared independence, Serbia and Montenegro remained united in the Federal Republic of Yugoslavia, which was succeeded in 2004 by the unified state of Serbia and Montenegro, before both Serbia and Montenegro finally became independent states in 2006. However, both had become fairly autonomous political systems many years before. Each developed fully autonomous party systems in the early 1990s, and while initially there were common direct elections to the federal assembly, the last such elections were held in 1997 with Serbian and Montenegrin politics following very different paths largely independent from one another. This allows us to treat both Republics as quasi-independent entities.

The new Serbian Constitution of 2006

Shortly after Serbia became an independent state in 2006, it gave itself a new constitution replacing Milošević's Constitution of 1990. While the new Constitution introduces certain practices of good governance such as the office of an ombudsman, abolition of the death penalty, and provision for parliamentary control when the army is to be deployed abroad, other provisions with regard to the division of state powers are problematic and do not fit into the picture of a liberal state. Namely, there are drawbacks regarding legislative control over the country's judiciary, and the power of the central government to dissolve municipal assemblies has been controversial (see for instance Venice Commission, 2007). The International Crisis Group attests that the new Constitution falls short in several aspects that are relevant for civic and minority rights. Serbia is defined as a nation state (while Milošević's Constitution had defined Serbia as a civic state), and the Serbian language and the Cyrillic alphabet are established as the only national language, despite numerous linguistic minorities living in the country. The preamble describes Kosovo as an integral part of Serbia, so that a recognition of Kosovo's independence would be unconstitutional (International Crisis Group 2006b: 13–14). The expectations of the pro-European and non-nationalist parties in regard to the Constitution were widely disappointed. Namely, the Democratic Party (DS) favoured a constitution with emphasis on greater decentralisation, with restoration of autonomy to the Vojvodina province, and 'liberal democratic values in a civic state' (International Crisis Group 2006b: 2). These points were opposed by the largest governing party at the time, the Democratic Party of Serbia (DSS), which attempted to assemble a large coalition in support of the new Constitution encompassing all relevant parliamentary parties, including the nationalist ones. 'Koštunica [Prime Minister, DSS] used the preamble's statement that Kosovo is a part of Serbia to force other parties to support the draft lest he accuse them publicly of insufficient loyalty at a time when the province is in danger of being lost' (International Crisis Group 2006b: 4). This helped him to gather the support of the main opposition parties, the pro-European DS and the ultra-nationalist Serbian Radical Party (SRS) for the Constitution, while opponents were branded as promoting Albanian separatism. Only the coalition around the Liberal Democratic Party (LDP), along with a few minority parties, were opposed to the new Constitution and called for a boycott of the referendum,[3] but many registered voters stayed away from the polls. Allegedly the turnout amounted to 55 per cent, but according to reports of fraud and manipulation, the real turnout was below 50 per cent (International Crisis Group 2006b), which would mean that the Constitution would have failed. A new autonomy statute for the Vojvodina region was still under discussion in autumn 2008.

Like many democracies in Central and Eastern Europe, Serbia can be characterised as a semi-presidential system. This institutional order was introduced in 1990, but the powers of the presidents varied widely. Particularly in periods when the president's party was also in control of the cabinet – mostly during the presidency of Milošević from 1990 to 1997[4] – the role of the president was much more important (Orlović 2005: 35). The main competences of the popularly elected president are foreign policy and defence. Under the new Constitution, the president can veto laws, but the parliament can suspend his veto. Based on a governmental proposal, the president can dissolve parliament. Until 2006, the president could enact emergency legislation as well (Orlović 2005).

Like other post-communist countries, dealing with the authoritarian past is an important political issue in Serbia after Milošević, and the responsibility of the regime for violation of rights towards its own people is mixed with war crimes abroad and crimes against internal ethnic minorities. Trials for political crimes committed in the authoritarian period were limited to prosecutions by the ICTY, where among others the leader of the Socialist Party of Serbia (SPS), Slobodan Milošević, and the SRS leader, Vojislav Šešelj, stood trial. These were not accompanied by any prosecution for crimes not related to the wars. On the contrary, both party leaders kept their positions at the top of the SPS and the SRS, in the case of Milošević until his death in 2006. Domestic courts opened trials for only a few acts of political violence. In sum, there was no lustration in Serbia, but rather a continuity of personnel within the old regime parties.

Contrary to the widespread impression, the political changes of 5 October 2000 were far from complete. Key players at the head of the secret service and the army were allowed to keep their posts under the new government. The head of the secret service stayed on at the insistence of the DSS for four more months, and the head of the army for two more years. Milošević appointees were able to keep these key positions against a possible lustration with respect to the possible persecution of war crimes and political crimes. During this period the secret service was involved with a massive destruction of documents.[5] With the Socialists' support for the first minority government of Vojislav Koštunica (DSS) in 2004, and their entry into coalition with the DS in 2008, the main protagonists of the authoritarian 1990s soon returned to political power, and their exponents occupied sensitive positions in the Serbian state.

Electoral systems at the national level

While multi-party elections were held in Serbia and in the Federal Republic of Yugoslavia throughout the 1990s, many civil liberties that are essential for a functioning democracy were severely restricted, and elections were not considered free and fair. This changed only in 2000, with the 'bulldozer revolution' of 5 October. Milošević was forced by the pressure of the street and the lack of support among the Serbian security forces, to acknowledge his electoral defeat and step down from power. This brought a wave of liberalisation into the Serbian political system.

The electoral system used for the elections of the Serbian parliament has largely remained the same since 2000, except for the rules on ethnic minority representation. The parliament consists of 250 seats, and is elected for a four-year-term by closed-list proportional representation with the D'Hondt formula in a single national district with a 5 per cent threshold (Jovanović 2005). Unlike many other cases in post-communist Europe, Serbia does not have a different threshold for multi-party coalitions, so the larger parties often gather a bunch of micro parties around themselves in broad electoral coalitions. The Serbian party leadership has far-reaching powers in determining the composition of the parliamentary group. Even if the parties ran closed candidate lists in the elections, their leaderships can decide freely after the elections which candidates will receive mandates.[6]

The access of ethnic minorities to parliament was facilitated in 2007 by a major change in the electoral law: for the first time, parties of national minorities (a term not precisely defined) did not need to pass the 5 per cent threshold (Jovanović, 2005: 191). The move came during a period of international pressure on Serbia because of the many anti-minority incidents. Moreover, in the 2003 elections, a broad coalition that consisted mostly of ethnic minority parties, Together for Tolerance (*Zajedno za toleranciju*, ZZT) failed to pass the 5 per cent threshold, leaving minorities poorly represented in parliament. The lifting of the threshold changed this. Whereas previously 10,000 signatures of eligible citizens had been required to submit an electoral list, the electoral commission lowered this number for minority parties to 3,000, against the provisions of the electoral law.[7]

The Serbian president is elected in a two-round run-off system for a five-year term. In the first round, only candidates who win an absolute majority of the votes are elected. The minimal turnout requirement was dropped in 2004, after three elections in 2002 and 2003 had been declared invalid due to insufficient participation (OSCE ODIHR 2004b). Presidential elections are called by the Parliament Speaker. To register its candidate, a party needs to present the signatures of 10,000 supporters (1.5 per cent of the electorate) to the Electoral Commission.

Election campaigns in Serbia are partially state-funded. In the 2007 parliamentary elections, public funding amounted to 323 million Serbian Dinars (around €4 million), with each electoral list receiving three million Dinars at the beginning of the campaign, and the major part of the funds allocated ex post in relation to the number of seats won in the new parliament.[8] Other, private donations vary widely, however.

Ethnic Serbian voters in the UN-administered Kosovo can participate in elections, whereas ethnic Albanian voters in Kosovo have been erased from the voter register, even if Serbia considers them as its own citizens. Since the 1990s, the Albanians in Kosovo have always boycotted Serbian elections, and their boycott would have lowered the turnout in presidential elections and in the constitution referendum below the 50 per cent threshold.

The main dimensions of party orientation

The bulldozer revolution in 2000

In the development of party systems in post-communist democracies in Europe, two phases can be distinguished. The period from the first to the second election was often characterised by a complete change in the character of party competition (Bielasiak 1997: 33; Bochsler 2007b; Olson 1998). In the first multi-party elections in post-communist countries, heterogeneous umbrella coalitions uniting a broad alliance of reform-oriented parties usually won a landslide victory against the old regime parties. The most relevant question in such elections was usually regime change, occasionally linked to issues related to the country's borders. In the Serbian case, a broad alliance of reform parties (Democratic Opposition Serbia/*Demokratska opozicija Srbije*, DOS) won a landslide victory over the old regime parties in the first reasonably free parliamentary elections on 23 December 2000, following the *bulldozer revolution* earlier the same year. Not only in Serbia, but in all the countries of the region, the umbrella movements soon broke up, leading to a process of dispersion, with numerous new parties competing independently, each occupying a specific location in the political space. This opens a second phase, the shakedown period, where the number of parties diminishes. Parties that did not find an electorate were abandoned by voters and politicians, or forced to merge with other parties.[9]

There are four main political conflicts which are addressed by political parties in Serbia and which seem relevant to voters when choosing a party to vote for. The four issue dimensions have been highly correlated within the party system.[10]

The *regime conflict* refers to the conflict between politicians close to the authoritarian Milošević regime versus the democratically oriented reform parties. Specifically, the SPS and the SRS have been the main pillars of the Milošević regime, while the pro-European reform parties (DS and the Serbian Renewal Movement, SPO), the nationalist-conservative parties (DSS and New Serbia, NS), and the parties of the ethnic minorities belonging to the DOS movement. The later-emerging parties, G17+ and LDP, have joined the reform side of the political spectrum. The division is regularly apparent when the reform parties commemorate important events in the public resistance against the regime, or in the few court cases regarding political violence committed during the authoritarian period.

Nationalist–authoritarian values are a second important dimension of Serbian politics. Attempts to create a Greater Serbia, the promotion of the Serbs as the dominant ethnic group, and authoritarian rejection of civic liberalism have been highly salient on the Serbian political agenda in the 1990s, and these have been a priority of both the regime parties, SPS and SRS, and likewise of the democratic reform party SPO, while the DSS 'oscillated between the nationalist and democratic opposition', and the DS adopted a nationalist agenda in 1994–1995 (Bieber 2003b: 75). The opposite view of Serbia as a non-nationalist civic–liberal state has been supported in most periods by the DS, but only the Civic Alliance of Serbia (*Građanski savez Srbije*, GSS) consistently defended this view throughout the 1990s. In the post-Milošević period, several issues related to the national question have dominated the agenda, namely the question of how to deal with the past and how to cooperate with the International Criminal Tribunal for the former Yugoslavia (ICTY), as well as relations with neighbouring states, human and minority rights, non-discrimination policies, and the achievement of a democratic system. Most parties belonging to the DOS movement tend to take civic–liberal stands, with the exception of the DSS and the small NS, which both tend towards nationalist positions, promote strong ties between the state and the Serbian Orthodox Church, and can be characterised as nationalist–conservative (Đurković, 2007; Komšić, 2003: 48).

Nationalist–authoritarian issues are closely related to Serbian *foreign policy*, since the EU integration process (and to some extent cooperation with NATO) is conditional on cooperation with the ICTY and civic rights. The most prominent pro-European parties are the civic liberal parties around the DS, along with G17+ and SPO. The DSS and NS moved away from the project of Western integration in 2007 when the DSS joined a cooperation agreement with United Russia, the Russian party in power; the DSS spoke out against NATO membership, and in 2008 both the DSS and NS rejected the possibility of EU integration after a majority of EU member states recognised Kosovo and the EU took over the UN mandate in Kosovo. The ultra-nationalist parties turn rather to Moscow than to Brussels, but the Radicals have struggled over their position on this issue (see below), and the Socialists took a more positive stand towards EU integration at their 2003 party congress.[11]

Finally, the parties' positioning on the *economic conflict* has been rather fuzzy. A clear advocate of a strong role for the state in the economy is the SPS, along with a few minor parties that declare themselves as social democrats, whereas G17+ favours radical liberal economic reforms. Other parties have less clear-cut positions: the SRS, which declares itself on the right side of the political spectrum, has increasingly campaigned for the losers in the economic transition, promising price controls and an increase in the welfare state. The DS has rather a moderate position, neither clearly in the reform camp nor promoting a strong welfare state, while the DSS has changed its position (see below).

In sum, the positioning of the parties on these four dimensions has been to a great extent correlated in the period after 2000. While the most reformist parties have mainly shared anti-nationalistic values, been united in their opposition to the old regime, and favoured EU integration and liberal economic reforms, the old regime parties have taken the opposite stands.

Political parties in Serbia

Serbian party politics after 2000 has been dominated by two large and fairly polarised parties. On one hand there is the pro-European DS, which was the main protagonist of the 2000 revolution and the party of the Prime Minister in 2000–2004 and from 2008. On the other extreme, the SRS has been Serbia's largest party for some time, replacing the Socialists as the main player of the old regime forces since 2003. Between these two poles, the DSS was not only able to profit from the DS's electoral weakness in the parliamentary elections of 2003, but for a long time held a comfortable position as king maker in the centre of the political spectrum; no majority was possible without the DSS's support. This helped the DSS, even as it continued to lose voters, to lead coalition governments from 2004 until 2008.

Political parties in Serbia give wide powers to the party presidency, and in many cases these powers have increased over time. In the case of the SRS, party organs appear as fairly marginal compared to the extensive presidential powers, which include interpretation of the party programme and policy decisions, as well as the nomination and dismissal of the general secretary and the four deputy presidents. Similarly, the president of the SPO, after the reform of the party statute in 1998, was empowered to nominate the party presidency and a third of the members of the party's executive committee. The only exceptions are the SPS and the G17+, whose presidents have mainly the role of party coordinator and representative (Goati 2004: 127–30).

The strong position of the party leaderships emanates not only from the parties' own statutes, but also from the electoral system and the system of resignation as it is practiced in the Serbian parliament. The party can decide, on its own, after the elections, on the composition of the parliamentary delegation. This enables the party leaderships to nominate deputies who did not compete in the elections, and to punish disliked candidates. Furthermore, several parties ask their deputies for blank letters of resignation that they can use against the members of their parliamentary group if the latter should decide to switch parties. However, such a practice is more understandable if we take into account that party switches are very common in post-communist legislatures, and not only in Serbia (Orlović 2006: 110–14).

Democratic Party (Demokratska stranka, DS)

The Democratic Party was the first opposition party in Serbia after 1989, and until the Socialists' rise that led to the formation of a government coalition after the 2008 elections, this party was always one of the main opponents of the Socialists. The DS leader Zoran Đinđić was one of the most prominent figures of the Serbian opposition throughout the 1990s, and the party was one of the key players in the 2000 revolution and the single largest member of the DOS opposition coalition. After taking office as Prime Minister in 2000, Đinđić was assassinated in March 2003, and he then became a symbol for the new liberal period afterwards: for democratic and economic reforms, and for leading Serbia towards the European Union.

Placing the DS purely at the anti-nationalist pole, however, would be misleading: in certain periods in the 1990s, the party clearly supported the national project of a Greater Serbia, calling for partition of Bosnia and Herzegovina in 1994 and 1995, and the creation of an independent Serbian Republic there (Goati 2004: 41). Đinđić's successor in party office, Boris Tadić, tended to follow a conciliatory course of compromises with the national conservative parties, in line with the party's new role in the institutional system. As of 2004 it held the presidential office in the person of Boris Tadić, and it needed first to cooperate with a government coalition led by the nationalist–conservative DSS and was later (2007–2008) included in a DSS-led cabinet. In the period until 2007, Prime Minister Koštunica (DSS) was perceived to have substantial influence over

Tadić. Examples of the DS's policy of appeasement toward the nationalists are the DS's approval of an important role of the Serbian Orthodox Church in the state (Gajić 2005), Tadić's half-hearted excuses for Serbian mass crimes,[12] or his radical rhetoric on the Kosovo issue for domestic consumption, symbolised by his visit to the Kosovo Serbs in March 2005.[13] One of the most damaging flirtations with the nationalists and the supposed opinion of the majority was DS support for the new Serbian constitution in the 2006 referendum.

In economic terms the DS favours liberal reforms, while promising socially egalitarian policies (Stojiljković 2007a: 144–5). Under the leadership of Zoran Đinđić and the interim Prime Minister after the Đinđić murder, Zoran Živković, the willingness to undertake rapid reforms was more pronounced than in the Tadić period. The party advocates civic rights and minority rights, and has expressed its willingness to support a strong autonomy for Vojvodina.

After 2006, the DS made several policy moves and created symbolic events in order to re-position itself as a pronounced pro-reformist force, and not to leave this field to the newly emerging LDP, which positioned itself close to the DS but with a more decided pro-reform direction. In the 2007 elections the DS tried to attach itself to the legacy of Đinđić, calling for the renaming of a Belgrade boulevard after the murdered Prime Minister, and putting his widow Ružica Đinđić at the top of its electoral list (although she did not join the DS parliamentary delegation after the elections). In terms of its programme, the DS emphasised its reform credentials through the nomination of Božidar Đelić as its candidate for Prime Minister; he was finance minister in the Đinđić government and is seen as being committed to drastic economic reforms.[14] The pro-European and reformist credentials of the DS were underlined by the visit of EU enlargement commissar Oliver Rehn to president Boris Tadić in the last days of the campaign.

Differences within the DS-DSS coalition on the European issue were a major issue in the campaign for the presidential elections in 2008. Koštunica refused to support the candidacy of Tadić, and even though the presidential elections were supposed to be part of the DS-DSS coalition agreement, the DSS supported the minister of infrastructure, Velimir Ilić, in these elections (Bochsler 2008b: 746). Shortly after Tadić was re-elected and soon after the proclamation of Kosovo independence, the DS-DSS coalition broke over the question of whether the integration process should be continued. The nationalist–conservative parties, led by Prime Minister Koštunica, tried to link the issue of Kosovo independence to Serbian foreign policy and the issue of EU integration. Accordingly, the nationalist–conservatives demanded a stop to Serbian integration into the EU, and advocated re-orienting Serbian foreign policy towards Russia; Serbia withdrew its ambassadors from all those countries which recognised Kosovo. The DS, however, took a clear position against international isolation and the stalling of the EU integration process. Against the votes of the nationalist–conservative ministers in the government, the pro-European cabinet majority decided to sign the Stabilisation and Association Agreement with the European Union, which led to the break-up of the governing coalition and early elections in May 2008. The elections, fought mainly over EU integration, were won by a pro-European reform coalition around the DS, including G17+, SPO, and the League of Vojvodina Social Democrats (*Liga socialdemokrata Vojvodine*, LSV). Since then the DS has been back in government, forming a coalition with the Socialist Party (see below) under Prime Minister Mirko Cvetković (DS). The DS is a member of the Socialist International and has been an observer in the Party of European Socialists since 2006.

Liberal Democratic Party *(*Liberalno demokratska partija, *LDP)*

With the Liberal Democratic Party, a new pro-reform player has emerged, five years after the start of Serbia's transition. The creation and positioning of the party can only be understood by looking at the larger pro-reform party, the DS. The DS membership was always strongly pro-European and pro-reform, but as one of the largest parties it held differing roles of governmental responsibility in the period after 2000, and has behaved to some extent pragmatically. After the Đinđić murder, the circle of people around Đinđić was replaced by other currents in the party. Boris Tadić became party president in February 2004, and the DS moved towards pragmatic cooperation with the DSS. This caused dissatisfaction in the reformist wing of the party. At the 2004 DS party congress, Čedomir Jovanović, deputy Prime Minister in the interim government in 2003, attacked the DS leadership for its cooperation with Prime Minister Koštunica, whom he labelled the 'new Milošević'. In the aftermath, a group around Jovanović tried to form a Liberal Democratic Fraction inside the DS. The DS expelled Jovanović for this attempt (cf. Goati 2006: 172), and he in turn founded the new LDP on 5 November 2005.

The party presents itself as the only advocate of a continuation of the Đinđić reform programme, charging that the DS has stalled its own pro-European reforms. Accordingly, reform and change are the first priorities in the party programme[15] and a solution to the questions of The Hague and Kosovo – problems inherited from the Milošević regime – figure among the first points on this path of reform and European integration. The party argues that Serbia must face its recent past and deal with war crimes committed in the 1990s as the basis of societal modernisation. Issues such as lustration, human rights, autonomy for multicultural regions, and Western integration (into EU, NATO, and through increased cooperation with neighbouring states) take an important place in the programme. With regards to economic issues, the party takes clearly liberal–conservative stands, and wants to reduce the size of government. The party favours an accelerated transition, increased efforts in privatisation, the transfer of state regulatory activities to independent, market-oriented regulatory bodies, and the abolition of state-controlled prices, which should lead to economic growth and reduce poverty. With regards to social welfare, the party favours a reform of the Serbian education system, wants to replace the state-controlled health care with mandatory health insurance, and under the title 'social policies' the programme speaks of equal opportunity instead of criminal networks and clientelism, as well as increased quality and efficacy instead of direct social subsidies. For the fight against poverty, the party does not advocate redistributive programmes, but instead accuses the government of feudal attitudes, and 'fascist, racist, and xenophobe tendencies' excluding parts of the population from social and economic life.

The new party takes positions close to, but more radical than those of the DS, and accuses the DS programme of being too compromising. The DS leader Tadić in turn said that the LDP was not acceptable as a coalition partner because it would accept Kosovo's independence. While this might partly be understood as a restatement of the DS's clear position against Kosovo independence, the rejection was also seen as a signal that the LDP had no chance of getting into any governing coalition. In 2008 the party became a member of the European Liberal, Democratic and Reformist Group.[16]

Democratic Party of Serbia (Demokratska stranka Srbije, DSS) and New Serbia (Nova Srbija, NS)

The Democratic Party of Serbia of Vojislav Koštunica was brought to life in 1992, when it split from the DS due to disagreements about the alliance strategies, and mainly due to political differences on nationalist questions. The party wanted to redraw the country's borders according to the ethnic principle; that is to say, it supported the Greater Serbia project based on the idea that Serbia is everywhere where Serbians live.[17] This also meant that it opposed the peace treaties of Dayton and Erdut agreed to by Slobodan Milošević that ended the wars in Bosnia and Herzegovina and Croatia, and that it was not willing to recognise the new state borders (Goati 2004: 43). From 2000 to 2007, the DSS used much more conciliatory rhetoric towards neighbouring states and internal minorities. It remained sceptical about cooperation with the ICTY, but its position fluctuated. Koštunica, now in the position of president of the Former Republic of Yugoslavia (2000–2003), vetoed the extradition of Slobodan Milošević, which then took place against his will, provoked a state crisis, and initiated the DSS's breakaway from the DOS movement in 2001 (Goati 2004: 196). While Koštunica repeatedly accused the ICTY of being an anti-Serbian institution, after taking office as Prime Minister (heading two governments in 2004–2007 and 2007–2008), he officially declared his government's willingness to cooperate. However, the record has been rather mixed, and EU accession has stalled due to official incapability (or perhaps unwillingness) to extradite the highest-ranked accused war leaders. The DSS as well has continued its clerical policy towards the Serbian Orthodox Church. The DSS has a tradition as a right-wing party representing the interests of an economic elite, but due to structural changes in the party electorate, its economic direction changed after 2000 (Goati 2004: 208–9).

The DSS's membership before these changes could best be characterised as a nationalistic, intellectual and economic elite, and it did not change significantly until the democratic period after 2000 when the party became more successful in elections and could address a wider public. The DSS has been an associate member of the European People's Party since 2005.[18]

Since 2007, the DSS has competed in national elections jointly with the New Serbia Party (NS) of Velimir Ilić. The latter party is strong in a few localities, and its foremost stronghold is Ilić's hometown of Čačak in Southern Serbia. While before 2006 the party was characterised as having a position similar to that of the SPO (Goati 2006), and was in coalition with the SPO at that time, it has since moved towards a more conservative and nationalist point of view. Politically, New Serbia is usually on the side of Vojislav Koštunica, although it uses more radical rhetoric. In 2008, the DSS and NS formed a joint electoral list together with United Serbia (*Jedinstvena Srbija*, JS), a splinter group from an ultra-nationalist party that was founded by Željko Ražnjatović, a prominent war criminal.

G17+

G17+ was formed as a party in 2002, originating from an economic think-tank of the same name that had been politically close to the parties of the DOS movement. Its first party president, Miroljub Labus, was a former DS member. G17+ has the profile of a liberal political party (Vujačić 2007: 167–8), with a strong accent on economic reforms and development, market liberalisation, favouring budget austerity and tax cuts over a generous welfare state.

The party is clearly located at the liberal and anti-nationalist pole, speaking out for a strengthening of civic rights regardless of ethnicity, and stressing the EU membership process as the foremost important goal of Serbian politics. The party has been positive about Montenegro gaining independence from Serbia, arguing that in the confederation of Serbia and Montenegro, the small confederate had political power that was much greater than its importance in terms of economic power and fiscal contributions to the common institutions.[19] G17+ has been an associate member of the European People's Party since 2005.

G17+ has been in government constantly since its first appearance in the national parliamentary elections in 2003, first as part of the two Koštunica cabinets, and then in 2008 on a joint list with the DS. The party provoked the break-up of the first Koštunica cabinet in autumn 2006 over its disappointment about the stalled EU integration process. The EU had suspended negotiations over a Stabilisation and Association Agreement following the Serbian authorities' failure to arrest the fugitive ex-General Ratko Mladić and hand him over to the Hague Tribunal. The fiasco of the EU integration process irritated G17+, which left the government in September 2006, thus depriving Koštunica's cabinet of its majority and leading to early parliamentary elections in January 2007. Nevertheless, the party agreed to join a new coalition with Koštunica as Prime Minister, this time however with the participation of the DS, which is closer to G17+ in many aspects.

Serbian Renewal Movement (*Srpski pokret obnove, SPO*)

The Serbian Renewal Movement is arguably the most flexible party in uniting a Serbian nationalist background and a decidedly pro-European and anti-chauvinist programme under the same roof. Although it occupies conservative ideological territory on many issues, advocating the return of the monarchy and orthodox clericalism, on the most important political questions the SPO today identifies with the most liberal and pro-European positions, and in its 2001 programme it accepted the territorial reality of Serbia's borders and the defeat of the Greater Serbia idea.

The party was founded in 1990 as an extreme nationalist, revisionist and anti-communist force, defining itself as a party of all Serbs, applying a similarly ethnically exclusive concept to the definition of the Serbian state, and using insulting language for ethnic minorities.[20] The party pursued a Greater Serbia policy, stating that

> no piece of land drenched in Serbian blood and marked with Serbian churches and graves can be detached or confederated. No one can separate from Yugoslavia the territories which on the day when Yugoslavia was created in 1918 were part of the Kingdom of Serbia, or from the territories where Serbs were in a majority before the genocide carried out by the Croatian Ustashi.[21]

The later founder of the Serbian Radical Party, Vojislav Šešelj, was briefly a founding member of SPO. In the late 1980s and early 1990s, the party oriented historically upon the Serbian Chetniks, the royalist and nationalist Serbian militia in the Second World War. Twice, the party recruited its own paramilitary force, the White Eagles (*Beli orlovi*) in 1990 and the Serbian Guard (*Srpska garda*) in 1991 (NIOD 2002). After 1992 and until 1997, as well as after 2000, the party is said to have taken a pro-Western position (Goati 2004: 47).

The party is mainly oriented upon Vuk Drašković, party president since its foundation. He served as foreign minister of Serbia and Montenegro, and later of Serbia, from 2004 to 2007. He is a well-known figure due to his role in the democracy movements of the 1990s and the pro-democracy protests. However, in that role the party was rather erratic. In 1997, right after the student protests, the party sought to enter a coalition with Milošević, and finally did so in 1999 (Bieber 2003b). This was followed by assassination attempts by the regime against Drašković in 1999 and 2000, after which the party switched back to the anti-regime camp; but it did not officially support the 2000 pro-democracy protest movement, although its supporters were present in those protests. Given the party's history of vacillation, the SPO's absence might possibly have strengthened rather than weakened the credibility of the Democratic Opposition Movement in 2000.

Serbian Radical Party (Srpska radikalna stranka, SRS) and Serbian Progress Party (Srpska napredna stranka, SNS)

In the 1990s, the Serbian Radical Party was pushing for a more aggressive confrontation by the Serbian state and the Yugoslav army against its neighbours and its internal minorities, not only in politics but on the battlefield as well. Party leader Vojislav Šešelj ran the parallel paramilitary Serbian Chetnik Movement (*Srpski četnički pokret*, SČP), which organised ethnic cleansing, persecutions, deportations and the spread of hatred in Croatia, Bosnia, and in Vojvodina, (ICTY 2004: 2); among other things it called for Croats residing in Vojvodina to have their eyes gouged out with rusty spoons. The Serbian Radicals criticised Milošević repeatedly for not contributing enough to the war for a Greater Serbia. In the party's programme Greater Serbia is described as including regions in neighbouring countries such as 'Serbian Macedonia, Serbian Montenegro, Serbian Bosnia, Serbian Herzegovina, the Serbian town of Dubrovnik, Serbian Dalmatia, Serbian Lika, Serbian Kordun, Serbian Banija, Serbian Slavonia, and Serbian Baranja', often referred as the *Virovitica–Karlovac–Karlobag* line.[22]

After the end of the war and the changes of 2000, the party did not change its goal of a Greater Serbia. In 2003, Šešelj surrendered to the ICTY, accused of war crimes; party officials in Belgrade meanwhile have instead focused on different policy fields and tried to become more acceptable to the Serbian voters and the international community, which continues its embargo on all contacts with SRS officials at all levels.[23] Deputy party leader Tomislav Nikolić, now leading party manager, has attempted to position the Radicals as a conservative European party, trying to imitate the metamorphosis of other formerly fascist or ultra-nationalist parties such as the National Alliance (*Alleanza nazionale*, AN) in Italy, or the Croatian Democratic Union (*Hrvatska demokratska zajednica*, HDZ), now both accepted parties in the European environment. But this strategy has shown little success, either because the party is stuck deeper in the mire than its Croat counterpart, or because the party is commanded by its war-lord Šešelj, albeit now from a prison cell of the ICTY in the Netherlands. Šešelj continues to be an active personality in the political debate in Serbia, mainly through his political defence in the Hague Court, and through his sporadic orders that reach his party back in Belgrade. Important events staged by Šešelj include his hunger strike, which opened the SRS campaign for the 2007 parliamentary elections. In December 2006 Šešelj published his 'political testament', advising his party to oppose integration into the EU and NATO, and to re-open territorial issues of a Greater Serbia.[24]

Nikolić emphasised social and economic issues. The party campaigned increasingly for the losers of the economic transition. In the presidential campaign of 2008, Nikolić as the Radical candidate and other party members dropped the Šešelj badge that they had always worn in public, and tried to appeal to voters with the promise of change, to fight against criminality and the rampant corruption in Serbia. However, this can sound irritating, since his party is seen as being close to Serbian organised crime, including the assassins of Đinđić (it is expected of the party that it would grant an amnesty to them if it were to get such power).[25]

In electoral terms, the party was able to quickly recover from its losses in 2000, when it dropped to 8.8 per cent of the votes, and re-emerged as the largest Serbian party with up to 29 per cent of the vote in 2007 and 2008. The SRS has been highly successful in areas with an ethnically mixed population, where nationalist issues are much more salient among ethnic Serbian voters. The party scores particularly well in Kosovo and in multi-ethnic Vojivodina, and the cliché is that the party profits heavily from the voters of refugees from Bosnia and Kosovo who were settled there by Slobodan Milošević in order to change the ethnic make-up of the region and reinforce the ethnic Serbian dominance.[26]

The Radicals have not got back into government – they have repeatedly ruled out being part of a coalition government – but they were an inch away from a come-back in 2007 when, in a tactical move, the DSS backed the election of SRS deputy president Tomislav Nikolić as parliament speaker. This was understood as the threat of a possible formation of a DSS-SRS cabinet, provoking a domestic and international outcry. However, the SRS cooperates with almost all Serbian parties at the local level, in coalitions in 63 out of the 144 Serbian municipalities: its most frequent partners are the SPS and DSS, while DS-SRS coalitions are rare.[27]

The Radicals have lately suffered two quite relevant split-offs by members who were disappointed by their failed attempt to convert the party into an acceptable conservative party. On the one hand, after the SRS won the mayoral office in Novi Sad with Maja Gojković in 2004, certainly the most important public office the SRS had held in the post-2000 period, Gojković quit the party to found the People's Party (*Narodna partija*), and allied with the DSS and NS. Shortly after the 2008 national parliamentary elections, the SRS was hit by a further exodus when the party's deputy president, Tomislav Nikolić, and general secretary of the party, Aleksandar Vučić, stepped down from their offices along with 18 other Radical MPs[28] and formed the new Serbian Progress Party (SNS). The split in the SNS was provoked by Šešelj's intervention in 2008 after Tomislav Nikolić had negotiated with the DS-led government in order to pass legislation that would allow the signing of the Stabilisation and Association Agreement (SAA) with the European Union. The agreement between the Radicals and the government was celebrated as a breakthrough in the internal logjam of Serbian politics (the SRS had blocked parliamentary work through the use of procedural objections and motions for urgent debates, imitating filibusters in the US senate), and as a first step for the rehabilitation of the Radicals. But the plan was knocked down by Šešelj, who vetoed any agreement with the DS-led government, resulting in the internal splintering of the party.

Usually, party split-offs are hindered through the practice of submitting undated letters of resignation, but in this case it was Nikolić who controlled these documents, and he alleged that he had lost them. Once again, it was to the advantage of Nikolić that he could count on the support of the parliamentary majority in the event of a conflict about the mandates of the split-off deputies.

With the DSS-NS coalition moving towards a strongly nationalist position, along with the People's Party of Novi Sad ex-mayor Maja Gojković, the SNS and the SRS, there is strong competition for the nationalist voters in Serbia, and some parties will find it hard to pass the 5 per cent threshold by themselves. In its first test, in repeated local elections in four municipalities on 9 November 2008, the SNS became the second largest party behind the DS in three out of four municipalities. The SRS was devastated, failing to pass the threshold in two out of four municipalities, and losing most of its mandates in two others, including one of its foremost strongholds, Ruma. Upcoming elections may cause a reordering of powers in the nationalist field. At the time of writing, it appears plausible that the DSS-NS, the People's Party, and the SNS will agree on political cooperation.[29] The international community would be relieved if the new nationalist parties would win out over the Serbian Radicals, and has shown this clearly, for instance by symbolically attending the SNS founding congress while continuing to avoid all contacts with the SRS.

*Socialist Party of Serbia (*Socijalistička partija srbije*, SPS)*

The Socialist Party of Serbia has a long legacy, being the successor of the Union of Communists in Serbia (*Savez komunista Srbije*, SKS). It was re-named in 1990, but remained under the leadership of the previous secretary of the Serbian communists, Slobodan Milošević. The party was the main force on the economic left in Serbia, but it was known in the 1990s mainly for its authoritarian and nationalist policies. After 1991 the party began to advocate a Greater Serbia,[30] and in the programme of 1992 it called the Northern-Atlantic and European institutions of EU, OSCE, and NATO, imperialist organisations and enemies of Serbia (Vykoupilová and Stojarová 2007). The Socialists rejected any autonomy for Vojvodina and Kosovo in the 1996 programme, and minority-friendly statements existed only on paper, with no impact on implemented policies (Goati 2004: 50–1). With this programme of international isolation, hatred, and authoritarianism, the SPS's popularity dropped, and in the reasonably free and fair elections of December 2000 the party could no longer use electoral fraud as a substitute for popularity.[31]

The first few elections after the liberalisation of the regime were difficult for almost all of the former communist parties, which could neither attract many voters nor enter any coalition. Having lost their political monopoly, they were often discredited with substantial parts of the electorate. The old regime conflict still overwhelms, and with very few exceptions, elections are won in landslide victories by the reform parties, which usually compete in a broad umbrella coalition (Bochsler 2007a; Olson 1998). The situation in Serbia was no different. In the first reasonably free elections in 2000, the Socialists fell back to some 14 per cent of the vote, and in later elections they just barely passed the 5 per cent threshold.

The nationalist programme of the Socialist party did not pay off, post-2000, in terms of votes. The issue might have lost salience, since everyday economic problems had gained a higher priority for many citizens, and most importantly, the Socialists were not the sole owners of the nationalist issue. For authoritarian–nationalist voters, the Serbian Radical Party offered a more credible alternative than the Socialists, and moreover they have become more and more similar on most other issues, such as the demand for a strong welfare state. By 2008, the space at the authoritarian end of the political axis had become increasingly crowded, given an accentuation of the nationalist aspects of the programme by Prime Minister Koštunica's coalition of DSS and NS. The lack of ownership of the Socialist Party on nationalist issues was further reflected by its relationship to Milošević. He and his fellow prisoner Šešelj on trial at the ICTY were able to promote in their televised defences a Serbian nationalist view of recent history, and thus were able to increase their symbolic importance for the nationalists back home. However, while the Radical leader Šešelj stayed in close contact with his SRS, regularly giving orders as to the direction of the party, the same could not be said about the Socialist leader, Slobodan Milošević, who, in the 2004 presidential elections, even supported a Radical instead of his own SPS candidate.[32] The Radicals thus increasingly became the only dominant party that could represent the hardcore nationalist vote.

Its difficult electoral position, and the uncertain future direction of its support, may have prompted the party leadership to readjust its position after the death of Milošević in March 2006, most importantly around the parliamentary elections in 2008. The party attempted to re-position and to cut (to some extent) its ties to its past, in order to address new segments of voters, but also to become a possible coalition partner for the pro-Europeans. This meant that they could play the role of the pivotal voter in the national parliament as well as in local assemblies all across Serbia, since they were acceptable as a coalition partner both to the pro-Europeans around the DS, and to the nationalists around the DSS and SRS. This gave the party much more power in coalition negotiations. The main element of the SPS' new direction was a new accent on social welfare policies, and while it previously had a rather ambivalent view of the EU integration process, it now clearly approved the EU perspective. As far back as its party congress in 2003, the party had switched its position with regard to the European Union,[33] a position re-confirmed at the congress of December 2006. There, ahead of the 2007 elections, the Socialists stressed their new social orientation, putting the accent on economic policies and an extension of the welfare state. The SPS repeatedly declared itself to be the only relevant left-wing party in Serbia, pointing to its left-wing economic programme. The party promised to reintroduce the social welfare system of the early 1990s. It spoke out in favour of a regulation of the market, a mixed property structure, and full employment. More specifically, it based its economic and welfare policies on the importance of collective employment agreements and on participation of employees at their workplaces. It spoke of a better, more just and humane society, and democratic socialism (Stojiljković 2007b: 189). Furthermore, the party no longer campaigned on nationalist issues. The party was still negative towards cooperation with NATO, but it stepped back from its firm rejection of the 1990s and stated in 2006 that it would accept the people's verdict on this question.[34]

For the electorate of the SPS, the new orientation is certainly a major rupture, and the party risks losing part of its voters on the way to its new pro-European identity. However, and most importantly, the party could use the strengthening of social redistribution as one of its main pillars in any coalition agreement, and make 'social justice' one of the most frequently used phrases in Serbian politics. This label positions the SPS in the public perception as the issue-leader in favour of a strong social welfare state. Welfare policies are very popular with many

Serbian citizens, who are still used to a state that takes care of citizens 'from the cradle to the grave' (Stojiljković 2007a: 135).

In its new programme of 2006, the Socialist Party writes that its goal is membership in the Socialist International (SI).[35] However, it has so far been refused membership because of the party's historical legacies, the enduring link to Slobodan Milošević, and the lack of reform (Stojiljković 2007a: 132–3). The SI has been reluctant to accept members with a nationalist–authoritarian programme, so that parties with such a direction have only been able to become an SI member through mergers with other social democratic parties with whom they shared some economic stands. In the Serbian case, there is strong competition for the label of being *the* social democratic party. Besides several small social democratic parties (see below), the Democratic Party of Boris Tadić also attempts to position itself in this field, and it is also a member of the SI.

For the SPS, one of the latest steps towards an SI membership and democratic reconciliation was fulfilled on 18 October 2008, when DS leader Boris Tadić and SPS leader Ivica Dačić signed an agreement of reconciliation, declaring that they wanted to settle their former conflict, which can be seen as a rehabilitation of the Serbian Socialists.[36]

The social democratic party family

Several parties aspire to hold the position of *the* social democratic party in Serbia. There are several parties which not only call themselves social democrats, but are also oriented toward the Western European model of social democrats, with civic–liberal values and a social–redistributive programme. The most important party in this field is the Social Democratic Party (*Socijaldemokratska partija*, SDP), which is an SI member. But these parties are short of votes; none is able pass the electoral threshold either on its own or even as the leader of a party coalition. Apart from these parties, the social democratic space is occupied by the DS, another SI member. Finally, several regional Vojvodina parties, the most important among them being the LSV, locate themselves in the social democratic realm (see Chapter 9).

Administrative obstacles and the failure of the Movement of Serbian Force

Many party systems in Central and Eastern Europe saw the emergence of new parties that quickly won a considerable number of votes, often getting into the governments after their first electoral appearance: Res Publica in Estonia, New Era in Latvia, the New Union (Social Liberals) and the National Resurrection Party in Lithuania; or in Bulgaria, with the National Movement of Simeon II or the Citizens for a European Development of Bulgaria (Sikk 2006; Taagepera 2006). Unlike in Western Europe, these parties do not mobilise around newly emerging social–political divides, such as the post-materialist cleavage or anti-immigration or regional issues (Harmel and Robertson 1985; Meguid 2005).

As Sikk (2006) showed, they more frequently choose a position in the centre of the pre-existing party system – a strategy that in the West might possibly be best compared to Silvio Berlusconi's *Forza Italia*. Without having major political differences with them, they campaign with newness as their main issue, which presumably makes them highly successful with voters who are generally disappointed by the old parties. (Needless to say, in the subsequent elections, voters will switch again to another party, or abstain.) The success of new parties also depends on their financial resources, and on the resources that the old parties use in order to hinder the entry of new competitors that become dangerous to them.

Serbia has also had a new centrist political party, the Movement of Serbian Force (*Pokret snage Srbije*, PSS). Not only did the party name allude to *Forza Italia*, but as in the Italian case, the party functioned as an enterprise of the Serbian oligarch and media tycoon, Bogoljub Karić. The PSS gained parliamentary representation in 2005 when Karić allegedly paid MPs of other parties to join his parliamentary group.[37] In its campaigns the PSS could call upon Karić's own TV station, one of the most popular in Serbia at the time. With its appeals to national pride, a programme combining economic development and protectionism[38] with a nationalist–conservative position similar to that of the median voter in Serbia, the party was probably the closest and the most dangerous to the DSS. Survey results by Stojiljković (2007b) suggest that the PSS electorate is disillusioned by institutions, but does not prefer policies that are very different from those of the 'old' parties. In local elections the PSS was highly successful, and in the first round of the presidential elections in 2004, Karić won 18.2 per cent of the vote, just behind the Radical and the Democratic candidates, Nikolić and Tadić.

The Serbian case, however, is not only a textbook example of a popular new centrist party that draws heavily from its own financial capacities; it also shows what kind of barriers can be put up by the old parties, intimidated by the political success of the newcomer, and trying to hinder its rise. The comparative literature mentions the electoral legislation used by the old parties in order to conserve their political power – party registration rules, high legal thresholds in elections, or party financing rules unfavourable to the newcomers. But in the Serbian case the PSS's ascent was stopped at once when in 2006 the Serbian authorities smashed Karić's financial and media empire on criminal charges, and withdrew the frequency of his TV station. The motives for this move will perhaps never be completely clear, but many observers saw this as an attempt to block Karić's political career before he could win a landslide victory in the parliamentary elections in 2007. Karić fled the country, and with him went the PSS's chances, despite having more private funding than any other party in the election campaign.

Conclusion and outlook

Eight years after 5 October 2000, the Serbian party system is still in a process of consolidation. The main motor of European integration, the Democratic Party

(DS), has returned to power as the largest political party and dominant force of the pro-reform wing, similar to the situation after 2000. However, following a re-shuffle of the party landscape, with the entry of the new pro-European parties G17+ and LDP, with the move of the DSS back to its nationalist roots, and with the rise of the Socialist Party, the sharp division into *old regime parties* and *pro-European reformers* has been broken up. The leadership of the nationalist part of the spectrum, after the split of the Serbian Radicals and the programmatic change of the DSS, will be determined in upcoming elections.

Unlike other countries in post-communist Europe, the emergence of a new, centre-oriented anti-establishment party has so far been hindered not least through the use of administrative measures against the leader of one such party, the Serbian oligarch Bogoljub Karić. This, however, does not eliminate the electoral potential for other new parties to campaign on issues of state mismanagement and governmental failure. The strong polarisation and pronounced programmatic differences of Serbian parties along four major political cleavages – old regime versus reform parties, authoritarian–nationalist versus civic–liberal values, foreign policy, and social–economic issues – might make it more difficult than in other post-communist countries for catch-all parties to attract a wide electorate with a fuzzy centrist programme.

Notes

1 I am grateful to Daniel Zollinger for his very valuable comments.
2 Monarchist resistance movement during the Second World War.
3 The vote would only be valid if more than half of the registered voters turn out.
4 Milošević could not run again in 1997, and instead became president of the Federal Republic of Yugoslavia. His successor Milan Milutinović had less power, and his role became almost symbolic after the democratically oriented parties took over the parliament in 2000.
5 TV B92, *Insajder*, 23 October 2008.
6 Adding to this, some parties oblige their MPs to hand in an undated letter of resignation, allowing the party leadership to replace them with another candidate at any time in the legislature, and this practice of enforced replacements is indeed practised (Goati 2006: 109).
7 *Danas*, 16 November 2006, 'Od danas – podizanje izbornih obrazaca'. The Supreme Court rejected a formal complaint against the lowering.
8 B92, 1 February 2007, 'RIK dobio 14 izveštaja'.
9 For the shakedown hypothesis, see O'Donnell and Schmitter (1986: 58); Taagepera and Shugart (1989: 147) and Cox (1997). Dawisha and Deets (2006) and Bochsler (2007b) investigated the hypothesis for countries in Central and Eastern Europe.
10 See Pantić (2006); Slavujević (2006); Mihailović (2006); Goati (2004) for more information on party positioning.
11 Deklaracija šestog kongresa Socijalističke partije Srbije, 18 January 2003, Belgrade, www.sps.org.yu/uploads/DEKLERACIJA%206%20KONGRESA.pdf.
12 His strategy relies on a recognition of Serbian war crimes, and excuses them with the common Serbian argument that war crimes were committed by all former Yugoslav countries (*Danas*, 7 December 2004, 'Tadić: Svi jedni drugima dugujemo izvinjenje'). Commenting on an assembly that was aimed at denying the crimes committed in Srebrenica, Tadić stressed freedom of opinion (Nin, 2 July 2005, *Ljiljana Smajlović*, 'Srebrenica kao sudbina').

13 When speaking to the Serbs in Kosovo and the international community, Tadić was apparently more moderate, sending certain signals of support for a multi-ethnic Kosovo. In particular, Tadić encouraged the Kosovo Serbs to participate in the 2004 parliamentary elections in Kosovo, and tried to cool down emotions after the Kosovo riots in March 2004 (Helsinki Committee for Human Rights in Serbia 2005).

14 *Nin*, 16 November 2006: 'Šta nudim Srbiji'.

15 Programme 'Drugačija Srbija' (Different Serbia), from 2007. Found on www.ldp.org. yu.

16 B92, 30 October 2008, 'LDP primljen među evropske liberale'.

17 DSS programme 1998, p. 6, cited in Goati (2004: 44).

18 Information on the affiliation with European political parties is taken from Milivojević (2007: 115).

19 Programme, G17+, 28. mart 2004. Available at www.g17plus.org.yu/download/doku-menti/program.pdf (last accessed on 26 October 2008).

20 The party programme and further information on the party can be found on www.spo. rs. More information was retrieved in Goati (2004: 47–8), Komšić (2002), and Vukomanović (2007).

21 *Velika Srbija* (A Greater Serbia), July 1990, no. 1, p. 18 (cited in Tomic 2008: 80).

22 Programme published in Velika Srbija, the organ of the Serbian Chetnik Movement, in July 1990, no. 1, pp. 2–3 (cited in Tomic, 2008: 81).

23 Spoerri (2008) discusses the boycott against the SRS and SPS.

24 B92, 4 December 2006, 'O Šešeljevom testamentu'.

25 *Politika*, 15 January 2008, 'Svim srcem, ali bez Šešeljevog bedža'; *Politika*, 24 January 2008, 'I Nikolić putuje u Rusiju'.

26 Stefanović (2008) shows some support for the ethnic hypothesis (however, his results do not really show the expected curvilinear pattern of ethnic minorities and SRS vote share), but his results support the rumour about the refugees only in certain elections, while in other cases, no such effect is visible.

27 Figures for the period 2004–2008, provided by CeSID *Niš*, 'Koaliciona moc SRS-a na lokalu'.

28 *Politika*, 2 October 2008, 'Paralelna stvarnost srpske skupštine'.

29 *Politika*, 27 October 2008, 'Desni centar sa dvojcem bez kormilara'; B92, 21 October 2008, 'Gojkovićeva s liderima DSS-a i NS-a'.

30 In the 1993–1997 period, when Slobodan Milošević was a central figure in the inter-national peace negotiations for Bosnia and Herzegovina, the party position on a Greater Serbia was more nuanced.

31 For details, see Todorović (2002).

32 *Vreme*, 7.12.2006: 'Izborna Kampanja: Dvojci i Kormilari'.

33 Deklaracija šestog kongresa Socijalističke partije Srbije, 18 January 2003, Belgrade, www.sps.org.yu/uploads/DEKLERACIJA%206%20KONGRESA.pdf.

34 Programska deklaracija sedmog kongresa Socijalističke partije Srbije, 3 December 2006, Belgrade, www.sps.org.yu/cms/index.php?option=com_content&task=blogsect ion&id=5&Itemid=77.

35 Programska deklaracija sedmog kongresa Socijalističke partije Srbije, 3 December 2006, Belgrade, www.sps.org.yu/cms/index.php?option=com_content&task=blogsect ion&id=5&Itemid=77.

36 'Deklaracija o političkom pomirenju i zajedničkoj odgovornosti za ostvarivanje vizije Srbije kao demokratske, slobodne, celovite, ekonomski i kulturno razvijene i socijalno pravedne zemlje', *Politika*, 21 and 22 October 2008.

37 Danas, 20 May 2005, 'Aligrudić: Juče bio crn dan', 'Pokret Snaga Srbije očekuje nove poslanike'.

38 The party programme is presented in Stojiljković (2007a: 143).

8 The party system of Montenegro

Florian Bieber

Overview of the political system

Montenegro joined Yugoslavia as an independent country in 1918. Montenegro had already established autonomy under Ottoman rule, having formally become independent in 1878. However, the authoritarian rule of Prince Nikolai (from 1910 King) did not allow for the emergence of modern political parties (Roberts 2006: 271–3). During the first Yugoslavia, Montenegro did not enjoy any political autonomy. Some political forces in Montenegro supported a federal arrangement and opposed the centralist policies of the new state, whereas others opted for centralist parties (Banac 1984: 270–91). However, it was only after the Second World War that Montenegro was re-established as one of the six republics of Yugoslavia. Under the one-party rule of the League of Communists (*Savez komunista Jugoslavije*, SKJ) – until 1952 the Communist Party of Yugoslavia (*Komunistička partija Jugoslavije*, KPJ) – Montenegro saw rapid economic modernisation but still struggled with underdevelopment in relation to the other republics. Unlike in other parts of Yugoslavia, there was no significant dissident movement or opposition to communist rule. In 1989 the leadership of the League of Communists of Montenegro (*Savez komunista Crne Gore*, SK CG) had to resign following a series of protests and pressure from Serbia, where the regime of Slobodan Milošević sought to bring other regions of Yugoslavia under its control. While the new leadership tried to present themselves as democratic, free and fair elections were held in 1990s largely due to external pressure and the elections in other Yugoslav republics. The SK CG was able to gain more than 56 per cent of the vote and was thus able to retain absolute control of the political system. The SK CG transformed itself into the Democratic Party of Socialists (*Demokratska partija socijalista*, DPS) in 1991 and has been able to govern without interruption ever since. While the other Yugoslav republics sought their independence, Montenegro remained allied with Serbia, supporting a continuation of Yugoslavia. Though aligned with Serbia, Montenegro tried to pursue a less repressive policy. It participated in the Croatian war, in particular in the border region to Dubrovnik, but later did not contribute substantially to the Serbian side during the Bosnian war. The first post-authoritarian constitution of 1992 was considerably less flawed than its 1990 Serbian counterpart. In 1992 a referendum (95.4 per cent in favour, in a 66.04 per cent turnout) confirmed Montenegro's association with the new Federal Republic of Yugoslavia (*Savezna Republika Jugoslavija*, SRJ). Only after the DPS, under the leadership of Milo Đukanović, Prime Minister since 1991, broke ranks with Milošević in 1997, reforms and liberalisation were initiated, gradually, even though the political system continued to be dominated by the DPS. Between 1998 and 2002 Montenegro built up the features of a de facto state, replacing the Dinar with the German Mark (later Euro), remaining neutral during the Kosovo war in 1999, and pursuing a different foreign policy than Serbia. The fall of Milošević in 2000 did not bring about a shift in the Montenegrin government's pursuit of independence, resulting in Yugoslavia becoming the State Union of Serbia and Montenegro in 2002 (see Bieber 2003a: 11–43). Montenegro retained the right to hold a referendum on independence three years after the creation of the State Union in 2003. The referendum in May 2006, observed by international monitors and conducted under EU rules, resulted in a narrow majority for independence (55.5 per cent, turnout 86.5 per cent).[1] There were some challenges to the outcome by pro-Unionist parties, but independence was quickly recognised internationally, including by Serbia (ICG 2006a). Following independence, Montenegro held parliamentary (2006) and presidential elections (2008), and passed a new constitution in 2007. The new constitution was controversial on issues of identity, such as the official languages, the preamble and the symbols of the country.

Montenegro today is a parliamentary democracy with a directly elected president. The 81 members of parliament are elected according to proportional representation in a single electoral unit.[2] Five seats are won in specially designated polling stations in primarily Albanian inhabited regions. Thus, Albanians enjoy de facto reserved seats, unlike other minorities. This practice, with a varying number of reserved seats, has been criticised by international monitors since its establishment in 1998 (OSCE 2006a: 5, 16). The threshold for parliament is 3 per cent, down from 4 per cent (1990–1996) and seats are allocated according to the D'Hondt system. Only half of the seats have to be allocated according to the candidate lists, while the reminder can be freely assigned by parties. This rule and the single electoral unit favour a strong role of parties and their leadership. The parliament elects a government, while the president is directly elected. A candidate for the president has to obtain 50 per cent of the vote; if this is not achieved, a second round is required. Until 2003, there was a 50 per cent turnout requirement for the vote to be valid, but this threshold was dropped after two attempts to elect the president failed due to low turnout in 2002/3. The president is elected for five years and is the commander in chief. His competences are largely ceremonial and he can not veto legislation nor dissolve parliament nor dismiss the government (Bieber 2009; Pavićević et al. 2007: 13–82).

While there have been regular elections since 1990 and gradual political liberalisation since 1997, the political system remains skewed because the DPS has never gained less than 42 per cent of the vote and has continuously governed the country. As such, Montenegro can be classified as a dominant party system (Darmanović 2003: 145–53). During the period 1998–2002, Montenegro appeared to be moving towards a two-party system with two strong blocs, when in 2001, the opposition bloc centred on the *Socijalistička narodna partija*, SNP nearly obtained the same number of votes. However, the fragmentation of the opposition after the referendum reinforced the dominance of the DPS. Small parties which have support around or below the threshold have been able to enter parliament through the widespread practice of pre-election coalition. Thus in 1992, the governing Social Democratic Party (*Socijaldemokratska partija*, SDP) managed to enter parliament as an independent party but since 1998 has been part of a pre-election coalition with the DPS. As a result of this practice, the number of parliamentary parties by far exceeds the number of groups which cross the threshold. Thus, in 2006, eight lists gained seats but some 16 parties gained parliamentary representation. Fragmentation has been prominent among the pro-Serb parties, with seven parliamentary parties campaigning on this platform. The set-aside seats for Albanian voters also resulted in the fragmentation of Albanian minority parties, with three parties representing a minority of less than 6 per cent.

Development of party system

The party system is characterised by the dominance of the successor party to the League of Communists, the DPS. It has held power uninterrupted since the first multi-party elections in 1990. While the split of the party in 1997 over its position towards Slobodan Milošević and in regard to economic and political reforms reduced the dominance of the DPS, it has nevertheless retained its primary position. Between 1990 and 1997, the DPS was by far the largest political party, while opposition parties either argued for more reforms and independence from Serbia, such as the Reformists in 1990 and subsequently the Social Democratic Party and the Liberal Alliance (*Liberalni savez Crne Gore*, LSCG). On the conservative side of the political spectrum, the People's Party (*Narodna stranka*, NS) advocated a Serb nationalist line. In 1996, a coalition of the LSCG and the NS under the name of National Unity (*Narodna Sloga*), i.e. supporters of Montenegrin independence and Serb nationalism, was unable to effectively challenge the DPS. A reformist coalition brought together SDP, LSCG, NS and DPS after the pro-Milošević SNP split from the DPS in 1997. This steered the DPS towards economic and political reforms and also re-affirmed the link between reformists and supporters of independence. Apart from that split in 1997, the DPS has remained stable. As the governing party, it has been a broad technocratic party without a clear ideological profile, characterised by a great degree of flexibility. The SNP, closely linked to Serbia and Milošević's Socialist Party until 2000, retained some of the features of the DPS, being pragmatic and distancing itself from Milošević after 2000 and forming a coalition with the new Serbian governing coalition DOS, and especially the Democratic Party of Serbia (*Demokratska stranka Srbije*, DSS) of Yugoslav president Vojislav Koštunica. Consequently, the SNP was a coalition partner of the Yugoslav government between 1997 and 2003, giving it considerable influence at the Federal level.

Party families

The party system has displayed a certain degree of stability with most parliamentary political parties established for more than a decade. Nevertheless, party families have oriented themselves along issues pertaining to the political status of Montenegro (independent or as part of Yugoslavia), or the question of support to particular political leaders (for/against Slobodan Milošević, for/against Milo Đukanović). Although most parties formally and by name positioned themselves in a classic left-right spectrum, these labels often remained declaratory and without much substance. Between 1990 and 1996, the main line of orientation among parties themselves was on the relationship towards Serbia and the desired ties with the neighbouring republic. The dominant DPS sought close ties, while maintaining Montenegrin distinctiveness. Other more Serb nationalist parties, most prominently the NS, supported even closer links to Serbia. On the other hand, the SDP and LSCG advocated Montenegrin statehood and independence. These issues were also panned out on the topic of Montenegrin participation in the wars, in particular in the siege of Dubrovnik which was supported by parties aligning themselves with Serbia and rejected by pro-Montenegrin parties. A second theme which structured the party spectrum was the relationship towards the communist legacy. Unlike elsewhere, the explicitly anti-communist parties were less prominent, the most significant one being the NS. While the LSCG took a highly critical stance to the successor to the League of Communists, the DPS, it was not necessarily anti-communist, neither was the SDP. Between 1997 and 2000, the break of the DPS with the Milošević regime re-oriented the party system with parties either supporting Milošević and close ties to Serbia, or supporting greater autonomy for Montenegro and political and economic reforms. This development brought about the coalition of the NS and LSCG with the DPS, while the SNP and Serb People's Party (*Srpska narodna stranka*, SNS) aligned themselves with Serbia. After the fall of the Serbian regime, the main axis was the support for or against Montenegrin independence, the dominant issue until the referendum in 2006. Since then, parties have in part positioned themselves for or against the dominant role of the DPS, while some parties have also sought to emphasise ethnic Serb topics, i.e. identity politics.

Altogether, minority parties have been represented in parliament, but with the exception of the early phase of the Montenegrin multi-party system, there was little polarisation between minority and majority parties. In fact, most of the minorities, both from the Albanian and the Bosniak/Muslim community, consistently voted for multi-ethnic mainstream parties rather than ethnically defined parties. Albanian minority parties, the only ones with consistent representation in the Montenegrin parliament, thanks to preferential treatment in the electoral law, have been supporting the government since 1998. There are no extreme right-wing parties which define themselves as ethnic Montenegrin – Montenegrin identity has so far been to be too inclusive to allow for such a political agenda. Extreme right-wing parties have been proponents of an exclusive Serb nationalism, but with few exceptions have not fared well in elections. The

Radical Party only entered parliament independently in 1992, but has been represented in the Serb List, which has been the strongest opposition party since 2006.

Socialist and social-democratic parties

Social democratic and socialist parties emerged from either the League of Communists or the reform forces which were established by Yugoslav Prime Minister Ante Marković in 1990 to counter the rising nationalist forces in Yugoslavia. While Montenegrin society tends to be overall conservative, there is also a consensus beyond the political left on state intervention and gradual economic change. Thus, left–right political distinctions only partly capture the lines along which political parties have oriented themselves.

Democratic Party of Socialists (Demokratska partija socijalista, DPS)

The DPS has dominated the party system since the introduction of the multi-party system. It only endorsed multi-party democracy once this was inevitable. The DPS has been flexible in terms of policies and can only partly be considered a social democratic party. Mostly, it has been a pragmatic–technocratic governing party with a broad popular base. During the first half of the 1990s, it supported the regime of Milošević in Serbia and close ties with the larger republic. Nevertheless, it sought to maintain Montenegrin autonomy and never fully endorsed the isolationism of Serbia. After its support for the Dubrovnik campaign in Croatia, it largely sought to keep Montenegro out of the war in Bosnia and Herzegovina. In terms of economic policy, it also refrained from any far-reaching reforms before the late 1990s. Only after the departure of the more conservative pro-Serb wing in 1997 did the party begin to endorse a more liberal agenda, including close ties with Western Europe, democratic reforms and economic liberalisation (Bugajski 2002: 496–9). It gradually endorsed independence and began favouring Montenegrin identity over its earlier close ties to Serbia. In its programme it emphasises economic development, in particular in the field of tourism, and it endorses ethnic diversity and a civic state (*Demokratska partija socijalista* 2007).

However, it retained strong informal control over the administration and the economy, and many leading members, including its long-time president and Prime Minister (1991–1998, 2002–2007, 2008), and president (1998–2002), Milo Đukanović and his close associate at the party leadership, the president of the State Union of Serbia and Montenegro (2003–2006), Svetozar Marković, have been very influential and successful in private business.

Socialist People's Party (Socijalistička narodna partija, SNP)

The SNP was founded by Momir Bulatović after he lost the intra-party struggle in the DPS against Milo Đukanović in 1997. The party at first aligned itself closely with the Socialist Party of Serbia of Slobodan Milošević and pursued a similar mixture of social populism and affinity with Serb nationalism. Unlike the more Serb nationalist parties, it continued to support a distinct Montenegrin identity. After the fall of the Milošević regime in 2000, the more moderate wing of the party under Predrag Bulatović marginalised Momir Bulatović (no relation) and cooperated with the new Serbian democratic government at the Yugoslav level (Bugajski 2002: 499). Until 2006, the party remained the dominant pro-Yugoslav party. After the failure at the referendum, the party lost its dominance in the opposition to the Serbian List lead by the SNS and the PzP. Under the new leadership of Srđan Milić, the party's presidential candidate in 2008, the SNP sought to reinforce its moderate and pro-European credentials.

Thus, the SNP has emphasised the EU integration of Montenegro and abandoned its call for a joint state with Serbia. Instead, its main criticism of the government has focused on corruption and the latter's economic policy.[3] However, with the end of the joint state with Serbia, the party lost its defining feature; it could no longer pursue the joint state with Serbia as an effective political project, and no longer sought to cater for the Serb voters in Montenegro as did the SNS. As a result, the SNP lost its position as the largest opposition party and in the 2006 parliamentary and the 2008 presidential elections, it has been eclipsed by the SNS and the PzP.

*Social Democratic Party (*Socijaldemokratska partija*, SDP)*

The Social Democratic Party emerged out of parties affiliated with the Reformist Movement of the last Yugoslav Prime Minister, Ante Marković. It included some remnants from the League of Communists, which did not support the party's change of leadership initiated by Slobodan Milošević in 1989. The party was established in 1993 as a result of a merger of a number of small and regionally based reformist parties. The SDP supported Montenegrin independence and economic reforms (Bugajski 2002: 500–1). Together with the LSCG it was the main critic of the Serb nationalist policies of the early 1990s and opposed Montenegrin support for the war in Croatia.[4] It remained a small party, struggling to cross the threshold. After 1997, it became a close coalition partner of the DPS, participating in all governments since 1997, and it has not run independently in national/ republican elections. It has been a key force in the government coalition favouring Montenegrin independence, especially since the party has been headed by Ranko Krivokapić (since 2003). The party is a full member of the Socialist International and maintains close ties with other social democratic parties in the region.

Centrist and liberal parties

Amidst the polarisation between supporters and opponents of independence, there was little space for centrist policies. The PzP emerged as an alternative to this line of division, whereas the Liberal Alliance has been the most radical supporter of independence, combining Montenegrin nationalist rhetoric with rejection of exclusive nationalism and extremism.

*Movement for Change (*Pokret za promjene, *PzP)*

The Movement for Change emerged in 2006 out of the popular NGO Group for Changes (*Grupa za promjene*, GzP), led by the civil society activist Nebojša Medojević. It has modelled itself on the NGO and later party G17+ in Serbia, which sought to establish itself as a party of experts. Its main agenda has been a critique of the government for its economic policies and its involvement in corruption. The party programme focuses mainly on economic reforms and a break with the post-communist legacy (Pokret za Promjene 2006).

While many of its founding members were staunch supporters of independence and had been active in pro-independence parties earlier (such as SDP and LSCG), the PzP sought not to take sides in the debate but to appeal to both opponents and supporters of independence and to re-orient political debate. However, it has not been successful in making inroads in gathering support from DPS voters, but has split the opposition to the government.

*Liberal Party (*Liberalna stranka, *LS)*

The Liberal Party is the successor to the Liberal Alliance of Montenegro (*Liberalni Savez Crne Gore*, LSCG), which dissolved itself in March 2005. The LSCG had pursued a platform of independence since its foundation in 1991. It was one of the parties to emerge from the Reformist Forces of the last Yugoslav Prime Minister, Ante Marković. It was critical of the government and its support for Serbia. While it joined the government between 1998 and 2000 and supported a minority government in 2001, it remained critical of the DPS and Đukanović, and insisted on a referendum on independence.[5] It has also been associated with pro-independence institutions such as the Duklija Academy of Science and Arts (DANU) and the Montenegrin Orthodox Church. It sought to combine its support for Montenegrin nationalism with liberal policies (Bugajski 2002: 503–6). After 2002 the party formed coalitions at the local level with the SNP, opponents of Montenegrin independence, with the goal to end the dominance of the DPS. This, however, undermined its electoral basis. At a party congress in March 2005, the LSCG abolished itself. It is the only parliamentary party in the Western Balkans to abolish itself since the beginning of multi-party systems in 1990. The dissolution followed a corruption scandal and the split of the LS which was founded by former LSCG president, Miodrag Živković. The LS continued its support for independence while remaining at a critical distance towards the DPS and the official pro-independence campaign. The party's popular support declined from a peak in the 1990s as the DPS largely copied its party programme on independence. In the parliamentary elections in 2006, the LS formed a pre-election coalition with the Bosniak Party. The party platform emphasises economic reforms, EU integration and underlines its liberal orientation (*Liberalna partija* 2004), making its platform similar to the governing parties and some of the main opposition parties (PzP, SNP).

Conservative parties

The conservative party spectrum is occupied in the main by pro-Serbian parties. Most of them have drawn on a conservative electorate, often emphasising traditional values, close ties between the state, the Serb Orthodox Church and Serb nationalism.

People's Party (Narodna stranka, NS)

The NS was one of the main opposition parties in the 1990s, originally pursuing a Serb nationalist agenda with a staunchly anti-communist platform. It had close ties to the Serb Democratic Party (*Srpska demokratska stranka*, SDS) in Croatia and Bosnia and Herzegovina. It argued for Montenegro joining Serbia in a Greater Serbia. During the war in Bosnia and Herzegovina it moderated its position, largely under the influence of its founding president and writer, Novak Kilibarda. As such, in 1996, it formed an anti-DPS pre-election coalition with the LSCG and after Đukanović's break with Milošević, joined the first reformist DPS government 1998–2001. It lost some of the more nationalist vote to the SNS which split off in 1998, and to other more nationalist parties later on. Dragan Šoć, who replaced Kilibarda in 2000, and subsequent presidents have sought to re-affirm the conservative, pro-Serb aspects of the party, while keeping its distance from more extreme nationalist positions (Bugajski 2002: 506–7). This line has been largely maintained by Predrag Popović, who has headed the party since 2005. The party opposed Montenegrin independence during the referendum campaign and now promotes a conservative platform, emphasising the ethnic Serb identity in Montenegro and the role of the Serbian Orthodox Church; it also opposes Kosovo independence.

Democratic Serb Party (Demokratska Srpska stranka, DSS)

The Democratic Serb Party split off from the SNS after Božidar Bojović lost the election for party leader to Andrija Mandić. The party, lead by Ranko Kadić, has been a staunch opponent of independence and has formed close ties with the SNP and NS, i.e. the more moderate wing of the opponents of Montenegrin independence. Similar to the NS, it emphasises the Serb identity of Montenegro and has promoted a conservative political agenda. It has not run independently in national elections, and at the local level it has only achieved moderate results.

Democratic Party of Unity (Demokratska stranka jedinstva, DSJ)

The DSJ is a minor conservative party headed by Zoran Žižić, former Yugoslav Prime Minister (2000–2001) and member of the SNP. He coordinated the

Movement for European State Serbia and Montenegro, which was the main grouping leading the campaign against Montenegrin independence. He left the SNP when it adopted more moderate policies and aligned himself with the SNS.

*People's Socialist Party (*Narodna socijalistička stranka Crne Gore, *NSS)*

The NSS was formed by former president Momir Bulatović in 2001 after losing power in the SNP to the moderate reformist wing around Predrag Bulatović. The NSS failed to enter parliament until 2006 when it was part of the Serb List led by the SNS.

Radical right-wing parties

There has been limited support for extreme nationalist and radical right-wing parties. Only the Radical Party has been able to enter parliament in 1992 and again in 2006, however its basis remains limited. Some conservative and ethnic parties, especially the SNS, have sometimes taken radical nationalist positions.

*Serb Radical Party (*Srpska radikalna stranka dr. Vojislav Šešelj, *SRS)*

The SRS, an extreme Serb nationalist party, is part of the Serb List and represented in parliament. It is aligned with the Serb Radical Party in Serbia under the leadership of indicted war criminal Vojislav Šešelj, which combines nationalism (including a call for a Greater Serbia) with social populism. Throughout the 1990s, the Radical Party has been active in Montenegro, but managed to enter in parliament only in 1992, due to support from Serbia and the activities of para-military groups in Montenegro. Subsequently, the party has been weakened and suffered from a number of splits (Bugajski 2002: 508–9).

Ethnic parties

Ethnically defined parties have generally been less successful in Montenegro than in other countries of the former Yugoslavia. The main mainstream parties, which favoured Montenegrin independence, have been able to secure significant support from minorities. In particular the SDP has been able to gain votes among Bosniaks/Muslims, while a significant share of Albanians have voted for the DPS. Citizens who identified themselves as Serbs have in the past voted largely for parties favouring close ties with Serbia. Only since independence have these parties increasingly emphasised their ethnic Serb identity and in the case of the SNS distinguished it from the Montenegrin identity, as promoted by parties favouring statehood. As noted above, since 1998, Albanian ethnic parties have benefited from a special electoral unit which contains mostly Albanian polling stations. This has also led to a fragmentation of the Albanian vote into six different parties, three of which are represented in parliament.

*Serb People's Party (*Srpska narodna stranka, *SNS)*

The SNS split off from the NS in 1998, after the latter began supporting a more moderate platform and joined the government. The SNS, lead by Božidar Bojović until 2003 and since by Andrija Mandić, supported close ties with Serbia and a strong Serb nationalist line. The party belonged to the staunch opponents of Montenegrin independence and subsequently emerged as the main opposition party and the dominant force behind the Serb List (*Srpska lista*, SL). Since the referendum, it has positioned itself as a party representing the interests of the Serb community in Montenegro. The SNS has been attempting to combine endorsement of EU integration with a conservative platform of representing Serb national interests (*Srpska narodna stranka* 2007). It has formed close ties with New Serbia (*Nova Srbija*, NS), a conservative party in Serbia, and has emerged as a forceful critique of the Montenegrin government.

*Croat Civic Initiative (*Hrvatska građanska inicijativa, *HGI)*

The HGI was established in 2002 to represent the small Croat minority (about 1 per cent) in Montenegro (*Hrvatska građanska inicijativa* 2003). It has been able to gain seats in municipal assemblies of Tivat and Kotor, where most Croats live in Montenegro. As it would not be able to enter parliament independently, it formed a pre-election coalition with the DPS and gained one seat in parliament following the 2006 elections.

*Bosniak Party (*Bošnjačka Stranka, *BS)*

The BS was established shortly before the 2006 elections by the merger of four political parties representing the Bosniak minority. The main Muslim/Bosniak Party, the Party for Democratic Action, SDA, was able to gain representation in parliament in 1990, together with Albanian parties as part of the Democratic Coalition, and independently in 1996, but due to splits among Bosniak minority parties and strong support among Bosniak/Muslim voters for mainstream parties, especially the DPS, SDP and LSCG, the Bosniak parties failed to enter parliament until 2006. Under the leadership of Rafet Husović, the BS gained two seats in parliament as part of a pre-election coalition with the LS. The party is conservative and supports cross-border cooperation in the Sandžak region (Bošnjačka Stranka 2007).

*Democratic Alliance of Montenegro (*Demokratski savez u Crnoj Gori,
Lidhja Demokratike në Mal të Zi, *DSCG/LDMZ)*

The DSCG has been the first and long dominant Albanian minority party, led since its establishment in 1990 by Mehmet Bardhi. It has often taken nationalist positions, demanding a special status for Albanian inhabited regions and often criticising government policy towards minorities. Nevertheless, the party has supported the governing coalition and its members have held posts as deputy ministers (Lipsius 2008: 245; Bugajski 2002: 510–11).

*Democratic Union of Albanians (*Demokratska unija Albanaca, Unioni Demokratik i Shqiptarëve, *DUA/UDSH)*

The DUA, led by Ferhat Dinosha, has been a more moderate Albanian party, demanding cultural autonomy and in the main supporting the DPS governments since 1998. It has mostly been in control of the ministry for ethnic groups (since 2007 the Ministry for Human and Minority Rights) (Lipsius 2008: 245–6).

*Albanian Alternative (*Albanska Alternativa, Alternatives Shqiptare, *AA/AS)*

The Albanian Alternative was founded in the Albanian inhabited region of the capital Podgorica, Tuzi, in 2005. The AA was established as a civic group, primarily encompassing Catholic Albanian voters, who had often supported mainstream parties earlier (Lipsius 2008: 257). Its president Sinišaj Vaselj succeeded in 2006 to gain one seat for the group in parliament.

Conclusion

The party system of Montenegro remains unconsolidated. The DPS has been able to dominate the political system as opposition parties have increasingly fragmented. In the parliament elected in 2006, seven parties supported close ties to Serbia and represented Serb or pro-Serb voters. The role of ideology and programme remains subordinated to personality and differences on the question of identity. While the main line of division has shifted over the past decade, economic platforms and social policy have not been able to dominate electoral campaigns or programmes. Parties supporting continued ties with Serbia have been struggling to define their main policy positions since 2006. Currently no party actively supports the re-establishment of a joint state with Serbia, but pro-Serb parties do endorse closer ties with their neighbour. Some more moderate parties such as the PzP and SNP have focused on challenging the government on issues of corruption, while the more radical parties such as the SNS have sought to represent ethnic Serb interests and demand the protection of the Serb community as a constituent people in Montenegro. As the main line of confrontation has split the Montenegrin/Serb majority since 1990, minorities have often voted for mainstream parties, in particular parties supporting independence.

In addition to identity politics, some political parties have emphasised their opposition to the dominance of the DPS and associated nepotism and corruption. In particular, the PzP has been successful in channelling popular discontent associated with the visible wealth of a small economic–political elite. However, the rapid economic development since independence, largely driven by tourism and foreign investments, has been able to secure social peace, as sharply declining unemployment and rising salaries have brought greater prosperity to Montenegro.

Further development of the party system is going to depend largely on the dominance of the DPS. As long as the latter remains the largest party and continues to control government, many issues in the development of party platforms are likely to focus on support for or opposition to the DPS. However, if a change of government through elections were to come about, there would be potential for the development of alternative lines of orientation in the party spectrum. In addition to ideological distinctions, ethnic politics and the north–south divide (economic and cultural) are likely to remain or become relevant in the way political parties shape the agenda in Montenegro.

Notes

1 According to EU rules, at least 55 per cent had to vote in favour of independence and turnout had to exceed 50 per cent.
2 From 1992 to 2006, one seat was allocated for every 6,000 voters, but the 2007 constitution fixed the number of seats at 81.
3 www.snp.cg.yu/strana.asp?kat=1&id=394   see   also   www.srdjanmilic.com/strana.php?pid=55.
4 www.sdp.cg.yu/index1.php?module=1&sub=2.
5 See the website of the dissolved LSCG www.lscg.org/content/index2.asp.

9   Regional party systems in Serbia

Daniel Bochsler

Despite the high centralisation of the State, Serbia has developed a vivid political scene in its regions, including a wealth of political parties, namely in the three ethnically heterogeneous regions Vojvodina, Sandžak, and Preševo Valley. While previous work on the Serbian political landscape has concentrated on the national political landscape of Serbia (Komšić 2003; Goati 2004, 2006; Lutovac 2005; Bieber 2003b, etc.), regional parties have often been reduced to short paragraphs or footnotes, possibly because they appear to be not very crucial players on the national political level. Whereas the study of regionalism and regional party systems in many European countries has flourished in recent years (e.g. Heller 2002; Ishiyama 2002; De Winter and Türsan 1998, etc.), there is no such work known to the author on the Serbian case. Nevertheless, the study of regional parties in Serbia appears important because of two aspects. First, it might give new suggestions for research on territorial differences in party systems, such as the study of the importance of territorial ethnic divisions for party formation and electoral behaviour. Second, regional parties play an important part in Serbian political life, and should therefore be looked at more closely. The most important ethno-regional and regional parties in Serbia exist in Vojvodina, followed by the Sandžak, and then the Preševo Valley.

Since the emergence of regional parties is to a large extent (but not exclusively) related to the ethnic structure of the country, and to territorially concentrated ethnic groups, this chapter also offers a view on ethnically motivated party formation and electoral behaviour in Serbia. (For a view of other, not ethnicity- or region-related aspects, I refer to the chapter on Serbian parties in this book.) In this chapter, I first discuss the political institutions and social conflicts that are relevant for the creation of regional and ethno-regional parties. Building on this institutional and socio-economic framework, I discuss how territorial differences in the Serbian party system have developed since 1992, before having a closer look at the regional parties which play a role in the post-authoritarian period in Serbia, starting in 2000.

The institutional and socio-economic framework

Recently, two major contributions have proposed theoretical perspectives for the study of regional differences in party systems (Chhibber and Kollman 2004;

Caramani 2004). Both look at *party nationalisation*, which is defined as the homogeneity of the party system and party strengths across the territory. Strong regional and local parties and political organisations are understood as the contrary of a nationalised party system. In this section, the main arguments of these schools are reviewed, and their relevance is discussed for the Serbian case. This will help us to come up with theoretically based expectations about the occurrence and relevance of regional parties in Serbia.

The major school in this field contends that party nationalisation is a consequence of government institutions that incite the formation of a national party system. Chhibber and Kollman (2004: 222) relate party nationalisation mainly to the degree of centralisation of the government. In their view, when the main competences lie with the central government, then national political issues will dominate elections: 'Voters are more likely to support national political parties as the national government becomes more important in their lives', so that 'local parties are abandoned altogether and disappear'. On the other hand, decentralised political structures and most importantly substantial policy competences at lower levels of government, help to nurture local and regional parties that can make a difference to their voters on the local or regional level.

In contrast to this school, Caramani (2004) argues instead for a cleavage-based view of party nationalisation. In this approach, a party system becomes nationalised when the main social and economic divides become national in their character, thus overriding (almost) all territorial unities. This is typically the case for economic cleavage, which – among other things – explains the development of highly nationalised party systems in many West European party systems in the nineteenth and early twentieth centuries. Territorially based conflicts, however, would explain why a party system might not become nationalised, and why regional parties emerge.

Aside from these views, electoral systems have been discussed as an institutional feature that can shape the format of a party system, and, among other things, contribute to the nationalisation of party systems, or in contrast to the emergence of regional parties (Cox 1999; Van Cott 2003; Bochsler 2006).

The highly centralised Serbian institutional framework is rather unfavourable to the creation and success of regional parties. Like most post-communist countries in Europe, Serbia inherited a rather centralised administrative structure. The subnational level of administration relies on two levels, and on the special status of the Vojvodina region. On the one hand, Serbia consists of 144 rather large municipalities, with their own elected municipal assemblies and executive bodies. On the other hand, these municipalities are aggregated in 24 districts that do not have any important tasks, or any elected institutions. The capital city Belgrade is its own 25th district, with a city parliament and a mayor, and consists of 16 city municipalities.[1] The Northern Serbian province of Vojvodina was accorded broad autonomy under the Yugoslav constitution of 1974, and had almost the same competences as the republics. As in Kosovo, this autonomy was revoked in 1989, and less wide-ranging autonomy statutes were introduced only 12 years later. Vojvodina has two million inhabitants (27 per cent of the Serbian population), and its own directly elected parliamentary assembly and executive body.

After an 'omnibus law' that moved some of the competences back to the Vojvodina region and a revision of the Law on Local Self-Governance in 2001–2002, the policy competences and financial situation of the Serbian municipalities and Vojvodina have improved, but they still lack the funds to implement their own policies. The degree of financial decentralisation is estimated at 27 per cent: the Vojvodina region managed about 4.7 per cent of the overall budget, and the municipal level about 22.3 per cent, while the central government administers the remaining 73.0 per cent (in 2002/3, numbers taken from Marcou 2005: 41).

Apart from municipalities and the Vojvodina regions, the National Minority Councils offer a further political space where (ethno-)regional parties can be active. The Hungarian minority was the first to constitute such a body and by 2006, 14 ethnic minorities – all the minorities in Serbia with a substantial number of members, and a few extremely small minorities – had created such a body, except for the Albanian minority (Bašić and Crnjanski 2006: 90–4), but the competences of the Minority Councils remain unclear, and their funds limited. Because these councils are neither territorially based nor markedly dominated by political parties, they are outside the focus of this article.

Following Chhibber's and Kollman's view, the low level of decentralisation in Serbia should give only weak incentives for the creation of strong regional parties. But even if there is a correlation in many countries between decentralisation and regionalisation of the party system (Harbers 2008), this view is not uncontested: the causality may in fact be inverted. Decentralisation does not incite regional parties; instead, regional parties demand decentralisation (Caramani 2004). The processes of decentralisation in Central and Eastern Europe support this inverted causality (Bochsler 2006).

In this view, regional parties tend to emerge more along territorially-based social and economic differences (Caramani 2004) than along boundaries of subnational territorial units. This second approach borrows elements of the cleavage approach by Lipset and Rokkan (1967), which argues that a party system is the product of the underlying structure of social conflicts.

Serbia offers a number of differences that might form the basis for politicised social cleavages with a territorial dimension. On one hand, the Serbian regions bear a diverse cultural and historical heritage and economic power. When the rest of Serbia was under Ottoman rule, Vojvodina was part of the Kingdom of Hungary until the sixteenth century, and then, after two centuries under Ottoman rule, it was part of the Habsburg Empire, from the early eighteenth century until the First World War. The difference between Austro-Hungarian and Turkish influences is still visible today in local identities, in cultural aspects, and local dialects. Economically, the Vojvodina region (after the capital Belgrade) is still ahead of Central and Southern Serbia. And finally, the Austro-Hungarian experience contributed to shaping the ethnic structure of Vojvodina. It is ethnically much richer than the rather homogeneous central parts of Serbia,[2] and a number of ethnic groups that lived in the Austro-Hungarian empire now live in Vojvodina, mainly the Hungarian minority, followed by the Slovaks (see below for details). Ethnic engineering by Slobodan Milošević, who resettled ethnic Serbian refugees from Bosnia in Vojvodina, and the flight of many members of ethnic minorities during this period, changed the ethnic structure of Vojvodina, and allegedly contributed to ethnic tensions in the region (Kerenji 2005: 363). Finally, several smaller regions in Southern Serbia are distinguished by their ethnic structure: The Preševo Valley, at the border between Macedonia and Kosovo in Southern Serbia, is predominantly populated by ethnic Albanians. The Sandžak region, located partly in Serbia, partly in Montenegro, and connecting Bosnia and Kosovo, is home to the Bosniak minority, while ethnic Bulgarians constitute the local majority in the municipality Bosilegrad and the single largest community in the town Dimitrovgrad, both in the south-east near the Bulgarian border (see OSCE 2008). Both of these historic–cultural divides, and the partly territorially based ethnic divides, thus provide a basis for the emergence of regional differences in the party system.

Furthermore, we would expect that due to the high degree of centralisation and the importance of territorial divides, political pressure might be created for an enhancement of regional and local self-government. In that case the importance of strong autonomous institutions for the ethnic minorities becomes even more relevant, because in Serbia the state still plays a role in many spheres which are relevant for the minorities. For instance, the Serbian state (on all its levels) is (still) highly involved in public information: a slight majority of media outlets in minority languages are state-controlled, mostly funded by municipalities or the autonomous minority councils (*Fond za otvoreno društvo* 2007). Due to the importance of territorial divisions, and reluctant decentralisation in Serbia, we might ask whether the link between decentralisation and regional parties works as it does in other countries of the region, in the opposite manner to that suggested by Chhibber and Kollman. It is not necessarily the level of decentralisation that shapes the party system but, on the contrary, territorial social divides may provide the basis for mobilisation of those regional parties calling for decentralisation.

A third element worth mentioning that might affect the way regional political differences translate into the territorial structure of the party system, is the national electoral system. In the Serbian case, the electoral reform of 2000 appears to have a peculiar effect. The district-based system was abolished, and a new single countrywide electoral district was introduced; however, it is not the *size* of this electoral district that directly affects the chances of regional parties.[3] Rather, the change in the district structure also changed the effect of the legal threshold on the formation of regional parties. Already in the elections in the 1990s, a legal threshold of 5 per cent was applied on the share of the vote a party wins in the electoral district. With the electoral reform of 2000 and the introduction of the single nationwide electoral district, the 5 per cent threshold was applied at the national level. While it is easy for a regional party to pass the 5 per cent threshold in a *regional* district, 5 per cent *on the national level* is very difficult to achieve. As a consequence, regional parties no longer had a chance of being represented in parliament on their own, and instead joined electoral alliances. Only since the 2007 elections has the threshold been lifted for parties of ethnic minorities, but the law fails to define what is such an ethnic minority party (OSCE/ODIHR 2007a).

Finally, political parties in Serbia are highly centralised. Internal party democracy and local autonomy are not very developed (Goati 2004: 110–11, 127–9, 133), and the electoral system provides closed national lists so that the voters do not have the chance to favour candidates from their own region. Even if all the major national parties except the Serbian Radical Party (SRS) have their own Vojvodina organisation,[4] internal party autonomy is rather limited. The party leadership can decide who will occupy over two-thirds of the mandates in their parliamentary group ex post, irrespective of their order on the electoral list.[5] This is aggravated because of the parliamentary practice that mandates are not free; rather, most parties demand undated letters of resignation from every MP (Orlović 2006: 110), so that the party leadership can put elected MPs under pressure. In a system with such centralised power, it is difficult for local branches to follow their own policies, and parties can hardly credibly differentiate their programme according to regional differences in voter preferences. We might expect that as a consequence of the high degree of centralisation of the national parties, specific regional interests can only be expressed by specific regional parties, and not by the regional branches of national parties. Since party and electoral campaign financing is mostly concentrated on parties which are competing in national elections, local and regional parties have only a small state-funded income (Milosavljević 2005).[6]

Territorial heterogeneity in national elections

Before looking at the individual cases of regional parties, I will describe the territorial heterogeneity of the party *system* of Serbia. Measures of heterogeneity allow us to quantify the differences and similarities of party strength across the territory, and to compare them with other cases. In the early 1990s, there were still common Yugoslav elections to the Federal Assembly of the Federal Republic of Yugoslavia (FRY, including Serbia and Montenegro at the time). This allows a calculation of heterogeneity on the party system of FRY as a whole, as opposed to the heterogeneity of the Serbian party system. I employ the standardised party nationalisation score (Bochsler 2008a) and look at the electoral results of the national parliament. Since political parties compete either in Serbia or in Montenegro, values for the whole FRY reveal much stronger territorial differences than values only for Serbia (without Montenegro). In the case of perfect homogeneity across the territory, the employed measure would indicate a value of 1.00. This maximum is hardly ever reached, but the 2000 elections in Serbia, with a score of 0.94, came close to a very high level of party nationalisation (see Table 9.1). Otherwise, the party nationalisation score was around 0.85 to 0.87. This is a value that typically emerges in countries with few territorial differences, such as Bulgaria, Slovenia or Poland. It is higher than in countries with a general territorial split in the party system – such as was the case for FRY, whereas the Montenegrin party system was completely different from the Serbian one, reflected through lower levels of nationalisation on the FRY party system about 0.79–0.82.

The development of party nationalisation shall be discussed, and linked to aspects of party competition and of the electoral system. The main aspects that explain variance in party system nationalisation across the years are the legal electoral threshold and electoral coalitions.

The impact of the legal threshold

The first aspect to discuss is the legal electoral threshold of 5 per cent. It was already enacted in the 1990s and applied to electoral districts. This allowed Hungarians, Bosniaks, and Albanians to pass the threshold in the districts where they were concentrated. However, only the Hungarian minority parties had a constant representation in the Serbian parliament. In 1993 an alliance of two Albanian minority parties (Party of Democratic Action and Democratic Party of Albanians) won two mandates, and in 1997 one mandate was won by the Democratic Coalition Preševo-Bujanovac. Also, after discontinuing their electoral boycott in 1997, the Bosniak parties allied as '*Lista za Sandžak*' and won three parliamentary mandates. The shifting of the legal threshold in 2000 from the local to the national level excluded all these ethno-regional parties from running independently in elections. This has contributed to an increase in party nationalisation this

Table 9.1 Development of the party system nationalisation in the Federal Republic of Yugoslavia and in Serbia

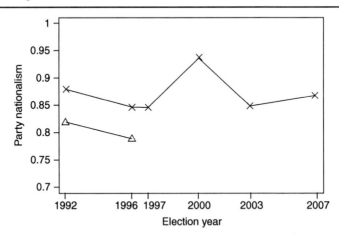

	1992	*1996*	*1997*	*2000*	*2003*	*2007*
FR Yugoslavia	0.82	0.79				
Serbia	0.88	0.85	0.85	0.94	0.85	0.87

Source: Bochsler 2009.

year. However, this does not necessarily mean that the regional parties have disappeared. As shall be shown later in detail, the introduction of a national legal threshold hinders regional parties from competing on their own in national elections, but they can still form electoral alliances, and remain represented in local and regional institutions. The consequences of the national legal threshold were partly reversed in 2007, when the threshold was lifted for parties of ethnic minorities, which explains why many ethno-regional parties run separately and that the degree of nationalisation has dropped.

The formation of an opposition umbrella coalition in 2000

The second reason, besides the electoral system, that explains the change in party nationalisation is the formation of a broad umbrella coalition in the 2000 elections. The elections in that year were exceptional, similar to the democratising elections in almost all post-communist countries in Europe. Almost all the democratically oriented opposition parties ran jointly within a broad umbrella coalition called Democratic Opposition of Serbia (*Demokratska opozicija Srbije*, DOS). This coalition included many regional parties, namely the Hungarian minority party SVM, the Bosniak minority SDP, and the regional Vojvodina parties LSV, RV and the short-living Vojvodina Coalition (*Koalicrja Vojvodine*, KV) (Goati 2006: 84). Since the conflict between the old regime and the democratic reformers is not territorially based, the umbrella coalition gathered a very homogeneous vote throughout the territory. After the elections, such umbrella coalitions everywhere quickly split up; Serbia is no exception to this rule, and thus party nationalisation has dropped again.

Coalition of regional parties

A very different type of coalition was formed in the subsequent elections in 2003, explaining a drop in party system nationalisation. In this election, ethnic minority and regional parties (namely the Vojvodina Party LSV and the Šumadija Party *'Liga za Šumadiju'*, see below) attempted to pass the electoral threshold jointly, forming a broad coalition under the label Together for Tolerance (*Zajedno za toleranciju*, ZZT). Although they failed to reach the necessary 5 per cent of the vote, their participation in elections has led to heterogeneity in the support level across Serbia: the party nationalisation degree of ZZT was about 0.45 (and has further negatively affected the party nationalisation degree of parties that are in electoral competition with ethnic and regional parties, which accordingly have lost votes in the regions where ZZT was strong). The exclusion of ZZT by the 5 per cent threshold becomes very substantial when we look at the numbers of *wasted votes* (votes cast for parties that fail to gain representation) by municipality. The national legal threshold has led to a fairly unequal representation of voters across the territory in parliament. In 13 municipalities with strong Hungarian or Bosniak minorities, the national legal threshold has – mainly due to the ZZT failure, and to a lesser extent due to the lack of success by other regional or small parties – excluded from between 30 per cent to 70 per cent of the voters from being represented in parliament. In other municipalities, where the ZZT was weaker (below 10 per cent), the rate of wasted votes was only about 12 per cent. The failure of the ZZT may have contributed to the exemption of ethnic minority parties from the threshold requirement after the 2003 elections (Bašić and Crnjanski 2006: 58).

(De)centralisation policies of parties in the National Assembly

The theoretically relevant question of the relationship between the nationalisation of the party system and decentralisation makes it worthwhile to devote some attention to party policies regarding decentralisation.[7] In regard to the autonomy of the Vojvodina region, this question separates the Serbian parties. After the victory of the Democratic Opposition in 2000, the main parties of the 'Democratic' bloc, the Democratic Party (*Demokratska stranka*, DS) and the Democratic Party of Serbia (*Demokratska stranka Srbije*, DSS), shifted their position regarding the autonomy of Vojvodina. In the 1990s both parties were in favour of a limited autonomy, but later the DS approved territorial autonomy for Vojvodina, with a full institutional system, but without specifying the policy competences that should be decentralised. In 2001 the DSS introduced a regionalist concept that did not explicitly mention Vojvodina, and the party position remained somewhat ambiguous; it was afraid of any elements that might be seen as limited statehood for autonomous regions. The reformist G17+ party expressed support for an expansion of the autonomous status of Vojvodina. However, this positioning was de facto reversed in 2006, when all three parties supported the new Serbian constitution establishing a more restrictive centralisation of the Serbian state, mainly as a concession to the nationalist parties (International Crisis Group 2006b: 4). The parties related to the Milošević regime, the Socialist (*Socijalistička partija Srbije*, SPS) and the Radical Party (*Srpska radikalna stranka*, SRS), reject any autonomy and favour a unitary state. Claims for territorial autonomy, particularly if they come from multi-ethnic areas, are often interpreted as the first steps towards separatism, both by the nationalist parties and by the media.

The lack of a particularly strong advocate for regional autonomies among the national parties in Serbia creates an opportunity for regional and ethnic minority parties to campaign on cultural and socio-economic differences, by pressuring for increased decentralisation. Due to the change in the electoral system, no such party could gain any mandates in the national parliament on its own in the 2000 and 2003 elections, but nevertheless they could retain a certain relevance in the Serbian party system. On the one hand, it allows them to join electoral alliances, so that a few members of regional parties became members of the national parliament on the lists of mainstream parties, and become integrated in the caucus of the list on which they became elected. On the other hand, regional and ethnic parties have retained power in the regional and local representative bodies, as will be shown in the next section.

Regional parties in Serbia

While regional parties have been only marginally represented in the Serbian national assembly, they have clearly shaped the political landscape in the regional and local institutions. Despite the limited importance of lower levels of administration, quite a colourful collection of ethno-regional and regional parties has developed. Ethno-regional parties are based on the support of ethnic minority groups. Three out of the four largest ethnic minorities in Serbia, the Hungarians (in the Vojvodina region), Albanians (in the Preševo valley), and Bosniaks (in the Sandžak region), have the richest set of relevant parties, but the multi-ethnic Vojvodina region also counts a few non-ethnically related regional parties, and parties of smaller minorities that are active mostly at the local level.

Three of the aspects shown in this section appear particularly relevant with regards to the underlying theoretical aspects. The first aspect shows how despite low decentralisation, regional parties are formed along ethnic divides and along political issues that create territorial divides in Serbian politics. Second, I argue that one of the main issues of regional political parties is the claim for territorial autonomy. Their strength partly relies on the opposition of the national parties to these claims, and this supports the view that decentralisation might rather be initiated by regional parties than vice versa. And third, a comparison of electoral results at the local and national level reveals the importance of local and regional institutions for the representation of local and regional parties, especially in cases where the electoral system hinders their representation in national institutions. In this section, I will discuss ethno-regional and regional parties that are active in the three mentioned regions of Serbia, and discuss their coalition strategies.

Vojvodina

Vojvodina is often portrayed as a multi-ethnic oasis in Serbia, with different historical–cultural roots, and the economic situation gives Vojvodina a particular profile. This is reflected politically as well in that there are a number of regional and ethnic parties that compete exclusively in Vojvodina. The political scene of the region will be discussed here with a view to the elections to the Assembly of Vojvodina, the Vojvodina parties' share of the vote in national parliamentary elections and their representation in the national parliament. Vojvodina is rich in its own parties, both those created along ethnic lines as well as those with a non-ethnic orientation. Unlike most Serbian mainstream parties, they advocate tolerance towards ethnic minorities and an improvement of their rights, and focus on decentralisation and territorial autonomy.

In the elections to the Assembly of the Vojvodina region (APV) in the years 1992–2000, the Socialist Party of Serbia dominated the political scene, partly due to the majoritarian electoral system that gave an advantage to the largest party and disadvantaged the non-unified democratic opposition. Only in the 2000 elections did the picture change, with DOS and the ethno-regional parties winning 117 of the 120 seats; this time the democratic victory was magnified by the majority vote system (Goati 2001: 248–9). The strength of the individual opposition parties and the regional parties is difficult to estimate for the elections before 2000, because they often formed electoral coalitions. In the 2004 elections to the APV, the electoral system was changed to a mixed non-compensatory electoral system,[8] with 60 mandates in each tier, so the strength of individual national parties and ethno-regional parties was for the first time clearly identifiable. Overall, the latter obtained some 20 per cent of the votes and seats in the Vojvodina elections (see Table 9.2). Furthermore, they became important players in many municipal governments.

In the national parliamentary elections, the vote shares of all large national parties in Vojvodina were lower than in the rest of Serbia (see chapter on Serbia in this volume),[9] with only one exception, the Serbian Radical Party. It is often argued that the SRS gets substantial support from the ethnic Serb refugees from Croatia and Bosnia, who settled in Vojvodina in the 1990s. Generally it is observed that through the polarisation of the ethnic conflict in multi-ethnic areas, the less radical parties lose votes to the Serbian Radical Party, which takes more radical stances on ethnic issues (Bochsler 2007a; Stefanovic 2008). Compared to the results in the local and regional elections, the ethno-regional parties get lower vote shares in national parliamentary elections. On the one hand, national parties might be more visible with their national campaigns in national elections; on the other hand, the national legal threshold of 5 per cent has hindered regional parties and (until 2007) ethnic parties from competing on their own.

Before discussing the ethnically oriented parties in detail, let us look at the non-ethnic regional parties. The largest party in this field is the League of Vojvodina Social Democrats (*Liga socijaldemokrata Vojvodine*, LSV), followed by the Vojvodina Reformists (*Reformisti Vojvodine*, RV), which merged in 2005 with smaller parties into the Vojvodina Party (*Vojvođanska stranka*, VP) (Goati 2006: 258). The most common denominator is an accent on strong regional autonomy and decentralisation as a main goal and priority of the parties' programs.[10] Together with two other non-ethnic parties, they asked in 1997 for broad autonomy for the Vojvodina region.[11] In a 1999 declaration the LSV demanded the federalisation of Serbia (Komšić 2007: 272–3). Unlike the national parties, the Vojvodina regionalist parties rejected the new constitution in 2006, due to its regressive measures on regional autonomy.

Otherwise, both the LSV and RV(VP) are among the democratically oriented parties. Some participated in the DOS alliance in 2000, and both declare themselves to be Social Democrats.[12] Mihić (2002, 2005) characterises LSV and RV supporters as standing politically close to the DS and G17+. They are opposed to social authoritarianism, tolerant on ethnic questions, favour a normalisation of relations with neighbouring states, and are strongly pro-European. LSV supporters seem to be left wing on welfare issues. The LSV electorate is ethnically mixed; ethnic identities are less important to average LSV supporters, but on the other hand they stress their Vojvodina identity.[13] They have remained weak in their national representative institutions, and never became dominant in regional

Table 9.2 Results of the elections to the autonomous assembly of the Vojvodina region, 2004, compared to the vote shares in the Vojvodina region in the national parliamentary elections of 2003

	Assembly of the Vojvodina region (APV) elections 2004				Local elections 2004		National parliamentary elections	
	PR seats	District seats	Seat share %	Vote share (PR) %	Local mayors	Seats in local assemblies	2003, vote share in Vojvodina %	2007, vote share in Vojvodina %
National parties								
DS	15	20	29.2	22.3	9[c]	338	9.9	24.1
SRS	21	15	30.0	30.4	14	442	31.9	32.3
SPS	4	4	6.7	6.0	3[c]	124[c]	5.1	4.0
DSS	4	2	5.0	7.0	2	112	12.2	9.9
PSS	4	3	5.8	6.9	1	101		1.7
G17+	–	2	1.7	5.0	2	89	13.6	6.3
'Clean hands Vojvodina'	–	–	–	2.4	–	15 (SPO)[b]	3.8 (SPO/NS) with SPO	2.1 (SPO) with DSS
NS	–	–	–	1.4	–	5		
Regional and ethnic parties								
SVM	6	5	9.2	8.8	2	73	13.0 (ZZT) partly in ZZT	5.0
Coalition 'Together for Vojvodina'[a]	6	1	5.8	9.8	–	74 (LSV)[c]		8.1 (with LDP)
RV	–	2	1.7	–	2	9	1.7 (with SDP and others)	–
DSVM	–	1	0.8	–	–	15	–	1.2 (with DZVM)
DZVM	–	–	–	–	–	13	–	–
Local coalitions and local citizens' groups	–	5	4.2	–	8	–	–	–
Others	–	–	–	–	2	313	8.8	5.3
Overall	60	60	100 (120)	100	45	1666	100	100

Sources: Vojvodina Government, Cesid, Statistical Yearbook of Serbia 2005, my own corrections for local coalitions and my own calculations.

Notes

a Vojvođanska unija – Vojvodina moj dom, Liga socijaldemokrata Vojvodine, Demokratska Vojvodina, Unija socijalista Vojvodine, Vojvodanski pokret, Građanski savez Srbije i So-jjademokratska unija.

b SPO, Vojvodina reformists.

c Three of the DS mayors were elected for a coalition of DS and SVM; one of the SPS mayors was elected in a coalition with SNS. The SPS figures for the local assembly include six members elected on a common list with SNS, and eight elected on SNS lists; four of the SPO local deputies were elected in coalitions with NS. The numbers for LSV include four members that were jointly elected in a broad coalition with minor parties.

politics, but they obtained 9.8 per cent of the PR votes in the 2004 regional elections and three direct seats, and are included in governing coalitions at the local and regional level in Vojvodina (see Table 9.2).

A second set of regional parties is related to ethnic minorities.[14] However, they are not the exclusive representatives of ethnic minorities, since the regional and some of the national non-ethnic parties also compete for the votes of minorities, and occasionally include minority members on their electoral lists (Lutovac 2007). The minority parties will now be discussed for the different minority groups living in Vojvodina.

The **Hungarians** are the largest ethnic minority in Serbia. They account for 4.0 per cent of the Serbian population, and almost all live in Vojvodina, where they account for 14.3 per cent of the population. They organised back in 1990 under the Democratic Union of the Vojvodina Hungarians (*Demokratska zajedinca Vojvođanskih Mađara*, DZVM). This party, led by András Ágoston, radicalised during the first year under increasing Serbian repression, and demanded a strong autonomy for Hungarians in Serbia, similar to the one that was being discussed in peace plans for Serbs in Croatia and Bosnia at this time (Jenne 2004: 742). Since Ágoston was perceived as too radical, several parties split off in 1994. One of those, the Union of the Vojvodina Hungarians (*Savez Vojvođanskih Mađara*, SVM), under the moderate Subotica mayor Jószef Kasza, became the dominant party of the Hungarian minority (Jenne 2004: 743). In 1997, the Democratic Party of the Vojvodina Hungarians (*Demokratska stranka Vojvođanskih Mađara*, DSVM) broke away from the DZVM (Bašić and Crnjanski 2006: 44).

The Hungarian minority parties are distinct from the previously discussed non-ethnic regional parties not only because of their exclusive orientation towards ethnic minority voters, but also with regards to their decentralisation programme. The non-ethnic parties favour substantial autonomy for the whole Vojvodina region, and SVM supports this position, while DZVM considers this a Serbian issue in which the ethnic Hungarians should not be involved.[15] However, the Hungarian parties do not put their main focus on the question of Vojvodina autonomy, but rather demand a substantial political and cultural autonomy for the eight municipalities with a high concentration of ethnic Hungarians in Northern Vojvodina. However, they have never adopted separatist claims. On most issues, SVM supporters are politically close to LSV voters (Mihić 2005), while the other parties are too small to be polled.

In the current decade the SVM has been the most relevant representative of the Hungarian minority. In the Serbian parliament of 2000, it received six seats as part of DOS, and its leader Kasza became deputy Prime Minister in charge of minority affairs and local governments (Jenne 2004: 744). Three years later the SVM failed in the national parliamentary elections (being part of the failed ZZT alliance); in 2007 it won three seats on its own list. In the 2004 elections to the Vojvodina assembly, the party won 8.8 per cent of the vote and became part of the governing coalition. And in the municipal elections of 2004, SVM was by far the strongest of all Hungarian parties, though both the other Hungarian parties were also able to win a few mandates in local assemblies (see Table 9.2).

Furthermore, the DSVM won one seat in the Vojvodina assembly in 2004 in one of the majority districts. Instead of presenting a common candidate in the 2008 Serbian presidential elections, the Hungarian minority parties refused to cooperate with each other.

The parties of other minorities were active more on the local level, or competed on the lists of mainstream parties.

Slovaks (0.8 per cent in Serbia; 2.8 per cent in Vojvodina) are the second-largest minority in Vojvodina, and quite a large minority in municipalities such as Kovačica or Bački Petrovac (where they are the single largest ethnic group), and a few other places. In the 2004 local elections, the Slovak People's Party (*Slovačka narodna stranka*), obtained two out of 31 mandates in the Bački Petrovac assembly. However, in municipalities with a high share of Slovaks, they mainly participate in political life through other parties with non-ethnic orientations. The head of the Slovak minority council and the ethnic Slovak mayor of Bački Petrovac were elected to the national assembly in 2007 as members of the DS.

The **Croat** minority (0.9 per cent of the Serbian population, 2.7 per cent in Vojvodina) live in a few parts of Vojvodina, namely in the districts of Northern Bačka and Srem. They form the Democratic Union of Croats in Vojvodina (*Demokratski savez Hrvata u Vojvodini, DSHV*). The party gained access to the Vojvodina assembly in 2004, where it forms a local governing coalition with SVM and DS, and to the national parliament in 2007 with one of three deputies elected on the DS list.[16] In the 2003 elections to the national parliament, the party competed on the unsuccessful minority parties' list.

Ethnic **Romanians** (0.5 per cent in Serbia, 1.5 per cent in Vojvodina) are concentrated in a number of municipalities in the Banat (South-Eastern Vojvodina), namely in Alibunar, Zrenjanin, Vršac, Kovačica, Kovin, Apatin and Žitište. There is a related minority of **Vlachs** (0.5 per cent in Serbia, not present in Vojvodina) who live mainly in Eastern Serbia and speak a Romanian dialect; their own ethnic status is disputed by the ethnic Romanians.[17] The Romanians and Vlachs share a common national minority council, and some minority parties address both Romanians and Vlachs jointly. The Movement of Romanians and Vlachs in Yugoslavia (*Pokret Rumuna i Vlaha u Srbiji*) competed in 2003 on the list of a minor political party for the national parliament, but without gaining any seats. In the national minority council two marginal parties are represented: the Alliance of Romanians from Vojvodina (*Alijansa Vojvođanskih Rumuna*), and the Democratic Union of Romanians (*Demokratski savez Rumuna*). Romanians and Vlachs tend to get elected on the lists of parties with a non-ethnic orientation, most notably in the town of Alibunar in Vojvodina on the DS, DSS and G17+ list.

The **Bunjevac** (0.3 per cent in Serbia, 1.0 per cent in Vojvodina) live mostly in the towns of Sombor and Subotica. They have a specific regional origin in the Dinara mountains (on the border between Croatia and Bosnia, cf. OSCE 2008), but as Croats they are Roman Catholics, and they speak the same language, so they are often perceived to be close to ethnic Croats. Bunjevac have their own national minority council, and they formed their own Bunjevac Party

(*Bunjevačka stranka*). While this party has remained without any larger electoral success, a descendant of a Bunjevac family, Oliver Dulić, became speaker of parliament in 2007, elected on the DS list. It might be indicative of the complexity of ethnic identities in the region that Dulić himself says that in his view, the Bunjevac belong rather to the Croats, but he declares himself to be a 'child of a Yugoslav family and a big "Yugo-nostalgic"'.[18]

Other, smaller minorities in Vojvodina are not represented by their own parties, or they are too marginal to be individually discussed.

At the local and regional level, the ethnic minority parties and the regional parties in Vojvodina cooperate mostly with DS and G17+, not least in the Vojvodina government: after 2000, the DOS alliance formed the Serbian government (however, the DSS quit the government and the alliance in 2001, both at the national and at the regional level). After the 2004 elections a coalition was formed of almost the same parties, namely DS, SVM, the LSV coalition Together for Vojvodina (*Zajedno za Vojvodinu*), and the Movement of Serbian Force (*Pokret snage Srbije*, PSS) (Goati 2006: 79).

The DS and SVM have cooperated closely on the local and regional level, and occasionally presented joint candidates in local elections, particularly in majoritarian elections. However, the two parties are fierce competitors for the same votes in areas that are ethnically mainly Hungarian (Lutovac 2007: 232). But cooperation is not limited to the democratically oriented parties. In the Bečej municipality, the DZVM enabled the Serbian Radicals to lead a governing coalition after 2004.[19]

Sandžak

Sandžak is a region covering 11 municipalities in both South-West Serbia and North-East Montenegro, between Kosovo and Bosnia.[20] The region is populated mostly by the Bosniak minority, who are Muslims speaking Serbo-Croat, and are the largest ethnic group in neighbouring Bosnia. The Serbian part of Sandžak consists of six municipalities that have been split into two districts, so that the Bosniaks are in a majority in neither (Schmidt 1996). Apart from the power in the municipalities, the Bosniak minority is also organised in the Bosniak National Council.

The first Bosniak party was organised in 1990 as a local branch of the dominant party of Bosniaks in Bosnia and Herzegovina, the Party of Democratic Action (*Stranka demokratske akcije*, SDA). With Bosnia's independence from Yugoslavia in 1992, the Sandžak SDA became its own organisation. The party, and its leader Sulejman Ugljanin, remained the dominant part of the umbrella organisation List for Sandžak (*Lista za Sandžak*) that was formed later. A referendum for political autonomy for the Sandžak region, organised by the SDA in 1991, affected and still affects the relations towards the Bosniak political organisations to this day. Ugljanin was accused of engineering Sandžak's secession from Serbia (ICG 1998: 8), even if all the relevant Bosniak leaders denied this (Bašić 2002: 58–9). In the same year, the Muslim National Council of Sandžak (*Muslimansko nacionalno vijeće Sandžaka*, MNVS) was formed as the representative body of the Bosniaks in the Sandžak region, later to be renamed as the Bosnian National Council of Sandžak (*Bošnjačko nacionalno vijeće Sandžaka*, BNVS).

In 1995, a leading member of the party, Rasim Ljajić, broke away and formed his own Sandžak Democratic Party (*Sandžacka demokratska partija*, SDP). The Bosniak political scene has remained deeply divided between Ugljanin and Ljajić, and until today (2008) has been overshadowed by physical violence between members of both main party blocs.[21] After the 2004 elections resulted in a change of the municipal government of the largest Sandžak municipality, Novi Pazar, the new office holders were only able to move into their offices after the central government had sent in special police forces. Apart from the personal rivalry, a major difference between both parties is the SDA's goal of substantial autonomy for the Sandžak municipalities both in Serbia and Montenegro. Unlike Ugljanin, Ljajić's SDP does not refer to the Montenegrin Sandžak, and appears to take more moderate stands (International Crisis Group 1998: 10–12; Schmidt 1996), which makes it a more suitable partner for coalitions with Serbian parties, both in the Sandžak municipalities and at the national level. After 2000, the SDP joined coalitions with DOS and later DS in the national parliament elections, and in exchange the SDP leader Ljajić became a minister in the Serbian government. Recently, Ljajić has been aiming at an electorate beyond the Sandžak region, and defines his party as a non-ethnic, mainstream party.[22] However, it has no offices and has never run in an election outside Sandžak.

Bosniak parties in the Sandžak profit from a strong alignment of voters, and in national elections they often join agreements with the non-ethnic national parties, which guarantee them a few seats in parliament in exchange. In the 2003 and 2007 elections, the Democratic Party (DS) aligned with a large Bosniak party (the SDA in 2003, the SDP in 2007) and helped the DS list to become the strongest in the six Sandžak municipalities (see Table 9.3). Of the other national parties, only the new pro-European and minority-friendly Liberal Democratic Party (*Liberalno-demokratska partija*, LDP) got a slightly better result in the Sandžak region than on the national average (Table 9.3).

Apart from the two major players, many small parties have formed and disappeared, among which the most prominent is the Liberal–Bosniak Organisation of the Sandžak (*Liberalno–Bošnjačka organizacija Sandžaka*).

Coalition politics in the Sandžak are to a large extent dominated by quarrels between Ljajić and Ugljanin. After the 2004 elections this even led to two remarkable anti-Ugljanin coalitions in the municipal assemblies of Novi Pazar and of Sjenica. In both cases, all the parties except the SDA participate in broad coalitions led by Ljajić's SDP; this even includes five deputies of the ultra-nationalist SRS.

Preševo Valley

The Preševo Valley, located in Southern Serbia near the border with Kosovo, consists of three municipalities. In two municipalities, Preševo and Bujanovac,

Table 9.3 Election results in the six Sandžak municipalities. Only parties over 5 per cent are considered

	Local elections 2004		National parliamentary elections	
	Number of seats in local assemblies	Number of local mayors	2003 %	2007 %
Lista za Sandžak/SDA (Ugljanin)	71	2	40.1 (with DS)	27.9 (own list)
SDP (Ljajić)	55	2	20.6 (with ZZT)	31.1 (with DS)
NPS	10	–	–	–
DS	21[a]	1	with Lista za S.	with SDP
SRS	23	–	18.1	14.1
DSS	18[a]	–	6.1	10.3
LDP	–	–	–	5.6
Other Serbian parties	39			
Others	15	SPS	15.1	11.0

Source: Cesid, own calculations.

Note
a Two DSS mandates in a broad coalition with other ethnic Serbian parties. Nine DS mandates in a coalition with two smaller parties.

ethnic Albanians (0.8 per cent of Serbia's population) are a local majority. In the Preševo Valley, they almost exclusively vote for their own ethnic parties, that or abstain. Since the introduction of the new electoral law and the abolition of gerrymandered districts in Bujanovac in 2002, ethnic Albanian parties have controlled the local authorities in both Preševo and Bujanovac. Among these parties is the largest, rather moderate Party of Democratic Action (*Partija za demokratsko delovanje*, PDD), the more nationalist Party for Democratic Progress (*Pokret za demokratski progres*, Albanian LDP/PDP), the Democratic Party of Albanians (*Demokratska Partija Albanaca*, PDSH/DPA), and the Party for Democratic Integration (*Pokret za demokratsku integraciju*, PDI).[23] Further breakaway parties have emerged, such as the PDD-splinter Democratic Union of the Valley (*Demokratska unija Doline*, BDL/DUD) (see Table 9.4 for their representation in local assemblies). These parties are politically oriented towards Kosovo, and have separatist programmes. They like to refer to an unofficial 1992 referendum in which most ethnic Albanians of the valley voted for unification with Kosovo. In a common platform in 2006, all the parties called for a high degree of decentralisation and territorial autonomy and, seconded by Kosovo leaders, for a unification with the Preševo Valley, if ever there should be any changes in the Kosovo borders (International Crisis Group 2007: 10). The party divisions are based on legacies from the 2000–2001 insurgence against Belgrade, personal rivalries, and differences in their willingness to cooperate with Belgrade (International Crisis Group 2007: 4–5). The radicalism in the claims seems to be an important electoral vehicle, an observation that is in line with the ethnic outbidding effect that has often been described for ethnically divided societies: when several parties of the same ethnic group exist, the most hard-line party wins most of the votes.[24] Local governing coalitions in the Preševo Valley are ethnically exclusive, and there is no cooperation between ethnic Albanians and ethnic Serbs. The electoral results from different levels of elections are difficult to compare due to the large-scale election boycott of national elections by the Albanian minority in Preševo. In the period 2000–2007, Albanian parties boycotted all national elections in Serbia, and only participated in local elections (International Crisis Group 2007). In 2007, and only due to international persuasion, two parties (PDD, BDL) participated in the elections as an alliance, and won a seat in the national parliament.

Ethnic parties in other regions

Other ethnic groups are not relevant for the emergence of regional parties and party systems. Either they are spread throughout the country, or they are organised within the national, mainstream political parties.

The **Roma** minority makes up 1.4 per cent of the Serbian population, according to the census, but the number of Roma might be several times that.[25] Roma live throughout the country. Their political behaviour, however, appears to be mostly non-homogeneous. Two Roma parties, the Union of Roma in Serbia (*Unija Roma Srbije*), and the Roma Party (*Romska partija*), gained representation in the Serbian national parliament in 2007, with one deputy each. There are several local councillors of Roma nationality, elected from different lists (OSCE 2008: 20).

Table 9.4 Results of the 2004/2006 municipal elections

	Bujenovac	*Medveđa*	*Preševo*
PDD	13	6	12
LDP	9		5
PDI			
BDL			5
PDSH			15
SRS	12	2	1
SPS		7	
DOS coalition	5		
DSS		3	
SPO		3	
Roma parties	2		
Other parties (ethnic Serbs)		11	

Sources: Cesid (Preševo, Medveđa 2004), and International Crisis Group (Bujanovac 2006).

Other minorities have only marginal parties, with a few municipal mandates.

Bulgarians make up 0.3 per cent of the population of Serbia, and live mainly in two towns in Eastern Serbia. Their vote distribution in the national elections does not substantially differ from the national average. The Democratic Party of Bulgarians (*Demokratska partija Bugara*) has entered local politics in Dimitrovgrad, and it was part of the minority parties' electoral list (ZZT) in the 2003 national elections, but in both Bulgarian-populated locations, the Serbian mainstream parties rule.

The **Gorani** (0.1 per cent of Serbia's population) live mainly in and around Belgrade. Their language is very similar to Serbo-Croatian, but they are Muslims, and further identified through their origin in the south-western part of Kosovo. The Civic Union of the Gorani (*Građanska inicijativa Goranaca*) was formed in 2006, under the same name as the Gorani Party in Kosovo.[26] It first competed on its own in the 2008 national elections.

Finally, the Šumadija Party (*Lista za Šumadiju*) is a tiny non-ethnic, regional party, which is related to the Šumadija region, south-east of Belgrade. It belongs to the democratic part of the political spectrum, and participated in 2003 in the ZZT coalition with regional and ethnic parties.

Summary

Despite its still strong centralisation, Serbia is a country that is rich in regional parties, some that compete with a regionalist programme, and others that appeal for the votes of ethnic groups territorially concentrated in a small area. This has given party politics in three Serbian regions a specific touch. In the Albanian-dominated Preševo Valley, mainly Albanian minority parties compete in elections, while Bosniak political parties play an important role in many of the municipalities in the Sandžak, where Bosniaks (Muslims) live. The largest regional parties, however, can be found in the multi-ethnic Vojvodina region.

The nature of these ethno-regional parties shows clearly that they are based more on social and economic conflicts than administrative lines: either they campaign along ethnic boundaries, or they are formed to demand the restoration of the previous autonomy of Vojvodina. Looking at theoretical explanations, the emergence of regional parties in Serbia fits well with cleavage-based explanations, and puts a question mark after the decentralisation approach. While for other areas of the world it has been argued that administrative decentralisation offers incentives for the creation of strong regional parties, the empirical evidence in Serbia looks rather the other way round: regional parties have been formed despite a lack of substantial decentralisation, or they could be attracting their voters precisely *because* the major national parties were advocating a centralisation of the state (and, after a short policy change with their support for the new Serbian constitution, have re-adopted this position). In any case, the stress of regional and ethnic minority parties on decentralisation can be a vehicle to put pressure on the political authorities to transfer more competences to autonomous provinces and municipalities. These parties might have remained weak in terms of seats, but they have been important coalition partners, especially for the democratically oriented parties in Serbia, in several national, regional and local government coalitions, and occasionally they have even helped the Serbian nationalists to obtain a governing majority. Their openness to coalitions on both sides puts ethnic and regional parties in a position that they might be able to use sooner or later to negotiate for a more decentralised system.

This is why the sequence of events in Serbia questions the commonly supported hypothesis, and instead leads to the following: if not during the process of state-building, when is the impact of the party system on the structure of a young democracy particularly strong? From the perspective of the growing body of literature on party nationalisation and decentralisation, it would therefore be relevant to keep a close eye on the further development of regional autonomies and ethno-regional parties in Serbia.

Notes

1 All the population statistics and financial statistics refer to Serbian territory without Kosovo, which has not been administered by Serbia since 1999. All population numbers are taken from the 2002 census.

2 When referring to central parts of Serbia here, I employ a geographical and not a political definition. The unit which is politically defined as 'Central Serbia' encompasses ethnically heterogeneous regions in Serbia's south.

3 With the same votes as a regional party gets in district-based elections, a party can gain approximately the same number of seats in a nationwide constituency, and there is little reason why a regional party should gain or lose a substantial number of votes if small electoral districts are replaced by a single countrywide one.

4 Many thanks to Vladimir Mihić for information on this aspect.

5 Electoral law (*Zakon o izboru narodnih poslanika*), art. 84. Available from www. cesid.org/zakoni/sr/poslanici.jsp (last accessed 6 April 2008).

6 Electoral campaign financing is fixed as a percentage (0.05 per cent at the local and regional level) of the budget of the relevant government authority, and due to the small budgets of local and regional governments, the state contributions for parties in local and regional elections are not very substantial.

7 Information on this aspect is taken from Komšić (2003: 83–8), Goati (2004: 42, 45–6, 52; 2006: 228–31), and the International Crisis Group (2006b).

8 In the literature, such systems are sometimes named mixed-member majoritarian; see Shugart and Wattenberg (2001) for a typology of mixed electoral systems.

9 My own calculations for parliamentary elections in 2003 and 2007, data taken from Cesid. In the second round of presidential elections, DS candidates got better results.

10 Found on www.lsv.org.yu/ and www.reformisti.org.yu/ (last accessed on 5 April 2008).

11 'Deklaracija o Vojvodini – Koalicija Vojvodina', *Novi Sad*, 1 March 1997. www. lsvsu.org.yu/dokumenti/deklaracija_koalicija_vojvodina.htm (last accessed on 6 April 2008).

12 There are many parties that compete for the Social Democratic label in Serbia. Stojiljković (2007a) considers LSV to belong to those parties which have a Social Democratic programme and anti-nationalist, anti-traditionalist positions.

13 Mihić provides some of the very rare studies that focus on voters in Vojvodina. The number of respondents (302, out of whom 14.2 per cent LSV supporters) is rather small, but still very useful, if considering that the number of respondents in national surveys would be too small to analyse Vojvodina parties. The non-random sampling

employed by the author does not follow standards employed in election studies. Most other Serbian party studies concentrate on the national parties, or on ethnically-oriented parties. The fact that the regional parties often competed in alliances in national elections means further that an analysis of aggregate electoral data from municipalities is difficult or impossible. Todosijević (2008) locates LSV similarly on the main political axis, based however on a survey of 120 students at the University of Novi Sad; a sample which might be seen as insufficiently representative, both in the choice of the locality and of the environment.

14 Information on these parties and their representation, where not stated differently, were taken from Bašić and Crnjanski (2006) and electoral results.

15 *Politika*, 23 December 2007, 'Tema nedelje: Šta žele stranke nacionalnih – Namigivanje lokalnih šerifa'.

16 *Danas*, 25 August 2004, 'Za evropsku Vojvodinu u evropskoj Srbiji'; *Danas*, 17 November 2006, 'Kuntić na listi DS'.

17 *Danas*, 15 October 2002, 'Rusini, Slovaci i Rumuni u 'elektorskoj groznici'. Do saveta u bar dve struje'.

18 Press, 27 May 2007, Oliver Dulić, predsednik Skupštine: Manjina.

19 *Politika*, 23 December 2007, 'Tema nedelje: Šta žele stranke nacionalnih – Namigivanje lokalnih šerifa'.

20 Information on the Sandžak draws mainly on a report by the International Crisis Group (2005b).

21 For one of the latest incidents, see B92, 25.2.2008, 'Bomba na kuću odbornika'.

22 *Politika*, 23 December 2007, 'Tema nedelje: Šta žele stranke nacionalnih – Ne predstavljam samo Bošnjake'.

23 Information on the Preševo valley from International Crisis Group (2003: 19–24, 2007: 4–5, 10).

24 See Mitchell (1995: 773), cf. Horowitz (1985: 291, 357–8).

25 See for instance the website of the European Roma Rights Centre, www.errc.org/cikk. php?cikk=398.

26 *Danas*, 4–5 November 2006, 'Osnovana Građanska Inicijativa Goranaca'.

10   The party system of Kosovo

Věra Stojarová

Overview of the political system

As a result of the Balkan wars and the subsequent London Conference (1913), Kosovo was divided between the Kingdom of Serbia and the Kingdom of Montenegro and later became part of the Kingdom of Serbs, Croats and Slovenes. During the Second World War it was under Italian and then German occupation, and after the end of the Second World War it was established as the autonomous province of Kosovo and Metohija (Kosmet). Under the 1974 constitution Kosovo was practically self-governing. Its extensive autonomy was considerably reduced in 1989, and only one year later a state of emergency was declared. Initially the local population[1] tried to gain independence in a peaceful way, but since 1995 there has emerged the paramilitary Kosovo Liberation Army (*Ushtria Çlirimtare e Kosovës*, UÇK, English acronym KLA). The conflict escalated in 1998, and culminated with the NATO air campaign in spring 1999.

From 1999 till the declaration of independence, Kosovo was ruled on the basis of Security Council Resolution 1244, which basically stated that Kosovo is *de jure* a Serbian autonomous province and de facto a UN protectorate. The fundamentals of the political system were embedded in the Constitutional Framework[2] which was adopted in May 2001. The Provisional Institutions of Self-government were comprised of legislative, executive and judicial bodies. The provisional Kosovo Assembly was composed of 120 members of parliament: 100 distributed among all parties, ten seats reserved for the Serbian minority, and ten seats for other (non-Serb) national minorities (a proportional system used in all).[3] Kosovo was treated as a single electoral district, and because it is a region undergoing rapid change, the electoral term was set at three years only. Interestingly, Kosovo together with Albania and Moldova are the only countries in the region where the president was elected indirectly by parliament.[4] The presidential mandate lasted for three years. The president nominated the Prime Minister, who in turn proposed a list of ministers to the Assembly; the Assembly then endorsed the government. In order to secure minority representation, the Constitutional Framework stated that

> at all times, at least two Ministers shall be from Communities other than the Community having a majority representation in the Assembly; at least one

of these Ministers shall be from the Kosovo Serb Community and one from another Community. In the event that there are more than twelve Ministers, a third Minister shall be from a non-majority Community.

(Constitutional Framework UNMIK 2001)

As for the judicial system, the Special Representative of the Secretary General appointed judges and prosecutors[5] from a list of candidates proposed by the Judicial and Prosecutorial Council and endorsed by the Assembly. The Office of the Special Representative of the Secretary-General (SRSG) was the Kosovo-wide oversight and advisory organ – the final authority in theatre.[6] Kosovo was divided into 30 municipalities (alb. *komuna*, srb. *opština*).

In November 2005, the Contact Group[7] released Guiding Principles[8] which opened the path towards independence. The negotiations over the future of Kosovo's status started in Vienna in February 2006 under the mediation of former Finnish president Martti Ahtissari. In September 2006 a new Serbian constitution was approved in a referendum which incorporated a clause on Serbian territorial integrity claiming the right to the territory of Kosovo, so if Kosovo wanted to secede, then, according to the Serbian legal system, a constitutional amendment or the adoption of a new Serbian constitution would be needed.[9] After the parliamentary elections in Serbia, the Ahtissari plan was proposed: Kosovo would have all the attributes of an independent state[10] (institutions, state symbols, army, and the possibility to join international organisations as an independent subject) and would be temporarily under the supervision of the International Civilian Office. The plan was discarded because it failed to secure the backing of Russia. As no compromise was reached by 10 December 2007 (the deadline set by the UN Secretary General Ban Ki-moon), the Kosovo Albanians declared independence on 17 February 2008.

The new constitution

A Commission was immediately established to draft a constitution for the newly born state. The draft of the Constitution was published and passed by the Parliamentary Assembly in April 2008, and came into force on 15 June 2008. The Constitution is clear from the beginning where, in Article 1, it bans any irredentist tendencies (mainly referring to Serbian areas in the north of Kosovo), annexation of other territories (possibly south-eastern Serbia or western Macedonia inhabited mainly by ethnic Albanians) or unification with any other state (Albania). For those fearing a new Islamic state in Europe, Article 8 states that 'The Republic of Kosovo is a secular state and is neutral in matters of religious beliefs'. The Albanian as well as the Serbian language are recognised as official state languages[11] while Article 59 stipulates a wide range of rights for communities and their members regarding the use of language, national symbols, education in these languages, the media, public associations etc. Nevertheless, both Serbs and Albanians are not really willing to approach each other, and life for the former remains autarkic, with no contacts with the state authorities or the majoritarian population.[12]

The composition of the Parliamentary Assembly remains very much the same: 120 deputies are elected on open ballots by proportional representation. The difference is that according to the old Constitution, the 20 seats for national minorities were added to the number of mandates the parties of national minorities gained in the elections. Under the new Constitution, the 20 seats are guaranteed for the national minorities, and no additional seats can be won (cf. Constitutional Framework, article 9.1.3.b and Kosovo Constitution, article 64).[13] The mandate of the Assembly remains for four years. Multiculturalism is also assured in the composition of the government[14] as well as the Kosovo Judicial Council, with more or fewer provisions as in the previously adopted Constitutional Framework.[15]

The mandate of the president of the republic was prolonged: the new Constitution sets the terms at five years, with the right of one re-election. The president is still elected by the parliament, though he has more powers than under the Constitutional Framework. Among other things, the president issues decrees in accordance with the Constitution, leads the foreign policy of the country, and addresses the Assembly of Kosovo at least once a year in regard to her/his scope of authority (Constitution of the Republic of Kosovo, article 84).

The presence of international civilian representatives is ensured in the transitional provisions of the Constitution, and is designed according to Martti Ahtisaari's Comprehensive Proposal for the Kosovo Status Settlement dated 26 March 2007.[16] This leaves the final authority to the international civilian representative, while the Head of the International Military Presence shall be the final authority in theatre regarding aspects concerning the international military presence.

The Serbian authorities announced their intention to hold Serbian parliamentary elections, in Kosovo, on 11 May 2008, but this was condemned by UNMIK authorities as illegal. The result was the holding of local elections in which the Serbian Radical Party won a majority in the municipalities. In the meantime, representatives of the Democratic Party of Serbia, the Serbian Radical Party, Democratic Party, Socialist Party of Serbia, and G17+ announced the formation of a provisional parliament[17] by June 28.

As for internal developments, after the first elections in 2001, all parties formed a grand coalition, and therefore there was no real opposition. Ibrahim Rugova was elected president, and Bajram Rexhepi became Prime Minister. The 2004 elections resulted in a restructuring of the political scene: a new coalition composed of the Democratic League of Kosovo (LDK) and the Alliance for the future of Kosovo (AAK), while Hashim Thaçi with the Democratic Party of Kosovo (PDK) and Ora of Veton Surroi stayed in the opposition. Ibrahim Rugova remained as president, and the leader of the AAK Ramush Haradinaj was approved as the new Prime Minister. As ICTY issued an indictment on Ramush Haradinaj, he resigned and was replaced by Bajram Kosumi from his party. At the beginning of 2006, Ibrahim Rugova passed away, and one month later a new president, Fatmir Sejdiu, appointed a new Prime Minister, the former KLA commander, Agim Çeku.[18] After the 2007 November elections,[19] Hashim

Thaçi announced the formation of a new government composed of the PDK and its former rival LDK.

International observers remarked in 2000 that the provisional governments and municipal representatives often use violence and coercion to try to control Kosovo's structures and society, while redistributing humanitarian aid only to those who swear allegiance and promise their votes. 'The media have also been subject to pressure in ways reminiscent of authoritarian forms of government. Local journalists have repeatedly received visits from "government officials", been called to "informative talks" or even subjected to direct threats' (International Crisis Group 2000: 5). These *Sicilian* methods have not disappeared, and assassinations of party officials remain a method of political competition. The suspects in the assassinations of LDK or Ora officials are usually PDK followers, and most violent attacks remain unsolved (International Crisis Group 2005a).

One of the most difficult disturbances to handle took place in March 2004, after a minor incident in northern Kosovo (International Crisis Group 2004a). Subsequent demonstrations led to violence, which quickly spread to other parts of Kosovo. Serbian communities were under attack: eight ethnic Serbs were killed during the unrest. Three years later, in February 2007, demonstrations again took place against the negotiations in Vienna and for an immediate declaration of independence, in which two people died of injuries suffered in the clashes. Against expectations, the unrest did not spread to the rest of Kosovo, and the situation was resolved with the resignation of the Minister of Interior Fatmir Rexhepi.

For internal development, a stable and secure environment is needed. Before 1999 the Albanians were the ones who did not feel secure, but then the tide turned, and now insecurity is felt mainly by the Serbs, Roma, Ashkali and Egyptians. The UNMIK Report from March 2003 concludes that 'a limited increase in the level of security in some areas for minority communities was observed; ... minority communities continue to face varying degrees of harassment, intimidation and provocation, as well as limited freedom of movement' (UNMIK 2003). Nevertheless it has to be remarked that ethnic Serbs are not willing to participate in or recognise the new state, rejecting its new IDs, passports, and refusing to vote or in any way take part in the political and social life of the new state. This point of view is supported by Serbia, especially by the Minister for Kosovo–Metohija, Goran Bogdanović.

Development of the party system

Although by the mid-1990s there were some 15 political parties in Kosovo, the Kosovo party system only began to be fully formed after 1999. The fractionalisation of the ethnic Albanian space has not changed, and the party system can not be considered to be consolidated. Many political parties are personality-based, and until recently, their only objective was the independence of Kosovo. They lack an internal structure and do not really strive to present a clear programme (other than on the issue of independence). The main differences between them are their affiliations with particular individuals. The smaller political parties are formed by the ethnic minorities – the Serbs, Turks, Goranji, Roma, Bosniaks, Egyptians and Ashkali. Last but not least we must mention that there are a couple of ethnic Albanian parties demanding the unification of Kosovo with Albania. However, their position remains marginal.

The oldest player on the Kosovo political scene is the Democratic League of Kosovo (LDK), which was founded back in 1989 by a group of intellectuals gathered around Ibrahim Rugova; the party still holds an important position in the system. After the passing of Ibrahim Rugova, a new leader was chosen: the current president of Kosovo, Fatmir Sejdiu. The party was weakened by an internal split and the foundation of a new formation – the Democratic League of Dardania (LDD);[20] this was formed in January 2007 by the former Speaker of the Assembly of Kosovo, Nexhat Daci, after his unsuccessful bid to become chief of the LDK. The second strongest party is the Democratic Party of Kosovo (PDK), which was formed a couple of months after the Kosovo war, in October 1999, by the former KLA leaders, the most prominent among them being Hashim Thaçi. The third important player was formed in 2000: the Alliance for the future of Kosovo (AAK), which is a loose alliance of five political parties.[21] The current leader, the former KLA warrior and former Prime Minister of Kosovo, Ramush Haradinaj, was indicted by the ICTY. The reformist Party Ora was formed a few months before the 2004 parliamentary elections by the chief of the Koha Ditore media group, Veton Surroi. Last but not least is the New Kosovo Alliance (AKR), which was founded only in March 2007 by the successful businessman, Behgjet Pacolli, and it already scores quite well in the opinion polls. The LDK and PDK remain the most important players in the system; nevertheless we can not rule out the formation of new successful political parties.[22]

There is a great polarisation between LDK followers and ex-KLA supporters that dates back to the pre-war situation. The KLA got its main support in the rural areas among the young population; and with the move into the cities the support for the LDK dropped. Already in the 1990s there was great hostility between the LDK and the newly formed KLA which resulted many times in violence and killings between these two groups. The International Crisis Group claims that some of the LDK supporters coming out of the Gorani community were suspected of providing the Yugoslav Secret Service with information about KLA activities. The same could be said about the Albanian Roman Catholic community in Kosovo (around 10 per cent), who in the mid 1990s already had strong reservations towards the KLA (mainly due to its former Marxist–Leninist orientation), and gave their support to the LDK (International Crisis Group 1999a).

After the 2001 elections, ethnic Serb parties had 22 representatives in parliament. After the 2004 contest, the number of seats dropped to the ten reserved seats – two seats for the Serbians Citizens' Initiative, and eight for the Serbian List for Kosovo and Metohija. In 2007 the ethnic Serbs again won ten seats – three for the

Independent Liberal Party, three for the Serb Democratic Party of Kosovo and Metohija, one for the Serb People's Party, one for the Serb Kosovo Metohija Party, and one for the Union of Independent Social Democrats of Kosovo–Metohija. Nevertheless, most of the Serbian representatives continue their boycott and do not take part in the work of the Assembly.

Analysing Kosovo's party system, one must not omit the tight connections between local politicians and organised crime – the result of the previous conflict, an environment with no experience of democracy, and the clan structure of Kosovo society. One example could be the long-term Speaker of the Kosovo Assembly (acting president in 2006 and the founder of the Democratic League of Dardania) Nexhat Daci, who was indentified by the media on several occasions for abusing public funds. A second example concerns the current (2008) Prime Minister Hashim Thaçi who allegedly was/is part of organised crime activities in the region that controls part of the criminal activities in Kosovo and cooperates with the Albanian mafia abroad. On the other hand, Thaçi in opposition had constantly accused the LDK government of nepotism, clientelism, corruption, abuse of state funds etc. Such allegations pertain not only to the ethnic Albanians. In November 2006 the Minister for Community and Return Slaviša Petković resigned due to allegations of corruption at his ministry.

Party families

The party system is by no means consolidated; most of the parties are single-issue (Kosovo independence vs. Kosovo to Serbia). The most visible cleavage is the ethnic one: Kosovo Albanians vote for ethnic Albanian parties, Kosovo Serbs vote for the ethnic Serbs, and other minorities (Turks, Bosniaks…) vote for political groups of their ethnicity. There is nothing like a pan-Kosovo political party that would try to attract all voters regardless of nationality. Besides the ethnic cleavage, there is internal division within each of the ethnic party systems. Kosovo Albanian politics is much more about belonging to a certain person, or rather a certain family (clan) stemming from one particular region. As the oldest party, the LDK was founded more as a movement for national liberation covering all segments of society; it does not really have one strong regional base from where the leaders emanated. Its electoral results are balanced, and the only regions where the party has little success are the ethnic Serbian regions (Zubin Potok, Leposaviq/Leposavić, Novobërdë/Novo Brdo) or the strongholds of the PDK. The PDK was founded by former KLA fighters, so its biggest support comes from the Drenica valley where the armed resistance actually began and where Hashim Thaçi comes from. The PDK receives most of its votes in Gllogoc/Glogovac and Skenderaj/Srbica, the centre of the valley. Its rival party, the AAK, is similar: it has its strong base in the Dukagjini region, the home of the Ramush Haradinaj family, and especially in the municipalities of Pejë/Peć, Deçan/Decani and Gjakovë/Djakovica (OSCE Elections Results 2000, 2001, 2002, 2004). The minor parties do not show such regional tendencies, though the LDD scored extremely well in the municipal elections in Zveçani/Zvečani,

Leposaviq/Leposavić and Ferizaj/Uroševac, while Ora is quite successful in bigger towns such as Prizren, Peja/Peć or Gjakovë/Djakovica.

There are strong animosities between the ethnic Albanian parties that date back to the 1998 pre-conflict situation. When the KLA was formed, there was another formation which claimed to be the only official representative of the armed resistance – the FARK (Armed Forces of the Republic of Kosovo, *Forcat e Armatosura të Republikës së Kosovës*) initiated by the exiled government of Bujar Bukoshi and backed by the LDK of Ibrahim Rugova. The rivalry has not disappeared, and when, after the 1999 bombing, Hasim Thaçi proclaimed himself Prime Minister, Bukoshi refused to recognise him. A series of violent murders followed.[23]

On the margin of the ethnic Albanian political spectrum are the parties which advocate unification of Kosovo with Albania. A typical example is the National Front of Kosovo (*Balli Kombëtar e Kosovës*), a party which evokes the nationalist party from the Second World War that fought for a Greater Albania. Another party was set up in July 2007 – the Movement for Unification (*Lëvizja për Bashkim*), which also demands the unification of all Albanians into one state (*Lëvizjes për Bashkim* 2007). These parties remain marginal at present, and do not attract popular support.

As for the Serbian parties, there are indigenous Kosovo parties and those whose mother parties are based in Belgrade; for the purpose of elections they unite in the wider lists such as the Serbian List for Kosovo and Metohija (*Srpska Lista za Kosovo i Metohija*) or the Civic Initiative Serbia (*Građanska iniciativa Srbije*). Another ten seats are reserved for the representatives of the Ashkali, Bosniak, Egyptian, Roma and Turkish communities, who form their own parties which are voted for by their respective national minorities (e.g. *Gradjanska inicijativa Gore, Demokratska partija Aškalija Kosova, Turska demokratska partija Kosova* or *Nova demokratska inicijativa*). However, these parties are quite small, and often struggle with financial resources.

The party system is not yet fully evolved: party families such as socialist, social democratic, liberal, agrarian etc. are completely lacking; the post-materialism dividing line is not present at all. The original KLA was formed by adherents to Marxism–Leninism, and the LDK was formed by many ex-communists; thus the political parties stemming from KLA together with the present LDK tend to the left. The only relevant cleavage is based on ethnic and family (clan) lines.

Ethnic Albanian political parties

*Democratic League of Kosovo (*Lidhja Demokratike te Kosovës, LDK*)*

The party was set up in 1989, more as a liberation movement rather than as a party; it was the leading force for a peaceful solution for Kosovo. With the institutionalisation of the political and party system after 1999, although it participated in all the governments, the party kept on losing voters, and in the 2007 elections, for the first time, it finished in second place, gaining just 25 seats in parliament. The Democratic League of Kosovo then formed a coalition with its rival PDK, in early 2008.[24] As the hostility between these two parties (or rather, between their leaders) dates to the conflict, no one really believed they could form a stable grand coalition. The current LDK party chairman, Fatmir Sejdiu, was elected president of Kosovo in 2006.[25]

The first part of the party programme from 2006 (LDK 2006) recalls 'Belgrade's oppressive and aggressive policies' and the services of the party's leaders in the war for independence. In the second part the party presents itself as a traditional party stressing humanity, solidarity and tolerance. Like all ethnic Albanian parties, the LDK strives for an independent and democratic Kosovo, and for its integration into Euro-Atlantic structures. The party programme does not deal with anything other than independence, and the party's stances towards the economy or other issues are unclear. In the pre-election campaign of 2007 the LDK stressed the computerisation of all schools, decentralisation of school finances, and improved social care for marginalised groups (BIRN, 8.11.2007).

At present the LDK's position is hurt by the fact that the party did not succeed in gaining independence in a peaceful way in the 1990s, and that independence was declared by the leader of the competing PDK, Hashim Thaçi. Besides that, as Fred Cocozzelli remarks, the LDK's goal was always national liberation, not democratisation, and even now the party's internal statutes do not conform to Kosovo party law (Cocozzelli 2004: 4). In order to become a standard modern political party, internal democratisation, a higher level of transparency, and the elaboration of a precise party programme (as prerequisites for becoming anchored on either the left or right side of the political spectrum) are needed.

Democratic League of Dardania (Lidhja Demokratike e Dardanisë, LDD)

The party was created after an unsuccessful candidacy by former Speaker of the Kosovo Assembly, Nexhat Daci, to become LDK party leader after Ibrahim Rugova's death. As his challenger won the majority of the votes and became the chief of LDK, Nexhat Daci[26] decided to form a new party, the Democratic League of Dardania. The party was founded in January 2007, and seven LDK members defected into the newly formed LDD. Together with the Albanian Christian Democratic Party of Kosovo, the party gained 11 seats in the Kosovo Assembly in the 2007 elections.

The motto of the party is 'Independence, peace and prosperity', and this party, too, advocates independence for Kosovo, integration into the EU and NATO, and good relations with the USA. The political platform states that the party respects diverse ethnicities, cultures, and religions, and will engage in guaranteeing the rights for all ethnic groups in Kosovo according to European as well as world standards (LDD 2007). The LDD plans to reform the education system, and in the social sphere promotes policies aimed at alleviating the plight of the unemployed (BIRN, 8.11.2007).

*Democratic Party of Kosovo (*Partia Demokratike e Kosovës, *PDK)*

The party is a successor to the Party of Democratic Progress of Kosovo (*Partia e Progresit Demokratik të Kosovës*, PPDK),[27] which held its first congress in May 2000. As the party was formed mainly by ex-KLA warriors, the party gets support largely from those who were behind the paramilitary organisation, mostly in the Drenica region. The party took part in the great coalition of 2001, and Prime Minister Bajram Rexhepi came from its ranks. After the subsequent elections, the PDK went into opposition, where it harshly attacked the government, blaming the LDK for corruption, nepotism, and involvement in organised crime. The elections in 2007 then changed the political situation completely: the PDK allied with its former rival the LDK and created a coalition government in January 2008. The PDK leader Hashim Thaçi became Prime Minister, and happened to be in power when Kosovo declared independence.

The party programme starts by recalling the heroism of KLA fighters and reminding the reader that it is the successor of this heroic paramilitary organisation. It claims that 'the independence of Kosovo is a necessary condition for the stability in the region'. The party programme is not as brief as the LDK's and seems to be more elaborate. The party demands Albanian integration in the region and Europe, integration into the EU, a Kosovo with democratic institutions, and personal rights and freedoms according to international standards; the right to life, information, and free elections, tolerance and inter-ethnic empathy. Besides the democratic claims, the party strives for the creation and modernisation of the Kosovo army in order to be able to integrate into Euro-Atlantic structures, and it stands against any politicisation of the Kosovo Protection Corps (KPC). The programme states that the PDK supports the private economy and the privatisation of state firms, and would like to guarantee a social minimum wage, as well as pensions for every retiree and financial support for war invalids. It declares that only independence can guarantee development of the economy. The programme goes on to deal with the special needs of children, education, equal rights for women, culture, and the health care system. The PDK stresses strict measures against corruption and organised crime and the importance of law and order. It proposes among other things free medicine for retirees, and the development of the pharmaceutical industry in Kosovo (PDK 2002).

*Alliance for the Future of Kosovo (*Aleanca për Ardhmërinë e Kosovës, AAK)*

The Alliance for the Future of Kosovo was set up before the municipal elections in 2000 as a coalition of five parties. Two of the parties withdrew from the coalition one year later by the time of the parliamentary elections. The rest of the coalition registered as an ordinary political party in 2002, with former KLA commander Ramush Haradinaj as leader. In the 2001 parliamentary elections, the party gained eight seats which enabled it to take part in the grand coalition government. Three years later, it gained nine seats and entered a coalition with the LDK while its leader was appointed as Prime Minister, where he stayed until he was charged with war crimes related to the Kosovo war.[28] The post of Prime Minister was then given to another AAK deputy, Bajram Kosumi.

The AAK is based in the Dukagjini region; Cocozzelli remarks that '[W]here the AAK is strong it most often displaces the PDK rather than the LDK'. The party presents itself as much more professionalised, with democratic internal governance, and as having a strong youth and female membership (Cocozzelli 2004: 6). The party is more radical arguing that if independence is not achieved in a peaceful way, the option of violence is not excluded. The programme does not mention relations with national minorities, stating in the first line of its programme: 'We are the owners and we will be the owners of Kosovo' (AAK 2006). Regarding other parts of the programme, the party wishes to increase funds for education and offer textbooks for free, develop the social services, and improve the level of care for persons with disabilities and special needs (BIRN, 8.11.2007).

Reformist party Ora

Ora was founded in 2004 by Veton Surroi,[29] who was dissatisfied with the current shape of politics and who claimed the time for change had come.[30] Since 2008 the party has been led by Teuta Sahatqija. Ora succeeded in gaining seven seats to the Kosovo assembly in 2004, but three years later it failed to gain a single seat. Party members are mainly businessmen and intellectuals. Surroi is the owner of the Kosovo newspaper *Koha Ditore* as well as the local television KTV. He was less confrontational and hostile towards Serbs than the other ethnic Albanian party leaders. Already in 1999 he condemned 'the organized and systematic intimidation of all Serbs simply because they are Serbs' calling such attitudes 'fascist'. The reaction was an article by the Kosovo press agency attacking Surroi and Koha Ditore editor Baton Haxhiu, saying that 'the two had a "Slav stink", and were supporters of Slobodan Milosevic. It said that they risked "eventual and very understandable revenge" for the Surroi commentary' (International Crisis Group 1999b: 13). Surroi is seen as Yugo-nostalgic or pro-Serbian, and as such undesirable for his opponents in Kosovo politics (Galtung 2005: 5).

Unlike the other parties, Ora does not mention 'the heroism of Kosovo warriors' or 'the brutality of the Serbian regime', but concentrates on the fundamentals that a Kosovo state should be based upon: the constitution, the judicial system, and the rule of law, security for the citizens, a modern army of Kosovo integrated into NATO, and a Kosovo police force complying with European and international standards. The programme further emphasises free education for everyone, improved health care, as well as a pension system. The party supports private as well as state ownership; however, it accentuates the role of the state and adds that the social security system shall be provided by the state and available for everyone. The party promotes the integration of Kosovo into the EU. Its second foreign policy priority concerns its relations with Albania, other neighbouring countries and the USA (*Partia reformiste* Ora undated). Ora advocates more accessible schools, and in the health and social sphere it envisages the creation of health insurance as well as pension funds.

New Kosovo Alliance *(*Aleanca Kosova e Re*, AKR)*

The split in the LDK party in December 2006 resulted in the creation of a new party, the AKR, which was founded by the controversial businessman Behgjet Pacolli. In the pre-election campaign of 2007, the AKR promoted increases in teachers' salaries, provision of health insurance, as well as health care for young people and the mentally handicapped. The party talked of raising pensions by 100 per cent, and priorities for marginalised groups. It campaigns on economic issues, capitalising on public dissatisfaction over poor economic performance, while being criticised by its competitors for Pacolli's business ties to Russia (NDI 2007). The party succeeded in gaining 13 mandates in the 2007 parliamentary elections, and so became the third largest player on the Kosovo political scene.

In its programme, the AKR is not very different from the other parties – it promotes the integration of Kosovo into the EU as well as NATO, and special ties with Albania, the USA, and neighbouring countries. Other goals are decentralisation, an efficient economy, a welfare state etc. There is one striking difference: the AKR is the only party that has an environmental plank in its platform, stating that it 'wishes to impose environmental taxes and special permits in order to encourage people [to] live in line with environmental protection requirements'. The programme is elaborately detailed and the party is evidently no mere single issue party. Also quite interesting is the part about religion: 'In God we believe … We consider religious diversity in Kosovo as our prize, and we will do everything possible to cultivate and preserve permanent religious harmony and tolerance in Kosova' (AKR 2007: 17, 30). Since its beginning the party has endeavoured to have a very modern and Western design in its PR campaigns, copying the market strategies of successful political parties both in Europe and the USA.

Ethnic Serb political parties

The Serbian political scene in Kosovo remains divided: some boycott the elections, while others participate. The offspring of Belgrade-based political parties usually wait for orders from Belgrade on whether or not to boycott elections or the post-electoral period. As a result, the seats reserved for the Kosovo Serbs in the Kosovo Assembly often remain partially or fully vacant. At present, some political parties run in the elections, take part in sessions of parliament or even in government. The others boycott according to their instructions from Belgrade (usually the Serbian Radical Party, the Democratic Party of Serbia, the Serbian Renewal Movement etc.) As the Serbian parties are discussed in the chapter on Serbia,[31] the next part will focus on the autochthonous ethnic Serb Kosovo political parties which do take part in the political process.

Independent Liberal Party *(*Samostalna Liberalna Stranka*, SLS)*

The SLS was founded in the beginning of 2006 in Dobrotin, and its first leader was Slobodan Petrović. It campaigns for the interests of the Serbs in Kosovo, and for a better life for all Kosovo inhabitants. The party participated in the 2007 elections and gained three mandates, and two of its highest officials take part in the newly formed Kosovo government – the Minister of Community and Return, Boban Stanković, and the Minister of Labour and Social Welfare, Nenad Rašić. The leader of the party stands against the manipulation of Kosovo Serbs from Belgrade, and maintains that there should be no ties between the Belgrade government and the Kosovo Serbs, so that the Serbs in Kosovo are not manipulated by patriotic lectures.[32] The programme declares that 'The SLS stands for full affirmation of Kosovo ... while the community of Kosovo Serbs shall be institutionally and through personal contacts tied to Serbia and the whole Serbian nation'. The whole document quite clearly accepts the current state of affairs in Kosovo, and is willing to participate in the new state. The party is marginal among the Serb community in terms of political support.

Other ethnic Serb parties

Besides the SLS, other parties also won seats in Kosovo's parliament in the 2007 parliamentary elections: the Serb Democratic Party of Kosovo and Metohija (*Srpska demokratska stranka Kosova i Metohije*), the Serb People's Party (*Srpska narodna stranka*), New Democracy (*Nova demokratija*), the Serb Kosovo–Metohija Party (*Srpska Kosovsko Metohijka stranka*) and the Union of Independent Social Democrats of Kosovo and Metohija (*Savez nezavisnih socijaldemokrata Kosova i Metohije*). Parties that take part in the political process usually address immediate concerns such as freedom of movement and the return of Serbian property.

Other minority parties

Seats in the Kosovo assembly are reserved for the Ashkali, Bosniak, Egyptian, Roma and Turkish communities. Most of these parties struggle financially, and focus merely on issues related to cultural preservation and better economic, political and social conditions for their respective minorities. Successful parties in the parliamentary elections in 2007 were the following: The Turkish Democratic Party of Kosovo (*Kosova Demokratik Türk Partisi*, KDTP), the Democratic Ashkali Party of Kosovo (*Partia Demokratike e Ashkanlive të Kosovës*, PDAK), the Bosniak Vakat Coalition (*Koalicija Vakat*) and the Party of Democratic Action (*Stranka demokratske akcije*), the Gorani Civic Initiative of Gora (*Građanska inicijativa Gore*), and the Egyptian New Democratic Initiative of Kosovo (*Iniciativa e re Demokrarike e Kosovës*).

Interim conclusion

All political parties in Kosovo offer very much the same: independence, prosperity and development. None of the parties offers a way to resolve the current problems, or how to deal with the controversial issues of the post-independence period. All of them talk about success and wealth for Kosovo in the future, and integration into the EU, but none of them says how it plans to achieve these goals. A typical example is the pre-election promise of the PDK to build 800 km of roads, while failing to give a detailed explanation of how this would be done. In the field of education, most of the parties offer increased funds, provision of free textbooks for pupils at elementary schools, and internet access. All the parties seem to be rather to the left of the political spectrum, promising full health protection for children, orphans, veterans or pensioners, and special welfare provisions for these marginalised groups. Most of the parties foresee the creation of health insurance funds and a functioning social welfare system. None talk about ways to achieve this.

None of the parties includes cooperation with the ICTY in its programme – the Albanians feel that they are the victors in the war and therefore do not see the reason for national reconciliation. They do not even think that they can be indicted by the ICTY and handed over to The Hague. There are only two parties who explicitly talk about the past in their programmes – the PDK and LDK. However, both talk only of Serbian aggression and the victorious Albanian patriotic war, with a black-and-white image of allies and enemies, victors and vanquished. Regarding foreign policy, all parties focus on the integration of an independent Kosovo into the European Union and NATO. Besides that, the AAK, LDD and Ora advocate special relations with the USA. All parties except the Democratic League of Dardania accentuate regional cooperation and integration. Special relations with Albania and the Albanian diaspora are emphasised in the programmes of all political parties except in that of the Alliance for the Future of Kosovo of Ramush Haradinaj.

As there are practically no differences among the parties, voters vote for the parties because of their leaders. Presumably this will change after Kosovo independence, when continuity in the system takes hold, along with party democratisation and consolidation of the party system as such. The national question will be replaced by economic and social issues important for the local citizens, who are looking forward to the prosperity and development envisaged by the political parties.

Notes

1 Kosovo's ethnic composition in 2000: Albanian 88 per cent, Serb 7 per cent, other ethnic groups 5 per cent of the population (Statistical office of Kosovo 2005). The Albanians in Kosovo (together with those in Macedonia, Montenegro and northern Albania) belong to the Geg ethnic subgroup. Before the transformation of the regime in Albania, the Albanians from Yugoslavia regarded Albania as the country they wished to live in. Nevertheless, with the fall of the borders, they realised that the standard of living in Yugoslavia is far higher than that of Albania, and that the identities of Kosovo Albanians and Albanian Albanians are quite different, as they had

had almost no contact for nearly half a century. The separate Kosovo Albanian identity evolved slowly, and it strengthened with the struggle for independence and the objections of opponents that the right of the Albanians to self-determination had already been fulfilled. Currently, a group of ethnic Albanians in Kosovo has emerged calling for the codification of a separate Kosovo Albanian language which would be codified according to the Geg dialect. (The standardised Albanian language was codified according to the Tosk dialect (southern Albania) in 1972.) With the declaration of independence, the use of the Albanian flag with a black eagle on a red field is slowly diminishing, being replaced or accompanied by the new Kosovo flag with yellow stars on a blue field. When asked, Kosovo Albanians regard themselves as the same but different – as Albanians, but Kosovo Albanians. Therefore both flags are usually used. The common answer as to a Greater Albania is usually that the Albanians will unite finally in the European Union, and that no such state is needed as they can already travel between these two countries with only their IDs, and therefore do not need a single bigger state.

2 The Albanians demanded a 'Constitution', while the Serbs strived for a 'Legal Framework'. A compromise was reached by adopting a 'Constitutional Framework'. A clause about a declaration of independence on the basis of a referendum was not included.

3 According to UNMIK Regulation 2001/9, for the purposes of elections to the Assembly, Kosovo shall be considered a single, multi-member electoral district. Distribution of the extra seats for the ethnic communities: four Roma, Ashkali and Egyptian, three Bosniak, two Turkish and one Gorani.

4 A nomination for president requires the support of the party having the largest number of seats or at least 25 members (UN Security Council Resolution 1244).

5 International as well as Kosovo judges, where the latter must reflect the ethnic diversity in Kosovo.

6 Since 1 September 2006 Joachim Rücker; list of former SRSGs: Søren Jessen-Pettersen, Harri Holkeri, Michael Steiner, Hans Haekkerup and Bernard Kouchner.

7 The Contact Group is a group of countries that have interest in the developments in Balkans. It is composed of USA, UK, Russia, France, Germany, Italy.

8 Kosovo does not return to the pre-March 1999 situation. There will be no changes in the current territory of Kosovo, i.e. no partition of Kosovo and no union of Kosovo with any country or part of any country. The territorial integrity and internal stability of regional neighbours will be fully respected (Guiding Principles of the Contact Group 2005).

9 The Constitution draft must be proposed by one-third of the members of the parliament, the president, government or 150,000 voters, and it can only be approved with the consent of two-thirds of all the MPs, along with approval in a referendum.

10 Though the word 'independence' was not mentioned.

11 Nevertheless, this clause is neglected in practice, as all official correspondence is performed mainly in the Albanian language (Interview with Head of Gračanica health centre Rada Trajković Gračanica, August 2008).

12 A typical example is that the Serbian communities use the mobile network operator from Serbia which does not communicate with the local networks, so it is not possible to phone or send an SMS from one to another. Life in the Serbian communities is financially supported from Serbia – these communities are not willing to approach Kosovo authorities, and thus they avoid recognising the existence of the Kosovo state.

13 Nevertheless, there is a transitional period for the first two Assembly mandates which shall be assigned according to the Kosovo Constitutional Framework. The mandate existing at the time of entry into the Constitution will be deemed to be the first electoral mandate of the Assembly, provided that such mandate continues for a period of at least two years from the date of entry into force of the Constitution (Kosovo Constitution, article 148).

14 There shall be at least one Minister from the Kosovo Serb Community and one Minister from another non-majority Community. If there are more than 12 Ministers, the Government shall have a third Minister representing a Kosovo non-majority community. Similar provision applies in regard to the deputy ministers (two Serbs, two others) (Constitution of the Republic of Kosovo, article 96).

15 Out of the 13 members of the Kosovo Juridical Council, two members shall be elected by the deputies of the Assembly holding reserved or guaranteed seats for the Kosovo Serb community and at least one of the two must be a judge (Constitution of the Republic of Kosovo, article 108).

16 Available online www.unosek.org/docref/Comprehensive_proposal-english.pdf.

17 The parliament shall have 45 delegates, 43 of whom will come from the local Kosovo assemblies, while two seats will be reserved for representatives of Muslims and Roma.

18 Before the Kosovo war, Çeku took part in the war in Croatia. He was arrested (and almost immediately released) on two occasions, at Ljubljana Airport in October 2003, and then at Budapest Airport in February 2004, on a warrant issued by the Serbian judiciary for allegations of war crimes. After 1999 he was responsible for the formation of the Kosovo Protection Corps – the Kosovo provisional army.

19 All the previous elections were held on the basis of closed lists, while in 2007 the voting lists were open so that citizens could vote for individual candidates.

20 There is a popular claim in ethnic Albanian territories that the inhabitants of Dardania (conquered by the Roman Empire in 6 AD) were the predecessors of Albanians, in order to prove that Albanian civilisation has a very long tradition. However, this idea is disputed.

21 The Civic Alliance of Kosovo, Parliamentary Party for Kosovo, National Movement for the Liberation of Kosovo, People's Movement of Kosovo, Party of National Albanian Union, and the Albanian Union of Christian Democrats.

22 In 2001 the LDK gained 47, PDK 26 and AAK eight seats of the 120 seats in the parliament. In 2004 elections, LDK gained 47, PDK 30, AAK nine and Ora seven seats out of the 120 seats. The LDK, PDK, AAK and the Coalition Povratak formed a government in 2002, and thus there was no opposition in the parliament during those three years; therefore the renewal of such a coalition seemed outdated in 2004. The LDK and AAK formed the government after the last elections in 2004.

23 For example, Idriz Balaj, the leader of the former KLA special unit Black Eagles, was convicted of murdering rival Kosovo Albanian soldiers of the FARK forces in the 'Dukagjini case'. The most often covered by the media was the alleged blood revenge between Musaj and Haradinaj families. The brother of former Prime Minister Ramush Haradinaj – Daut Haradinaj – was allegedly involved in the murder of Sinan Musaj in 1999. The last victim of the alleged vendetta was Enver Haradinaj who was killed in April 2005 (International Crisis Group 2005a).

24 The coalition agreement was controversial in a couple of aspects that openly conflict with the Constitutional Framework: the bar against launching no-confidence motions against the Prime Minister and the president; and the extension of the presidential mandate by two years to five years (Dugolli 2008).

25 According to the Constitutional Framework, the leading party position is incompatible with the presidential function. However, UNMIK authorities failed to persuade either Rugova or Sejdiu to step down as party chair.

26 Nexhat Daci was charged on an issue relating to legal financial controls, and the acquisition of an armoured vehicle for personal use at a cost of more €230,000. He was seen as the second most powerful figure in the LDK. After being charged, he nevertheless refused for more than ten days to resign from his post as President of the Assembly, and in this period used Assembly funds to purchase items for personal use.

27 Democratic Union Party (*Partia e Bashkimit Democratic*, PBD) merged in 1999 with the supporters of Hashim Thaçi, ex-UÇK fighters and former émigrés from Switzerland (who had formed in exile People's Movement of Kosovo, *Levizja Popullore e Kosovës*, PDK), and created a new party – the PPDK.

28 For the current state of the Haradinaj case see www.un.org/icty/cases-e/index-e.htm.

29 Veton Surroi was a member of the negotiating team over Kosovo status in Vienna.

30 Ora means 'time' in Albanian.

31 For the Serbian political parties see Chapter 7, the party system in Serbia.

32 http://sls-ks.org/index.php?option=com_content&task=view&id=129&Itemid=44.

11 The party system of Macedonia

Jakub Šedo

Overview of the political system

The territory of what is now the Republic of Macedonia is only a part of geographical Macedonia which was annexed by Serbia during the Balkan wars (1912–1913) and called Vardar Macedonia. After the First World War, the then Kingdom of Serbs, Croats and Slovenians was enlarged with a western part of Pirin Macedonia which belonged originally to Bulgaria. Macedonia was declared a republic of the future Yugoslavian federation during the Second World War, and Macedonia then became one of the republics of the Federal People's Republic of Yugoslavia (Rychlík and Kouba 2003: 191–210).

The secession process from Yugoslavia took place with a certain delay; independence was declared only after it began to appear that Macedonia as a part of Yugoslavia was in danger of being dragged into the growing civil wars in Croatia and Bosnia and Herzegovina, with all the adverse consequences for the citizens and the country's economy. A referendum on independence was held in September 1991, and thus Macedonia left the federation (Stojarová *et al.* 2007: 57, Rychlík and Kouba 2003: 248–55).

The process of becoming independent was peaceful, but the new state experienced difficulties in gaining international recognition. Greece refused to recognise Macedonia, including its state symbols, which originally referred back to the ancient Macedonia. Eventually, Greece recognised the new state under the provisional name the Former Yugoslav Republic of Macedonia (FYROM) (Stojarová *et al.* 2007: 57–8). The Greek attitude towards Macedonia, however, is still negative; at NATO's Bucharest summit in April 2008, Greece vetoed Macedonia's bid for membership.[1] Long-term negotiations between Greece and Macedonia have been unsuccessful. Greece has opposed any proposals which contain the word 'Macedonia'; Macedonian officials insist on identifying the country with the name 'Macedonia' (or, at least inside the country, 'Republic of Macedonia'), but there are some attempts to find a compromise name with an adjective or addition that distinguishes between the Greek province of Macedonia and the Republic of Macedonia (e.g. New Macedonia, the Republic of Skopje, or Upper Macedonia). The dispute over the name also threatens Macedonia's chances of EU membership, which is among the main goals of all the relevant Macedonian parties.[2]

Another complication for the future lies in the ethnic composition of the population. Only two-thirds of the inhabitants are ethnic Macedonians. The biggest difficulty concerns the Albanian minority, almost a quarter of the population, which is concentrated in the north-west of the country next to the borders of Kosovo and Albania. Another approximately 10 per cent of the population belongs to different ethnic groups such as Turks, Roma, Serbs, Bosniaks etc. (Ortakovski 2001: 26).

Macedonia was established as a republic, with a directly elected president (his formal position corresponds in the main to the parliamentary model of government), and a one-chamber parliament of 120 members. The electoral system underwent a complicated evolution. In 1990 and 1994, Macedonia used a plurality electoral system; in 1998 a parallel mixed system (85 seats elected in a two-round system with a run-off, 35 in a PR system in a single electoral district and a 5 per cent legal threshold); and since 2002, a PR system with no minimum threshold has been in use, with six electoral districts of the same size. The D'Hondt method is used for the distribution of seats (Šedo 2007: 72–4). In the 1990s, tensions between Macedonians and Albanians were visible but limited to minor incidents. In several cases, the Albanians attempted to establish their own institutions: one symbol for them was the University of Tetovo (Tetovë), which was not recognised by the Macedonian authorities. In 1997 there were disturbances that claimed three lives after Albanian flags were flown in front of town halls in Tetovo and Gostivar (Gostivari) (Ortakovski 2001: 34; Kapal 2004: 10). In spite of all these problems, the situation was successfully kept under control: the Albanians participated in state institutions, and Albanian parties have been included in all the Macedonian governments since 1992. Relations among Macedonian parties were also strained. In 1992 the caretaker cabinet of that time, headed by Nikola Kljusev, was replaced by a left-wing government under Branko Crvenkovski of the Social Democratic Union of Macedonia (SDSM), which was sharply attacked by the Internal Macedonian Revolutionary Organisation – Democratic Party for Macedonian National Unity (VMRO-DPMNE) and the Democratic Party (DP). In 1994, conflicts between the government and the opposition led to a boycott of the second round of the elections by the VMRO-DPMNE and the DP, which enabled the existing government coalition to continue. The reason for the boycott of the second round of the elections was an accusation of electoral manipulation (Šedo 2007: 255–6; Rychlík and Kouba 2003: 261).

In October 1995 there was an assassination attempt on president Kiro Gligorov (the background of which has never been solved). He nevertheless survived the car bomb attack and remained in office. During his hospitalisation, relations within the government worsened. Prime Minister Crvenkovski had a conflict with parliament and the leader of the Liberal Party (LP), Stojan Andov, who was the president's deputy and who hoped would become his successor. The conflict led to a re-shaping of the government headed by Crvenkovski, without LP participation (Pacák 2000: 35–7).

In 1998, the country experienced a peaceful changeover of power: the VMRO-DPMNE won the parliamentary elections and created a coalition with parties which had not yet participated in government. One year later, the VMRO-DPMNE candidate, Boris Trajkovski, also won the presidential elections (Rychlík and Kouba 2003: 264–7).

Stability was utterly undermined by the increasing tension in Kosovo. More than 300,000 Albanians from Kosovo fled into Macedonian territory, a quantity unmanageable for Macedonia considering its size and economic weakness. Some of the Macedonians adopted a negative attitude towards the NATO action against Serbia, while the Albanians supported it; this led to an escalation of the tensions so far hidden in the country (Ortakovski 2001: 38–40; Kapal 2004: 12–13). The international community totally failed Macedonia during the following months.

A certain preventive role could have been played by the UN mission UNPREDEP (UN Preventive Deployment Force, a mission established in 1995 by extending the preceding UNPROFOR mission in Macedonia); it monitored the borders in the north-west of the country, and their troops were deployed in regions with an Albanian majority. China, however, vetoed the extension of the mission mandate in 1999, because Macedonia had recognised Taiwan a short time before.[3] The international forces in Kosovo failed in the period when armed Albanian radicals streamed into Macedonia from Kosovo. In spring 2001, an Albanian uprising broke out in the north-west, headed by the Albanian National Liberation Army (UÇK), against whom Macedonian army forces were engaged. Fortunately, the conflict did not grow to the extent of the civil wars in Croatia, Bosnia and Herzegovina or Kosovo. In May 2001, a government of national unity was established in which all the main Macedonian and Albanian political parties participated, and after negotiations, the Ohrid Framework Agreement was concluded. It was agreed to make several changes to the Constitution and to enact certain other laws. The language of each ethnic group with at least 20 per cent of the population became an official language (this meaning, de facto, the Albanian language). The powers of local administration were significantly strengthened, and use of the symbols of the local majority community allowed. For changes to some articles of the Constitution, a double majority is required: besides two-thirds of all the representatives, they must also be approved by a majority of deputies representing the ethnic minorities. The share of individual ethnicities in the public sphere must be taken into consideration, and the Macedonian government must recognise the University of Tetovo as a state university. The Ohrid Framework Agreement brought a partial solution to the situation in the country, although it is criticised by the Macedonians, while the other minorities also see it as weakening their position (Brunnbauer 2002; Kapal 2004: 14–36; Ortakovski 2001: 40–2). So far it has been observed, and it enables the Macedonians and Albanians to live together in a single state, despite some incidents from time to time.[4]

In 2002, the left-wing parties returned to power and the government was joined by the Democratic Union for Integration (DUI), a new Albanian party whose representatives had headed the Albanian uprising. Crvenkovski became the Prime Minister again and, in 2004, he was elected president in early presidential elections (B. Trajkovski died in a plane crash in February 2004). The 2006 elections brought a return of VMRO-DPMNE to power, and their government continues after early elections were held in 2008, when Greece vetoed Macedonia's bid to join NATO.[5]

Development of the party system

The majority of relevant political parties were founded, or transformed from older parties already in existence, at the beginning or the 1990s. The League of Communists of Yugoslavia entered the first free elections as the League of Communists of Macedonia – Party for Democratic Changes (SKM-PDP); after completing its transformation in 1992, the party adopted the name Social Democratic Union of Macedonia (SDSM). The main rival for the SKM-PDP in the first elections was the nationalist Internal Macedonian Revolutionary Organisation – Democratic Party for Macedonian National Unity (VMRO-DPMNE). A potential centre of the political spectrum was represented by the Union of Democratic Forces in Macedonia (SRSM), which was part of the reform movement in Yugoslavia formed by the former Prime Minister of Yugoslavia, Ante Marković. The SRSM was transformed after the elections into the Liberal Party (LP). The Socialist Party of Macedonia (SPM) likewise came into existence through the transformation of the Socialist Alliance of the Working People of Macedonia, and managed to gain parliamentary representation. The Albanian minority was represented by the Party of Democratic Prosperity (PDP), and the parliament was also joined by several minor parties, some of which represented other ethnic minorities (Šedo 2007: 368; Allcock 1994: 280–1).

A most remarkable change took place prior to the 1994 elections, when the SDSM split: the party was abandoned by a fraction around Petar Gošev, who then founded the Democratic Party (DP) and ran in the elections in opposition to the existing left-wing government. In addition, there were conflicts inside the Albanian minority. The PDP, which had been a member of the governmental coalition since 1992, was criticised for being too moderate, and unsatisfied representatives defected to the Party of Democratic Prosperity of Albanians (PDPA) or the People's Democratic Party (NDP). These quarrels among the Albanians in 1994 resulted in their lowest representation since 1990; thanks to the plurality electoral system, their candidates suffered defeat even in regions with large Albanian populations. The 1994 elections were marred with a boycott of the second round by the VMRO-DPMNE and the DP, which led to a decisive victory for the coalition Union for Macedonia headed by the SDSM (Šedo 2007: 257; Pacák 2000: 30–6).

The main changes which took place before the 1998 elections were the termination of cooperation between the SDSM and the LP, which merged with the DP into the Liberal Democratic Party (LDP); and the merger of the PDPA and the NDP into the Democratic Party of Albanians (DPA). The elections proper further deepened the trend which had already been clear in the first half of the 1990s, the domination of the VMRO-DPMNE and the SDSM over the other Macedonian parties. The failures of the LDP (four seats) and the SPM (one seat) confirmed that outside a coalition led by one of the largest parties of both sides, there was no chance for any third Macedonian party to break through (Šedo 2007: 257–63).

The party spectrum was not substantially affected by the conflict in 2001 (the LDP split into the LDP and the Liberal Party of Macedonia, LPM, when both the newly established entities started to cooperate with a different large party, had taken place previously). On the other hand, the Albanian part changed greatly – the Democratic Union for Integration (DUI) was founded, supported by Albanian veterans from the struggles in Macedonia, and representing the radical Albanian element. The DUI became clearly the strongest representative of the Albanians (Šedo 2002b: 253–64; Šedo 2007: 368).

Before the 2006 elections, both the large parties suffered splits: the VMRO-DPMNE suffered the defection of the Internal Macedonian Revolutionary Organisation – People's Party (VMRO-NP), headed by the former party chairman and Prime Minister, Ljubčo Georgievski. The SDSM lost the New Social Democratic Party (NDSA), headed by a former prominent politician of the SDSM, Tito Petkovski.[6] The early elections in 2008 nevertheless proved the attractiveness of both the large blocs: the VMRO-NP was not allowed to run in the elections, and the NSDA ran within the bloc headed by the SDSM.[7]

Party families

The basic dividing line in Macedonia is the ethnic cleavage between Macedonian and Albanian parties. Parties of the other ethnic minorities are also active, but since 2002, the most important of them have been seeking partnerships among the main Macedonian parties. Both the Macedonian and the Albanian sides are divided into two blocs (in the case of the Macedonians) or parties (Albanians). Apart from these, there are dozens of minor, practically marginal subjects, mostly small Macedonian parties.[8] The assessment of relevance and also possible classification in a specific party family is complicated by the tendency to form big blocs around the strongest Macedonian parties. These alliances may contain more than ten entities of widely varying orientation, and in some cases a minority ideological orientation is declared by parties in both blocs (see Table 11.1).

Another problem concerns the relevance of the small parties which participate in these large electoral blocs. Most seats are assigned by the largest party of the bloc, and some (or even the majority) of their partners have no parliamentary representation at all.[9] Therefore attention will be devoted only to the parties which are represented in the parliament at present (2008), and those that in the past have been able to win more than two seats when acting independently.

Communist parties

Since the governing Communist Party has undergone transformation, this family has no relevant representatives. Some totally marginal subjects either do not participate in the elections, or their achievements are negligible, such as the Communist Party of Macedonia (*Komunisticka partija na Makedonija*, KPM), which won just 0.06 per cent of the vote in the 2006 elections.[10]

Table 11.1 Bloc of main Macedonian political parties in the 2006 elections

VMRO-DPMNE	SDSM
Liberal Party of Macedonia	Liberal Democratic Party
Socialist Party of Macedonia	
Democratic Union	
People's Movement of Macedonia	
Party of the Greens	Green Party of Macedonia
European Party of Macedonia	
	Workers' Agrarian Party
	Socialist Christian Party of Macedonia
Party for Democratic Movement of Turks in Macedonia	Democratic Party of Turks
Union of Roma in Macedonia	United Party of Roma in Macedonia
Party of Democratic Action in Macedonia	
Party of the Vlachs from Macedonia	Democratic Union of Vlachs
Bosniak Democratic Party	
Party of Democratic Forces of Roma in Macedonia	
Party for Integration of Roma	
	Democratic Party of Serbs

Source: www.sec.mk/parlamentarni/Листинакандидати/tabid/173/Default.aspx.

Socialist and Social democratic parties

Social Democratic Union of Macedonia (Socijaldemokratski sojuz na Makedonija, SDSM)

This party came into existence through the gradual transformation of the League of Communists of Yugoslavia (*Savez komunista Jugoslavie*, SKJ), first to the League of Communists of Macedonia – Party for Democratic Changes (*Savez komunista Makedonije – Partija za demokratska preobrazba*, SKM-PDP), and later on into the SDSM (Allcock 1994: 288–9; Šedo 2002b: 253–4). The post of chairman was won by Branko Crvenkovski in 1992 when he replaced Petar Gošev. Gošev and his supporters later founded the DP. Crvenkovski gave up his post in 2004 when he was elected president. His successor was Vlado Bučkovski, who was replaced by Radmila Šekerinska after the lost elections in 2006. Šekerinska resigned after electoral defeat in 2008; her successor is Zoran Zaev.[11]

The SDSM was the strongest government party in 1992–1998 and 2002–2006. It also participated in the nationwide coalition government led by VRMO-DPMNE in 2001. In 1994 it had created the Alliance of Macedonia (*Sojuz za Makedonija*) together with the SPM and the LP; and since 2002 it has always run in a coalition along with the LDP and several minor parties including the ethnic ones (Šedo 2002b: 254). In the 2002 and 2006 elections, this coalition was named Together for Macedonia (*Za Makedonija zajedno*); in the 2008 elections when also the LP and the NSDP took part, its name was changed to The Sun – Coalition for Europe (*Sonce – Koalicija za Evropa*).[12]

The SDSM defines itself as a social democratic party. It is an associate member of the Party of European Socialists. It supports a pro-Western orientation. Reflecting its decisive role in the economic transformation and privatisation under the SDSM-led governments, the party is closely connected with the business lobby, and its representatives have been involved in corruption scandals. The SDSM is therefore criticised for deviating from the classic social democratic orientation. When minority topics are negotiated, the SDSM usually presents itself as a moderate, tolerant partner willing to accept concessions (Šedo 2002b: 254). A high rate of unemployment, corruption scandals, and concessions in favour of the Albanians taken in order to implement the Ohrid Framework Agreement, were the main reasons for its electoral defeat in 2006 and the overall decrease in voter support for the party. In the 2008 early elections the SDSM-led Sun Coalition won 23.64 per cent of the vote and 27 seats (18 seats were won by the SDSM and nine by smaller parties).[13]

*New Social Democratic Party (*Nova socijaldemokratska partija*, NSDP)*

The NSDP was founded in the autumn of 2005 by Tito Petkovski, a former SDSM candidate for president in 1999.[14] Petkovski criticised the deviation of the SDSM from the social democratic programme. His new NSDP was to act as an authentically left-wing party with more emphasis on social issues, and this would have made a distinct difference from the policies conducted by previous governments and the SDSM.[15] The NSDP took part in the 2006 elections independently and won seven seats. After the elections they participated in the government headed by the VMRO-DPMNE. However, in the early elections in 2008 they ran as a member of the SDSM-led coalition and won three seats (out of the 27 seats won by that coalition).[16]

*Socialist Party of Macedonia (*Socialistička partija na Makedonija*, SPM)*

The SPM came into existence in 1990 through the transformation of the Socialist Alliance of the Working People of Macedonia (Pacák 2000: 62). In the 1990s its leader was Kiro Popovski, and under his leadership the SPM cooperated as a coalition partner of the SDSM in the governments of 1992–1998 (Šedo 2002b: 255). In 1994 it participated in an electoral alliance with the SDSM and the LP. With its new leader, Ljubislav Ivanov-Dzingo, the owner of one of the biggest private TV stations in Macedonia,[17] the SPM ran in a coalition with some small ethnic parties, and in 2002 it ran independently. In both elections it achieved the bare minimum of representation; its only seat was given to the party leader Ivanov-Dzingo. Thus marginalised, the SPM began to cooperate with the VMRO-DPMNE, and in 2006 and 2008, it participated both in the VMRO-DPMNE-led electoral alliances and in the right-wing government, although it presented itself as a party whose programme was rather to the left of the SDSM (Šedo 2007: 256–8; Šedo 2002b: 254–5). In the 2008 early elections, the SPM won three seats (out of 63 seats won by the VMRO-DPMNE-led coalition).[18]

Centrist and liberal parties

Liberal Democratic Party (Liberalno demokratska Partija, LDP)

The LDP was established in 1997 by a merger between the Liberal Party (*Liberalna partija*, LP) and the Democratic Party (*Demokratska partija*, DP). In 1999 a faction broke away led by the former party leader of the LP, Stojan Andov. Through a policy of cooperation with the SDSM, the LDP tended to follow the LP, but its personnel are more connected with the DP. The DP was founded in 1993 by the merger of several minor parties with a group of former SDSM members led by the former party leader Petar Gošev. The DP went into opposition against the left-wing government, and in 1994, it boycotted the second round of the parliamentary elections. When the LDP was established, Petar Gošev became its chairman and under his leadership the LDP failed in the 1998 elections when it refused to cooperate with the large parties and instead, it created a coalition with the marginal Democratic Party of Macedonia (*Demokratska partija na Makedonija*, DPM). In 1999 Gošev was replaced in his post by Risto Penov (Šedo 2002b: 255–7). Since 2002 the LDP has always participated in the SDSM-led electoral alliances (Šedo 2007: 368). In government, it was represented briefly in 1999; then it took part in the nation-wide coalition government in 2001. In 2002–2006 it was a partner in the SDSM governments. Since 2006 the leader of the party has been Jovan Manasijevski.[19] In the 2008 elections, the LDP won four seats as a member of the SDSM-led Sun Coalition.[20]

The party defines itself as liberal, and is a member of the European Liberal Democrat and Reform Party. In the 2008 elections, its programme included integration into Western structures, which would have been easier to put to practice if the Sun Coalition had won. It thus identified a negative consequence of the present domination by the VMRO-DPMNE.[21]

Liberal Party of Macedonia (Liberalna Partija na Makedonija, LPM)

The LPM was founded in 1999 by a faction led by former LP chairman, Stojan Andov (Šedo 2002b: 255–7). He led the party until 2008 when he was replaced by Borče Stojanovski.[22] The LP proper came into existence in 1991 through the merger of the Union of Reform Forces of Macedonia (*Sojuz na reformski sili na Makedonija*, SRSM) with two minor parties. The LP participated in the SDS-led governments in 1992–1996, and in the 1994 elections it formed an electoral alliance with the SDSM and the SPM. In 1996 it left for the opposition, and in 1997 it merged with the DP into the Liberal Democratic Party (LDP). A group of members headed by S. Andov defected from the LDP in 1999 and founded the LPM (Šedo 2002b: 255–6). Until 2008, the LPM cooperated with the VMRO-DPMNE in electoral alliances and government coalitions. In 2008 it switched partners and joined the SDSM-led Sun Coalition, winning one seat (out of 27 seats won by the Sun Coalition).[23]

The party declares its support for liberal policies, and is a member of the European Liberal Democrat and Reform Party. Their programme emphasises the citizenship principle against that of ethnicity, and suggests a series of reform measures which may be difficult to put into practice.[24]

Conservative and Christian democratic parties

*Internal Macedonian Revolutionary Organisation – Democratic Party for Macedonian National Unity (*Vnatrešno Makedonska revolucionerna organizacia – Demokratska partija za Makedonsko narodno edinstvo*, VMRO-DPMNE)*

This party was founded in summer 1990 as a nationalist and anti-communist party (Rychlík and Kouba 2003: 248–51; Allcock 1994: 284–5). Its name refers to the Internal Macedonian Revolutionary Organisation (VMRO) which was founded in 1893 and was active in the first half of the twentieth century as a revolutionary organisation fighting against the Turks and later against the Serbs for Macedonian autonomy (the VMRO often used terrorist methods) (Rychlík and Kouba 2003: 115–25, 146–8, 158–60, 165–7). Since 1990, the legacy of the VMRO has also been used as part of the party name by several other prevailingly right-wing nationalist parties. The VMRO-DPMNE's first chairman was Ljubčo Georgievski; he was replaced in 2003 by Nikola Gruevski who still heads the party today. Georgievski founded a nationalist party, the Internal Macedonian Revolutionary Organisation – People's Party (*Vnatrešno Makedonska revolucionerna organizacija – Narodnaja partija*, VMRO-NP), in 2004.[25]

The VMRO-DPMNE won in the 1990 elections, but it was not able to find partners for a government coalition. From the establishment of a left-wing government in 1992 until 1998, it was in opposition, and because of its boycott of the second round of elections in 1994, it had no parliamentary representation for four years. It took part in the 1998 elections as part of an alliance with the Democratic Alternative (*Demokratska alternativa*, DA). This time it won, and L. Georgievski became Prime Minister; moreover its candidate, Boris Trajkovski, won the 1999 presidential elections (Rychlík and Kouba 2003: 264–7; Šedo 2002b: 258–9). The period of the VMRO-DPMNE-led government was marked by the conflict with the Albanians, which concluded with the Ohrid Framework Agreement. In the 2002 elections the VMRO-DPMNE cooperated with the LPM; in the 2006 and 2008 elections it formed a coalition with minor parties, two of Macedonian ethnicity and others representing small ethnic minorities. The VMRO-DPMNE was the strongest party in government in 2006–2008, and it can be assumed that after the landslide in 2008, it will stay in the same position. The VMRO-DPMNE-led coalition got 48.78 per cent of votes and 63 seats (53 seats for VMRO-DPMNE, and ten for the smaller parties).[26]

In the first half of the 1990s, the VMRO-DPMNE presented itself as an extreme right-wing nationalist party with anti-Albanian attitudes. In the years 1996–1998, its programme evolved and its rhetoric became more moderate; the party began to define itself as Christian democratic (Pacák 2000: 51). After the 1998 elections it accepted an Albanian coalition partner, although it was possible to form the government without Albanian participation (see Šedo 2007: 257). Its pro-Western orientation was confirmed by a change of leadership: under Gruevski, the party is presented as a conservative Christian Democratic and moderate nationalist party.[27] It is an observer member of the European People's Party.

Radical right-wing parties

In the first half of the 1990s, it was possible to include the VMRO-DPMNE in this family. There were and still are several marginal parties with a similar orientation; their representation in parliament is at best minimal. The only exception was the Internal Macedonian Revolutionary Organisation – People's Party (*Vnatrešno – Makedonska revolucionerna organizacia – Narodna partija*, VMRO-NP), which was created from the nationalist wing of the VMRO-DPMNE in 2004. In the 2006 elections it succeeded in obtaining six seats.[28] Its campaign was focused on a criticism of the Ohrid Framework Agreement. When Georgievski left, the party was marginalised and before the 2008 elections failed to register its bank account for the campaign and its list for the elections was excluded.[29]

Agrarian parties

This orientation is claimed by totally marginal subjects only.

Green parties

Membership in this family is declared by two marginal parties – the Party of the Greens (*Partija na zelenite*, PZ) and the Green Party of Macedonia (*Zelena partija na Makedonija*, ZPM). The first of these has been participating in the VMRO-DPMNE-led coalitions since 2006, and the second one is in the SDSM-led coalitions.[30] Neither is involved in the European structures of green parties.

Ethnic Albanian parties

The Democratic Party of the Albanians *(*Partia Demokratike Shqiptarëve/Demokratska Partija na Albacite*, DPA/PDSh)*

In the early 1990s, the de facto role of the only Albanian party in Macedonia was played by the Party of Democratic Prosperity (*Partia per Prosperitet Demokratik/Partija za demokratski Prosperitet*, PDP/PPD). It participated in the left-wing government after 1992, and its moderate policies were criticised by many Albanians. Some of its dissatisfied supporters left for the People's Democratic Party (*Partis Demokratis Populore/Narodna demokratska partija*, NDP/PDP). The radical wing, led by Arben Xhaferi and Menduh Thaçi, then made an attempt to win control over the PDP. In the dispute with the moderate wing headed by Xheladin Murati, the PDP represented the moderates, and the radicals ran in the 1994 elections as independents. After the election the latter formed the Party of Democratic Prosperity of Albanians (*Partia per Prosperitet Demokratik Shqiptarëve/Partija za demokratski prosperitet na Albancite* – PDPA/PPDSh). In 1997 there was a merger between the PDPA and the NDP under the name of the DPA; the chairman of the party was A. Xhaferi. The present chairman of the DPA is Menduh Thaçi (Rychlík and Kouba: 2003: 260–1; Šedo 2002b: 261–2).[31]

In the 1998 elections, the DPA cooperated with the PDP. Its target was to avoid a failure similar to the one in the 1994 elections, when the Albanian parties won only 18 seats (including four independent seats), while in 1990 they had won 23 seats (Šedo 2007: 256–7). After the elections the PDP left for the opposition; the DPA on the contrary joined the right-wing government coalition until 2002 (Šedo 2002b: 261–2). The VMRO-DPMNE chose the DPA as a governmental partner in 2006 as well. The launch of the DUI brought a clear decline in support for the DPA. In the following years the DPA was the second strongest Albanian party. The PDP ran in 2006 as part of a coalition with the DUI, and in 2008 with 0.73 per cent of vote failed to win parliamentary representation. The DPA runs a permanent campaign against the DUI, and in pre-election periods, incidents of violence take place among the supporters of both parties. In the 2008 elections, the DPA got 8.26 per cent of the vote and won 11 seats.[32]

The DPA supports the conclusions of the Ohrid Framework Agreement, and their implementation corresponds with DPA goals. In some cases it adopts a harder rhetoric in order to attract voters from the DUI. In spite of this it remains an acceptable partner for the Macedonian parties, and it is the closest to the definition of a nationalist Albanian catch-all party.[33]

*Democratic Union for Integration (*Bashkimi Demokratik për Integrim/ Demokratska unija za integracija*, DUI/BDI)*

The DUI was founded in 2002 by former UÇK leader Ali Ahmeti, who today remains as head of the party. In the 2002 elections, the party became the strongest Albanian actor; in 2002–2006 it was a member of the left-wing government coalition (Šedo 200b: 263).[34] In 2006 it ran in coalition with the PDP, and succeeded in maintaining its position as the strongest Albanian party. However, after the elections, the VMRO-DPMNE preferred the DPA. This step was said by the DUI to be an infringement of the Ohrid Framework Agreement. A series of demonstrations took place in favour of the DUI, but in the end it had to leave for the opposition. However, its position as the strongest Albanian party was confirmed again in the early elections of 2008, when the party won 18 seats (12.82 per cent of the vote).[35]

The DUI supports the conclusions of the Ohrid Framework Agreement. Like the DPA, it can be classified as a nationalist Albanian catch-all party. Its principal policy and campaign concern an improvement of the position of former UÇK fighters.[36] Considering its past, the DUI is less acceptable as a partner than the DPA for the majority of Macedonians.

Parties of other minorities

In the early elections of 2008, 12 participating parties declared a connection with a minority; (ten of them joined in coalitions with either the VMRO-DPMNE or the SDSM). In 2006 there were 13 parties and again most had one of the large Macedonian parties as a partner. In the 2008 early elections, parties representing Turks, Serbs, Roma and Bosniaks each won one seat as members of the VMRO-DPMNE led coalition (for more details see Pacák 2000: 73–7).[37]

Interim conclusion

Macedonia has succeeded in managing several problematic situations since 1990, but the political system has not yet been stabilised. First of all, disturbances and incidents appear in the country during election campaigns. Another potential problem for the future is the Albanian minority, whose share of the population is growing, and which has already succeeded in pursing their political goals through violence.

The party system is relatively stable. The Macedonians are represented by two large parties around whom coalitions have been created. Parties outside of these coalitions can succeed only for a short time. The spectrum of Albanian parties is also divided into two, which compete very intensely. The limited number of relevant actors has so far not been altered even by the proportional representation system with its relatively high degree of inclusiveness.

Notes

1 See www.summitbucharest.ro/en/doc_202.html.
2 About the lastest development for example www.tanea.gr/default. asp?pid=2&ct=1&artId=1403491.
3 www.un.org/Depts/DPKO/Missions/unpred_r.htm.
4 For the full text of the Ohrid Framework Agreement see for example www.coe.int/t/e/ legal_affairs/legal_co-operation/police_and_internal_security/OHRID%20Agreement%2013august2001.asp.
5 www.osce.org/documents/odihr/2008/08/32619_en.pdf, pp. 5–6.
6 www.osce.org/documents/odihr/2006/09/20610_en.pdf, p. 10.
7 www.osce.org/documents/odihr/2008/08/32619_en.pdf.
8 See results of the 2006 and 2008 elections on www.sec.mk:90/2009.
9 See for example www.sobranie.mk/?ItemID=389F3043E8580843B6CD7A4BCF90D D9F.
10 www.sec.mk:90/2009.
11 www.sdsm.mk/?ItemID=5A2CE21D0D8A3C46A9B3598AD9DCD325.
12 www.sec.mk:90/2009.
13 www.sec.mk:90/2009 and www.sobranie.mk/?ItemID=389F3043E8580843B6CD7A 4BCF90DD9F.
14 www.osce.org/documents/odihr/2006/09/20610_en.pdf, p. 10.
15 For the party self-presentation see nsdp.org.mk/web.
16 www.sec.mk:90/2009 and www.sobranie.mk/?ItemID=389F3043E8580843B6CD7A 4BCF90DD9F.

17 http://unpan1.un.org/intradoc/groups/public/documents/NISPAcee/UNPAN008270. pdf, p. 7.
18 www.sec.mk:90/2009 and www.sobranie.mk/?ItemID=389F3043E8580843B6CD7A 4BCF90DD9F.
19 www.ldp.org.mk.
20 www.sec.mk:90/2009 and www.sobranie.mk/?ItemID=389F3043E8580843B6CD7A 4BCF90DD9F.
21 www.ldp.org.mk.
22 www.lp.org.mk.
23 www.sec.mk:90/2009 and www.sobranie.mk/?ItemID=389F3043E8580843B6CD7A 4BCF90DD9F.
24 www.lp.org.mk.
25 www.osce.org/documents/odihr/2006/09/20610_en.pdf, p. 10.
26 www.sec.mk:90/2009 and www.sobranie.mk/?ItemID=389F3043E8580843B6CD7A 4BCF90DD9F.
27 www.vmro-dpmne.org.mk/mk/index.asp.
28 www.sec.mk:90/2009.
29 www.osce.org/documents/odihr/2008/08/32619_en.pdf, p. 8.
30 www.sec.mk:90/2009.
31 www.pdsh.info.
32 www.sec.mk:90/2009 and www.sobranie.mk/?ItemID=389F3043E8580843B6CD7A 4BCF90DD9F.
33 For the party self-presentation see www.pdsh.info.
34 www.osce.org/documents/odihr/2006/09/20610_en.pdf, p. 4.
35 www.sec.mk:90/2009.
36 www.bdi.org.mk.
37 See also www.sec.mk:90/2009 and www.sobranie.mk/?ItemID=389F3043E8580843 B6CD7A4BCF90DD9F.

12 The party system of Albania

Věra Stojarová

Overview of the political system

Albania emerged as an independent state after the Balkan wars in 1912–1913. The quest for democracy, along with internal societal divisions, led to the proclamation of a monarchy in 1928 and the subsequent authoritarian regime of Ahmed Bey Zogu. The new king sought the patronage of Italy, which became fatal to him as the Italian protection was turned into a protectorate and the king was forced to leave the country. After the Second World War, the Communist Party usurped power, and under Enver Hoxha, Albania was governed by one of the most brutal totalitarian regimes in Europe, until his death in April 1985. For most of that time the country was in isolation,[1] and the standard of living remained one of the lowest in Europe. Even though we can trace a slow liberalisation all the way back to 1985, the first (semi-)democratic elections in Albania were held in 1991.[2] In the period 1992–1997 the country was governed by the Democratic Party of Albania (PDSh), with the leader of PDSh and former Albanian president attempting to govern in a not quite fully democratic manner.[3] In 1997 Albania was rocked by the collapse of the so-called pyramid schemes,[4] and fell into anarchy. Elections were then organised with the assistance of the OSCE, and these were won by the Socialist party of Albania (PSSh), which was the governing party until 2005 when it was replaced with a coalition of parties under PDSh leadership.

The presidency was held in 1992–1997 by PDSh leader Sali Berisha. In 1997 a new president was inaugurated, Rexhep Mejdani. In 2002 the presidential post was taken up by the former minister of defence, retired general Alfred Moisiu, and in 2007 the deputy chairman of the PDSh and former director of the Veterinary Institute, Bamir Topi, became president. As the Democratic Party received the majority of the votes in the elections of 2005,[5] its leader and former Albanian president Sali Berisha became Prime Minister. People loyal to the Socialist Party were immediately dismissed from their posts at all levels of the state administration, while the media as well as the courts and academic world come under attack by the new state authorities. Berisha decided to trim the executive powers of local government, and move some of its competences to the central government.[6] The latter also took control over the council for radio and TV broadcasting. One of the biggest scandals of the Berisha administration was the so-called *Albatrosgate*, which refers to the government's decision to shut down the *Albatros* airline (owned by Moisiu's nephew) in order to increase pressure on the president to agree to dismiss the prosecutor-general. Berisha was not successful, as the affair attracted the attention of the media as well as civil society, and the biggest NGO dealing with democracy and transparency issues, MJAFT, (Albanian for 'enough') then called for a protest against these government practices.[7] Berisha won out on the issue only after the newly elected president Bamir Topi dismissed the prosecutor general, Theorori Sollaku, in November 2007.

Today Albania is working under its seventh Constitution (including the Italian war-time one). The current Constitution, approved in a referendum in 1998, was amended in 2007[8] and again in April 2008. The last constitutional changes were passed through parliament in haste: Chapter XII of the Constitution on the *Central Election Commission*, specifically Articles 153 and 154, were annulled;[9] the electoral system was changed to one based on regional proportional representation. Under the new rules, voters no longer cast ballots for candidates but for parties, which then nominate their representatives to the Assembly.

> According to the reform, the electoral districts should coincide with one of the administrative levels of the country. This means that the number of voters, of deputies, as well as the threshold allowing the election of a parliamentarian will vary from one electoral sector to another. Thus, in the most populous areas, the threshold for getting an elected official will be relatively low, while in areas where the density of population is less, it will be much higher. We can say that according to one of the amendments, parties not getting past a threshold of 10 per cent of the votes, which in some regions can reach 20 per cent, will be deprived of representation.
>
> (Moniquet 2008: 2)

The reforms also allow for the election of the president by a majority vote in the fourth round of balloting, instead of the previously required three-fifths vote. The legislation sets the term of office for the state prosecutor, which was previously unlimited, to five years. It also requires the dissolution of parliament and new elections if the government loses a parliamentary vote of confidence.

The reform was agreed by the Democrats and Socialists, while the smaller parties demanded a referendum on the amendments and a wider debate, accompanied by a consultation with experts and interest groups; accordingly, they have started to collect the signatures needed to hold a plebiscite which would reject the constitutional changes.[10]

It remains unclear whether the constitutional amendments will be reversed; therefore the next section will be based on the Constitution as it was, before the amendments were passed. The president is elected by the parliament (three-fifths of all members of the parliament, so 84 votes are needed). If one is not elected even after a fifth round, the parliament is dissolved and the new parliament will elect the president by an absolute majority of all members).[11] The president is elected for a five-year term with the right of one re-election. The Constitution guarantees a strong position for the government, which can in an emergency issue laws without any further approval of the legislature. There is no collective responsibility; every minister is responsible for his/her resort. Change-overs of ministers are quite frequent, and the instability of governments is quite high.[12] Prosecution of former ministers by present ones is quite frequent.[13]

The Parliament of Albania consists of 140 deputies, 100 of whom are directly elected from single electoral districts with a similar number of electors, while 40 deputies are elected from multi-candidate lists of parties/or coalitions (2.5 per cent threshold for parties and 4 per cent for coalitions). The Parliament is elected for a four-year period (Constitution Article 75/2). Albania is divided into 12 counties (*qarque*), whose competences were limited in the beginning of the 1990s but then expanded in 1995.

Albania is striving to integrate into the Euro-Atlantic structures; its main protector and ally remains the USA. The country was invited to join NATO at the Bucharest summit, and it is hoping to join the Alliance in 2009. None of the governments have so far propagated the creation of a Greater Albania. Even though Albania has not endured any ethnic conflict, the democratisation of the country remains on a very low level, and EU membership remains more a dream than a reality.

Development of party system

Since the beginning of the transition, the Albanian political system has been highly polarised, with two dominant political parties – the Socialist Party of Albania (PSSh, in power 1997–2005) and the Democratic Party of Albania (PDSh, in power 1992–1997 and since 2005, cf. Biberaj 1999; Schmidt and Neke 2001). These two parties make up a strong component of the party system, but the same cannot be said of their coalition partners. The Democratic Party of Albania draws most of its support from northern Albania, while the Socialist party of Albania is more successful in the south.[14] Officially around 90 parties are registered, while 13 of them are at present (2008) in the parliament. The polarisation is accompanied with a distrust of the political actors, who only communicate with each other via the media or other channels. The biggest problem seems to be the personal animosity between the PDSh leader, Sali Berisha, the former PSSh leader Fatos Nano, and the present chief of the PSSh Edi Rama (cf. Schmidt 2000b).

The Democratic Party was set up as a classic catch-all party, and personal animosities quickly led to the rise of a faction led by Gramoz Pashko, Azem Hajdari and Arben Imami who were critical of Berisha. In 1992, some party members were dismissed from the party membership, which led to the creation of a new party, the Democratic Alliance, led by Neritan Çeka. After the 1997 elections a new internal split emerged: Genc Polo stood in opposition to Berisha, accused him of mafia practices, and announced the creation of a new Democratic Alternative within the party as a step towards party democratisation. However, the internal reformation was unsuccessful, and Genc Polo set up shop with his supporters in the New Democratic Party.

A schism emerged in the Socialist Party in 2001, when Fatos Nano accused party rival (and former Prime Minister) Ilyr Meta of corruption, and challenged him for the presidential post. After the calming of inter-party disputes, a new government was formed in March 2002 by Pandeli Majko, while a compromise was found in the election of a non-abrasive general in retirement, Alfred Moisiu. Fatos Nano pushed for a resolution that the leader of the party must be at the same time Prime Minister. Pandeli Majko was unsuccessful in his candidacy for the post of a PSSh chairman, so in June 2002, former party president Fatos Nano became Prime Minister. Ilyr Meta then left the party and set up the new Socialist Movement for Integration in September 2004. Nevertheless, Fatos Nano was removed from the party chairmanship one year later, when the popular former mayor of Tiran, Edi Rama, was elected to the party presidency. Fatos Nano announced the foundation of a faction within the part, the Movement for Institutional Politics, with the aim of revitalising the Socialist Party.[15]

Party families

It would be misleading to speak of right and left in Albanian politics; instead, we shall speak about the partners of PSSh and PDSh, though some of the party families could be depicted with reservations. Among the frequent allies of the Democratic Party are the Republican Party of Albania or Liberal Democratic Party, and sometimes the Legality Movement or the National Front. Among the parties which usually ally with the Socialists are the Social Democratic Party, the Party of Democratic Alliance, or the Movement for Unity and Human Rights.[16] The extreme right-wing party, the National Front, remains on the margin of the political spectrum. The monarchist party family is represented by the Legality Movement. However, the monarchist idea does not have wide support in Albania, and this party also remains on the margins. Much the same could be said about the extreme left-wing parties, and the radical left of the political spectrum is not represented in parliament. The green parties face a similar problem – the Environmental–Agrarian Party gained only four mandates in the last elections. The last elections were held in 2005,[17] after which the Democratic Party and its allies formed a government.

Communist parties

*Albanian Party of Labour (*Partia e Punës e Shqipërisë*, PPSh) and*
*Communist Party of Albania (*Partia e Komunistëve e Shqipërisë*, PKSh)*

With the transformation of the Albanian Party of Labour into the Socialist party (PSSh) and its abandonment of Marxism–Leninism, the hard core wing decided to set up the Communist Party of Albania (PKSh). After the 1992 elections (in which the party gained 0.32 per cent of the votes), parties based on Enverism (the policies of the Enver Hoxha regime) and Stalinism were banned, and so the party went underground and split into factions. In August 1998, the Ministry of

Justice officially recognised the Renewed Communist Party (*Partia Komuniste e Shqipërisë e Rindertuar*, PKShR) and the New Albanian Party of Labour (*Partia e Re e Punës së Shqipërisë*, PRPSh). In 2002, the Communist Party of Albania, the Albanian Party of Labour, and other small Enverist formations merged and formed a renewed Albanian Party of Labour. Support for communist parties remains minimal; none of them have succeeded in passing the electoral threshold. The parties' common ideological core lies in the legacy of Enver Hoxha and 'the dedication to the Albanian people, fatherland and the national question'.[18]

Socialist and social-democratic parties

Socialist Party of Albania (Partia Socialiste e Shqipërisë, PSSh)

Even though the party abandoned its communist past at its tenth party congress and adopted a new party name, it is not willing to acknowledge responsibility for the crimes of the communist past. After electoral defeat in 1992, the party stood in opposition to the Democratic Party, and tried to hinder the transformation process. People tied to the previous communist regime remained in the leadership of the party. The chairman of the party, Fatos Nano, was imprisoned after the victory of the Democratic Party in 1992, but after the rebellion in 1997 he became Prime Minister. The Socialists remained in power till 2005, when they gained only 42 mandates in the elections and left for the opposition. The party's programme includes integration of Albania into the European Union, while maintaining social rights and policies of justice for all, and public as well as private forms of property (PS 2007). The party remains internally split: in 2007, Fatos Nano broke away and founded a new party, the Movement for Institutional Politics (sometimes referred to as Movement for Solidarity) with the aim of regaining his lost position in the government.

Social Democratic Party of Albania (Partia Socialdemokrate e Shqipërisë, PSDSh)

The PSDSh was the third largest party in the Albanian parliament in 1992–1996 (seven mandates). Although the party participated in the government led by the Democratic Party, it also criticised the latter and very often sided with the opposition Socialists, mainly on economic issues. In 1997–2005 it was part of the Socialist governments. In the 2005 elections, the party gained seven mandates. The party's leader is Skënder Gjinushi. The party describes itself as a European leftist party positioned on the centre-left of the spectrum of Albanian politics; it is a full member of the Socialist International; it advocates freedom and democracy, equality and social rights, solidarity and national ideals (PSDSh undated: B1). The party declares that the national question is among its priorities, though it states that the integration of all Albanians shall be implemented through the integration of the region into the EU, as the PSDSh is against changing the borders by violence, and respects all international acts and documents dealing with the issue (PSDSh undated: C1).

*Party of Social Democracy (*Partia Demokracia Sociale e Shqiperise,
PDSSh)

Originally a faction from PSDSh, the PDSSh was set up in 2003. It is led by
Paskal Milo, and in 2005 it gained two mandates. The PDSSh cooperates with
the parties of the Socialist International, and identifies itself as a party of the
centre-left. Its programme gives special attention to the depoliticisation and
modernisation of the armed forces, the police and intelligence agencies. Quite
naturally, a large part of the programme is devoted to social policies – their
implementation is envisioned through decentralisation and introducing social
policies at the regional and communal level (PDSSh undated: 3.1.).

*Socialist Movement for Integration (*Lëvizja Socialiste për Intigrim,
LSI)

The party was founded by former Albanian Prime Minister Ilir Meta (1999–2002)
in 2004, from a faction within the PSSh.[19] The party declares a liberal democratic
orientation as well as social democratic values; it is unique in the system as it
strives to introduce civic values in the clientelist Albanian system. Nevertheless,
the primary declared aim is the integration of Albania into Euro-Atlantic structures. The party gained five mandates in the 2005 parliamentary elections.

Centrist and liberal parties

*Party of Democratic Alliance (*Partia Aleanca Demokratike, *PAD)*

The party was founded in 1992 by former members of the Democratic Party; its
chairman was Neritan Çeka. The party was very critical of the governments the
Democrats took part in, and often voted with the Socialists. It was the only party
in Albania which advocated the consolidation of bilateral relations with Serbia
to the detriment of the Kosovo Albanians. In 1993, Çeka visited Belgrade, which
was perceived as national treason. The party was in favour of improving bilateral
relations with Greece, and blamed the government for its bad relations with its
southern neighbour. The PAD has adopted a strongly anti-Islamic stance.
Though the party claims to stand for liberalism, it has been part of the socialist
governments of 1997–2005. The current chairman is Gramoz Pashko. The party
has held three mandates in parliament since 2005.

*Democratic Party of Albania (*Partia Demokratike e Shqipërisë, *PDSh)*

The Democratic Party was founded in 1990 and quickly evolved into a classic
catch-all party. It describes itself as a centre-right party, though in some vital
economic issues it acts in a leftist manner. The party is strongly centralised: the
main power remains in the hands of the party chairman and former president
(1992–1997) and Prime Minister (since 2005), Sali Berisha. The PDSh was the

strongest party in 1992–1996; after its defeat in the 1997 elections, it began to boycott sessions of parliament, and moved from the centre of the political scene. In 2002, after an internal schism in the party, its chief Berisha acknowledged that a constructive dialogue was the way to solve political conflicts. Fearing another defeat, the PDSh formed the Union for Victory (*Bashkimi Për Fitore*, BF), which was composed of right-wing to centre-right political parties. This coalition gained 46 mandates in the 140-seat parliament, so it stayed in opposition. Berisha could not accept the defeat, and began again to boycott parliament. The next elections, however, were victorious for the PDSh: the party together with its allies won 79 mandates (PDSh itself won 56 mandates) and it then formed a coalition government under the chairmanship of Berisha.[20]

*Republican Party of Albania (*Partia Republikane e Shqipërisë, *PRSh)*

The PRSh was the second party to run against the Albanian Party of Labour under the chairmanship of Sabri Godo. The party remains fragmented and does not achieve significant results in elections. The main slogan of the 1994 campaign was the return of property confiscated under the Hoxha regime. In 2005 with its allies, it formed the Alliance for Freedom, Justice and Welfare (*Aliansa për Liri, Drejtësi dhe Mirëqenie*, ALDM). The party is a natural ally of the Democratic Party[21]; it won 11 seats in parliament in 2005. The present chairman is former defence minister Fatmir Mediu.

*New Democratic Party (*Partia Demokrate e Re, *PDR)*

The party was set up only six months before the 2001 elections, in which it succeeded in gaining six mandates. It is led by Genz Pollo. The creation of the PD was a result of an internal split in the PDSh, which among other things was caused by the insistence of the party's president on boycotting parliamentary sessions. The party is an observer member of the European People's Party. The party gained four seats in the 2005 parliamentary elections.

*Christian Democratic Party of Albania (*Partia Demokristiane e Shqipërisë, *PDK)*

The party was founded in 1991, and draws most of its support from northern Albania. The party won two seats in the July 2005 parliamentary elections. The leader of the PDK is Nard Ndoka. In 2007, the party suffered an internal split from which a new party emerged, the Albanian Christian Democratic Movement.

*Liberal Democratic Union (*Bashkimi Liberal Demokrat, *BLD)*

The party was founded in 1995 as the Social Democratic Union of Albania (*Bashkimi i Social Demokratikët i Shqipërisë*). The BLD won one parliamentary seat. The leader of the party is Arjan Starova.

Agrarian and environmental parties

*Agrarian Environmental Party (*Partia Agrare Ambjentaliste, *PAA)*

Set up in 1991 as the Agrarian Party of Albania, the PAA focuses on rural populations, addressing mainly property rights. It secured four parliamentary seats in the July 2005 election. The party leader is Lufter Xhuveli.

Monarchist Parties

*Legality Movement (*Partia Levizja e Legalitetit, *PLL)*

The party supports the restoration of the monarchy and the return to power of the House of Zogu. Crown Prince Leka returned to Albania in 1997 before the planned referendum on the restoration of the monarchy (the result of the referendum was that most voters favoured a parliamentary republic). Leka has been living in Albania since 2002 and has been trying to move the opinion polls in favour of the monarchy. Even though he was indicted for illegal weapons smuggling, after a long debate he gained a diplomatic passport as an expression of Albania's effort to re-integrate the royal family into post-communist society. The party advocates awarding the royal family special status, and returning their property. The party has very little support in society; it allies with the PDSh and usually scores one or two mandates.

Radical nationalist parties

*Party of the National Front (*Partia Balli Kombëtar, *BK) and the*
*Democratic National Front Party (*Partia Balli Kombëtar Demokrat,*
PBKD)

The Party of the National Front is a radical right-wing party and successor of the party of the same name which during the Second World War fought with the Axis powers for the unification of lands inhabited by ethnic Albanians. The party has been a strong supporter of the restitution of property confiscated under the previous regime, and it demands the complete de-communisation of society. The programme has a strong nationalist component, advocating the unification of Albania with Kosovo, northern Epirus, western Macedonia, south-eastern Serbia and part of Montenegro. The party split in 1997 due to internal personal disagreements between Hysen Selfo and Abaz Ermenji, when the former decided to set up the new Democratic National Front. The PBK did not gain any seats in the 2005 elections, as the Central Electoral Commission denied the PBK's request to join the Alliance for Freedom, Justice and Well-Being, because it missed the deadline to apply. Instead, the PBKD joined the Alliance coalition, but it did not gain any seats either.[22] There have been repeated proposals to merge the two parties, but they remain un-implemented.

Ethnic parties

*Party for Unity and Human Rights (*Partia Bashkimi për të Drejtat e Njeriut, *PBDNJ,* Κόμμα Ένωσης Ανθρωπίνων Δικαιωμάτων*)*

This party evolved from the Omonia party. Its electorate is composed of ethnic Greeks living in the south of Albania, as well as other minorities (Vlach, Roma, Serb, Macedonian, Bulgarian, etc.) The party usually gains from one to three seats in the parliament. It is led by Vangjel Dule.

Interim conclusion

The political system in Albania remains very fragile even nearly twenty years after the beginning of the transition. Governments are weak, while the political culture remains on a very low level. Although the political system remains unstable and the country is among the poorest in Europe, Albania has been quite successful in its foreign policy. Its restraint on the Greater Albania question, as well as the Albanian engagement in Bosnia and Herzegovina, Afghanistan and Iraq, has persuaded NATO to invite Albania to join its structures. Integration into the EU remains the next goal of Albanian foreign policy.

The party system is quite stable: two main political rivals, the Democrats and the Socialists, form alternate governments with other small allies. The rivalry of the parties has been very intense, and their relations remain antagonistic, as they lack the will to cooperate. Outside these two big parties the political spectrum remains fragmented, and after the 2005 elections 12 parties sent representatives to the People's Assembly. The power in the hands of the two parties might even become absolute if constitutional amendments are not blocked. There is a whole spectrum of party families, but all remain on the political margins. The stance of the main parties towards the issue of unification of ethnic Albanian lands is rather neutral, respecting the sovereignty of neighbouring states while stating in the same breath that Albanians will unite anyway, in the European Union.

Notes

1 Until 1948 Albania was allied with Yugoslavia, next with USSR until 1956, and then until approximately 1978 with China.
2 For the early period of the emerging party system, see e.g. Hoppe 1993.
3 More about the form of the regime see Balík and Stojarová 2005.
4 For further information, see Jarvis 2000.
5 Freedom House described it as the 'first change of power without significant violence'. Nevertheless, the elections were marred by multiple voting, security breaches, and electoral violence which resulted in one death. Cited from Immigration and Refugee Board of Canada. *Country fact sheet Albania 2007.* Available online at www.unhcr.org/cgi-bin/texis/vtx/refworld/rwmain/opendocpdf.pdf?docid=47de299b0.
6 These were mainly competences regarding building permits, town planning, and public works.
7 *Protest of 'Civil Action', in defense of Democracy* 29th of September, 2006. MJAFT. Available online at www.mjaft.org/news_al.php?faqe=news&newsid=771.

8 The changes related to local elections (the mandate of mayors and local governments was prolonged to four years) and the Central Electoral Commission (nine members instead of seven).

9 CEC announced that 'it continues to operate as an institution, whose organization, functions and powers are established in the Electoral Code'. Available online at www. cec.org.al/2004/eng/veprimtaria/2008/Prill.htm.

10 See Venice Commission 2008.

11 The new Albanian president thanked his re-election to ten votes from the ranks of the opposition, so he was able to gain 85 votes in favour.

12 The reasons are usually allegations of corruption and ties to organised crime. There are many examples from both governing sides. In November 1993, the Minister of Economy and Finance, Genc Ruli, was forced to resign due to allegations of cigarette smuggling and other financial scandals with a French national, Nicolas Arsidi. In December 2001, three more ministers had to resign due to allegations of corruption and abuse of power.

13 The Socialist chairman Fatos Nano was imprisoned in June 1993 and accused of misappropriating US$8 million. The former Prime Minister Vilson Ahmeti was sentenced to two years for abuse of power in 1995.

14 The Albanians are internally divided into southerners (Tosks, Labs, Chams) and the northerners (Gegs). The pre-Second World War ruler King Zog came from the north whereas Enver Hoxha came from the south, and the Communist Party (Albanian Party of Labour) drew most of its support from southern Albania. Even though the Democratic Party of Albania is traditionally a northern party, it achieved good results in the 2003 local elections, even in some southern municipalities.

15 www.tiranaobserver.com.al/al/index.php?option=com_content&task=view&id=2558 &Itemid=42.

16 The party has been in the coalition government with PDSh since 2005.

17 The results of the 2005 elections in the next section are taken from the Central Electoral Commission www.cec.org.al/2004/Zgjedhejekuvendfiles/Rez-zgjedhje2005/ rezultatetper cent20vendore/linke/perberjaper cent20eper cent20kuvendit_grafiku.pdf.

18 www.pksh.org/.

19 www.ilirmeta.com/index.php?page=cv.

20 www.partiademokratike.al.

21 Nevertheless, the leader of the party warned in October 2008 that it may run on its own in the 2009 elections, as it has its own electorate and potential. www.setimes. com/cocoon/setimes/xhtml/en_GB/newsbriefs/setimes/newsbriefs/2008/10/01/nb-09.

22 The coalition gained 18 seats altogether.

Conclusion

Věra Stojarová

In the context of the dissolution of the former Yugoslavia and the turbulence of the transition from stone-age communism in Albania, the countries of the Western Balkans have encountered special problems in building viable political communities and avoiding various forms of warfare and civic violence (Lewis 2001: 152). Despite the lack of a solid democratic tradition, the parties had to find a way to adapt to the new conditions, institutionalise, and re-discover paths towards conflict resolution found in the previously established democracies in Western Europe (c.f. Katz and Crotty 2006; Bartolini and Mair 1990; Epstein 1967; Diamandouros and Gunther 2001; Niedermayer *et al.* 2006 etc.). Heterogeneous umbrella coalitions uniting reform-minded parties were not found in many of the Balkan countries, as they were in other CEE countries. Opportunist politicians took advantage of the new era, and presented democracy to their voters through the prism of ethnicity, and transmutation rather than transformation was the result.

After almost two decades in the new environment, some of the systems have come to resemble their Western European counterparts, while others are still struggling, and display the same structure of a competition based on ethnicity, as in the beginning of the 1990s. Delayed institutionalisation was caused mainly by conflicts (Croatia, Bosnia and Herzegovina, Kosovo and partially Macedonia) and later by democratisation. In Croatia and in Serbia, a second attempt at democratisation took place around the start of the new millennium; but the Albanian regime could not be depicted as fully democratic until the 1997 uprising. Both Bosnia and Herzegovina and Kosovo are special cases, as they are still under international supervision; Macedonian politics is hindered by great struggles among political leaders; and in the case of Montenegro, a real change of the party system has to occur to make it comparable with its Western counterparts.

The shape of the party systems has been partially influenced by electoral reforms. The chapter dealing with electoral systems has shown how they varied from country to country, with an overall trend moving from majoritarian, either directly or in stages, to full proportionality. There has also been a trend to ensure representation of minorities by introducing set-aside seats for national minorities (Kosovo), creating special countrywide electoral districts for minorities (Croatia), establishing special polling units in the geographical area where most

Albanians live (Montenegro), or eliminating the mandate threshold for the political parties of national minorities (Serbia).

The second chapter revealed that in most cases, the successor communist parties managed to transform into socialist or socio-democratic groupings, except for the Communist League of Kosovo which ceased to exist in 1990. The Albanian PSSh kept its socialist ideology until the second half of 1990s, and then changed more towards social democracy. The Macedonian and Croatian post-communists successfully reformed, while the former retained power and the latter returned to government at a later stage of the transition. Social democracy with a nationalist attribute was adopted in the case of Serbia and Montenegro, and thus those parties held on to power. All the post-communist parties in the Western Balkans are members of the Socialist International, with the exception of the Serbian SPS; only the Croatian SDP and Macedonian SDSM are associate PES members.

As the third chapter showed, nationalist parties in the region of the Western Balkans are usually xenophobic towards local ethnicities, and typically strive for mono-ethnic countries within expanded borders. Croatian nationalism is on the decline: the HDZ is slowly distancing itself from nationalism and has moved to the centre of the political spectrum, while the rest of the extreme right is scattered with only the HSP being represented regularly in parliament. This is not the case in Serbia where the position of the SRS is stable (with the exception of 2000 elections), reaching 29 per cent in the 2008 elections while retaining the idea of a Greater Serbia in its programme. Ethnic Albanian political parties advocating a Greater Albania are not relevant, neither in Kosovo nor in Albania and Macedonia. Nor is ethnic Macedonian nationalism represented by any political party in Macedonia. The parties in BiH, Kosovo, and Montenegro, however, are still divided along ethnic lines.

The chapter dealing with national minorities in the party systems has shown that with the partial exception of Montenegro, the majority of mainstream parties have been unable to attract the votes of minorities. Florian Bieber remarks that the configuration of party systems along ethnic lines is largely a consequence of the unwillingness of majority parties to seriously incorporate minority community concerns, often due to fears of alienating the majority. In order to secure ethnic minority representation, the regional trend seems to be the inclusion of set-aside seats on the basis of ethnic affiliation: Croatia, Bosnia and Herzegovina, Montenegro, and Kosovo have reserved seats for their ethnic minorities in parliament. Despite these efforts, there is one ethnic group that remains consistently underrepresented in the region – the Roma. Nevertheless, as the author notes, this seems to be rather the result of the political and social marginalisation of the community.

However, it would not be wise to generalise, as the countries followed different patterns. Croatia's democratisation was a rather protracted process, and the country was criticised by human rights watchers for limiting the freedom of the press and restricting civil and political rights. The situation improved after the death of Franjo Tuđman, the subsequent elections, and the victory of the opposition SDP and its allies. The subsequent change in the HDZ leadership and its defeat in the 2000 elections gave the party time to restructure and remedy its democratic deficit. Meanwhile the ruling SDP succeeded in changing some of the relics of the previous regime; since then, the country has been rated as free, while gaining a rating of two for political liberties and civil liberties.[1]

Until 2000 we would probably speak of a not fully competitive system, and the predominance of the HDZ, with only one pole of the political axis being occupied. The significant change occurred prior to the elections in 2000, when the opposition parties maximised their effort to defeat the ruling HDZ, resulting in a broad coalition consisting of six parties. In 2003, the SDP's motivation for finding more coalition partners decreased, and the results showed two poles occupied, one by the HDZ and the other by the SDP. A similar pattern as in 2000 arose from the 2007 elections – we find six relevant parties in the system (the HDZ, HSS, HSLS, SDS, SDSS and HNS). The system remains bipolar, and competition somewhat centripetal; there is no radical left party represented in the parliament, and since 2007, there is only one representative of the radical right, (the HSP), which has very low coalition potential and an ever-decreasing electoral result.

The smaller parties tend to re-group and enter a winning coalition, whether right or left; and the two big parties find themselves with different coalition partners (for example, the HSLS was in coalition with the SDP in 2000, and now it is in the HDZ coalition government and holding the ministry of internal affairs; the SDP ran in coalition with the liberals and the IDS before the 2003 elections, and then alone in the 2007 elections). The structure of the competition in Croatia is relatively open, but the competition takes place only among the existing players, which could be due to the polarisation caused by the long dominance of the HDZ (Šedo 2007: 222). The average duration of governments in the period June 1990–December 2008 is 23.4 months. This low number is mainly due, first, to unstable formations in the early 1990s, and second, because of the situation in the coalition after the 2000 elections; while the HDZ-led governments from 1995 and from 2003 prop up the average length of government duration.[2]

The current arrangement in Bosnia and Herzegovina stems mainly from the Dayton Peace Agreement concluded in Dayton and signed in Paris in 1995. The country has been divided into two entities, the Federation of Bosnia and Herzegovina (Croat–Muslim entity) and Republika Srpska. The self-governing District of Brčko was established as a third independent unit enjoying special status outside the entities since 1999. The international community plays an important role in post-conflict reconstruction, and the High Representative for Bosnia and Herzegovina is the final authority in the country. Despite considerable efforts, most aspects of political, economic and social life remain divided along ethnic lines. The country is rated as partially free, scoring four for political rights and three for civil liberties (Freedom House 2008). There are actually two party systems in the country which meet on the national level, and the systems remain open.

The main parties which were formed at the beginning of 1990s (or their splinter parties) have survived and still prevail, even in the post-war environment. There has been a great number of conflicts (usually personal rather than programmatic) within the parties, and these usually lead to a split in the party and the creation of a new one. New parties are successful to a certain extent; but intra-party democracy remains very limited, and the parties tend to be personality based rather than programmatic.

The SDA, HDZ and SDS were dominant before the civil war and until shortly after the war ended, when their main competitors arose, mostly from splinter parties. At present we can conclude, with a little simplification, that Bosniak voters vote mainly for the SDA, SBiH or SDP; the Croat vote for either the HDZ or HDZ-1990; and the Serbs cast their ballots either for SNSD, SDS, PDP or SRS. Any research or analysis of the parties' orientation is complicated, as the parties tend not to have a firm programme or ideological orientation, and some of their proclamations or policies are not included in their programmes due to bans or suppression by the OHR. Classification of the parties according to party families becomes complicated and, as Jakub Šedo notes, it is better when analysing the party families to define a party first by its connection with the appropriate ethnicity, and to consider its programmatic orientation as secondary. Except for the SDP, which is the closest of all the relevant parties to having a non-ethnic character, the primary classification of the parties follows the criterion of the constituent nation each party belongs to. The assessment of stability of the governments is highly problematic, as the first elections held according to a four-year cycle took place only in 2006. Nevertheless, no government has made it through a two-year cycle without any changes in its composition. The average government lasted 16.1 months, while the greatest stability was achieved during the second half of the war and in the first four-year period 2002–2006.

The Serbian transition was the most complicated and uneasy one. The splintered opposition was unable to overcome the SPS in the (not very fair) elections and to dismantle the undemocratic regime. National reconciliation has still not taken place, and the situation is further complicated by the Kosovo issue (which was not solved for the Serbian side on 17 February 2008). The democracy ratings do not really reflect the state of affairs in Serbia, as they were given for Serbia and Montenegro until 2006, and incorporated conditions in Kosovo as well. In 2001, the country was still rated as partially free, rating four for both political and civil liberties; in the 2003 report the countries were rated as free for the very first time, and in 2008 the rating for civil liberties improved to two (Freedom House).

As Daniel Bochsler clearly pointed out in his chapter, there are four political conflicts which seem relevant for Serbian voters. The most reformist parties have been united in opposition to the Milošević regime; many of them favour EU integration and share a civic–liberal view of the state; they are open to critically reassessing recent Serbian history, and promote liberal economic reforms, while the old regime party is rather Moscow-oriented in its foreign policy, pursues nationalist–authoritarian values, is not open to dealing with the past, and its position on economic issues is not a united one.

There is a relatively small number of new parties entering the Serbian political spectrum, and the players remain much the same as in the mid-1990s. Despite this, the party scene has re-grouped with every election, and the number of poles keeps changing as well. Already in 1992, the SPS and SRS were the two strongest parties; thus the system pointed to two extreme poles under different conditions and different environments. However, the nationalism of both, and their (in)formal coalitions, point to the SPS and SRS as occupying one pole, or the dominant SPS on the main pole while the SRS represented a minor pole. The rest of the parties occupied many small poles. The elections in 2000 marked a change: the previously opposition parties made up the main pole, with the SPS as a second main pole, and the SRS as an additional one. In the 2003 elections, the parties failed to have a common goal, and we could observe the SRS as occupying the main pole, with an additional pole occupied by the DSS and SPO/NS, the DS and the G17+ in the centre, and SPS as a second main pole. The year 2007 again featured the SRS as occupying the main pole, while the rest of the parties occupied other, minor poles. The stalemate after 2008 and the slow change in the SPS resulted in a coalition government of the DS and its allies; finally the SPS with its coalition parties and the minority parties created one pole, with the second main pole occupied by the SRS, and two small ones taken by the DSS and the LDP. As the system remained undemocratic till 2000, the concept of anti-systemic parties is not relevant until then. The situation after the October revolution shows the post-communist SPS as well as the SRS as anti-systemic, so a short glance at the party system would point to centrifugal tendencies and the occupation of two remote poles by anti-systemic parties. The results of the 2008 elections showed the SPS tending to move towards the centre, and the only remaining anti-systemic parliamentary party is the SRS. The Serbian party system together with the Albanian one are the only systems in the Western Balkans where the monarchist parties regularly gain some percentage in the elections, either in coalitions or alone, though they remain on the margins (SPO, NS). Notwithstanding, it is highly disputable whether the voters of these parties really wish to install a monarchy or whether they vote for these parties because of their activities during the 1990s and the Chetnik tradition. During the 1990s, majority governments alternated with minority or majority coalition governments. The governments after 2000 have been characterised by a high number of parties and members.[3] The average length of governments is 19.5 months (Šedo 2007: 247). The structure of competition in the Serbian party system remains open and unpredictable.

Serbia is a country rich in regional parties despite its strong centralisation. Some parties run on a regionalist programme, while others appeal for the votes of ethnic groups territorially concentrated in a small area. The largest regional parties can be found in the multi-ethnic Vojvodina region; the Albanian minority mainly competes in the Preševo Valley, and Bosniak political parties are most important in the Sandžak region. These ethno-regional parties tend to compete along ethnic lines, or demand the decentralisation of Serbia. As Daniel Bochsler remarks, the openness of the regional parties to coalitions puts ethnic and regional parties in a position from which, sooner or later, they might be able to negotiate for a more decentralised system.

Montenegrin democratisation has been complicated, as many of the factors which would lead to the democratisation of the country were superseded by the Serbian/Montenegrin cleavage on the question of Yugoslavian engagement in the wars in Slovenia, Croatia, BiH and Kosovo. The tight results of the referendum on Montenegrin independence in 2006 show the persistence of the ethnic cleavage. The post-communists succeeded in remaining in power, and there has not been any real alternation in power. In the 1990s, the dominant DPS CG occupied one pole, until in 1998 a second pole was created with the split in the party and the creation of the SNP CG. Competition is relatively open; nevertheless this is not reflected in the results, which are rather predictable, although this could be due to the unfinished process of democratisation, low political culture, clientelism and nepotism. The two main poles remain occupied; there has not been any relevant extreme left party represented in the parliament, and the extreme right SRS CG was represented in the parliament with eight mandates after the 1992 elections and with one mandate after 2006 elections. The Freedom House labelled Montenegro as partially free, scoring three for political as well as civil liberties (Freedom House 2008).

The two main Montenegrin parties remained technocratic; the governing DPS exhibited a chameleonic nature, adapting to different situations along no clear lines. Therefore, even though the parties claim to be right or left, there is no really clear identification and positioning on the right–left axis. The main cleavage during the 1990s remained the question – *to be or not to be with Serbia?* – while the next most significant issues of division was support for one or other political leader. As Florian Bieber points out, as long as the DPS remains the largest governing party, many issues in the development of the party scene are likely to focus on support for or opposition to the DPS. However, if a change in government comes about, there is the potential for the development of alternative lines of orientation in the party spectrum; in that case ideological distinctions, ethnic politics, and the north–south divide (economic and cultural) are likely to shape the agenda of political parties. Determining the stability of Montenegrin governments could be complicated as there are differences in sources used, and some of the changes in the governments which are cited do not necessarily mean a fully new government. In this case, seven governments would make an average of 27.1 months per government. As early elections have been called for 29 March 2009, the number could slightly fall.

In June 1999, the United Nations was tasked with governing Kosovo through UNMIK, with a mandate to oversee the democratisation process. The Kosovo Albanians' relationship with the international community began to deteriorate after the declaration of independence in February 2008, when the six point plan was proposed.[4] The Kosovo representatives resisted the plan, and regional security experts pointed to the risk of destabilising the region if the plan were implemented (Six-point plan on Kosovo will destabilise Balkans, UN six-point plan 2008). At present (2008), 54 countries have recognised the independence of

Kosovo while Serbia, Russia and four EU countries, among others, have refused to do so. The future of international missions as well as the internal administration of Kosovo remain open, but should be clarified by the upcoming plan currently being negotiated. The Freedom House rating for Kosovo remains the worst of the countries analysed so far, scoring six for political rights and five for civil liberties (Freedom House 2008).

The political party scene in Kosovo is quite young, compared to others in the Western Balkans. The first political parties in Kosovo were founded at the end of 1980s; nevertheless, the political party scene began to flourish only after 1999. After the first elections, a grand coalition consisting of LDK, PDK, AAK and the (Serbian and Turkish) minority parties was formed. The next elections saw a change, when LDK formed a coalition with the AAK and the minority parties only. Ramush Haradinaj left the post of Prime Minister due to allegations of war crimes from the ICTY, and Bajram Kosumi was elected and remained in the post until 2006, when former UÇK commandant Agim Çeku took over. After the 2007 elections another broad coalition composed of the PDK, LDK and the minority parties emerged. The average length of the governments in the period March 2002–January 2008 was 23.05 months.[5]

The LDK and PDK seem to have stabilised on the party scene, while the others keep re-grouping. The structure of the competition remains open. The parties do not profile themselves on socio-economic issues, but are personality based, and do not show any ideological profile, thus the pattern of polarisation remains unclear. Currently, the only cleavage is probably the ethnic one – Albanians do have a wide range of parties to vote for; the Serbs can decide whether to vote for the pro-Belgrade parties or for one which is willing to participate in the new Kosovo administration. Then there is a range of parties affiliated to ethnic minorities – Turks, Egyptians, Bosniaks, Ashkali, Gorani and Roma. All of the parties offer prosperity, development etc.; although there is still some uncertainty as to how to achieve these aims. Once there is no more common enemy, one might expect a re-grouping of the party scene, and attempts at different strategies. However, this could last longer than expected, as Kosovo will probably have no seat at the United Nations in the short run, and the EULEX mission will initially stay in the country, which could eventually turn public opinion against the mentors from the Western hemisphere. To conclude, the party scene in Kosovo is not yet consolidated, and will be shaped by internal as well as external actors and issues.

During the whole of the 1990s, Macedonia was labelled as an oasis of peace, and used to be cited as an example of the transformation of a multi-ethnic country. However, the crisis in Kosovo led to increased demands by the ethnic Albanian minority in Macedonia, and to the awaking of latent tensions. The conflict escalated in 2001; international mediators managed to force the parties to sit down to the negotiating table and sign an agreement. The Ohrid Framework Agreement significantly strengthened the position of the Albanian minority, giving it veto rights on sensitive issues debated in the parliament. A second thorny issue for Macedonia has been the dispute with Greece over the name of the country. However, an interim solution was found (FYROM is used in international organisations and bilateral relations, while Republic of Macedonia is used in bilateral relations with those countries who recognise the country under its constitutional name). Negotiations are still ongoing and unless the issue is resolved, it seems Greece will veto Macedonian entry into Euro-Atlantic institutions. The rating from Freedom House is very similar to the scores in neighbouring countries: three for political rights as well as for civil liberties (Freedom House 2008). The political system suffers from repeated boycotts of the elections or of parliament (last time in 2007 over disapproval of the integration of an ethnic Albanian party into government that did not gain a majority of the votes of the ethnic Albanians), allegations of electoral discrepancies, and constant allegations of corruption on the part of politicians.

The party system in Macedonia is relatively stable. The main division line in the party system remains the ethnic issue. Ethnic Macedonian political parties tend to create great blocs around the core party, while ethnic Albanian political parties tend to act rather unilaterally, and compete with each other intensely. Parties of other ethnic minorities are more or less represented as well (Turks, Romas, Serbs, Bosniaks). As Jakub Šedo notes, the main competition on the ethnic Macedonian side takes place between two blocs organised around two main political rivals – VMRO-DPMNE and the post-communist SDSM. There is no relevant extreme left political party in Macedonia. The VMRO-NP could be cautiously labelled as extreme right, while in the early 1990s the VMRO-DPMNE was classified as inclining towards the extreme right. The average Macedonian government lasts 15.5 months (in the period 1991–2006); no government has lasted without changes until the end of its electoral period.

Since the beginning of its transformation, Albania has experienced capital political, economic, institutional, and societal changes. A completely isolated country opened up to the world, and its citizens were permitted to travel freely without any hindrance, not only in the country itself but abroad. The country started literally from scratch – infrastructure was lacking, industry and the whole society was based on the phobic policies of the former dictator, with numerous secret police officers a part of everyday life. Since the borders were first opened, Albania has been suffering from a great outflow of people – a brain drain. Considering the initial conditions, Albania has achieved great development. However, in comparison with other countries in the CEE, it still has a long way to go. Albania is labelled as partially free by Freedom House, with a rating of three for political rights as well as civil liberties (Freedom House 2008).

The political actors in Albania are rather stable and any new political parties entering the legislative body for the first time remain marginal. During the 1990s, parties entered electoral contests rather unilaterally, but after the turn of the millennium, some have tried to create electoral coalitions. The system remains bipolar, with two main parties, the PSSh and PDSh (either as the main pole or as the core of a coalition). In the early 1990s, both political parties represented the cleavage of old regime vs. transformation. The actions of Sali Berisha as the leader of PDSh and winner of the 1992 elections led to a popular uprising in 1997, and since then the cleavage has been personalised between the two leaders of the main: Berisha and Nano (and later on with Rama). There is no extreme left political party represented in parliament, while the extreme right (BK) is usually represented with one or two mandates. There is stability among the ethnic minority parties, the Greek minority being represented by the PBDNJ (former Omonia). As in Serbia, there is a monarchist party striving for restoration of the monarchy, though again it is represented by only one or two mandates. The average length of the governments is rather short: in the period 1991–2005, they averaged 15.6 months. All the governments were composed of broad coalitions – since 1996 there have always been more than four coalition partners – and there has never been a government formed by only one party. In 1991–1992, the country experienced a transitional non-party government (ZPC European Governments).

The party systems do not demonstrate similar paths or similar results. With simplification we can conclude that the Croatian, Macedonian, Albanian, and since 1998 the Montenegrin systems are all shaped in a bipolar way, while Serbia and BiH demonstrate multi-polarism. Kosovo's structure is not yet clearly enough evolved to fall into a pattern. The Croatian, Bosnian, and Kosovo parliaments are significant for the high number of political parties present in the parliaments; after the 2007 elections, Kosovo has the high score of 18 parties. In Montenegro, the effective number of parties at the parliamentary level reached its highest mark after the 2006 elections; nevertheless the numbers are low only at first glance; parties unite under party lists, so in the 2006 elections the eight lists represented 16 political parties, and fragmentation in the parliament is quite high. Albania scores somewhere in the middle; the nominal number of political parties is rather lower, while the only exception was the 1997 elections when 11 parties entered parliament. The nominal number of parties entering the Serbian parliament was highest in 1990 (15 parties) and lowest in 2000 (four parties); Serbia together with Macedonia have the lowest levels in region in both the nominal as well as effective number of parliamentary parties.

As elsewhere in the post-communist region, politics in the Balkans is characterised by numerous parties, weak political actors, and floating constituencies. Meanwhile, weakly institutionalised party systems function in very different

Table C.1 Effective and nominal number of parties at the parliamentary level after the last three elections

	Year/effective/nominal	Year/effective/nominal	Year/effective/nominal
Croatia	2000/4.01/11	2003/3.56/13	2007/3.07/10
BiH	2000/7.30/13	2002/7.96/14	2006/7.17/12
Serbia	2000/1.89/4	2003/4.8/6	2007/4.55/11
Montenegro	2001/2.44/5	2002/2.30/4	2006/3.16/8
Macedonia	1998/2.76/6	2002/2.88/7	2006/4.06/8
Kosovo	2001/4.15/14	2004/4.31/17	2007/5.90/18
Albania	1997/2.18/11+3	2001/2.60/7+2	2005/3.68/9+1

ways from well-established ones, and this has significant implications for democracy (Bielasiak 2005; Mainwaring 1998). Most of the Balkan political systems are among the less institutionalised, as the parties are fluid and suffer from internal fracturing which usually leads to the establishment of new parties. Party leaders tend to be autonomous agents, and party platforms are not clearly established. Thus politics tends to be personalised, and in most of the cases, ethnic issues dominate the agenda. Democratic accountability is rather low, and there is declining trust of the citizens in the institutions of the state (Stojarová *et al.* 2007). Nevertheless, it must be remarked that even where systems remain open and new parties do enter parliament, most of the latter remain marginal, and unlike in other CEE countries, the main actors remain more or less the same. The only real changes take place in the domain of strategies and configuration of the competition.[6] The range of actors is therefore more or less the same, and only the parties themselves and the setting are changing. The high degree of personalisation reflects weak party roots in society. There still seems to be a space for the institutionalisation of party politics, and this would seem to be one of the main prerequisites for the development of full democracy.

Notes

1 A score of one indicates the highest degree of freedom and seven the lowest level of freedom (Freedom House 2002–2008).
2 Not counting government reconstructions.
3 If we take DOS (2000) as one electoral alliance we would be talking about a single-party government.
4 The plan included provisions for police, customs, justice, transport and infrastructure, boundaries and Serbian patrimony (UN six-point plan 2008).
5 The government of acting Prime Minister Adem Salihaj (8 March 2005–23 March 2005) was not counted.
6 This seems to be result of a pattern of democratisation where a strong actor prevailed, while the rest of the political spectrum tried to reverse the situation by using different strategies and seeking different allies.

Bibliography

Akademia ë shkencavë ë shqiperisë (1998) *Platformë për Zgjidhjene Çësthjes Kombetarë Shqiptarë*, Akademia ë shkencavë ë shqiperisë: Tirana.

Albanian Institute for International Studies (AIIS) (2003) *Albania and European Union: Perceptions and Realities*, Tirana: AIIS. Online. Available at http://pdc.ceu.hu/archive/00002055/01/Albania_+_EU,_perceptions_and_realities.pdf.

Aleanca për Ardhmërinë e Kosovës (2006) *Dokument-platformë i përbërë nga: Vizioni, Objektivat, Plani i punës, Plani zbatues*. Prishtina. Online. Available at www.aleanca.info/dokumente/.

Aleanca për Ardhmërinë e Kosovës (2007) *Ramush Haradinaj – Intervistë*. Online. Available at www.aleanca.info/media/index.html.

Alionescu, C.-C. (2004) 'Parliamentary representation of minorities in Romania', *Southeast European Politics*, 5(1): 60–75.

Allcock, J.B. (1994) 'Macedonia', in B. Szajkowski (ed.) *Political Parties of Eastern Europe, Russia and the Successor States*, London: Longman.

Antić, M. and Gruičić, M.D. (2008) 'The parliamentary election in Croatia, November 2007', *Electoral Studies*, 27(4): 752–5.

Arnautović, S. (1996) *Izbori u Bosni i Hercegovini '90: Analiza izbornog procesa*, Sarajevo: Promocult.

Balík, S. and Stýskalíková, V. (2005) 'Berishovská a postberishovská Albánie: Případová studie defektního režimu', *Středoevropské politické studie*, 7(4): 366–88. Online. Available at www.cepsr.com/dwnld/albanie052.pdf.

Balli Kombëtar (2001) *Program i partisë Balli Kombëtar Kosovë*, Prishtinë, electronic version obtained by approaching BK.

Balli Kombëtar (2006) *Dekalogu – Programi i Ballit Kombëtar*. Online. Available at www.ballikombit.org/index.php?option=com_content&task=view&id=27&Itemid=39.

Balli Kombëtar (not dated) *Platforma politike, ekonomike dhe sociale e partisë 'Balli Kombëtar'*. Online. Available at www.ballikombit.org/Platforma.html.

Banac, I. (1984) *The National Question in Yugoslavia: Origins, History, Politics*, Ithaca: Cornell University Press.

Barić, N. (2005) *Srpska pobuna u Hrvatskoj 1990–1995*, Zagreb: Golden marketing – Tehnička knjiga.

Bartolini, S. and Mair, P. (1990) *Identity, Competition, and Electoral Availability: The Stabilisation of European Electorates 1885–1985*, Cambridge: Cambridge University Press.

Bašić, G. (2002) *Položaj Bošnjaka u Sandžaku*, Beograd: Centar za antiratnu akciju.

Bašić, G. and Crnjanski, K. (2006) *Politička participacija i kulturna autonomija nacionalnih manjina u Srbiji*, Beograd: Friedrich Ebert Stiftung/Fakultet političkih nauka.

Bennett, C. (1995) *Yugoslavia's Bloody Collapse: Causes, Course and Consequences*, London: Hurst & Company.

Beqiri, I. (2002) 'Nacionalizmi Shqiptar kërkon ribashkim kombëtar', *Pasqyra*, 1 November. Online. Available at www.pasqyra.com/arkivi/2002/01112002/faqe/nacionaliz-mishqiptarkerkonribashkimkombetar.htm.

Beyme, K. (1996) *Transition to Democracy in Eastern Europe*, Houndmills: Macmillan.

Biberaj, E. (1999) *Albania in Transition: The Rocky Road to Democracy*, Oxford: West-view Press.

Bieber, F. (2003a) 'Montenegrin politics since the disintegration of Yugoslavia', in F. Bieber (ed.) *Montenegro in Transition: Problems of Identity and Statehood*, Baden-Baden: Nomos.

Bieber, F. (2003b) 'The Serbian opposition and civil society: Roots of the delayed trans-ition in Serbia', *International Journal of Politics, Culture and Society*, 17(1): 73–90.

Bieber, F. (ed.) (2003c) *Montenegro in Transition: Problems of Identity and Statehood*, Baden-Baden: Nomos.

Bieber, F. (2006) *Post-War Bosnia: Ethnicity, Inequality and Public Sector Governance*, London: Palgrave Macmillan.

Bieber, F. (2008a) 'Introduction: Minority participation and political parties', in *Political Parties and Minority Participation*, Skopje: Friedrich Ebert Stiftung. Online. Available at www.fes.org.mk/pdf/Political%20Parties%20and%20Minority%20 Participation.pdf.

Bieber, F. (2008b) 'Regulating minority parties in Central and South-Eastern Europe', in B. Reilly and P. Nordlund (eds) *Political Parties in Conflict-Prone Societies: Regula-tion, Engineering and Democratic Development*, Tokyo: United Nations University Press.

Bieber, F. (forthcoming) 'Das politische System Montenegros', in W. Ismayr (ed.) *Die politischen Systeme Osteuropas*, Wiesbaden: VS Verlag für Sozialwissenschaften.

Bielasiak, J. (1997) 'Substance and process in the development of party systems in East Central Europe', *Communist and Post-Communist Studies*, 30(1): 23–44.

Bielasiak, J. (2005) 'Party competition in emerging democracies: Representation and effectiveness in post-communism and beyond', *Democratization*, 12(3): 331–56.

Bilic, V. (1998) 'U Sarajevu osnovana Nova hrvatska inicijativa', *Voice of America*, 27 June. Online. Available at www.voa.gov/miscl/croatia/inchrv.html.

Bochsler, D. (2006) 'Ethnic diversity, electoral system constraints and the nationalization of political parties: A triangle model, applied on the Central and Eastern European countries', *CEU Political Science Journal*, 1(4): 6–37.

Bochsler, D. (2007a) 'The majority vote and ethnic radicalization: The case of Serbian municipal elections 2004', paper presented at the SVPW Annual Conference, Balsthal, 22–23 November 2007.

Bochsler, D. (2007b) 'Umbrellas and rainbows – the early development of party systems in new European democracies', paper presented at the 8th Postgraduate Conference on Slavonic and Eastern European Studies, Brno, 28–30 June 2007. Online. Available at www.bochsler.eu/publi/bochsler_umbrella050607.pdf.

Bochsler, D. (2008) 'The presidential election in Serbia, January–February 2008', *Elect-oral Studies*, 27(4): 745–8.

Bochsler, D. (2009) 'Territory and electoral rules in post-communist democracies', Houndmills: Palgrave (forthcoming).

'Bosnian PM resigns over reforms', *BBC News* (1 November 2007). Online. Available at news.bbc.co.uk/2/hi/europe/7072908.stm.

Bošnjačka stranka (2007) *Program*, Rožaje. Online. Available at www.bosnjackastranka. org/bs/17-Program.html.

Bozóki, A. and Ishiyama, J.T. (eds) (2002) *The Communist Successor Parties of Central and Eastern Europe*, New York: M.E. Sharpe.

'Bucharest Summit Declaration' (2008). Online. Available at www.summitbucharest.ro/ en/doc_202.html.

Brunnbauer, U. (2002) *The Implementation of the Ohrid Agreement: Macedonian Resentments*, Center for the Study of Balkan Societies and Cultures, Graz: University of Graz. Online. Available at www.ecmi.de/jemie/download/Focus1-2002Brunnbauer.pdf.

Bugajski, J. (2002) *Political Parties of Eastern Europe: A Guide to Politics in the Post-Communist Era*, Armonk, NY: M.E. Sharpe.

Buljan, I. and Duka, Z. (2003) *Izbori: Duh stranaka i duše političara: Vodič kroz hrvatsku političku scenu*, Zagreb: Profil International.

Burwitz, B. (2004) 'The elections in Bosnia-Herzegovina, October 2002', *Electoral Studies*, 23(2): 329–38.

Caramani, D. (2004) *The Nationalization of Politics: The Formation of National Electorates and Party Systems in Western Europe*, Cambridge: Cambridge University Press.

Caspersen, N. (2006) 'Contingent nationalist dominance: Intra-Serb challenges to the Serb Democratic Party', *Nationalities Papers*, 34(1): 51–69.

Central Election Commission Kosovo (2007a) *Election Results 2007 C&CR Election Results*. Online. Available at http://internet.cec-ko.org/al/zgjedhjetekosoves/materiale/ rezultatet/listaekandidatevevotatefituara.pdf.

Central Election Commission Kosovo (2007b) *Results – Elections 2007*. Online. Available at http://internet.cec-ko.org/en/informacione/rezultatet.html.

CeSID (not dated) *Model Law on Political Parties/Model Law on Financing of Political Parties*, 2nd edn, Belgrade: CeSID. Online. Available at www.cesid.org/pdf/model_ zakona_eng.pdf.

Chhibber, P. and Kollman, K. (2004) *The Formation of National Party Systems: Federalism and Party Competition in Canada, Great Britain, India, and the United States*, Princeton: Princeton University Press.

Chytilek, R. (2005) 'Podněty a výsledky: Volební a stranické systémy v evropských zemích', in M. Strmiska, V. Hloušek, L. Kopeček and R. Chytilek, *Politické strany moderní Evropy: Analýza stranicko-politických systémů*, Praha: Portál.

Cocozzelli, F. (2004) 'Political parties in Kosovo, 2003', *GSC Quarterly*, 11. Online. Available at http://programs.ssrc.org/gsc/publications/quarterly11/cocozzelli.pdf.

Cohen, L.J. (1995) *Broken Bonds: Yugoslavia's Disintegration and Balkan Politics in Transition*, Boulder, CO: Westview Press.

Cohen, L.J. (1997) 'Embattled democracy: Postcommunist Croatia in transition', in K. Dawisha and B. Parrot (eds) *Politics, Power, and the Struggle for Democracy in South-East Europe*, Cambridge: Cambridge University Press.

'Constitution of Albania' (1991). Online. Available at www.servat.unibe.ch/law/icl/ al00t___.html.

'Constitution of Albania' (1998), amended on 13 January 2007. Online. Available at www.legislationline.org/documents/id/8775.

'Constitution of Albania' (1998). Online. Available at www.ipls.org/services/kusht/contents.html.

'Constitution of Croatia' (1990). Online. Available at www.servat.unibe.ch/icl/hr00000_. html.

'Constitution of Kosovo' (2008). Online. Available at www.kosovoconstitution.info.

'Constitution of the Republic of Kosovo' (2008). Online. Available at www.kushtetuta-kosoves.info/repository/docs/Constitution.of.the.Republic.of.Kosovo.pdf.

Cox, G.W. (1997) *Making Votes Count: Strategic Coordination in the World's Electoral Systems*, Cambridge: Cambridge University Press.

Cox, G.W. (1999) 'Electoral rules and electoral coordination', *Annual Review of Political Science*, 2: 145–61.

Čular, G. (ed.) (2005) *Izbori i konsolidacija demokracije u Hrvatskoj*, Zagreb: Fakultet političkih znanosti.

Darmanović, S. (2003) 'Montenegro: Dilemmas of a small republic', *Journal of Democracy*, 14(1): 145–53.

Daskalovski, Ž. (1999) 'Elite transformation and democratic transition in Macedonia and Slovenia', *Balkanologie, Revue d'études pluridisciplinaires*, 3(1): 5–32. Online. Available at http://balkanologie.revues.org/index281.html#quotation.

Dawisha, K. and Deets, S. (2006) 'Political learning in post-communist elections', *East European Politics and Societies*, 20(4): 691–728.

Dawisha, K. and Parrot, B. (eds) (1997) *Politics, Power, and the Struggle for Democracy in South-East Europe*, Cambridge: Cambridge University Press.

'Dayton Peace Agreement (The General Framework Agreement for Peace in Bosnia and Herzegovina)' (1995). Online. Available at www.ohr.int/dpa/default.asp?content_id=380.

De Bréadún, D. (2008) *The Far Side of Revenge: Making Peace in Northern Ireland*, Dublin: Collins.

De Winter, L. and Türsan, H. (eds) (1998) *Regionalist Parties in Western Europe*, London: Routledge.

Demokratska partija socijalista Crne Gore (2007) *Za evropski kvalitet života: Program*, Podgorica. Online. Available at www.dpscg.org/5kongres/ProgramDPS.pdf.

Diamandouros, P.N. and Gunther, R. (eds) (2001) *Parties, Politics and Democracy in the New Southern Europe*, Baltimore, London: John Hopkins University Press.

Donia, R.J. and Fine, Jr, J.V.A. (1994) *Bosnia and Herzegovina: A Tradition Betrayed*, New York: Columbia University Press.

Državna izborna komisija (2006) *Listi na kandidati 2006*. Online. Available at www.sec.mk/parlamentarni/Листинакандидати/tabid/173/Default.aspx.

Dugolli, I. (2008) 'Kosovo Coalition Pact harms democracy', *BIRN Kosovo*, 10 January. Online. Available at http://kosovo.birn.eu.com/en/1/70/7318/.

Đurković, M. (2007) 'Narodnjaštvo u političkim strankama Srbije', in Z. Lutovac (ed.) *Ideologija i političke stranke u Srbiji*, Beograd: Friedrich Ebert Stiftung/Institut društvenih nauka.

Duverger, M. (1954) *Political Parties: Their Organization and Activity in the Modern State*, London: Methuen.

Duverger, M. (1972) 'Factors in a two-party and multiparty system', in *Party Politics and Pressure Groups*, New York: Thomas Y. Crowell.

Eban, A.S. (1998) *Diplomacy for the Next Century*, New Haven: Yale University Press.

'[Election Debate] Life in Kosovo debates political parties' plans on education, health and social welfare', *BIRN (Balkan Investigative Reporting Network)* (8 November 2007). Online. Available at www.birn.eu.com/en/1/50/5834/.

El Khazen, F. (1998) *Lebanon's First Postwar Parliamentary Election, 1992: An Imposed Choice*, Oxford: Centre for Lebanese Studies.

Emerson, B.C. (1926) 'The New Albanian Constitution', *American Political Science Review*, 20(1): 120–3.

Emerson, P.J. (2000) *From Belfast to the Balkans*, Belfast: The de Borda Institute.

Emerson, P.J. (2002) *Defining Democracy*, Belfast: The de Borda Institute.

Emerson, P.J. (ed.) (2007) *Designing an All-Inclusive Democracy: Consensual Voting Procedures for Use in Parliaments, Councils and Committees*, Berlin: Springer.

Epstein, L.D. (1967) *Political Parties in Western Democracies*, New York: Praeger.

European Commission for Democracy through Law (Venice Commission) (2007) *Opinion on the Constitution of Serbia: Adopted by the Commission at its 70th plenary session (Venice, 17–18 March 2007)*, Opinion No. 405/2006, Strasbourg: Council of Europe. Online. Available at www.venice.coe.int/docs/2007/CDL-AD(2007)004-e.pdf.

Fiala, P., Mareš, M. and Sokol, P. (2007) *Eurostrany: Politické strany na evropské úrovni*, Brno: Barrister & Principal.

Fink Hafner, Danica – Pejanović Mirko (eds) (2006) Razvoj političkog pluralizma u Sloveniji i Bosni i Hercegovini Ljubljana-Sarajero: Fakultet za družbenevede.

Fond za otvoreno društvo (2007) *Informisanje na jezicima nacionalnih manjina*, Beograd: Fond za otvoreno društvo.

Friedman, E. (2005) 'Electoral system design and minority representation in Slovakia and Macedonia', *Ethnopolitics*, 4(4): 381–96.

Gajić, S. (2005) 'Odnosi države i crkve: nužnosti i granice "politizacije"', *Nova srpska politička misao Analize*, 1(4): 29–35.

Gallagher, M. (2008) *Election Indices*. Online. Available at www.tcd.ie/Political_Science/staff/michael_gallagher/ElSystems/Docts/ElectionIndices.pdf.

Galtung, B.H. (2005) *Kosovo: Assembly Elections October 2004*, NORDEM Report 02/2005. Online. Available at www.humanrights.uio.no/forskning/publikasjoner/nordem-rapport/2005/0205.pdf.

Glavaš, B (2006) *Curriculum Vitae of Branimir Glavaš*. Online. Available at www.branimirglavas.com/index.php?option=com_content&task=view&id=22&Itemid=2.

Glenny, M. (1992, 3rd edn 1996) *The Fall of Yugoslavia: The Third Balkan War*, London: Penguin.

Glenny, M. (1999) *The Balkans 1804–1999: Nationalism, War and the Great Powers*, London: Granta Books.

Goati, V. (1999) *Izbori u SRJ od 1990 do 1998: volja građana ili izborna manipulacija*, Beograd: CeSID.

Goati, V. (2001) *Elections in FRY. From 1990 to 1998: Will of People or Electoral Manipulation?*, Beograd: CeSID.

Goati, V. (2004) *Partije i partijski sistem u Srbiji*, Niš: OGI Centar.

Goati, V. (2006) *Partijske borbe u Srbiji u postoktobarskom razdoblju*, Beograd: Friedrich Ebert Stiftung/Institut društvenih nauka.

Goati, V., Nenadić, N. and Jovanović, P. (2004) *Financing Presidential Electoral Campaign in Serbia 2004: A Blow to Political Corruption or Preservation of Status Quo?*, Belgrade: Transparency Serbia. Online. Available at www.transparentnost.org.rs/english/PUBLICATIONS/presidential_electoral_2004.pdf.

'Guiding principles of the Contact Group for a settlement of the status of Kosovo' (not dated). Online. Available at www.unosek.org/docref/Contact%20Group%20-%20Ten%20Guiding%20principles%20for%20Ahtisaari.pdf.

Haas, M., Niedermayer, O. and Stöss, R. (eds) (2006) *Die Parteiensysteme Westeuropas*, Wiesbaden: VS Verlag für Sozialwissenschaften.

Hafner, D.F. and Pejanović, M. (2006) *Razvoj političkog pluralizma u Sloveniji i Bosni i*

Hercegovini, Ljubljana: Fakulteta za družbene vede, Založba FDV, Sarajevo: Fakultet političkih nauka.

Harbers, I. (2008) 'Decentralization as a condition of party system nationalization: Evidence from Latin America and Central and Eastern Europe', paper prepared for presentation at the 2008 ECPR Joint Sessions of Workshops, Rennes, 11–16 April 2008.

Harmel, R. and Robertson, J.D. (1985) 'Formation and success of new parties: A cross-national analysis', *International Political Science Review*, 6(4): 501–23.

Harris, P. and Reilly, B. (eds) (1998) *Democracy and Deep-Rooted Conflict: Options for Negotiators*, Stockholm: International IDEA. Online. Available at www.idea.int/publications/democracy_and_deep_rooted_conflict/upload/Intro.pdf.

Hatschikjan, M., Reljić, D. and Šebek, N. (eds) (2005) *Disclosing Hidden History: Lustration in the Western Balkans: A Project Documentation*, Thessaloniki: Center for Democracy and Reconciliation in Southeast Europe, Belgrade: Cicero. Online. Available at www.lustration.net/lustration_documentation.pdf.

Haughton, T. and Fisher, S. (2008) 'From the politics of state-building to programmatic politics: The post-federal experience and the development of centre–right party politics in Croatia and Slovakia', *Party Politics*, 14(4): 435–54.

HDZ-1990 (2006) *HDZ 1990 – Programska Deklaracija*, Mostar. Online. Available at www.hdz1990.org/dokumenti/Programskapercent20deklaracijapercent20HDZpercent201990.doc.

Heller, W.B. (2002) 'Regional parties and national politics in Europe: Spain's Estado De Las Autonomías, 1993 to 2000', *Comparative Political Studies*, 35(6): 657–85.

Helmerich, A. (2008) 'Kroatien: Vom "faktischen" Einparteiensystem zum polarisierten Pluralismus', in E. Bos and D. Segert (eds) *Osteuropäische Demokratien als Trendsetter*, Opladen & Farmington Hills: Verlag Barbara Budrich.

Helsinki Committee for Human Rights in Serbia (2005) *Human Rights and Collective Identity: Serbia 2004*, Belgrade: Helsinki Committee for Human Rights in Serbia. Online. Available at www.helsinki.org.yu/doc/AnnualReport2004.pdf.

Herceg, N. and Tomić, Z. (1998) *Izbori u Bosni i Hercegovini, Drugo dopunjeno izdanje*, Mostar: Sveučilište u Mostaru, Centar za studije novinarstva.

Hladký, L. (2005) *Bosenská otázka v 19. a 20. století*, Brno: MPÚ MU.

Hloušek, V. (2002) 'Republika Chorvatsko', in P. Fiala, J. Holzer and M. Strmiska (eds) *Politické strany ve střední a východní Evropě*, Brno: MPÚ MU.

Hloušek, V. (2003) 'Budování stranických systémů: Stranické systémy a konfliktní linie ve Slovinsku, Chorvatsku, Estonsku, Litvě a Lotyšsku', unpublished PhD dissertation, Brno: Masarykova univerzita.

Holbrooke, R. (1998) *To End a War*, New York: Random House.

Hoppe, H.-J. (1993) *Das Profil der neuen politischen Elite Albaniens*, Bericht des BIOst Nr. 5/1993, Köln: Bundesinstitut für ostwissenschaftliche und internationale Studien.

Horowitz, D.L. (1985) *Ethnic Groups in Conflict*, Berkeley, CA: University of California Press.

Hrvatska čista stranka prava (2007) *Deklaracija opcega sabora starčevićanske mladeži HČSP-a*. Online. Available at www.hcsp.hr/priopcenja.php?subaction=showfull&id=1192350474&archive=&start_from=&ucat=3&.

Hrvatska čista stranka prava (2007a) *Izborni program*. Online. Available at www.hcsp.hr/priopcenja.php?subaction=showfull&id=1192350129&archive=&start_from=&ucat=3&.

Hrvatska čista stranka prava (2007b) *Negirati zločine nad Hrvatima koje su počinili antifašisti, isto je kao da netko negira holokaust!*. Online. Available at www.hcsp.hr/

priopcenja.php?subaction=showfull&id=1188368245&archive=&start_from=&ucat
=3&.

Hrvatska čista stranka prava (2007c) *Temeljna načela*. Online. Available at www.hcsp.hr/
nacela.php.

Hrvatska demokratska zajednica (HDZ) (2002) *Program Hrvatske demokratske zajednice*. Online. Available at www.hdz.hr/images/site/upload/program.pdf.

Hrvatska demokratska zajednica BiH (2007) *Program Hrvatske demokratske zajednice
Bosne i Hercegovine*, Mostar. Online. Available at www.hdzbih.org/webroot/js/
uploaded/xx_program.pdf.

Hrvatska građanska inicijativa (2003) *Politički program*, Tivat. Online. Available at
www.hgi.co.me/files/docs/Politicki%20program.pdf.

Hrvatska narodna zajednica (2005) *Žo HNZ HNŽ: BiH treba biti decentralizirana država
Hrvata, Bošnjaka, Srba i svih njezinih građana*, Mostar. Online. Available at www.
hnzbih.org/news.htm.

Hrvatska seljačka stranka (2006) *Pogled u budućnost: Sažetak izbornog programa*.
Online. Available at www.hss.hr/onama_prog.php?id=1.

Hrvatska stranka prava (2007) *Govor predsjednika Hrvatske stranke prava na konvenciji
16.IX.2007*. Online. Available at www.hsp.hr/content/view/90/137/lang,hr/.

Hrvatska stranka prava 1861 (2003) *Temeljna načela Hrvatske stranke prava – 1861*.
Online. Available at www.hsp1861.hr/1temeljna.htm.

Hrvatska stranka prava 1861 (not dated) *Vijesti iz medija*. Available at www.hsp1861.hr/
Ostalo.html.

Hrvatska stranka prava BiH Đapić – dr. Jurišić (2005) *Programska načela*, Mostar.
Online. Available at hsp-bih.ba/PDF/programska%20nacela.pdf.

Hrvatski blok – pokret za modernu Hrvatsku (2003a) *100 pitanja i odgovora*, Zagreb.
Online. Available at www.hrvatski-blok.hr/doc1/100pitanja.pdf.

Hrvatski blok – pokret za modernu Hrvatsku (2003b) *Deklaracija izborne koalicije 'Za
modernu Hrvatsku'*, Zagreb. Online. Available at hrvatski-blok.hr/doc1/Deklaracija.doc.

Hrvatski blok (2006) *Program Hrvatskoga bloka*, Zagreb. Online. Available at hrvatski-
blok.hr/doc1/program.pdf.

Hrvatski blok BiH (2005) *Politička sudbina Hrvata u BiH*, Mostar. Online. Available at
www.hrvatski-blok.hr/doc1/PolitickaSudbina-kb.pdf.

Hrvatski istinski preporod (2001a) *Politički profil*, Zagreb. Online. Available at hidra.
srce.hr/arhiva/392/5980/www.hipnet.hr/kategorije.phppercent3fKATEGORIJA_IDper-
cent3d33.html.

Hrvatski istinski preporod (2001b) *Program stranke*, Zagreb. Online. Available at http://
hidra.srce.hr/arhiva/392/5980/www.hipnet.hr/kategorije.php%3fKATEGORIJA_
ID%3d19.html.

Hrvatski istinski preporod (2005a) 'Ne vjerujem u Mikšićevu ideju o zajedničkom bloku:
Intervju Miroslav Tuđman', *Večernji list*, 7 May. Online. Available at hidra.srce.hr/
arhiva/392/5980/www.hipnet.hr/kategorije.php%3fKATEGORIJA_ID%3d27.html.

Hrvatski istinski preporod (2005b) 'Pritisci su način funkcioniranja međunarodne zajednice:
Intervju Miroslav Tuđman', *Posavska Hrvatska*, 4 March. Online. Available at hidra.srce.
hr/arhiva/392/5980/www.hipnet.hr/kategorije.php%3fKATEGORIJA_ID%3d27.html.

Hrvatski pravaši – Hrvatski pravaški pokret (2004) *Temeljna načela*, Zagreb. Online.
Available at www.hrvatskipravasi.hr/index.php?id=m&lnk=2.

Hrvatsko pravaško bratstvo (2004) *Programska deklaracija političke stranke Hrvatsko
pravaško bratstvo*, Arbanija. Online. Available at www.hpb-makarska.com/content/
view/6/11/.

Ignazi, P. (1995) *The Re-emergence of the Extreme Right in Europe*. Reihe Politikwissen-schaft, No. 21, Wien: Institut für Höhere Studien. Online. Available at www.ihs.ac.at/publications/pol/pw_21.pdf.

Imami, A. (1996) 'Freedom of thought and expression in Albania: The post-communist situation', *Südosteuropa*, 45(2): 168–78.

Immigration and Refugee Board of Canada (2007) *Country Fact Sheet: Albania*. Online. Available at www.unhcr.org/cgi-bin/texis/vtx/refworld/rwmain/opendocpdf. pdf?docid=47de299b0.

Index Kosovo (2007) *Current political affairs in Kosova*, April 2007. Available at www. indexkosova.com.

International Criminal Tribunal for the former Yugoslavia (ICTY) (2004) *Prosecutor v. Radislav Krstić: Case No: IT-98–33-A*. Online. Available at www.icty.org/x/cases/krstic/acjug/en/krs-aj040419e.pdf.

International Crisis Group (1998) *Sandžak: Calm for Now*, Europe Report No. 48, Sarajevo: ICG. Online. Available at www.crisisgroup.org/home/index.cfm?l=1&id=1731.

International Crisis Group (1999a) *Unifying the Kosovar Factions: The Way Forward*, Europe Report No. 58, Brussels/Tirana: ICG. Online. Available at www.crisisgroup.org/home/index.cfm?id=1599&l=1.

International Crisis Group (1999b) *Violence in Kosovo: Who's Killing Whom?*, Europe Report No. 78, Pristina/London/Washington: ICG. Online. Available at www.crisisgroup.org/home/index.cfm?l=1&id=1581.

International Crisis Group (2000) *What Happened to the KLA?*, Europe Report No. 88, Pristina/Washington/Brussels: ICG. Online. Available at www.crisisgroup.org/home/index.cfm?l=1&id=1582.

International Crisis Group (2003) *Southern Serbia's Fragile Peace*, Europe Report No. 152, Belgrade/Brussels: ICG. Online. Available at www.crisisgroup.org/home/index.cfm?id=2414.

International Crisis Group (2004a) *Collapse in Kosovo*, Europe Report No. 155, Pristina/Belgrade/Brussels: ICG. Online. Available at www.crisisgroup.org/home/index.cfm?id=2627&l=1.

International Crisis Group (2004b) *Pan-Albanianism: How Big a Threat to Balkan Stability?*, Europe Report No. 153, Tirana/Brussels: ICG. Online. Available at www.crisisgroup.org/home/index.cfm?l=1&id=2523.

International Crisis Group (2005a) *Kosovo after Haradinaj*, Europe Report No. 163, Pristina/Brussels: ICG. Online. Available at www.crisisgroup.org/home/index.cfm?id=3474.

International Crisis Group (2005b) *Serbia's Sandžak: Still Forgotten*, Europe Report No. 162, Belgrade/Brussels: ICG. Online. Available at www.crisisgroup.org/home/index.cfm?l=1&id=3361.

International Crisis Group (2006a) *Montenegro's Referendum*, Europe Briefing No. 42, Podgorica/Belgrade/Brussels: ICG. Online. Available at www.crisisgroup.org/home/index.cfm?id=4144.

International Crisis Group (2006b) *Serbia's New Constitution: Democracy Going Backwards*, Europe Briefing No. 44, Belgrade/Brussels: ICG. Online. Available at www.crisisgroup.org/home/index.cfm?id=4494.

International Crisis Group (2007) *Serbia: Maintaining Peace in the Presevo Valley*, Europe Report No. 186, Belgrade/Pristina/Brussels: ICG. Online. Available at www.crisisgroup.org/home/index.cfm?id=5126.

Irvine, J.A. (1996) *Extreme Right Parties and the Extremist Electorate in Croatia*,

1990–1995, report solicited by the National Council for Soviet and East European Research.

Ishiyama, J.T. (1998) 'Strange bedfellows: Explaining political cooperation between communist successor parties and nationalists in Eastern Europe', *Nations and Nationalism*, 4(1): 61–85.

Ishiyama, J.T. (ed.) (1999) *Communist Successor Parties in Post-Communist Politics*, Huntington, NY: Nova Science Publishers.

Ishiyama, J.T. (2002) 'Regionalism and the nationalization of the legislative vote in post-communist Russian politics', *Communist and Post-communist Studies*, 35(2): 155–68.

Ishiyama, J.T. (2006) 'Europeanization and the communist successor parties in post-communist politics', *Politics & Policy*, 34(1): 3–29.

Istarski demokratski sabor (2007) *Programska deklaracija IDS*. Online. Available at www.ids-ddi.com/ids-ddi/dokumenti/programska-deklaracija/.

Jarvis, C. (2000) 'The rise and fall of Albania's pyramid schemes', *Finance and Development*. Online. Available at www.imf.org/external/pubs/ft/fandd/2000/03/pdf/jarvis.pdf.

Jenne, E. (2004) 'A bargaining theory of minority demands: Explaining the dog that did not bite in 1990s Yugoslavia', *International Studies Quarterly*, 48(4): 729–54.

Jovanović, M. (2005) 'Izborni prag i stranački sistem', in Z. Lutovac (ed.) *Političke stranke u Srbiji: Struktura i funkcionisanje*, Beograd: Friedrich Ebert Stiftung/Institut društvenih nauka.

Kapal, R. (2004) 'Ochridská dohoda a její vliv na politický systém Makedonie', unpublished bachelor thesis, Brno: Masarykova univerzita.

Karasimeonov, G. (ed.) (2004) *Political Parties and the Consolidation of Democracy in South Eastern Europe*, Sofia: Friedrich Ebert Stiftung.

Kasapović, M. (1997) '1996 parliamentary elections in Bosnia and Herzegovina', *Electoral Studies*, 16(1): 117-21.

Kasapović, M. (2000) 'Electoral politics in Croatia 1990–2000', *Politička misao*, 37(5): 3–20.

Kasapović, M. (2005) 'Koalicijske vlade u Hrvatskoj: Prva iskustva u komparativnoj perspektivi', in G. Čular (ed.) *Izbori i konsolidacija demokracije u Hrvatskoj*, Zagreb: Fakultet političkih znanosti.

Kasapović, M. and Nohlen, D. (1996) 'Wahlsysteme und Systemwechsel in Osteuropa', in W. Merkel, E. Sandschneider and D. Segert (eds) *Systemwechsel 2. Die Institutionalisierung der Demokratie*, Opladen: Leske & Budrich.

Kasum, D. (2006) 'Vývoj politického systému Bosny a Hercegoviny po Daytonu a jeho současná podoba', *Středoevropské politické studie*, 8(2–3): 327–41. Online. Available at www.cepsr.com/dwnld/kas10.pdf.

Kasum, D. (2007) 'Etnický konflikt v Bosně a Hercegovině', in T. Šmíd and V. Vaďura (eds) *Etnické konflikty v postkomunistickém prostoru*, Brno: CDK.

Katz, R.S. and Crotty, W. (eds) (2006) *Handbook of Party Politics*, London: Sage.

Kerenji, E. (2005) 'Vojvodina since 1988', in S.P. Ramet and V. Pavlaković (eds) *Serbia Since 1989: Politics and Society under Milošević and After*, Seattle, WA: University of Washington Press.

Kim, L. (1994) 'The free press in the new Albania', *Südosteuropa*, 43(9–10): 570–5.

Kitschelt, H. (1995) 'Formation of party cleavages in post-communist democracies: Theoretical propositions', *Party Politics*, 1(4): 447–72.

Kitschelt, H. (2000) 'Linkages between citizens and politicians in democratic polities', *Comparative Political Studies*, 33(6–7): 845–79.

Kola, P. (2003) *The Search for Greater Albania*, London: Hurst & Company.

Komšić, J. (2002) 'Programska evolucija partija', in V. Goati (ed.) *Partijska scena Srbije posle 5. oktobra 2000*, Beograd: Friedrich Ebert Stiftung/Institut društvenih nauka.

Komšić, J. (2003) 'Istorijsko-etnički rascepi i politička pregrupisavanja u Srbiji', in J. Komšić, D. Pantić and Z.Đ. Slavujević (eds) *Osnovne linije partijskih podela i mogući pravci političkog pregrupisavanja u Srbiji*, Beograd: Friedrich Ebert Stiftung/Institut društvenih nauka.

Komšić, J. (2006) *Dileme demokratske nacije i autonomije: Ogledi o političkoj tranziciji u Srbiji*, Beograd: Službeni glasnik.

Komšić, J. (2007) 'Ideje autonomije i regionalizma među političkim strankama Srbije', in Z. Lutovac (ed.) *Ideologija i političke stranke u Srbiji*, Beograd: Friedrich Ebert Stiftung/Institut društvenih nauka.

Komunist (2005) *Šta hoće komunisti za Bosnu i Hercegovinu? Politički manifest Radničko-komunističke partije Bosne i Hercegovine*. Online. Available at komunist. free.fr/arhiva/feb2005/rkp-bih.html.

Komunistička partija Hrvatske (KPH) (2005): *Program Komunističke partije Hrvatske*. Online. Available at www.komunisti-hrvatske.com/prilozi/ProgramKPH.doc.

'Konačni podaci RIK o broju mandata', *B92 Vesti*, 30 December 2003. Online. Available at www.b92.net/specijal/izbori2003/izborne_liste.php?nav_id=127234.

Kosovo Compromise Staff (2008) 'UN six-point Plan 2008', *Kosovo Compromise*, 26 November. Online. Available at www.kosovocompromise.com/cms/item/latestnews/en .html?view=story&id=1571&sectionId=1.

Leaković, K. (2004) 'Political party quotas in the Croatian Social Democratic Party', paper presented at the IDEA/CEE Network for Gender Issues Conference on The Implementation of Quotas: European Experiences, Budapest, October 2004. Online. Available at www.quotaproject.org/CS/Croatia.pdf.

Lebeda, T. (2004) 'Stručný přehled volebních systémů', in M. Novák and T. Lebeda *et al.*, *Volební a stranické systémy: ČR v mezinárodním srovnání*, Dobrá Voda: Aleš Čeněk.

Lëvizja për Bashkim (not dated) *Programi politik i Lëvizjes për Bashkim (LB)*. Online. Available at www.levizjaperbashkim.com/Menyja%20kryesore/Programi/programi. html.

Lewis, P.G. (2001) *Political Parties in Post-Communist Eastern Europe*, London: Routledge.

Liberalna Partija Crne Gore (2004) *Program*, Podgorica. Online. Available at www.lpcg. org/index1.php?module=1&sub=11.

Lidhja Demokratike e Dardanisë (2007) *Platforma politike e Lidhjes Demokratike të Dardanisë*. Online. Available at www.ldd-kosova.org/.

Lidhja Demokratike e Kosovës (2006) *Programi i Lidhjes demokratike të Kosovës*. Online. Available at http://ldk-kosova.eu/programi.php.

Lijphart, A. (1994) *Electoral Systems and Party Systems: A Study of Twenty-Seven Democracies, 1945–1990*, Oxford: Oxford University Press.

Lijphart, A. (1999) *Patterns of Democracy: Government Forms and Performance in Thirty-Six Countries*, New Haven: Yale University Press.

Linz, J.J. and Stepan, A.C. (1996) *Problems of Democratic Transition and Consolidation: Southern Europe, South America and Post-Communist Europe*, Baltimore: Johns Hopkins University Press.

Lipset, Seymour Martin and Rokkan, Stein (1967) *Party Systems and Voter Alignments: Cross-national Perspectives*, New York: The Free Press.

Lipsius, S. (1998) 'Kommunistische Parteien in Albanien und Kosovo – Vorbild Enver Hoxha?', *Südosteuropa*, 47(10–11): 536–45.

Lipsius, S. (2008) 'Die albanische Minderheit in Montenegro', in U. Brunnbauer and C. Voss (eds) *Inklusion und Exklusion auf dem Westbalkan*, München: Verlag Otto Sagner.

Lutovac, Z. (ed.) (2005) *Političke stranke u Srbiji: Struktura i funkcionisanje*, Beograd: Friedrich Ebert Stiftung/Institut društvenih nauka.

Lutovac, Z. (ed.) (2006) *Demokratija u političkim strankama Srbije*, Beograd: Friedrich Ebert Stiftung/Institut društvenih nauka.

Lutovac, Z. (2007) 'Nacionalne manjine u evropskim standardima i političkom životu Srbije', in Z. Lutovac (ed.) *Političke stranke u Srbiji i Evropska unija*, Beograd: Friedrich Ebert Stiftung/Fakultet političkih nauka.

'Macedonia', *Nations in Transit*. Online. Available at http://unpan1.un.org/intradoc/groups/public/documents/NISPAcee/UNPAN008270.pdf.

Mainwaring, S. (1998) 'Rethinking party systems theory in the third wave of democratization: The importance of party system institutionalization', The Kellog Institute Working Paper No. 260, October 1998. Online. Available at www.nd.edu/~kellogg/publications/workingpapers/WPS/260.pdf.

Mandela, N. (1994) *Long Walk to Freedom: The Autobiography of Nelson Mandela*, New York: Little, Brown and Company.

March, L. and Mudde, C. (2005) 'What's left of the radical left? The European radical left after 1989: Decline and mutation', *Comparative European Politics*, 3(1): 23–49.

Marcou, G. (2005) 'The state of local and regional democracy in South-Eastern Europe', in The Council of Europe *et al.* (eds) *Effective Democratic Governance at Local and Regional Level*, Budapest: Open Society Institute/The Council of Europe.

Meguid, B.M. (2005) 'Competition between unequals: The role of mainstream party strategy in niche party success', *American Political Science Review*, 99(3): 347–59.

Merkel, W. (1999) *Systemtransformation: Eine Einführung in die Theorie und Empirie der Transformationsforschung*, Opladen: Leske & Budrich.

Mihailović, S. (2006) 'Vrednosne orijentacije stranačkih pristalica', in Z. Lutovac (ed.) *Demokratija u političkim strankama Srbije*, Beograd: Friedrich Ebert Stiftung/Institut društvenih nauka.

Mihić, V. (2002) 'Razlike među biračima različitih stranaka u Vojvodini u odnosu na dimenzije političkih stavova po Ajzenku', saopštenje na 8. naučnom skupu Empirijska istraživanja u psihologiji, Beograd, 7–8 februar 2002, knjiga rezimea. Beograd: Insitut za psihologiju Filozofski fakultet.

Mihić, V. (2005) 'Povezanost biračkog opredeljenja i nekih političkih stavova stanovnika Vojvodine', *Psihologija*, 38(2): 197–212.

Milardović, A., Lalić, D. and Malenica, Z. (2007) *Kriza i transformacija političkih stranaka*, Zagreb: Centar za politološka istraživanja.

Milivojević, K. (2007) 'Saradnja političkih stranaka u Srbiji sa institucijama Evropske Unije', in Z. Lutovac (ed.) *Političke stranke u Srbiji i Evropska unija*, Beograd: Friedrich Ebert Stiftung/Fakultet političkih nauka.

Miller, N.J. (1997) 'A failed transition: The case of Serbia', in K. Dawisha and B. Parrot (eds) *Politics, Power, and the Struggle for Democracy in South-East Europe*, Cambridge: Cambridge University Press.

Milosavljević, M. (2005) 'Finansiranje političkih stranaka u Srbiji iz javnih izvora: norme i praksa', in Z. Lutovac (ed.) *Političke stranke u Srbiji: Struktura i funkcionisanje*, Beograd: Friedrich Ebert Stiftung/Institut društvenih nauka.

MINA (2005) 'Montenegrin Liberal Alliance folds after 15-year independence fight', *MINA*, 24 March.

Miščević, N. (2006) 'Ante Starčević – između liberalizma i rasizma', *Novi list*, 25 February. Online. Available at www.novilist.hr/default.asp?WCI=Pretrazivac&WCU=285A 28602863285A2863285A28582858285E2863286328632852928602858285E285B2858 28632863286328592863E.

Mitchell, P. (1995) 'Party competition in an ethnic dual party system', *Ethnic and Racial Studies*, 18(4): 773–96.

Moniquet, C. (2008) *Albania: When a Reform of the Electoral Code Weakens Democracy*, ESICS. Online. Available at www.esisc.org/documents/pdf/en/albania-reform-of-the-electoral-code-414.pdf.

Mudde, C. (2000) 'Extreme-right parties in Eastern Europe', *Patterns of Prejudice*, 34(1): 5–27.

Mudde, C. (2007) *Populist Radical Right Parties in Europe*, Cambridge: Cambridge University Press.

Narodna Stranka (not dated) *Politički program*. Online. Available at www.narodnas-tranka.com/program/politicki%20program.htm.

National Democratic Institute (2007) *Kosovo general elections 2007: Pre-Election Report*. Online. Available at www.accessdemocracy.org/library/2222_reports_kosovo_pre-elect_11152007.pdf.

Nederlands Institut voor Oorlogsdocumentatie (NIOD) (2002) *Srebrenica – a 'safe' area: Reconstruction, background, consequences and analyses of the fall of a Safe Area*, Amsterdam: NIOD. Online. Available at www.srebrenica.nl.

New Kosova Alliance (2007) *The Programme of New Kosova Alliance (AKR)*, Prishtina. Online. Available at http://akr-ks.com/www.akr-ks.com%20e%20reja/statuti%20dhe%20 programi%20eng%20ver/programi%20ne%20gjuhen%20angleze%2016.10.2007.pdf.

Niedermayer, Oskar, Stöss, Richard and Haas, Melanie (eds) (2006) *Die Parteiensysteme in Westeuropa*, Opladen: Verlag für Sozialwissenschaften.

O'Donnell, G. and Schmitter, P.C. (1986) *Transitions from Authoritarian Rule: Tentative Conclusions about Uncertain Democracies*, Baltimore, London: Johns Hopkins University Press.

'Ohrid Framework Agreement' (2001) Online. Available at www.coe.int/t/e/legal_affairs/ legal_co-operation/police_and_internal_security/OHRID%20Agreement%20 13august2001.asp.

Olson, D.M. (1998) 'Party formation and party system consolidation in the new democracies of Central Europe', *Political Studies*, 46(3): 432–64.

Orlović, S. (2005) 'Polupredsednički sistem i partijski sistem Srbije', in Z. Lutovac (ed.) *Političke stranke u Srbiji: Struktura i funkcionisanje*, Beograd: Friedrich Ebert Stiftung/Institut društvenih nauka.

Orlović, S. (2006) 'Nedemokratičnost partija i demokratizacija društva', in Z. Lutovac (ed.) *Demokratija u političkim strankama Srbije*, Beograd: Friedrich Ebert Stiftung/ Institut društvenih nauka.

Ortakovski, V.T. (2001) 'Interethnic relations and minorities in the Republic of Macedonia', *Southeast European Politics*, 2(1): 24–45. Online. Available at www.seep.ceu.hu/ issue21/ortakovski.pdf.

OSCE (2000, 2001, 2002, 2004) *Kosovo Elections Results*, OSCE Mission to Kosovo. Online. Available at www.osce.org/kosovo/13208.html.

OSCE (2005) *Background Report on Refugee Return in Croatia and the Status of Implementation of the January 2005 Sarajevo Ministerial Declaration on Refugee Returns*, OSCE Mission to Croatia. Online. Available at www.osce.org/documents/ mc/2005/07/15886_en.pdf.

OSCE (2008) *Ethnic Minorities in Serbia: An Overview*, OSCE Mission to Serbia. Online. Available at www.osce.org/documents/srb/2008/02/29908_en.pdf.

OSCE/ODIHR (1996) *The Elections in Bosnia and Herzegovina: 14 September 1996: Second Statement of the Co-ordinator for International Monitoring (CIM)*, Sarajevo. Online. Available at www.osce.org/documents/odihr/1996/09/1194_en.pdf.

OSCE/ODIHR (1998) *Parliamentary Elections in the Former Yugoslav Republic of Macedonia: 18 October and 1 November 1998*, OSCE/ODIHR Election Observation Mission Report, Warsaw. Online. Available at www.osce.org/documents/odihr/1998/12/1395_en.pdf.

OSCE/ODIHR (2000) *Republic of Croatia: Parliamentary Elections (House of Representatives): 2 and 3 January 2000*, OSCE/ODIHR Election Observation Mission Report, Warsaw. Online. Available at www.osce.org/documents/odihr/2000/04/1368_en.pdf.

OSCE/ODIHR (2004a) *Republic of Croatia: Parliamentary Elections: 23 November 2003*, OSCE/ODIHR Election Observation Mission Report, Warsaw. Online. Available at www.osce.org/documents/odihr/2004/01/1897_en.pdf.

OSCE/ODIHR (2004b) *Republic of Serbia: Serbia and Montenegro: Presidential Election: 13 and 27 June 2004*, OSCE/ODIHR Election Observation Mission Report, Warsaw. Online. Available at www.osce.org/documents/odihr/2004/09/3620_en.pdf.

OSCE/ODIHR (2006a) *Former Yugoslav Republic of Macedonia: Parliamentary Elections: 5 July 2006*, OSCE/ODIHR Election Observation Mission Report, Warsaw. Online. Available at www.osce.org/documents/odihr/2006/09/20610_en.pdf.

OSCE/ODIHR (2006b) *Republic of Montenegro: Parliamentary Elections: 10 September 2006*, OSCE/ODIHR Election Observation Mission Report, Warsaw. Online. Available at www.osce.org/documents/odihr/2006/12/22841_en.pdf.

OSCE/ODIHR (2007a) *Republic of Serbia: Parliamentary Elections: 21 January 2007*, OSCE/ODIHR Election Observation Mission Report, Warsaw. Online. Available at www.osce.org/documents/odihr/2007/04/24171_en.pdf.

OSCE/ODIHR (2007b) *Republika Hrvatska: Parlamentarni izbori: 25. studenog 2007*, Izvješ_e OESS/ODIHR-ove Ograni_ene misije za promatranje izbora, Varšava. Online. Available at www.osce.org/documents/odihr/2008/04/30928_hr.pdf.

OSCE/ODIHR (2008) *The Former Yugoslav Republic of Macedonia: Early Parliamentary Elections: 1 June 2008*, OSCE/ODIHR Election Observation Mission Report, Warsaw. Online. Available at www.osce.org/documents/odihr/2008/08/32619_en.pdf.

Pacák, J. (2000) 'Systém politických stran Makedonie', unpublished master thesis, Brno: Masarykova univerzita.

Pantić, D. (2006) 'Vrednosna i stavovska homogenost i heterogenost pristalica političkih partija u Srbiji na kraju 2005', in Z. Lutovac (ed.) *Demokratija u političkim strankama Srbije*, Beograd: Friedrich Ebert Stiftung/Institut društvenih nauka.

Partia demokracia Sociale (not dated) *Programi politik i Partisë Demokracia Sociale*. Online. Available at www.pds.al/?fq=mesi&m=shfaqart&aid=1.

Partia demokratike Shqiptare (2007) *Perspektiva e Maqedonisë varet nga të drejtat e Shqiptarëve*. Zv-kryetari i PDSH-së z Menduh Thaçi ekskluzivisht në 'SHQIP' Top-Channel, 28 March. Available at http://pdsh.info/index.php?option=com_content&task=view&id=530&Itemid=7.

Partia demokratke e Kosovës (2002) *Programi. Partia Demokratike e Kosovës*. Online. Available at www.pdk-ks.org/site/?id=8,0,0,57,a.

Partia per Drejtesi dhe Integrim (2006) *Shekulli PBDNJ*. Online. Available at www.pdi-al.com/shekulli_PBDNJ.html.

Partia reformiste Ora (undated) *Program i Parties reformiste Ora*. Online. Available at www.ora-kosova.org/programi.htm.

Partia socialdemokrate e Shqipërisë (PSDSh) (not dated) *Programi i Partise Social-demokrate te Shqipërisë*. Online. Available at www.psd-al.org/index-2.html.

Partia socialiste e Shqipërisë (2007) *Programi i PS*. Online. Available at ps.al//index. php?option=com_content&task=view&id=64&Itemid=129.

Partija podunavskih Srba (not dated) *Povijest i program – sažetak*. Online. Available at www.hidra.hr/STRANKE/programi/028426.htm.

Partos, G. (1997) *Albania: Conflict Prevention and Crisis Management*, Briefing Paper No. 16, London: The International Security Information Service.

Pavićević, V. (2002) *Izborni sistem: Distributivni činioci izbornog sistema na primeru izbora u Crnoj Gori: 1990–2001*, Beograd: CeSID.

Pavićević, V., Darmanović, S., Komar, O. and Vujović, Z. (2007) *Izbori i izborno zakon-odavstvo u Crnoj Gori 1990–2006*, Podgorica: Centar za monitoring – CEMI. Online. Available at www.cemi.cg.yu/publikacije/download/IzboriIzbornoZakonodavstvo CG2007.pdf.

Pejanović, M. (2005) *Politički razvitak Bosne i Hercegovine u postdejtonskom periodu*, Sarajevo: TKD Šahinpašić.

Petak, Z. (2003) 'Financing political parties in Croatia: Parliamentary elections 2003', *Politička misao*, 40(5): 68–74.

Petričušić, A. (2002/2003) 'Constitutional law on the rights of national minorities in the Republic of Croatia', *European Yearbook of Minority Issues*, 2: 607–29, Leiden, Boston: Martinus Nijhoff Publishers.

Pickering, P.M. and Baskin, M. (2008) 'What is to be done? Succession from the League of Communists of Croatia', *Communist and Post-Communist Studies*, 41(4): 521–40.

Pleše, M. (2003) 'Anto Djapić and Miroslav Tudjman – together in the elections', *Nacional*, No. 395, 10 June. Online. Available at www.nacional.hr/en/articles/view/18225/.

Pokret za promjene (2006) *Program*, Cetinje. Online. Available at www.promjene.org/ pdf/3.%20program_pzp.pdf.

'Povećan broj potpisa za manjine', *B92 Vesti*, 9 April 2008. Online. Available at www. b92.net/info/vesti/index.php?yyyy=2008&mm=04&dd=09&nav_category=418&nav_ id=293145.

Pridham, G. and Vanhanen, T. (1994) *Democratization in Eastern Europe: Domestic and International Perspectives*, London: Routledge.

Radelić, Z. *et al.* (2006) *Stvaranje hrvatske države i Domovinski rat*, Zagreb: Školska knjiga.

Ramet, S.P. (ed.) (1999) *The Radical Right in Central and Eastern Europe since 1989*, University Park, PA: Pennsylvania State University Press.

Republic Statistical Office of Serbia (2002) *Final Results of the Census 2002: Population by national or ethnic group, gender and age groups in the Republic of Serbia, by municipali-ties*, Communication No. 295. Online. Available at www.statserb.sr.gov.yu/zip/esn31.pdf.

Republika Hrvatska: Državni zavod za statistiku (2007) *Žene i muškarci u Hrvatskoj 2007*, Zagreb. Online. Available at www.dzs.hr/.

Republika Hrvatska: Državno izborno povjerenstvo Republike Hrvatske (2007) *Službeni rezultati izbora za zastupnike u Hrvatski sabor*. Online. Available at www.izbori. hr/2007Sabor/rezultati/rezultati_izbora_sluzbeni.pdf.

Reynolds, A. and Reilly, B. (eds) (1997) *The International IDEA Handbook of Electoral System Design*, Stockholm: International IDEA. Online. Available at http://twistedma-trix.com/users/z3p/files/esd_english.pdf.

Ristić, I. (2008) 'The Socialist Party of Serbia', in U. Backes and P. Moreau (eds) *Communist and Post-Communist Parties in Europe*, Göttingen: Vandenhoeck & Ruprecht.

Roberts, E. (2006) *Realm of the Black Mountains: A History of Montenegro*, London: Hurst & Company.

Robinson, G.M. and Pobrić, A. (2006) 'Nationalism and identity in post-Dayton accords: Bosnia–Hercegovina', *Tijdschrift voor economische en sociale geografie*, 97(3): 237–52.

Rusi, I. (2004) 'From army to party: The politics of the NLA', in J. Pettifer *et al.* (eds) *The 2001 Conflict in FYROM*, Surrey: Conflict Studies Research Centre.

Rychlík, J. and Kouba, M. (2003) *Dějiny Makedonie*, Praha: Nakladatelství Lidové noviny.

Samostalna demokratska Srpska stranka (not dated) *Program samostalne demokratske Srpske stranke*. Online. Available at www.sdss.hr/dokumenti/PROGRAM%20SDSS-a. doc.

Samostalna liberalna stranka (2006) *Program samostalne liberalne stranke*. Online. Available at http://sls-ks.org/index.php?option=com_content&task=view&id=36&Item id=41.

Šandor, P. (1994) *Koncept manjinske samouprave Demokratske zajednice Vojvođanskih Mađara*, Beograd. Online. Available at www.vmdk.org.yu/content/hu/koncman.html.

Sartori, G. (2001) *Srovnávací ústavní inženýrství: Zkoumání struktur, podnětů a výsledků*, Praha: SLON.

Savez nezavisnih socijaldemokrata (not dated) *Istorijat*. Online. Available at www.snsd. org/dnn/Default.aspx?tabid=54&language=en-US.

Savez nezavisnih socijaldemokrata (not dated) *Program saveza nezavisnih socijaldemokrata*. Online. Available at www.snsd.org/lat_program.html.

Schirdewan, M. (2004) 'Die Europäische Linkspartei – Partei der europäischen Linken?', *Zeitschrift Marxistische Erneuerung*, 15(58): 151–60.

Schmidt, F. (1996) 'Dayton at midpoint: Sandzak Muslims pin hopes on elections', *Transition*, 2(14).

Schmidt, F. (2000a) 'Die "Albanische Frage" im Spiegel der regional-albanischen Diskussion', *Südosteuropa*, 49(7–8): 375–400.

Schmidt, F. (2000b) 'Generationskonflikte in Albaniens großen Parteien', *Südosteuropa*, 49(1–2): 32–50.

Schmidt, F. (2002) 'Conspiracy theories in Albanian politics and media', in S. Schwandner-Sievers and B.J. Fischer (eds) *Albanian Identities: Myth and History*, London: Hurst & Company.

Schmidt-Neke, M. (1994) 'Schwierige Nachbarschaft: Albanien zwischen Griechenland und Makedonien', *Südosteuropa*, 43(11–12): 666–83.

Schmidt-Neke, M. (1995) 'Albanien vor einer neuen Wende? Das Verfassungsreferendum und seine Konsequenzen', *Südosteuropa*, 44(1–2): 63–88.

Schmidt-Neke, M. (1996) 'Die albanischen Parlamentswahlen vom 26 Mai 1996: Geburtsstunde eines autoritären Systems?', *Südosteuropa*, 45(8): 567–88.

Schmidt-Neke, M. (1998) 'Regierungswechsel in Albanien: die Rückkehr der Krise', *Südosteuropa*, 47(10–11): 516–35.

Schmidt-Neke, M. (2001) 'Die Normalität als Ereignis: Die Parlamentswahlen in Albanien 2001', *Südosteuropa*, 50(7–9): 324–45.

Schubert, P. (2001) 'Reflexionen zur politischen Kultur in Albanien', *Südosteuropa*, 50(10–12): 461–71.

SDSM (not dated) *Zoran Zaev*. Online. Available at www.sdsm.mk/?ItemID=5A2CE21D 0D8A3C46A9B3598AD9DCD325.

Šedo, J. (2002a) 'Bosna a Hercegovina', in P. Fiala, J. Holzer and M. Strmiska (eds) *Politické strany ve střední a východní Evropě*, Brno: MPÚ MU.

Šedo, J. (2002b) 'Republika Makedonie', in P. Fiala, J. Holzer and M. Strmiska (eds) *Politické strany ve střední a východní Evropě*, Brno: MPÚ MU.

Šedo, J. (2006) 'Stranický systém Bosny a Hercegoviny', *Středoevropské politické studie*, 8(2–3): 342–60. Online. Available at www.cepsr.com/dwnld/sedo11.pdf.

Šedo, J. (2007) *Volební systémy postkomunistických zemí*, Brno: CDK.

'Serbia captures fugitive Karadzic', *BBC News* (22 July 2008). Online. Available at news.bbc.co.uk/2/hi/europe/7518543.stm.

Šešelj, V. (2000) *Hajka na heretika (Hunt for heretic)*, Beograd: Srpska radikalna stranka.

Šešelj, V. (2007) *Ili Karlin svedok ili smrt (Either Carla's witness or death)*, Beograd: Srpska radikalna stranka.

Shugart, M.S. and Wattenberg, M.P. (2001) 'Mixed-member electoral systems: A definition and typology', in M.S. Shugart and M.P. Wattenberg (eds) *Mixed Member Electoral Systems. The Best of Both Worlds?*, Oxford: Oxford University Press.

Šiber, I. (2007) *Političko ponašanje: Istraživanja hrvatskog društva*, Zagreb: Politička kultura.

Sikk, A. (2006) *Highways to Power: New Party Success in Three Young Democracies*, Tartu: Tartu University Press.

Silber, L. and Little, A. (1995) *The Death of Yugoslavia*, London: Penguin.

'Six-point plan on Kosovo will destabilize the Balkans', *New Kosova Report* (21 November 2008). Online. Available at www.newkosovareport.com/200811211431/Politics/Six-point-plan-on-Kosovo-will-destablize-the-Balkans.html.

Slavujević, Z.Đ. (2006) 'Razvrstavanje biračkog tela i relevantnih stranaka Srbije na osi levica – desnica', in J. Komšić, D. Pantić and Z.Đ. Slavujević (eds) *Osnovne linije partijskih podela i mogući pravci političkog pregrupisavanja u Srbiji*, Beograd: Friedrich Ebert Stiftung/Institut društvenih nauka.

Søberg, M. (2006) 'Hrvatska nakon 1989. godine. HDZ i politika tranzicije', in S.P. Ramet and D. Matić (eds) *Demokratska tranzicija u Hrvatskoj: Transformacija vrijednosti, obrazovanje mediji*, Zagreb: Alinea.

Sobranie na Republika Makedonija (not dated) *Pratelnički sostav 2008–2012*. Online. Available at www.sobranie.mk/?ItemID=389F3043E8580843B6CD7A4BCF90DD9F.

Socijaldemokratska partija Bosne i Hercegovine (2003) *Program partije*. Online. Available at www.sdp.ba/Default.aspx?categoryid=27&sub1=5.

Socijaldemokratska partija Hrvatske (2007) *Izborni program SDP-a 2007. Nova snaga*. Online. Available at www.sdp.hr/ljudi_i_politike/nase_politike/izborni_program_sdp_a_nova_snaga.

Socijalistička radnička partija Hrvatske (SRPH) (2002) *Program Socialističke radničke partije Hrvatske*, Zagreb. Online. Available at www.srp.hr/.

Spiro, Butko (2004) 'Pan-Albanianism: How big a threat to Balkan stability?', *ICG Europe*, 153, 25 February. Available at www.crisisweb.org.

Spoerri, M. (2008) 'US policy towards ultranationalist political parties in Serbia: The policy of non-engagement examined', *CEU Political Science Journal*, 3(1): 25–48.

Srpska demokratska stranka (2007) *Politička platforma Srpske demokratske stranke: Prijedlog*. Online. Available at www.sdsrs.com/index.php?option=com_content&task=view&id=25&Itemid=32.

Srpska napredna stranka Republike Srpske (1997) *Programski ciljevi Srpske napredne stranke*. Online. Available at http://snsrs.org/onama.html.

Srpska napredna stranka Republike Srpske (2006) *Zajedniška izjava*. Online. Available at http://snsrs.org/centar/slike/duma.html.

Srpska narodna stranka (2006) *Program SNS*. Online. Available at www.sns.cg.yu/dokumenti/program.doc.

Srpska radikalna stranka (not dated) *Program Srpske radikalne stranke*.

Statistical Office of Kosovo (2006) *Series 1: General Statistics: Kosovo in figures 2005*. Online. Available at www.unmikonline.org/archives/EUinKosovo/upload/Kosovo%20 in%20figures%202005%20-%20General%20statistics.pdf.

Stefanovic, D. (2008) 'The path to Weimar Serbia? Explaining the resurgence of the Serbian far right after the fall of Milosevic', *Ethnic and Racial Studies*, 31(7): 1195–221.

Stojar, R. (2006) 'Vnitřní makedonská revoluční organizace (VMRO)', in E. Souleimanov (ed.) *Terorismus: Válka proti státu*, Praha: Eurolex Bohemia.

Stojarová, V. (forthcoming) 'The far right in Croatia, Bosnia and Herzegovina and Serbia', in A. Mammone, E. Godin and B. Jenkins (eds) *Mapping the Far Right in Contemporary Europe: Local, National, Comparative, Transnational*, Oxford: Berghahn.

Stojarová, V., Šedo, J., Kopeček, L. and Chytilek, R. (2007) *Political Parties in Central and Eastern Europe: In Search of Consolidation: Central and Eastern Europe Regional Report: Based on Research and Dialogue with Political Parties*, Stockholm: International IDEA. Online. Available at www.idea.int/publications/pp_c_and_e_europe/index.cfm.

Stojiljković, Z. (2006) *Partijski sistem Srbije*, Beograd: Službeni glasnik.

Stojiljković, Z. (2007a) 'Socijaldemokratija i političke stranke Srbije', in Z. Lutovac (ed.) *Ideologija i političke stranke u Srbiji*, Beograd: Friedrich Ebert Stiftung/Institut društvenih nauka.

Stojiljković, Z. (2007b) 'Srbija i evropski socijalni model(i)', in Z. Lutovac (ed.) *Političke stranke u Srbiji i Evropska unija*, Beograd: Friedrich Ebert Stiftung/Fakultet političkih nauka.

Stranka demokratske akcije (2005) *Programska deklaracija*. Online. Available at www. sda.ba/list.php?id=2.

Stranka za Bosnu i Hercegovinu (not dated) *Izborna platforma Stranke za Bosnu i Hercegovinu*. Online. Available at www.zabih.ba/downloads/24_1.pdf.

Sud Bosne i Hercegovine (2008) *Izrečena presuda u predmetu Dragan Čović i drugi*. Online. Available at www.sudbih.gov.ba/?id=896&jezik=h.

Taagepera, R. (2006) 'Meteoric trajectory: The Res Publica Party in Estonia', *Democratization*, 13(1): 78–94.

Taagepera, R. and Shugart, M.S. (1989) *Seats and Votes: The Effects and Determinants of Electoral Systems*, New Haven: Yale University Press.

Thompson, M. (1992) *A Paper House: The Ending of Yugoslavia*, London: Vintage.

Todorović, M. (2002) *Izborne manipulacije*, Beograd: CeSID.

Todosijević, B. (2008) Politics of World Views: Ideology and Political Behavior in Serbia 1990–2002, Saarbrücken: VDM Verlag.

Todosijević, B. (2008) 'The structure of political attitudes in Hungary and Serbia', *East European Politics and Societies*, 22(4): 879–900.

Tomic, Y. (2008) *The Ideology of a Greater Serbia in the Nineteenth and Twentieth Centuries*, Expert Report, International Criminal Tribunal for the former Yugoslavia. Online. Available at www.helsinki.org.yu/doc/expert%20report%20-%20yves%20tomic. pdf.

Trimçev, E. (2003) 'Organized crime in Albania: An unconventional security threat', *Connections, The Quarterly Journal*, 2(2): 61–8.

UN Security Council (1999) *Resolution 1244*, adopted by the Security Council at its 4011th meeting, 10 June. Online. Available at www.nato.int/Kosovo/docu/u990610a.htm.

UN Security Council (2007) *Comprehensive Proposal for the Kosovo Status Settlement*. Online. Available at www.unosek.org/docref/Comprehensive_proposal-english.pdf.

UNMIK (2001) *Constitutional Framework for Provisional Self-Government in Kosovo*. Online. Available at www.unmikonline.org/pub/misc/FrameworkPocket_ENG_Dec2002.pdf.

UNMIK (2003) *Tenth Assessment of the Situation of Ethnic Minorities in Kosovo (Period covering May 2002 to December 2002)*. Online. Available at www.unmikonline.org/press/reports/MinorityAssessmentReport10ENG.pdf.

UNPREDEP (not dated) *UNPREDEP Recent Development*. Online. Available at www.un.org/Depts/DPKO/Missions/unpred_r.htm.

Van Cott, D.L. (2003) 'Institutional change and ethnic parties in South America', *Latin American Politics and Society*, 45(2): 1–39.

Venice Commission (2000) *Electoral Law and National Minorities*, CDL-INF (2000) 4, Strasbourg. Online. Available at www.venice.coe.int/docs/2000/CDL-INF(2000)004-e.asp.

Vickers, M. and Pettifer, J. (1999) *Albania: From Anarchy to a Balkan Identity*, London: Hurst & Company.

VMRO-NP (2006) *Idnina namesto sudbina: Izborna programa*. Online. Available at www.vmro-np.org.mk/upload/dokumenti/ip2006vmronp.pdf.

Vujačić, I. (2007) 'Liberalizam i političke stranke u Srbiji', in Z. Lutovac (ed.) *Ideologija i političke stranke u Srbiji*, Beograd: Friedrich Ebert Stiftung/Institut društvenih nauka.

Vujović, Z. *et al.* (2007) *Financing Political Parties in Montenegro: Report for Year 2005*, Podgorica: Centar za monitoring – CEMI. Online. Available at http://213.149.103.11/download/financing_political_parties_2005.pdf.

Vukomanović, D. (2007) 'Ideološke matrice političkih partija u Srbiji 1990–2007', in Z. Lutovac (ed.) *Ideologija i političke stranke u Srbiji*, Beograd: Friedrich Ebert Stiftung/Institut društvenih nauka.

Vykoupilová, H. and Stojarová, V. (2007) 'Populism in the Balkans: Case of Serbia', paper presented at ECPR 4th General Conference, Pisa.

Wolinetz, S.B. (2004) 'Classifying party systems: Where have all the typologies gone?', paper prepared for the Annual Meeting of the Canadian Political Science Association, Winnipeg, Manitoba, June 2004. Online. Available at www.cpsa-acsp.ca/papers-2004/Wolinetz.pdf.

Woodward, S.L. (1995) *Balkan Tragedy: Chaos and Dissolution after the Cold War*, Washington: Brookings Institution.

'Zakon o političkim strankama' (1993) Online. Available at narodne-novine.nn.hr/clanci/sluzbeni/259441.html.

'Zakon o političkim strankama' (1999) Online. Available at www.sabor.hr/fgs.axd?id=1846.

Zavod za statistiku Crne Gore (2004) *Popis stanovnistva, domacinstava i stanova u Republici Crnoj Gori u 2003*. Online Available at www.monstat.cg.yu/Popis.htm.

ZPC European Governments (not dated) *Leaders of Bosnia and Herzegovina*. Online. Available at www.terra.es/personal2/monolith/bosnia.htm.

Zrinjski, M. (2007) 'Picula iz protesta napustio HTV-ovu emisiju, *Nacional* (16 November). Online. Available at www.nacional.hr/clanak/39960/picula-iz-protesta-napustio-htv-ovu-emisiju.

Electronic sources

Albanian Central Elections Commission (Komisioni Qendror i Zgjedhjeve). Available at www.cec.org.al/.

Albanian Helsinki Committee (Komiteti Shqiptar i Helsinkit, KSHH). Available at www.ahc.org.al/kshh/eng/def.html.

Albanian Statistical Office (Instituti i Statistikës. Republika e Shqipërisë). Available at www.instat.gov.al/.

Albanska Alternativa (Alternativa Shqiptare, Albanian Alternative, AA). Available at http://alternativa-shqiptare.org/.

Alliance for the future of Kosovo (Aleanca për Ardhmërinë e Kosovës, AAK). Available at www.aleanca.info/.

Ante Gotovina. Available at www.antegotovina.com/.

Antiglobalizam.com. Available at www.antiglobalizam.com/.

Arhiv Jugoslavije. Available at www.arhiv.sv.gov.yu/.

Armata Kombëtare Shqipëtare (AKSh). Available at http://akshalb.ifrance.com/.

Armata kombëtare Shqiptare (AKSh). Available at http://akshalb.ifrance.com/statuti.htm.

Army for the Independence of Kosovo (Ushtria për Pavarësinë ë Kosovës UPK). Available at http://sweb.cz/messin/upk.htm.

Assembly: Republic of Kosovo. Available at www.assembly-kosova.org/.

Balli i Kombit. Available at http://ballikombit.albanet.org/.

Bashkimi Demokratik për Integrim. Available at www.bdi.org.mk.

BiH Central Electoral Commission. Available at www.izbori.ba/eng/default.asp.

BiH Statistical Office Agency for Statistics of Bosnia and Herzegovina (Agencija za statistiku Bosne i Hercegovine). Available at www.bhas.ba/new/.

Blood and Honour Serbia (Krv i čast Srbija). Available at www.bhserbia.org/.

Bosna i Hercegovina: Centralna izborna komisija: Središnje izborno povjerenstvo. Available at www.izbori.ba.

Bosniak Party (Bošnjačka stranka, BS). Available at www.bosnjackastranka.org/.

CEDEM (Center for Democracy and Human Rights Montenegro). Available at www.cedem.cg.yu/.

CEMI (The Monitoring Center). Available at www.cemi.cg.yu/vijesti/index.php.

Center for Democratic Transition (Centar za demokratsku tranziciju). Available at www.cdtmn.org.

Center for Research and Policy Making. Available at www.crpm.org.mk.

CeSID (Centar za slobodne izbore i demokratiju). Available at www.cesid.org/.

Citizen's Advocacy Office. Available at www.cao.al.

Communist Party of Croatia (Komunistička partija Hrvatske, KPH). Available at www.komunisti-hrvatske.com/.

Conference of Communist and Workers' Parties of the Balkans. Available at www.balkanconference.net/english/index.html.

Council of Ministers: Republic of Albania. Available at www.keshilliministrave.al/english/default.asp.

Croat Civic Initiative (Hrvatska građanska inicijativa, HGI). Available at www.hgi.co.me/.

Croatian Agrarian Party (Hrvatska seljačka stranka, HSS). Available at www.hss.hr/.

Croatian Bloc (Hrvatski blok, HB). Available at www.hrvatski-blok.hr/.

Croatian Democratic Union (Hrvatska demokratska zajednica, HDZ). Available at www.hdz.hr/.

Croatian Democratic Union of BiH (Hrvatska demokratska zajednica BiH, HDZ BiH). Available at www.hdzbih.org/.

Croatian Elections (Hrvatski izborni podaci). Available at www.fpzg.hr/hip/.

Croatian Information Documentation Referral Agency (Hrvatska informacijsko doku-mentacijska referalna agencija). Available at www.hidra.hr/.

Croatian National Community (Hrvatska narodna zajednica, HNZ). Available at http://hnzbih.org/.

Croatian Party of Rights (Hrvatska stranka prava, HSP). Available at www.hsp.hr/.

Croatian Party of Rights (in Bavaria) (Hrvatska stranka prava Bavarska). Available at www.hsp-bavarska.de/hsp/index.php.

Croatian Party of Rights 1861 (Hrvatska stranka prava 1861). Available at www.hsp1861.hr/.

Croatian Party of Rights of BiH Đapić-dr. Jurišić (Hrvatska stranka prava BiH Đapić-dr. Jurišić). Available at www.hsp-bih.ba/.

Croatian Pure Party of Rights (Hrvatska čista stranka prava, HSČP). Available at www.hcsp.hr/.

Croatian Rightist Brotherhood (Hrvatsko Pravaško Bratstvo, HPB). Available at www.hpb-makarska.com/.

Croatian Rightists – Croatian Rightist Movement (Hrvatski pravaši – Hrvatski pravaški pokret, HP-HPP). Available at www.hrvatskipravasi.hr/.

Croatian State Archives (Hrvatski državni arhiv). Available at www.arhiv.hr/.

Croatian Statistical Office Republic of Croatia – Central Bureau of Statistics (Republika Hrvatska – Državni zavod za statistiku). Available at www.dzs.hr/.

Croatian True Revival (Hrvatski istinski preporod, HIP). Available at http://hidra.srce.hr/arhiva/392/5980/www.hipnet.hr/.

Democratic Albanian Party (Partia Demokratike Shqiptare, PDSh). Available at www.pdsh.org/; www.gurra-pdsh.org/.

Democratic League of Dardania (Lidhja Demokratike e Dardanisë, LDD). Available at www.ldd-kosova.org/.

Democratic Party of Kosovo (Demokratska Stranka Kosova, Partia Demokratike e Kosovës, PDK). Available at www.pdk-ks.org/site/?id=1,0,0,1,a.

Democratic Party of Socialists of Montenegro (Demokratska partija socijalista Crne Gore, DPS). Available at www.dpscg.org/.

Državna izborna komisija. Available at www.sec.mk:90/2009.

Državno izborno povjerenstvo Republike Hrvatske. Available at www.izbori.hr.

FBKSh. Available at www.fbksh-aksh.org/.

Forum 2015. Available at www.forumi2015.org.

Freedom House. Available at www.freedomhouse.org/.

Government of Montenegro (Vlada Crne Gore). Available at www.gov.me/.

Government: Republic of Kosovo. Available at www.ks-gov.net/.

HDZ-1990. Available at www.hdz1990.org.

Hrvatska narodna stranka – liberalni demokrati. Available at www.hns.hr/.

Hrvatska seljačka stranka. Available at www.hss.hr.

Hrvatska socijalno-liberalna stranka. Available at www.hsls.hr.

Hrvatska stranka prava. Available at www.hsp.hr.

Hrvatska stranka umirovjenika. Available at www.hsu.hr.

Hrvatski demokratski savez Slavonije i Baranje (HDSSB). Available at www.hdssb.hr.

I Am Voting (Unë votoj). Available at www.unevotoj.com.

IDRA (Institute for Development Research and Alternatives). Available at www.idra-al.org/.

Ilir Meta. Available at www.ilirmeta.com.

Independent Democratic Serbian Party (Samostalna demokratska srpska stranka, SDSS). Available at www.sdss.hr.

Independent Liberal Party (Samostalna liberalna stranka, SLS). Available at http://sls-ks. org/.

Institute for Policy & Legal Studies (IPLS). Available at www.ipls.org/.

International Conference of Marxist–Leninist Parties and Organizations. Available at www.icmlpo.de/.

Istarski demokratski sabor. Available at www.ids-ddi.com.

Komunist. Available at http://komunist.free.fr/.

Kontra-punkt (Serbian anarchists). Available at www.kontra-punkt.info/.

Kosovar Center for Gender Studies (Qendra Kosovare për Studime Gjinore). Available at www.kgscenter.org/index.php?lng=1.

Kosovo Democratic Turk Party (Kosova Demokratik Türk Partisi). Available at www. kdtp.org/kdtp/.

Labour Communist Party of BiH. Available at www.rkp-bih.org/.

Leftist Parties of the World: Albania. Available at www.broadleft.org/al.htm.

Leftist Parties of the World: Serbia and Monte Negro. Available at www.broadleft.org/ yu.htm.

Liberal Party of Montenegro (Liberalna parija Crne Gore, LP). Available at www.lpcg. org/.

Liberalna partija na Makedonija. Available at www.lp.org.mk.

Liberalno–Demokratska partija. Available at www.ldp.org.mk.

Lidhja Demokratike e Kosovës (Democratic League of Kosovo, LDK). Available at ldk-kosova.eu/.

Lustration in the Western Balkans. Available at www.lustration.net/.

MIPT Terrorism Knowledge Base. Available at www.tkb.org/.

MJAFT. Available at www.mjaft.org.

Movement for Changes (Pokret za promjene, PzP). Available at www.promjene.org/.

Movement for unification (Lëvizja për bashkim). Available at www.levizjaperbashkim. com/.

National Movement for the Liberation of Kosovo. Available at www.lkck.net.

Network for the Affirmation of the Non-Governmental Sector (Mreža za afirmaciju nev-ladinin sektor, MANS). Available at www.mans.cg.yu/.

New Communist Party of Yugoslavia (Nova komunistička partija Jugoslavije). Available at http://members.tripod.com/nkpj/.

New Kosovoa Alliance (Aleanca Kosova e Re). Available at www.akr-ks.info/.

Nova socijaldemokratska partija. Available at http://nsdp.org.mk/web/.

Novi Plamen. Available at www.noviplamen.org/.

Opium za narod: Optimirano za komuniste. Available at http://de.geocities.com/opium-zanarod/.

OSCE (The Organization for Security and Co-operation in Europe). Available at http:// www.osce.org.

(The) Parliament of Montenegro (Skupština Crne Gore). Available at www.skupstina.cg. yu/.

Partia demokratike e Shqipërisë (PDSh). Available at www.partiademokratike.al/.

Partia Demokratike Shquiptare. Available at www.pdsh.info.

Partia socialdemokrate e Shqipërisë (PSDSh). Available at www.psd-al.org/.

Party for Bosnia and Herzegovina (Stranka za Bosnu i Hercegovinu). Available at www. zabih.ba.

Party of Democratic Action (Stranka demokratske akcije, SDA). Available at www.sda. ba/naslovna.php.

Party of Labour. Available at www.partijarada.org.yu/.

Party of Social Democracy (Partia Demokracia Sociale, PDSSh). Available at www.pds. al/.

People's Party (Nardona stranka, NS). Available at www.narodnastranka.com/.

Pionirov Glasnik. Available at www.pionirovglasnik.com/.

PKSh. Available at www.pksh.org/.

Pobunjeni Um. Available at http://yu.marxist.com/.

President of Montenegro (Predsjednik Crne Gore). Available at www.predsjednik.cg.yu/.

Radio Free Europe/Radio Liberty. Available at www.rferl.org.

Reformist Party Ora (Partia Reformiste Ora). Available at www.ora-kosova.org/.

Register of Political Parties in Croatia (Registar političkih stranaka). Available at www. uprava.hr/RegistarPolitickihStranaka/.

Samostalna demokratska srpska stranka. Available at www.sdss.hr.

Serbian Democratic Party (Srpska demokratska stranka, SDS). Available at www.sdsrs. com/.

Serbian National Party (Srpska narodna stranka, SNS). Available at www.sns.cg.yu.

Serbian Progressive Party of RS (Srpska napredna stranka Republike Srpske, SNS RS). Available at //snsrs.org/.

Serbian Radical Party (Srpska radikalna stranka, SRS). Available at www.srs.org.yu/ index.php.

Serbian Radical Party of RS (Srpska radikalna stranka Republike Srpske, SRS RS). Available at www.srsrs-ugljevik.com/index.php?option=com_frontpage&Itemid=1.

Serbian Statistical Office (Republički zavod za statistiku). Available at http://webrzs.stat-serb.sr.gov.yu/axd/index.php.

Serbianna. Available at www.serbianna.com/.

Social Democratic Party (Socijaldemokratska partija Bosne i Hercegovine). Available at www.sdp.ba.

Social Democratic Union of Macedonia. Available at www.sdsm.org.mk/.

Socialdemocratic Party (Socijaldemokratska partija Crne Gore, SDP). Available at www.sdp.cg.yu/.

Socialist Labour Party (Socijalistička radnička partija Hrvatske). Available at www.srp. hr/.

Socialist National Party of Montenegro (Socijalistička narodna partija Crne Gore, SNP). Available at www.snp.cg.yu/; www.snp.co.me/.

Socialist Party of Albania (Partia socialiste e Shqipërisë, PSSh). Available at www.ps.al/.

Socialisticka Federativna Republika Jugosavija (SFRJ). Available at www.sfrj4ever.ch/.

Socijaldemokratska partija Hrvatske. Available at www.sdp.hr.

Solidnet. Available at www.solidnet.org/.

Srpska demokratska stranka Republike Srpske. Available at www.sdsrs.com.

State Electoral Commission: Republika Makedonija. Available at www.sec.mk:90/2009/.

Statistical Office of Montenegro (Zavod za statistiku Crne Gore). Available at www. monstat.cg.yu/.

Stranka demokratske akcije. Available at www.sda.ba.

Stranka nezavisnih socijaldemokrata. Available at www.snsd.org.

Stranka za Bosnu i Hercegovinu. Available at www.zabih.ba.

UÇK (Ushtria Çlirimtare e Kosovës, KLA Kosovo Liberation Army, OVK Oslobodilačka vojska Kosova).

Union of Independent Social Democrats. Available at www.snsd.org/dnn/.

Union of Yugoslavian Communists in Serbia. Available at www.komunistisubotice.org. yu/.

United Albania. Available at www.shqiperiaebashkuar.org/.

United Albania. Available at www.unitedalbania.org/.

VMRO – National party (VMRO-Narodna partija). Available at www.vmro-np.org.mk/#.

Vnatrešna makedonska revolucionerna organizacija – Demokratska partija za makedon-sko nacionalno edinstvo. Available at www.vmro-dpmne.org.mk/mk/index.asp.

Vojislav Seselj. Available at www.vojislavseselj.org.yu/.

Workers Party of Yugoslavia (Partija rada). Available at www.angelfire.com/extreme/ partijarada/.

ZPC European Governments. Available at www.terra.es/personal2/monolith/00europa. htm.

Electronic materials and sources accessed June–December 2008.

Index

Numbers in *italic* refer to illustrations